Premature Adolescent Pregnancy
and Parenthood

MONOGRAPHS IN NEONATALOGY

Thomas K. Oliver, Jr., M.D.
Series Editor

ANTIMICROBIAL THERAPY FOR NEWBORNS: PRACTICAL
APPLICATION OF PHARMACOLOGY TO CLINICAL USE
by George H. McCracken, Jr., M.D., and
John D. Nelson, M.D.

TEMPERATURE REGULATION AND ENERGY METABOLISM
IN THE NEWBORN
edited by John C. Sinclair, M.D.

HOST DEFENSES IN THE HUMAN NEONATE
by Michael E. Miller, M.D.

PERINATAL COAGULATION
by William E. Hathaway, M.D., and John Bonnar, M.D.

NEONATAL NECROTIZING ENTEROCOLITIS
edited by Edwin G. Brown, M.D., and
Avron Y. Sweet, M.D.

NEONATAL HYPERBILIRUBINEMIA
by Gerard B. Odell, M.D.

RETROLENTAL FIBROPLASIA: A MODERN PARABLE
by William A. Silverman, M.D.

PARENT–INFANT RELATIONSHIPS
edited by Paul M. Taylor, M.D.

THE EXPANDING ROLE OF THE NURSE IN NEONATAL
INTENSIVE CARE
edited by Roger E. Sheldon, M.D., and
Pati Sellers Dominiak, R.N., M.S.

NEONATAL ORTHOPAEDICS
by Robert N. Hensinger, M.D., and
Eric T. Jones, M.D., Ph.D.

Premature Adolescent Pregnancy and Parenthood

Edited by
Elizabeth R. McAnarney, M.D.
George Washington Goler Associate Professor of Pediatrics
Division of Biosocial Pediatrics and Adolescent Medicine
University of Rochester Medical Center
Rochester, New York

GRUNE & STRATTON
A Subsidiary of Harcourt Brace Jovanovich, Publishers
New York   London
Paris   San Diego   San Francisco   São Paulo
Sydney   Tokyo   Toronto

Library of Congress Cataloging in Publication Data
Main entry under title:

Premature adolescent pregnancy and parenthood.

(Monographs in neonatalogy)
Bibliography
Includes index.
1. Pregnancy, Adolescent—Addresses, essays, lectures.
2. Adolescent parents—Addresses, essays, lectures.
3. Adolescent parents—Services for—Addresses, essays,
lectures.   I. McAnarney, Elizabeth R.   II. Series.
[DNLM: 1. Pregnancy in adolescence.   2. Parent–child
relations.   WS 462 P925]
RG556.5.P74   1983   618.2′0088055   82-20995
ISBN 0-8089-1518-5

Grune & Stratton, Inc.
111 Fifth Avenue
New York, New York 10003

Distributed in the United Kingdom by
Academic Press Inc. (London) Ltd.
24/28 Oval Road, London NW 1

Library of Congress Catalog Number 82-20995
International Standard Book Number 0-8089-1518-5
Printed in the United States of America

This book is dedicated to
Gilbert B. Forbes,
physician, scholar, and friend,
to commemorate his retirement.

It is most fitting that this book is dedicated to Gilbert Forbes. Dr. Forbes is a distinguished scholar and teacher of pediatrics and nutrition. He has, through his research, made major contributions to our understanding of human body compositions. His studies have contributed significantly in generating recommendations for meeting optimum daily nutritional requirements for infants, children, adolescents, and adults and in helping us to understand better the pathophysiology of many nutritional diseases and the methods we should use in their prevention, diagnosis, and treatment.

Dr. Forbes has included growth during adolescence and during adolescent pregnancy in his many investigative efforts.[1-3] He has demonstrated sustained interest in the nutritional problems of adolescents, particularly obesity and anorexia nervosa, and continues to make rounds on the adolescent unit of the University of Rochester Medical Center–Strong Memorial Hospital.

Recognized as one of this country's foremost scholars, Dr. Forbes has served on several National Institutes of Health study sections and committees, as well as on advisory boards of the National Research Council, the

---

[1]Forbes GB: Growth of the lean body mass during childhood and adolescence. J Pediatr 64:822–827, 1964

[2]Forbes GB: Puberty: Body composition. In SR Berenberg (ed): Puberty, Biologic and Psychosocial Components. Proceedings of the Macy Conference on Puberty, Paris, France. Leiden, Netherlands, H.E. Stenfert Kroese B.V., 1975, pp 132–145

[3]Forbes GB: Biological implications of the adolescent growth process: Body composition. In JI McKigney, HN Munro (eds): Nutritional Requirements in Adolescence. Cambridge, Mass, MIT Press, 1976, pp 57–70

v

American Academy of Pediatrics, and several private foundations. He has been elected to the presidency of the Society for Pediatric Research, appointed Editor of the *American Journal of Diseases of Children,* received the Research Career Award from the National Institute of Child Health and Development and the Borden Award for Outstanding Contributions to Nutrition in Children, and selected as the second Distinguished Alumni Professor at the University of Rochester School of Medicine and Dentistry.

Although officially retired, Dr. Forbes will remain at the University of Rochester and carry on with his research, writing, and teaching. Those of us who are privileged to be his colleagues and friends will continue to turn to him for his sage counsel in academic and personal matters. He has always given this with thoughtfulness, clarity, and good will, reflecting his wise, gentle, and kind nature.

Robert A. Hoekelman, M.D.

Contents

Foreword

It is appropriate to ask whether we need another book about adolescent pregnancy and parenthood. As Dr. McAnarney points out in the preface to this volume, and as the extensive bibliography included herein attests, these subjects have received more than their share of attention in the medical, nursing, and social science literature during the 1960s and 1970s, albeit not much before that. One may ask why this is so and why yet another compendium on these matters has been published.

We have turned so much of our attention to adolescent sexuality, sexual activity, pregnancy, and parenthood because they have consumed such a large portion of our professional energies and community resources. Despite some opinion to the contrary, young men and women (boys and girls, if you choose) are more active sexually than they were a generation or two ago, and epidemiologic data show beyond question that even though contraceptives are more readily available to young people and more effective than in earlier years, the incidence of pregnancy among adolescents has risen to record levels. This has led to greater numbers of children being born to adolescents and to an increase in the problems that attend this outcome, despite the ready availability of safe and legal abortions. These are problems that cannot be ignored. Society no longer denies their presence and now wishes to do something to reduce their prevalence, for adolescent pregnancy is a high-risk condition: high risk for the adolescent mother (and father), high risk for the infant, and high risk for everyone else concerned—family, professionals, and the public. Its biologic, psychologic, sociologic, and economic consequences are enormous.

This book was written because heretofore all of the knowledge concerning the origin, process, and outcomes of adolescent pregnancy has not been published in one work. This book was written by health professionals and social scientists with expertise in all aspects of adolescent pregnancy and experience in its prevention and management. It was written for all professionals involved in this area and for all students who will become involved in such prevention and management. It will surely be of great help to them and to those they serve.

The information contained in this volume undoubtedly can be applied successfully to clinical situations we encounter every day in caring for adolescents and their offspring, who will benefit in terms of reduced biologic and psychosocial morbidity. How effective we can be, however, depends in large part on the resources that will be available to us. These, in turn, are dependent on both professional and political circumstances.

Currently, adolescents receive less than their proportionate share of medical attention for persons residing in the United States. During 1978, persons 14 through 20 years of age accounted for 9.3 percent (52.6 million) of all ambulatory visits made to physicians practicing in the United States.[1] During that year, adolescents 14 through 20 years of age constituted 13.7 percent of the population of the United States.[2] Only 6.8 percent (3.9 million) of the visits made to pediatricians (who aspire to provide comprehensive care to adolescents) during this same year were made by persons 14 through 20 years of age; 68.8 percent (39.3 million) were made by children less than 7 years of age, and 23.4 percent (13.4 million) were made by children 7 through 13 years of age. Thus, during 1978, visits to pediatricians accounted for only 7.4 percent of all visits made by patients 14 through 20 years of age.[1]

There are not many physicians, pediatricians, or others who have made a concerted effort to reach out and incorporate the care of adolescents within their practices. In 1982 the American Academy of Pediatrics, long an advocate of the comprehensive care of adolescents by pediatricians, revised its minimal standards for health supervision during the first 21 years of life. The number of recommended visits for health screening, disease prevention, anticipatory guidance, and counseling on biomedical and psychosocial issues during the 21-year span increased from 14 to 20. This adds 2 visits between 13 and 21 years of age (4 instead of 2) and 4 visits between birth and 12 years of age (16 instead of 12). Even though the percentage of scheduled

[1]National Center for Health Statistics: 1978 National Ambulatory Medical Care Survey (NAMCS) Micro Data Tape Documentation. Prepared by Raymond O. Gagnon, Ambulatory Care Statistics Branch, Hyattsville, Md

[2]U.S. Bureau of the Census: Statistical Abstract of the United States: 1979 (ed 100). Washington, DC, 1979

visits for adolescents rises from 14 to 20 percent, if these standards are used, pediatricians will have less time to devote to the problems of adolescents, including the prevention of adolescent pregnancy, because the 43 percent overall increase in the number of recommended visits will result in fewer patients served by each practitioner. This will not help improve the performance of pediatricians in providing anticipatory guidance and counseling to adolescents, which have been repeatedly shown in practice surveys to be little or nonexistent during health supervision visits.[3] If pediatricians, whose numbers are falling relative to other medical specialties (despite predictions to the contrary by the Graduate Medical Education National Advisory Council), are to help adolescents avoid early childbearing, they will have to change their practice priorities. To do so, as with other health care professionals who have difficulty finding time in their workday to address the needs of adolescents, they will have to determine which tasks they currently perform that can be performed by others, that they do not need to perform as often, and that they do not need to perform at all. Only in these ways will they be able to find the time needed to help their adolescent patients.

What, then, of the political circumstances that influence our ability to reach out and help reduce adolescent pregnancies and their consequences? In the last 2 years, we have seen marked reductions in federal funding of programs established over the past 20 years to improve maternal and child health. These programs have provided services to mothers of all ages, adolescents included, and at least one piece of legislation—PL 95-625—was designed specifically to provide comprehensive services to prevent and manage adolescent pregnancies. Federal maternal and child health programs, if not eliminated entirely, will be turned over to the states to administer under block grants. Most state executive and legislative leaders have indicated that they will be unable to support these programs at the levels at which they have been funded, and some programs will receive no support at all. Unless this trend is reversed, federal, state, and local monies will not be available to assist us in dealing with adolescent pregnancies.

Further, abortions may well be outlawed, as may the use of certain contraceptives (the IUD and the pill) and the provision by federally funded family planning programs of contraceptive information to adolescents without informing their parents. These federal legislative and administrative actions will make our work in dealing with adolescent pregnancy much more difficult, if not impossible, than it is currently.

I do not wish to seem discouraging—only to be realistic—in citing the professional and political circumstances that exist and need to be overcome if we are to carry out the recommendations detailed in this book. To overcome

---

[3]Hoekelman RA: Got a minute? Pediatrics 66:1013, 1980

those circumstances, we must individually and collectively work within the boundaries of our professions to effect changes that will enhance our abilities to deal with the problems of adolescent pregnancies. We must also, as Bob Haggerty has advised,[4] go beyond those boundaries and become involved in the political and social arenas that will influence, more than anything else, how often adolescents become pregnant and how well or poorly they fare thereafter.

Robert A. Hoekelman, M.D.
Professor and Associate Chairman
Department of Pediatrics
School of Medicine and Dentistry
University of Rochester Medical Center
Rochester, New York

---

[4]Haggerty RJ: The boundaries of health care. Pharos, July 1972, pp 106–111

Preface

Adolescent pregnancy and adolescent parenthood have received considerable national attention since 1970. Despite the availability of several books and numerous journal articles addressing these topics, I thought there still was a need for a book combining a clinical and an investigative approach to adolescent pregnancy and parenthood that was directed primarily toward professionals in perinatology. It is my belief that pregnancy, childbearing, and parenthood during the adolescent years are premature events for some young mothers, young fathers, and their infants. Even though young mothers who receive adequate prenatal care may not be at greater obstetric risk than adult women of the same background, adolescent mothers and fathers suffer severe psychosocial and developmental disadvantages as a consequence of adolescent childbearing. In addition, infants born to adolescent mothers, especially mothers less than 15 years old, are more likely to be born prematurely than infants born to adult mothers of similar backgrounds.

This book contains information about the epidemiology of adolescent pregnancy, childbearing, and sexual activity; prevention of adolescent pregnancy; the biology of adolescent pregnancy and childbearing; the psychosocial aspects of adolescent pregnancy and parenthood; and several intervention approaches. Several authors emphasize the importance of considering adolescence as a developmental stage, consisting of the substages of early, middle, and late adolescence. The developmental stage strongly influences adolescents' sexual behavior, their understanding of pregnancy, the prevention of pregnancy, and their expectations of parenthood. The unique developmental aspects of the different substages of adolescence make the clinical care and study of adolescents particularly enjoyable for some professionals and especially problematic for others. Several chapters on adolescent parenting are included as this is a major area for future investigation about the risks of adolescent childbearing. Even though the topic of abortion is somewhat peripheral to the main thrust of the book, its discussion is included for completeness.

The chapters comprise individual essays on specific topics. I have purposely avoided making major changes in them because although such changes might result in a more homogeneous book, they would risk losing the contributors' diverse ways of approaching the health care of adolescents. The same data may be interpreted differently by authors, as shown, for example, in Chapters 12 and 17. Some overlap of subject matter between chapters has been eliminated; some was retained for reinforcement of important concepts.

This volume would not have been possible without the efforts of the authors who enthusiastically contributed their expertise to its development, and I am most grateful to them. I would also like to express my appreciation for the continued support of three individuals with whom I have worked closely at the University of Rochester: David H. Smith, M.D., the Chairman of the Department of Pediatrics; Robert J. Haggerty, M.D., a former Chairman of the Department of Pediatrics; and Henry A. Thiede, M.D., the Chairman of the Department of Obstetrics-Gynecology. All three have encouraged our efforts over the past decade to improve the perinatal health of adolescents in Rochester, New York, and its environs. I would also like to recognize my many colleagues in Rochester, particularly the dedicated staff of the Rochester Adolescent Maternity Project, who have provided special care to the community's pregnant adolescents.

My personal gratitude is extended to Mrs. Carole M. Berger, who coordinated our efforts across the country and between the University of Rochester and Cornell University, the site of my sabbatical leave during the academic year 1981–1982. Her devotion to this project has been instrumental in its successful completion.

Gilbert B. Forbes, M.D. (J. Lowell Orbison Alumni Distinguished Service Professor of Pediatrics), to whom this book is dedicated, is a trusted and beloved colleague of his many friends at the University of Rochester. His hours of generous and optimistic consultation serve as an inspiration to many of us.

Elizabeth R. McAnarney, M.D.

Contributors

Wendy Baldwin, Ph.D., Chief, Social and Behavioral Sciences Branch, Center for Population Research, National Institute of Child Health and Human Development, Bethesda, Maryland

William Baldwin Carey, M.D., Ch.B, M.P.H., Assistant Professor of Obstetrics and Gynecology, Charles R. Drew Postgraduate Medical School, Los Angeles, California

Ezra C. Davidson, Jr., M.D., Professor and Chairman of Obstetrics and Gynecology, Charles R. Drew Postgraduate Medical School, Los Angeles, California

Arthur B. Elster, M.D., Assistant Professor of Pediatrics, School of Medicine, University of Utah, Salt Lake City, Utah

Marianne E. Felice, M.D., Assistant Professor of Pediatrics, Division of Adolescent Medicine, School of Medicine, University of California at San Diego, La Jolla, California

Stanford B. Friedman, M.D., Professor of Psychiatry and Human Development, Professor of Pediatrics, Division of Behavioral Pediatrics, Division of Child and Adolescent Psychiatry, School of Medicine, University of Maryland, Baltimore, Maryland

Donald E. Greydanus, M.D., Assistant Professor of Pediatrics, Division of Biosocial Pediatrics and Adolescent Medicine, University of Rochester Medical Center, Rochester, New York

Lisa B. Handwerker, M.D., Medical Director, Threshold Center for Alternative Youth Services, Inc.; Clinical Instructor of Pediatrics, University of Rochester Medical Center, Rochester, New York

Felix P. Heald, M.D., Professor of Pediatrics and Director, Division of Adolescent Medicine, School of Medicine, University of Maryland, Baltimore, Maryland

Christopher H. Hodgman, M.D., Associate Professor of Psychiatry and Pediatrics, Division of Child and Adolescent Psychiatry, University of Rochester Medical Center, Rochester, New York

Dorothy R. Hollingsworth, M.D., Professor of Reproductive Medicine and Medicine, School of Medicine, University of California at San Diego, La Jolla, California

Marc S. Jacobson, M.D., Assistant Professor of Pediatrics, Division of Adolescent Medicine, School of Medicine, University of Maryland, Baltimore, Maryland

James F. Jekel, M.D., M.P.H., Professor of Epidemiology and Public Health, School of Medicine, Yale University, New Haven, Connecticut

E. Milling Kinard, Ph.D., Adjunct Lecturer, The Florence Heller Graduate School for Advanced Studies in Social Welfare, Brandeis University, Waltham, Massachusetts

Lorraine V. Klerman, Dr.P.H., Professor of Public Health, The Florence Heller Graduate School for Advanced Studies in Social Welfare, Brandeis University, Waltham, Massachusetts

Jane Morley Kotchen, M.D., Associate Professor of Medicine, School of Medicine, University of Kentucky, Lexington, Kentucky

Richard E. Kreipe, M.D., Assistant Professor of Pediatrics, Division of Biosocial Pediatrics and Adolescent Medicine, University of Rochester Medical Center, Rochester, New York

Ruth A. Lawrence, M.D., Associate Professor of Pediatrics and Obstetrics-Gynecology, Division of Neonatal Medicine, University of Rochester Medical Center, Rochester, New York

Elizabeth R. McAnarney, M.D., George Washington Goler Associate Professor of Pediatrics, Division of Biosocial Pediatrics and Adolescent

Medicine, University of Rochester Medical Center, Rochester, New York

Thurma McCann-Sanford, M.D., Assistant Professor of Obstetrics and Gynecology, Charles R. Drew Postgraduate Medical School, Los Angeles, California

James McCarthy, Ph.D., Assistant Professor of Population Dynamics, School of Hygiene and Public Health, The Johns Hopkins University, Baltimore, Maryland

T. Allen Merritt, M.D., Assistant Professor of Pediatrics, Division of Neonatology, University Hospital, University of California at San Diego, San Diego, California

Howard J. Osofsky, M.D., Ph.D., Staff and Research Psychiatrist, The Menninger Foundation, Topeka, Kansas; Clinical Professor of Gynecology-Obstetrics, College of Health Science and Hospital, University of Kansas, Kansas City, Kansas

Joy D. Osofsky, Ph.D., Staff and Research Psychologist, The Menninger Foundation, Topeka, Kansas; Adjunct Associate Professor of Human Development, University of Kansas, Kansas City, Kansas

Susan Panzarine, R.N., M.S., College of Nursing, University of Utah, Salt Lake City, Utah

Sheridan Phillips, Ph.D., Associate Professor of Pediatrics and Psychiatry, Division of Child and Adolescent Psychiatry, Division of Behavioral Pediatrics, School of Medicine, University of Maryland, Baltimore, Maryland

Keith R. Powell, M.D., Assistant Professor of Pediatrics, Division of Infectious Diseases and Immunology, University of Rochester Medical Center, Rochester, New York

Ellen S. Radish, B.A., Doctoral Student, Department of Population Dynamics, School of Hygiene and Public Health, The Johns Hopkins University, Baltimore, Maryland

Nancy Jo Reedy, C.N.M, M.P.H., Instructor, Department of Obstetrics and Gynecology, Northwestern University Medical School, Chicago, Illinois

Olle Jane Z. Sahler, M.D., Assistant Professor of Pediatrics and Psychiatry, Division of Biosocial Pediatrics and Adolescent Medicine, University of Rochester Medical Center, Rochester, New York

Henry A. Thiede, M.D., Professor and Chairman of Obstetrics-Gynecology, Department of Obstetrics-Gynecology, University of Rochester Medical Center, Rochester, New York

Melvin Zelnik, Ph.D., Professor of Population Dynamics, School of Hygiene and Public Health, The Johns Hopkins University, Baltimore, Maryland

Part I

INTRODUCTION: ADOLESCENT PREGNANCY AND SEXUAL ACTIVITY

births to teenagers was the result of continued high numbers of births to teens in the face of reductions in the fertility of older women. There are many good reasons, however, for the recent wave of attention to early childbearing.

Since 1960 the decline in the number of births to teenagers has been concentrated in the older ages, the number of out-of-wedlock births to teenagers has risen, and the illegitimacy rate (number of out-of-wedlock births per 1000 unmarried women) has risen for teenagers (Table 1-1). Births

Table 1-2. Births per 1000 Women 14–19 Years of Age: 1920–1979

Period	14	15	16	17	18	19
1920–1924	3.6	11.9	28.6	57.9	93.1	125.4
1925–1929	3.9	12.3	28.5	55.6	86.9	114.0
1930–1934	3.4	10.9	25.2	48.6	75.3	99.0
1935–1939	3.7	11.5	26.0	49.0	75.0	97.9
1940–1944	4.0	12.7	27.8	52.2	81.7	109.2
1945–1949	4.9	15.5	34.1	63.7	99.4	133.0
1950–1954	5.9	19.3	43.1	79.7	123.1	162.6
1955–1959	6.0	20.1	45.7*	85.8*	136.2*	184.0*
1960–1964	5.4	17.8	40.2	75.8	122.7	169.2
1965	5.2	16.5	36.0	66.4	105.4	142.4
1966	5.3	16.4	35.5	64.8	101.8	136.1
1967	5.3	16.5	35.3	63.2	97.5	129.5
1968	5.7	16.7	35.2	62.6	95.7	125.2
1969	6.0	17.4	35.8	63.1	95.7	124.5
1970	6.6	19.2	38.8	66.6	98.3	126.0
1971	6.7	19.2	38.3	64.2	92.4	116.1
1972	7.1	20.1	39.3	63.5	87.1	105.0
1973	7.4*	20.2*	38.8	61.5	83.1	98.5
1974	7.2	19.7	37.7	59.7	80.5	96.2
1975	7.1	19.4	36.4	57.3	77.5	92.7
1976	6.8	18.6	34.6	54.2	73.3	88.7
1977	6.7	18.2	34.5	54.2	73.8	89.5
1978	6.3	17.2	32.7	52.4	72.2	88.0
1979	6.4	17.2	32.8	52.5	73.5	90.4
Decline from highest rate (*) to 1979	14%	15%	28%	39%	46%	51%

Data from National Center for Health Statistics.[7-10]

to young teenagers and to unmarried women are generally viewed as the most problematic, that is, most likely to be unwanted and to require public support. The trend in birth rates by single year of age confirms that during the 1960s and early 1970s the rate rose for young adolescents (15–16) and declined for older teenagers. In the late 1970s the birth rate for even the youngest teens began to decline and that for older teenagers (18–19) dropped to the lowest ever observed for that age group (Table 1-2).

There are substantial differences in fertility and fertility-related behavior between blacks and whites; the younger the adolescents, the greater are the racial differences in behavior. White teenage birth rates are compared with nonwhite rates (92 percent of nonwhite births are to blacks) by single year of age in Table 1-3. The ratio of nonwhite to white rates is over 1 at all ages, but is highest at the youngest ages. Since black adolescents begin childbearing at younger ages than whites, it is not surprising that they experience more second and higher order births during the teenage years (Table 1-4).

The rise in illegitimacy has largely been a function of increases in rates for whites. While the rate is higher for blacks, there has been a definite downward trend during the 1970s. Whites have shown a steady rise in the rate of births to unmarried women aged 15–19[2,4,5] (Table 1-5). The growth of out-of-wedlock childbearing raises concern because the marital status of the mother often affects access to both economic and social support. The number of out-of-wedlock births to women under age 20 increased from under 100,000 in 1960 to over 250,000 in 1979. During this time, the illegitimacy rate rose from 15.3 to 26.9 for women 15–19, a 76 percent increase. The percentage of births out of wedlock rose for all ages under 20 (Table 1-6) and for blacks as well as whites (data not shown). The increase in out-of-wedlock childbearing has been occurring simultaneously with an apparent reduction in the number of babies placed for adoption. In a 1976 survey of unmarried women 15–19 who had borne a child, 93 percent

Table 1-3. Teenage Births per 1000 Women Age and Race: 1979

Age	White	Nonwhite	Ratio of Nonwhite to White
14	3.9	18.8	4.8:1
15	11.7	44.6	3.8:1
16	25.0	73.0	2.9:1
17	42.8	103.3	2.4:1
18	62.9	129.5	2.1:1
19	80.0	144.9	1.8:1

Data from National Center for Health Statistics.[5]

Table 1-4. Teenage Births by Age, Race, and Birth Order: 1979

Age	White			Black			All Others		
	First Birth	Second and Higher*	Percentage First Births	First Birth	Second and Higher*	Percentage First Births	First Birth	Second and Higher*	Percentage First Births
Under 15	4,271	131	97	5,813	326	91	152	6	96
15	14,406	751	95	11,498	1,162	91	531	29	95
16	36,467	3,050	92	19,680	3,387	85	1,228	134	90
17	63,657	9,639	87	24,416	7,585	76	2,070	447	82
18	87,315	22,429	80	26,665	13,166	67	2,821	893	76
19	105,230	40,863	72	26,138	19,108	58	3,160	1,547	67

Data from National Center for Health Statistics.[5]
*Includes births for which order was not stated.

Table 1-5. Births per 1000 Unmarried Women 15–19 Years of Age, by Race: 1970–1979

Year	Black	White
1970	96.9	10.9
1971	99.1	10.3
1972	98.8	10.5
1973	96.0	10.7
1974	95.1	11.1
1975	95.1	12.1
1976	91.6	12.4
1977	93.2	13.6
1978	90.3	13.8
1979	93.7	14.9

Data from National Center for Health Statistics.[2,4,5]

reported that the child resided with them. This is an increase from 86 percent in 1971, a change which reflects the growing trend for white adolescents to keep their babies.[11] There may be increased social acceptance of a young single mother raising her baby; placing a child for adoption may be regarded as a solution of last resort that is not widely used when abortion or unmarried motherhood are seen as viable options.

ABORTION RATES

No overview of adolescent childbearing would be complete without a discussion of abortion. Adolescents account for one-third of the legal abortions performed each year in the United States. In 1979 there were over 400,000 abortions to teenagers; since there were fewer than 600,000 births to adolescents in 1979, abortion is clearly a significant aspect of teenage fertility behavior.

Table 1-6. Out-of-Wedlock Births among Adolescents: 1960, 1970, and 1979

Age	1960	1970	1979
Under 15	4,600 (68)*	9,500 (81)	9,500 (89)
15	8,700 (44)	19,300 (65)	21,800 (77)
16	15,100 (28)	34,000 (48)	41,300 (65)
17	19,900 (18)	42,800 (35)	56,900 (53)
18	21,800 (13)	47,500 (26)	66,400 (43)
19	21,600 (9)	46,800 (20)	66,600 (34)

Data from National Center for Health Statistics.[2,5,6]
*Percentage of births out of wedlock is shown in parentheses.

Table 1-7. Teenage Abortions: 1973–1978

Age	1973	1974	1975	1976	1977	1978
Under 15	11,630 (1.6)*	13,420 (1.5)	15,260 (1.5)	15,820 (1.3)	15,690 (1.2)	15,110 (1.1)
15–19	232,440 (31.2)	278,280 (31.0)	324,930 (31.4)	362,689 (30.8)	397,720 (30.1)	418,790 (29.7)
20–24	240,610 (32.3)	286,600 (31.9)	331,640 (32.1)	392,280 (33.3)	450,900 (34.2)	489,410 (34.7)
25+	259,930 (34.9)	320,270 (35.6)	362,340 (35.0)	408,511 (35.4)	456,010 (34.5)	486,290 (34.5)
Total	744,610	898,570	1,034,170	1,179,300	1,320,320	1,409,600

Adapted from Forrest JD, Sullivan E, Tietze C: Abortion in the United States, 1977–1978. Fam Plann Perspect 11:329–341, 1979. Henshaw S, Forrest JD, Sullivan E, et al: Abortion in the United States, 1978–1979. Fam Plann Perspect 13:6–18, 1981.
*Percentage of abortions by age is shown in parentheses.

Data on abortion come from two major sources. The Centers for Disease Control reports abortion surveillance data compiled from central state agencies and from hospitals or facilities in which abortions are performed. The Alan Guttmacher Institute reports the number of abortions based on a survey of health institutions and private physicians providing abortion services. Because the latter figure includes abortions performed in physicians' offices, it is higher than the Centers for Disease Control figure. The distribution of abortions by characteristics of the women is available from the Centers for Disease Control, and the two data sources may be combined to give estimates of the total number of abortions performed on women with given characteristics, such as age or marital status.[12,13]

The data presented in Table 1-7 show the increase in the number of abortions performed on teenagers from 1973 to 1978. Since the likelihood of a spontaneous abortion or stillbirth is unlikely to change over such a short time period, the number of births and abortions can be used as an estimate of the number of conceptions. Analyses of trends in adolescent behavior can be misleading, however, if the extent of sexual activity is not taken into account. The data from two national surveys conducted in 1971 and 1976 (Table 1-8) and a third survey of women living in metropolitan areas conducted in 1979 (Table 1-9) show substantial increases in sexual activity. The size of the population at risk of conception should not include the number of women in an age group, but rather the number of sexually active women. With a few assumptions, one can compare the "risk of conception" for broad age groups over several years. In Table 1-10 various data for the years 1974 and 1979 are compared. The proportion of women who were sexually active was estimated by a simple interpolation and extrapolation of the 1971 and 1976 data and an adjustment of the 1976 figures as a function of the 1979 metropolitan area study. Because many technical issues cannot be dealt with accurately, these estimates should be used for heuristic purposes

Table 1-8. Percentage of Never Married Women 15–19 Years of Age Experiencing Sexual Intercourse: 1971 and 1976

Age	1971	1976	Percentage Increase
15	13.8	18.0	30.4
16	21.2	25.4	19.8
17	26.6	40.9	53.8
18	36.8	45.2	22.8
19	46.8	55.2	17.9
Total	26.8	36.1	30.2

Adapted from Zelnik M, Kantner JF: Sexual and contraceptive experience of young unmarried women. Fam Plann Perspect 9:55–71, 1977.

Table 1-9. Percentage of Never Married Women 15–19 Years of Age Experiencing Sexual Intercourse, Metropolitan Only: 1971, 1976, and 1979

Age	1971	1976	1979	Percentage Increase 1971–1979
15	14.4	18.6	22.5	56.2
16	20.9	28.9	37.8	80.9
17	26.1	42.9	48.5	85.8
18	39.7	51.4	56.9	43.3
19	46.4	59.5	69.0	48.7
Total	27.6	39.2	46.0	66.7

Adapted from Zelnik M, Kantner JF: Sexual Activity, Contraceptive use and pregnancy among metropolitan-area teenagers: 1971–1979. Fam Plann Perspec 12:230–237, 1980.

Table 1-10. Trends in Conception among Women 15–19 Years of Age: 1974 and 1979

Item	1974	1979	Percentage Change
1. Women 15–19	10,186,000	10,145,000	—
2. Birth rate (per 1000)	58.7	53.4	−9.0
3. Sexual activity			
Ever married	1,272,000	894,000	−29.7
Never married women who are sexually active	2,888,000	3,922,000	+35.8
Percentage never married who are sexually active	32.4	42.4	+30.9
4. Women at risk of pregnancy (ever married and sexually active never married)	4,160,000	4,816,000	+15.8
5. Births	594,400	549,500	−7.7
6. Births per 1000 sexually active	143.1	114.1	−20.3
7. Induced abortions	278,300	449,500	+61.5
8. Estimated conceptions (births and induced abortions)	873,700	999,000	+14.3
9. Conceptions per 1000 women	85.8	98.5	+14.8
10. Conceptions per 1000 sexually active women	210.0	207.4	−1.2
11. Abortions per 1000 sexually active women	66.9	93.3	+39.5

Adapted from Baldwin W: Adolescent pregnancy and Childbearing—Growing concerns for Americans. Popul Bull 31:1–36, 1980 (updated reprint).

rather than as precise estimates of the risk of pregnancy. For sexually active women aged 15–19, the risk of bearing a child fell even in the short period under review (line 6). Failure to take into account the increased likelihood of sexual activity would lead to underestimates of the decline in rates of childbearing (lines 2 and 6) and overestimates of a rising risk of conception (lines 9 and 10).

Although there has been a substantial increase in the number of abortions, there has been a smaller increase in the number of abortions per 1000 sexually active women (lines 4 and 11). The risk of conception has fallen only slightly, while the risk of bearing a child has fallen considerably because of an increased tendency to abort unwanted pregnancies. The role of induced abortion in the control of adolescent fertility should not be underestimated.

CONTRACEPTION

Patterns of Contraception

This analysis cannot address the extent to which contraception is responsible for the prevention of unwanted pregnancies, only the change over time. Zelnik and Kantner estimated the likely impact of current patterns of adolescent contraceptive practices on the number of premarital pregnancies in 1976.[14] While there were over 1 million pregnancies that year to women 15–19 (78 percent of them premarital), there would have been an additonal 680,000 in the absence of the use of contraceptives. On the other hand, if all who did not intend to become pregnant had been consistent users of contraceptives, there would have been about 40 percent fewer unintended pregnancies. A life table analysis by Zabin illustrated the potential reduction in premarital pregnancies achieved by the use of medically prescribed contraceptives.[15] If a method were begun 1, 6, or 12 months after first intercourse, pregnancies would be reduced by 60, 30, or 20 percent, respectively.

Other analyses indicated that contraceptive practice improved between 1971 and 1976 but that the risk of pregnancy remained about the same. According to the data from the 1971 and 1976 national surveys, about 28 percent of teenagers who had sexual intercourse experienced a premarital pregnancy; that rate was much higher for blacks (40 percent) than for whites (25 percent)[16] Only 11 percent of the teenagers who always used contraceptives experienced a pregnancy (6 percent for those using medical methods), whereas 24 percent of those who were irregular users became pregnant. Although contraception clearly reduces the risk of pregnancy, only 27 percent of the teenagers were regular users and 42 percent were irregular users.

Given the differences in birth rates by race, it is not surprising to find higher rates of sexual activity reported by black adolescents (Table 1-11).

Table 1-11. Percentage of Unmarried Women 15–19 Years of Age Having Experienced Sexual Intercourse by Age and Race: 1976

Age	Black	White	Ratio of Black to White
15	38.4	13.8	2.8:1
16	52.6	22.6	2.3:1
17	68.4	36.1	1.9:1
18	74.1	43.6	1.7:1
19	83.6	48.7	1.7:1

Adapted from Zelnik M, Kantner JF: Sexual and contraceptive experience of young unmarried women in the United States, 1976 and 1971. Fam Plann Perspect 9:55–71, 1977.

One indicator of sexual activity is rarely enough to give an accurate view of subgroup differences. White adolescents were more likely to have many partners (six or more) and to report having had sex six or more times in the 4 weeks preceding the survey.[14] This pattern was also found in a study of family planning clinic patients.[17] Black adolescents were less likely to have ever used a contraceptive (57 percent of blacks versus 72 percent of whites) and less likely to have used a method at first intercourse (34 percent versus 40 percent). However, black and white adolescents were equally likely to be regular users if they began using a contraceptive method at first intercourse (72 percent versus 69 percent), and blacks were more likely to have used a medical method as their first method (47 percent versus 20 percent). Among teenagers who were regular users, there were small differences in the likelihood of pregnancy among blacks and whites (11.2 percent versus 9.6 percent). Among irregular users, blacks experienced a higher risk of pregnancy (30.0 percent versus 22.6 percent), and among nonusers their risk was much higher (71.2 percent versus 52.2 percent). Similar proportions of blacks (29.8 percent) and whites (28.3 percent) reported that premarital pregnancies were intended. Among those not intending a pregnancy, more blacks than whites were not using a contraceptive at the time they became pregnant (89.0 percent versus 74.5 percent).[14]

Are teenagers using abortion in place of contraception? While many teenagers who obtain abortions were not using a contraceptive at the time they became pregnant, the aborters are twice as likely to have used a contraceptive previously than are women with other pregnancy outcomes. Luker examined the risk-taking by women of all ages who engage in unprotected intercourse.[18] The woman's perception of her risk of becoming pregnant, the availability of contraceptives, the cost of contraceptive use both in monetary terms and in terms of the sexual relationship, and the dynamics of the sexual relationship appear to influence whether a woman, or more rightly a couple, takes a chance on unprotected intercourse.

Inaccurate information regarding fecundity, the sporadic nature of adolescent sexual relationships, and the newness of dealing with such relationships may make teenagers especially vulnerable to miscalculations of the risk. In addition, some adolescents may not be sufficiently motivated to avoid pregnancy even when they are aware of the risk of conception. Zelnik and Kantner found that almost one-half of the nonvirgin women they interviewed had not had sex in the 4 weeks preceding the interview—51 percent among the 15- to 17-year-olds and 44 percent among the 18- to 19-year-olds.[16] Only 41 percent knew the time during the menstrual cycle of greatest risk of pregnancy. The teenagers' leading reasons for nonuse of contraception were a belief that it was the time of month of low risk, their youth, infrequent sex, or general belief that they could not get pregnant. These reasons were followed by the difficulty of obtaining contraceptives.[19] Even among those who had been contracepting regularly when they had an unintended pregnancy, 41 percent thought there was a good chance they might become pregnant despite their attempts to prevent it. This proportion is not much lower than the 55 percent of noncontraceptors who also felt there was a good chance they would become pregnant.

Unintended pregnancies appear to be associated with interesting patterns of perception about risk and also with interesting consequences. Data for whites in 1976 show that, as one would expect, unintended pregnancies were much more likely to result in induced abortion than were intended pregnancies (52.7 percent versus 11.8 percent); however, they were also much more likely to be reported as ending in miscarriage (17.1 percent versus 5.9 percent). It is difficult to tell whether these were really induced abortions or the result of actions that might have raised the likelihood of miscarriage.[11]

The woman's age has a strong impact on contraceptive behavior and consequently on the risk of pregnancy. Less than one-quarter of the girls under age 15 used a contraceptive at first intercourse, as opposed to 41 percent of the 15- to 17-year-olds and 55 percent of the 18- to 19-year-olds. The younger teenagers were more likely to begin contracepting with a nonmedical method than were the older teenagers, a factor which also contributed to the young teenagers' risk of conception. Zabin et al. studied 18- to 19-year-old women and looked at their experience with pregnancy soon after first intercourse: "nearly one-fifth became pregnant within six months of beginning sexual intercourse." Of those who became pregnant, nearly half of the pregnancies occurred during the first 6 months of exposure and one-fifth during the first month.[20] The first months of sexual activity are most risky because contraceptive behavior is often not yet established, and this risk is greatest for the youngest women. If a girl is under 15 when she first engages in sexual intercourse, she is nearly twice as likely to become pregnant in the first 6 months of exposure than if she is over age 17. Almost

10 percent of sexually active girls under age 15 become pregnant in the first month of exposure. Although it may be generally true that the risk of pregnancy is less when one is very young, especially during the first year after menarche, even for the youngest sexually active girls menarche generally precedes intercourse by 2 or 3 years.

Clinic Attendance

Research reports of the time between the initiation of intercourse and first clinic attendance often show delays of 6 months to 1 year. It is appropriate to focus on the delay in coming to a clinic since it is through the medical care system that teenagers get access to the most reliable methods of fertility control. Detailed data about the use of private physicians is not available, but adolescents use clinics for family planning services much more than do older women. A study conducted in 1980 by Zabin and Clark in a variety of family planning clinics sheds some light on the patterns and reasons for teenagers' delay in coming to clinics for contraceptives.[17] Some teenagers came for services before they were sexually active; this group included twice as many blacks (19.6 percent of the teenagers who attended the clinics studied by Zabin and Clark) as whites (10.1 percent). However, since more whites came within 2 months of first intercourse (10.9 percent as opposed to 5.7 percent for blacks), there were not large racial differences in the proportion arriving early in their exposure to the risk of pregnancy. The suspicion of pregnancy was the reason given by 36 percent of the young women for their first clinic visit. Zabin and Clark noted that "the mean interval from first intercourse to the first contraceptive visit of all sexually active clinic patients is 16.6 months, even though these are the select group of sexually active young women who do make it to a clinic and who have not been pregnant during their prior interval of exposure.[17] Nearly three-quarters of these young women had prior experience with contraception, either folk methods or reliable nonprescription methods. The time prior to coming to the clinic may also have been a period of low exposure to the risk of pregnancy given the sporadic nature of adolescent sexual activity. In general, the young women who were contraceptors before coming to the clinic were the ones who came relatively early; those who were poorer contraceptors or came in response to a pregnancy scare had delayed the longest.

Fear of pregnancy is clearly a powerful motivator for clinic attendance— for one-quarter of the young women surveyed it was the most important reason. Another major reason was that the relationship with the partner was becoming closer, a finding echoed in other studies. Other important reasons were that they expected to begin having sex, had just begun to have sex, or were having sex more often. For 10 percent of the women, another person (partner, parents, or another) helped motivate them to come. The main reason they had delayed coming so long was that they just "didn't get around to it;" this response, Zabin and Clark noted, may indicate simple procrastination or a more complex ambivalence toward seeking contraceptives. The second most prevalent reason for delay was fear that their families would find out if they came. Others waited for the relationship with the partner to develop, possibly to see if they would be in need of contraceptive protection, while others expressed fear of a pelvic exam or a belief that birth control was dangerous. Some gave reasons that reflected an apparent disbelief in the risk of pregnancy either because they felt they were too young or because the other method they were using was sufficient. [17]

In light of the current interest in parental notification or consent for family-planning services for minors, it is interesting to compare the proportion of adolescents who reported fear of parental discovery delaying their first visit (31 percent) with those who reported that a parent suggested the visit (7.3 percent). More whites reported fear of discovery (35.2 percent) than blacks (25.4 percent), and more blacks reported parental urging (11.5 percent) than whites (3.0 percent). Fear of discovery was a prominent reason among those who came only under suspicion of pregnancy (40.2 percent) but did not discriminate between those who delayed a short while and those who came promptly. Teenagers whose parents suggested the visit were more highly represented among those who came while still virgins (12.0 percent); over 17 percent of the black but less than 2 percent of the white virgins reported being referred by a parent. [17]

Despite widespread concern about parental involvement, few clinics require notification or consent and they may only require it when the patient is quite young. A 1980 study by Torres et al. revealed that only 10 percent of the clinics surveyed had such requirements (excluding those with a requirement for consent or notification for IUD insertions only) when the patient was aged 16 or 17. [21] Almost none required it for those 18 or older, and 20 percent required it for patients 15 or younger. In this study of clinic attendees, 54 percent of those under age 18 reported that their parents knew of their attendance: 30 percent reported they told their parents voluntarily and 21 percent reported that their parents suggested the visit. The proportion who told their parents voluntarily was unaffected by whether the clinic had a consent or notification requirement, but the proportion of parent-suggested visits was higher in clinics requiring notification or consent.

Of the 41 percent who reported they were sure their parents did not know, 18 percent said they would come to the clinic even if notification were required, and 23 percent said they would not come. Most of those who would stop coming (15 percent of the total) said they would resort to nonprescription methods, 4 percent would have unprotected sex, and 2 percent would cease sexual activity. The authors noted that by extrapolating the findings of this survey to all teenagers less than 18 served by clinics, it could be estimated that requiring parental notification or consent would result in 100,000 patients telling their parents about their use of contraceptives, but it would also result in 125,000 patients ceasing to use effective methods of contraception while continuing to be at risk of pregnancy. The teenagers who would stop contracepting or switch to less reliable methods would be at increased risk of an unwanted pregnancy and, by extension, to abortion. This survey indicated that 55 percent of girls under 18 who obtain abortions do so with the knowledge of their parents.

CONCLUSIONS

The role of parents in regard to adolescent sexual, contraceptive, and abortion behavior is complex. It is axiomatic in the social sciences that the family is a vitally important vehicle for socialization, and research points to the role of parental factors in influencing adolescent behavior. This influence appears in the transmission of general values and norms regarding the timing of marriage and childbearing. Parental characteristics relate to adolescents' involvement in school and their educational and occupational aspirations, which research shows are associated with fertility-related behavior. However, the role of parents in influencing the specifics of fertility control and sexual behavior is less clear.

Perhaps the most important conclusion from this analysis is the need to reach adolescents early, preferably before they have begun sexual intercourse. If parents and providers wait for the adolescent to seek a service, the adolescent may already be pregnant. This is especially true for the youngest adolescents, who may be the most difficult to reach. The likelihood of sexual activity among unmarried adolescents is fairly high and increasing—although it is not until age 19 that half are sexually active. Adolescents give many indications of wanting to control their fertility but have considerable difficulty in doing so. The youngest adolescents are the least likely to control their fertility, and they are more likely to end a pregnancy with an induced abortion than with any other outcome.

Given that the risk of pregnancy is high in the first months of exposure to sexual intercourse, and that teenagers tend to delay coming for an initial clinic visit (partly the result of their misperception of the risk of pregnancy and their difficulties in dealing with contraception and the health care delivery system), the focus should be on ways to reach adolescents before they are sexually active. The difficulties of such a plan are not trivial. For such an outreach program to occur via parents they have to become more willing and able to discuss sex and contraception and acquire an improved sense of when their child is "old enough" to be a candidate for sexual intercourse. In order for schools or other institutions to undertake such a campaign parents' support would be required. The programs would have to reach age groups in which only a small percentage of the pupils would be genuine candidates for information about pregnancy risk and contraception. Service systems and/or counseling programs would be necessary to back up information. One possible step might be to target contraception education efforts at males since the male partner is likely to be a little older than the female. There is another major obstacle to reaching adolescents before they are sexually active. Parents and providers may believe that sexual activity is wrong or at least inappropriate for young adolescents, and therefore be reluctant to offer counsel about how to manage such activity. It is possible, however, for them to point out that for a young adolescent sex may be risky from a physical or psychological perspective, but still urge responsible contraceptive behavior should the adolescent become sexually active.

REFERENCES

1. National Center for Health Statistics: Vital Statistics of the United States, vol 1: Natality 1960. Rockville, Md, National Center for Health Statistics, 1962
2. National Center for Health Statistics: Final natality statistics, 1970. Monthly Vital Statistics Report [Suppl] 22(12), 1974 (DHEW Publ No (HRA) 74-1120)
3. National Center for Health Statistics: Final natality statistics, 1973. Monthly Vital Statistics Report [Suppl] 23(1), 1975 (DHEW Publ No (HRA) 75-1120)
4. National Center for Health Statistics: Final natality statistics, 1978. Monthly Vital Statistics Report [Suppl] 29(1), 1980 (DHHS Publ No (PHS) 80-1120)
5. National Center for Health Statistics: Advance report of final natality statistics, 1979. Monthly Vital Statistics Report [Suppl 2] 30(6), 1981 (DHHS Publ No (PHS) 81-1120)
6. National Center for Health Statistics: Trends in illegitimacy—United States 1940–1965. Vital and Health Statistics, Series 21, No 15, 1968
7. National Center for Health Statistics: Fertility Tables for Birth Cohorts by Color: United States, 1917–1973 (DHEW Publ No (HRA) 76-1152). Washington, DC, US Government Printing Office, 1976
8. National Center for Health Statistics: Vital Statistics of the United States: 1974, vol 1: Natality (DHEW Publ No (PHS) 78-1120). Washington, DC, US Government Printing Office, 1978
9. National Center for Health Statistics: Vital Statistics of the United States: 1975, vol 1: Natality. (DHEW Publ No (PHS) 78-1113)
10. National Center for Health Statistics: Unpublished tabulations of adolescent birth rates, 1976–1979
11. Zelnik M, Kantner JF: First pregnancies to women aged 15–19: 1976 and 1971. Fam Plann Perspect 10:11–20, 1978
12. Forrest JD, Sullivan E, Tietze C: Abortion in the United States, 1977–1978. Fam Plann Perspect 11:329–341, 1979
13. Centers for Disease Control: Abortion Surveillance, 1977. Atlanta, Ga, CDC, 1979
14. Zelnik M, Kantner JF: Contraceptive patterns and premarital pregnancy among women aged 15–19 in 1976. Fam Plann Perspect 10:135–142, 1978

15. Zabin LS: The impact of early use of prescription contraceptives on reducing premarital teenage pregnancies. Fam Plann Perspect 13:72–79, 1981
16. Zelnik M, Kantner JF: Sexual and contraceptive experience of young unmarried women in the United States, 1976 and 1971. Fam Plann Perspect 9:55–71, 1977
17. Zabin LS, Clark SD Jr: Why they delay: A study of teenage family planning clinic patients. Fam Plann Perspect 13:205–217, 1981
18. Luker, K: Taking Chances. Berkeley, University of California Press, 1975
19. Shah F, Zelnik M, Kantner JF: Unprotected intercourse among unwed teenagers. Fam Plann Perspect 7:39–44, 1975
20. Zabin LS, Kantner JF, Zelnik M: The risk of adolescent pregnancy in the first months of intercourse. Fam Plann Perspect 11:215–222, 1979
21. Torres A, Forrest JD, Eisman S: Telling parents: Clinic policies and adolescents' use of family planning and abortion services. Fam Plann Perspect 12:284–292, 1980

additional and more specific event-related lines of inquiry. As a result, the amount of information available about sexual activity increased with each survey. Comparative data are provided wherever possible.

EXTENT OF PREMARITAL SEXUAL ACTIVITY

Investigators disagree about the pattern of premarital sexual activity over the 50-year period preceding the 1970s: some argue for relative stability (combined with greater willingness to talk about sex), whereas others argue for continued increases in premarital intercourse. (Although it may be incorrect to speak of "premarital" intercourse with respect to never married women, since some of them will not marry, common usage and ease of exposition justify doing so.) Whatever the case may have been in the past, we can speak with more authority about the 1970s, during which time there was a substantial and continued increase in the prevalence of premarital sexual activity. The proportion of young women who had premarital intercourse increased from 30 percent in 1971 to 43 percent in 1976 and to 50 percent in 1979 (Table 2-1). Whereas blacks showed an increase from 54 percent in 1971 to 66 percent in 1976 with no subsequent change, whites show a continued increase from 26 percent in 1971 to 38 percent in 1976 and 47 percent in 1979. Although the racial difference has narrowed, blacks in 1979 were still 40 percent more likely than whites to be sexually active. There is a clear and consistent pattern of an increase in the proportion sexually active with an increase in current age. In each survey, 19-year-old women were about three times as likely to have had intercourse as 15-year-olds.

Not surprisingly, the proportion of ever married young women who had premarital intercourse is considerably greater than the proportion of never married women who had done so, with larger differences for whites than for blacks. A close examination of the data in Table 2-1 reveals that all of the increase in sexual activity between 1976 and 1979 is attributable to the increase that occurred among never married white women.

FIRST INTERCOURSE

Age

In spite of the increase in sexual activity that occurred among whites between 1976 and 1979, there was no change in their mean age at first intercourse; nor was there any change for blacks (Table 2-2). Thus, there appears to have been a leveling off in the age at which sexual activity begins,

Table 2-1. Percentage of Women 15–19 Years of Age Who Had Premarital Intercourse, by Age, Marital Status, and Race: 1971, 1976, and 1979

Age and Marital Status	1971			1976			1979		
	Total	White	Black	Total	White	Black	Total	White	Black
All	30.4	26.4	53.7	43.4	38.3	66.3	49.8	46.6	66.2
	(2739)*	(1758)	(981)	(1452)	(881)	(571)	(1717)	(1034)	(683)
15	14.8	11.8	31.2	18.9	14.2	38.9	22.8	18.5	41.7
16	21.8	17.8	46.4	30.0	25.2	55.1	39.5	37.4	50.9
17	28.2	23.2	58.4	46.0	40.0	71.9	50.1	45.8	74.6
18	42.6	38.8	62.4	56.7	52.1	78.4	63.0	60.3	77.0
19	48.2	43.8	76.2	64.1	59.2	85.3	71.4	68.0	88.7
Never married	27.6	23.2	52.4	39.2	33.6	64.3	46.0	42.3	64.8
	(2512)	(1584)	(928)	(1298)	(760)	(538)	(1571)	(928)	(643)
Ever married	55.0	53.2	72.7	86.3	85.0	93.9	86.7	86.2	91.2
	(227)	(174)	(53)	(154)	(121)	(33)	(146)	(106)	(40)

*Unweighted sample size is shown in parentheses; $n \geq 107$ for each age–race cell.

Table 2-2. Mean Age at First Premarital Intercourse, by Race: 1971, 1976 and 1979

Year and Race	Age	n
1971		
White	16.6	435
Black	15.9	501
Total	16.4	936
1976		
White	16.3	350
Black	15.6	376
Total	16.1	726
1979		
White	16.4	478
Black	15.5	455
Total	16.2	933

following a small decline that occurred between 1971 and 1976. The racial difference in the prevalence of sexual activity carries over to the initiation of that activity, with blacks starting their sexual careers at a somewhat younger age, on the average, than whites. Obviously, as these cohorts of young women get older and more of those not sexually active begin to have sex, the mean age at first intercourse will increase. As this occurs, the difference between blacks and whites will become larger than it is.

Locale

For years Americans have suffered through jokes about the importance of the back seat of the automobile in sexual encounters among young people. Whether the automobile was as widely used in the past for sexual purposes as the jokes suggested cannot now be determined. It is useful, however, to consider where sex takes place as a means of telling us something about society and the changes occurring around us—if not by revealing new social patterns then by illustrating and illuminating in new ways what we already know.

The distribution of where first intercourse occurred is given in Table 2-3 for 1976 and 1979 (this information was not collected in 1971). In both surveys about 80 percent of the premaritally sexually active young women reported that their first sexual experience (of intercourse) took place in a home—their own home, their partner's home, or the home of a relative or friend, with the partner's home being the most common. Interestingly, this location gained in popularity between the two surveys, while the use of a

Table 2-3. Distribution (in Percentages) of Locale of First Premarital Intercourse, by Race: 1976 and 1979

Locale	1976			1979		
	Total ($n = 713$)	White ($n = 345$)	Black ($n = 368$)	Total ($n = 923$)	White ($n = 469$)	Black ($n = 454$)
Respondent's home	17.6	16.2	21.2	18.5	17.9	20.7
Partner's home	43.5	43.8	43.1	49.2	48.4	51.7
Home of relative/friend	21.1	21.5	20.2	12.3	12.6	11.5
Motel/hotel	5.5	3.3	11.5	4.2	2.2	11.7
Car	7.1	8.9	2.0	8.9	10.6	2.7
Elsewhere	5.2	6.3	2.0	6.9	8.3	1.7

relative's or friend's home declined. The remaining 20 percent were divided among motels or hotels, cars, and "elsewhere" (largely outdoors in parks or camping grounds). The major differences between blacks and whites were that blacks made greater relative use of motels, whereas whites more commonly used cars and "elsewhere." The age at which sexual initiation occurred seems to have made little difference as to where it occurred—with the exception that the younger the age at first intercourse the more likely the home was the young girl's or a relative's and the less likely it was the partner's, whereas the older the age at first intercourse the more likely it was the partner's home (data not shown).

The degree to which sex begins at home may be surprising to some, but it is certainly consistent with the changes that have occurred with respect to working wives, declining neighborhoods, and the general lessening of parental surveillance and control. Homes unoccupied by parents are far more attractive as places for sexual dalliance than cars or the great outdoors; and presumably something other than studying together (or listening to music together) is going on behind closed doors while parents sit downstairs congratulating themselves for treating their children as responsible and mature individuals entitled to privacy.

First Partner

If a home is the most likely place for the onset of sexual activity, then what relationship does the male partner have with the young woman? Information on this issue was collected in the 1979 survey but not in the two earlier studies. The distribution of the type of relationship the young woman had with her first sexual partner at the time of her first intercourse is presented in Table 2-4. About 80 percent of the young women reported that they were going steady with or dating their initial sexual partner. (Although the terms "going steady with" and "dating" may strike some as anachronistic, our respondents had no difficulty understanding them or distinguishing

Table 2-4. Distribution (in Percentages) of Type of Relationship with First Premarital Sexual Partner, by Race: 1979

Relationship	Total ($n = 931$)	White ($n = 477$)	Black ($n = 454$)
Engaged	9.3	9.6	8.2
Going steady	55.3	57.6	46.5
Dating	24.4	22.2	32.6
Friends	6.7	6.0	9.4
Just met	3.3	3.4	3.2
Other	1.0	1.2	0.1

between these and other types of relationships, i.e., "engaged" or "friend.") Blacks and whites were similar in this respect, but blacks were more likely than whites to have sex the first time with someone they were dating, whereas whites were more likely than blacks to be going steady with their first sexual partner. Only 9 percent reported they were engaged to their first partner. Here again there was very little variation by age at first intercourse, with the exception that those who first had intercourse at age 18 or 19 were somewhat more likely than those who began sex earlier to be engaged to their partner when sexual intercourse first took place (data not shown). Even among those who first had intercourse at age 15 or younger, 79 percent reported they were going steady with or dating their first partner.

Whatever the case may have been in the past, it does not now appear that sex is the "gateway" to marriage—unless we want to make the unlikely assumption that persons going steady or dating will eventually marry each other. The phenomenon of early dating (including going steady) has over the years aroused much discussion among social commentators. Some have ridiculed and scorned it, others have found much good in it, while still others have found it cute but meaningless and harmless. We cannot with our data determine what the psychic benefits or disadvantages of early dating may be, but the data do suggest that in the current social environment one consequence of early dating is early initiation of sexual activity.

Planned or Unplanned Occurrence

The 1979 survey provides information on whether the first intercourse was planned or "just happened," at least as seen retrospectively through the eyes of the young woman. Just under 20 percent of the young women reported that they planned their first intercourse; there was virtually no difference in this respect between whites and blacks (Table 2-5). Surprisingly, there was no systematic variation in planning by age at time of first intercourse; the

Table 2-5. Percentage of Premaritally Sexually Active Women 15–19 Years of Age Whose First Intercourse Was Planned, by Age At First Intercourse and Race: 1979

Age at First Intercourse	Total	White	Black
All	17.5 (928)*	17.1 (476)	18.8 (452)
15 and under	17.3 (485)	16.7 (213)	18.9 (272)
16	21.6 (214)	20.8 (116)	25.0 (98)
17	10.6 (127)	10.6 (73)	10.5 (54)
18–19	18.7 (102)	18.8 (74)	17.1 (28)

*Number in sample is shown in parentheses.

relatively high proportion who engaged in planned first intercourse at age 16, for both whites and blacks, may reflect determination on the part of some young women to acknowledge that "celebrated" age with more than just a kiss.

Does type of relationship with first partner have an effect on whether first intercourse was planned? The highest proportion who engaged in a planned first intercourse were those who reported they were going steady with their first partner; 22 percent of these women planned their first intercourse. Here again, there was no difference between blacks and whites. Among blacks, those who were engaged had an equally high rate of planned first intercourse, whereas among whites this category had the lowest proportion of planning except for the "just met" category. Thus, while there were some differences in distribution among the first partner categories, for the overwhelming majority of young women first intercourse "just happened" regardless of the relationship the couple had.

TOTAL NUMBER OF PARTNERS AND FREQUENCY OF INTERCOURSE

Many, if not most, young people go through a series of dating and/or going steady relationships. We do not have data on how many relationships a respondent had, but we do have data for each respondent on the total number of (premarital) sexual partners (Table 2-6). Although the modal number of partners in each survey was one, the number of young women who had only one partner diminished between 1971 and 1976, and the number who had multiple partners increased, indicating an increase in the average number of partners. Between 1976 and 1979 the mean number of partners declined slightly, a result of a decline among whites. Even among whites, however, the proportion who had only one partner declined (as did the proportion who had four or more partners). One-half of all sexually active young women in 1979 had had more than one partner and 16 percent had had four or more partners.

In the 1971 and 1976 surveys whites tended to have more partners on the average than blacks; by 1979 the two groups had essentially the same average number of partners. Given that blacks begin to have sex earlier on the average than whites, it is perhaps surprising that the longer duration of sexual activity on the part of blacks does not lead to their having more sexual partners than whites.

Whereas the total number of partners increased between 1971 and 1976 and declined slightly between 1976 and 1979, frequency of intercourse (in the 4 weeks preceding interview and among never married women only) apparently decreased between 1971 and 1976 and then increased between

Table 2-6. Distribution (in Percentages) of Total Number of Premarital Sexual Partners, by Race: 1971, 1976, and 1979

No. of Partners*	1971			1976			1979		
	Total (*n* = 919)	White (*n* = 431)	Black (*n* = 488)	Total (*n* = 714)	White (*n* = 344)	Black (*n* = 370)	Total (*n* = 933)	White (*n* = 476)	Black (*n* = 457)
1	61.7	61.8	61.4	52.5	56.2	42.8	48.9	51.1	40.9
2–3	24.6	23.0	29.5	27.7	23.0	40.0	35.1	33.0	42.7
4–5	6.8	7.4	5.1	9.1	8.2	11.6	7.9	7.0	11.4
6 or more	6.9	7.8	4.0	10.7	12.6	5.6	8.1	8.9	5.0
Mean	NA†	NA	NA	2.9	3.0	2.4	2.6	2.7	2.5

*In the 1971 survey these precoded categories were used; in the 1976 and 1979 surveys individual responses were recorded.
†NA: not available.

Table 2-7. Distribution (in Percentages) of Frequency of Intercourse in the 4 Weeks Preceding Interview among Never Married Women, by Race: 1971, 1976, and 1979

Frequency of Intercourse*	1971			1976			1979		
	Total ($n = 777$)	White ($n = 330$)	Black ($n = 447$)	Total ($n = 590$)	White ($n = 247$)	Black ($n = 343$)	Total ($n = 809$)	White ($n = 388$)	Black ($n = 421$)
0	38.3	36.9	41.7	47.5	45.7	51.8	41.8	40.2	46.8
1–2	31.1	30.6	32.3	22.2	19.7	28.0	24.6	23.9	26.7
3–5	17.7	17.5	18.1	15.0	15.9	13.0	14.1	13.3	16.5
6 or more	12.9	15.0	7.9	15.3	18.8	7.2	19.5	22.6	10.0
Mean	NA†	NA	NA	2.9	3.4	1.7	3.7	4.1	2.3

*In the 1971 survey these precoded categories were used; in the 1976 and 1979 surveys individual responses were recorded.
†NA: not available.

1976 and 1979 (Table 2-7). Thus, for all sexually active women, the number of partners and frequency of intercourse appear to be inversely related. Over all three surveys the major changes resulted from shifts between the zero and the one or two times categories, whereas approximately the same proportions had intercourse three or more times (during the reference period). Whites had higher frequencies at each date than blacks, with no narrowing of the difference in 1979, as was the case with number of partners.

The modal frequency of intercourse for each race at each survey was zero, with 40–50 percent falling in this category. Another 20–30 percent had intercourse only once or twice during the 4-week period—fairly high proportions at very low frequencies. On the other hand, if we exclude the large proportion of the temporarily abstinent (i.e., the zero category) and consider mean frequency only among those who had intercourse at least once in the 4-week period preceding interview, we get a somewhat different picture. Taking white women for illustrative purposes, mean frequency of intercourse over the 4-week period among those young women who had it at least once during that interval was 6.9 in 1979 and 6.3 in 1976. These are fairly high levels considering that the women were young and single.

CONCLUSIONS

We have considered several aspects of premarital sexual activity among adolescent women in the United States during the 1970s. The proportion of young women having premarital sexual intercourse increased over this period, and by 1979 one-half of the young women were sexually active. The average age at first intercourse was just over 16 years, with no change in this respect during the latter part of the decade. The overwhelming majority of young women had their first sexual experience in a home and with someone they were dating or going steady with. For most young women the initiation into sex was spontaneous or unplanned. Among the sexually active, about one-half had only one partner, although over the decade there was a continued decrease in the proportion having only one partner and a continued increase in the proportion having two or three partners. For about 40 percent of the sexually active, intercourse appeared to be a relatively sporadic and infrequent event, at least as measured by the frequency of intercourse in a 4-week period preceding interview. For a smaller but still substantial fraction of young women, however, sexual intercourse presumably was a more frequent and regular activity. In 1979, 20 percent of the young women had sex six or more times in the 4-week reference period, an increase at this level of sexual activity from 13 percent in 1971.

At a societal level, sex among the young is of concern because it often has an undesired and unintended consequence, namely, pregnancy. The proportion of sexually active young women who had a premarital pregnancy increased from 28 percent in 1971 to 33 percent in 1979—during the same period premarital pregnancy among all young women doubled, from 8 to 16 percent. The visibility of premarital pregnancy was further heightened during the 1970s by a continued reduction in the proportion marrying while pregnant and a continued increase in the proportion of pregnancies ending in abortion.[1]

The increase in premarital pregnancy occurred in spite of an increase in the proportion of sexually active young women who consistently used contraception, an increase in the proportion who used contraception at first intercourse, a decrease in the proportion who never used contraception, a decline in the proportion who wanted to become pregnant, and an increase, among those who did not want to become pregnant, in the proportion using contraception at the time of conception.[1] Thus, there is evidence that young women are increasingly trying to avoid pregnancy out of wedlock. That they are having less success in doing so may in part be a result of a change in the profile of initial contraceptive methods used, with greater reliance on the condom and withdrawal and less on the pill,[1] but other factors also are involved. What these factors and those underlying the changes in the initial contraceptive method profile may be requires further investigation. It is within this context—the delineation of the reasons for the increasing level of out-of-wedlock pregnancy—that patterns of sexual behavior take on their significance.

REFERENCES

1. Zelnik M, Kantner JF: Sexual activity, contraceptive use and pregnancy among metropolitan-area teenagers: 1971–1979. Fam Plann Perspect 12:230–237, 1980
2. Zelnik M, Kantner JF, Ford K: Sex and Pregnancy in Adolescence. Beverly Hills, Calif, Sage, 1981

3

Prevention of Adolescent Pregnancy: A Developmental Approach

Richard E. Kreipe

*It is not the biological aspect of age that is relevant in our society; it is the social significance. In some other time and place, sexual intercourse leading to early reproduction might not be a problem; it might even be an advantage. However, early reproduction in our society has a contemporary disadvantage, the result of modern life.**

Although this book is based on the premise that childbearing during adolescence places the youth at a social disadvantage, not all members of society share similar goals in preventing adolescent pregnancy. Some people argue that only illegitimate pregnancies should be avoided, since pregnancy within marriage is appropriate. Others feel that attention should be focused on unintended conceptions, irrespective of marital status. Still others contend that unwanted pregnancies should be aborted, while wanted pregnancies should be supported. Libertarians consider the idea of limiting personal freedom officious; authoritarians consider the idea of adolescent sexual behavior unacceptable. Controversy abounds, and one's viewpoint will necessarily influence one's approach to the issue.

Epidemiologists define three levels of prevention that tend to overlap to some extent. The promotion of abstinence, sex education, and effective

---

*From Morris NM: The biological advantages and social disadvantages of teenage pregnancy. Am J Public Health 71:796, 1981. With permission.

birth control are all examples of primary prevention, the prevention of conception. Secondary prevention is the avoidance of "disability" once a pregnancy occurs. The disabilities associated with early childbearing are discussed elsewhere in this book (see Parts II and III); at this level of prevention, abortion or adoption are two options presently available for those youth who choose to not keep their babies. Secondary prevention also includes continuing education, developing support systems and parenting skills, as well as preventing a repeat pregnancy while an adolescent. Tertiary prevention applies to those adolescents who have become pregnant and have experienced some disability as a result. Rehabilitation is the objective at this level of prevention, exemplified by various intervention programs directed toward restoring normal adolescent growth and development.

Since individual adolescent growth and development need to be fostered irrespective of one's preventive goals, in this chapter we first examine adolescence with an emphasis on aspects of development relevant to teenage pregnancy. Adolescents are neither children nor adults, but are transitional with respect to their bodies, their minds, and their social development; they are vulnerable to a number of internal and external influences that can lead to early sexual activity and pregnancy. It is therefore important to discuss a developmental framework that takes these considerations into account.

It is also important to be aware of the evolution of attitudes and beliefs about adolescent sexuality and childbearing over the past several decades. Key historical events in this process are presented in an effort to establish an understanding of the changing cultural milieu in which adolescents have been developing. In addition to attitudes about adolescent pregnancy, programs to prevent adolescent pregnancy have developed over the years. Rather than dissect numerous specific programs, we examine approaches of various programs, attempting to extract the key elements that relate to success. Successful prevention also requires individualization. Hence we discuss individual adolescent sexual decision making and suggest ways that responsible decision making can be fostered.

DEVELOPMENTAL CONSIDERATIONS

Many theorists have described various developmental "tasks" of adolescence; failure to complete those tasks precludes the attainment of a responsible adulthood. Havighurst has defined 12 such tasks,[1] and Erikson has defined one "phase-specific" task.[2] In this discussion we focus on four tasks that reflect dynamic forces with direct influence on adolescent sexual expression and pregnancy. These interactive forces help to explain many of the apparent incongruencies associated with premature sexuality or parenthood: the 17-year-old searching for independence who encounters nothing but restrictions with her 5-month-old son; the 15-year-old groping for security who finds only one-night stands; or the 13-year-old seeking mothering who becomes a mother herself. Potentially successful preventive strategies become more obvious when these developmental forces are appreciated.

The tasks include the acceptance of physical maturation, the attainment of adult thinking skills in a cognitive transition, the achievement of independence, and the establishment of an adult identity. Obviously, successful prevention also requires attention to familial, community and societal influences on adolescent sexual behavior; the primary focus of this chapter is individual adolescent development. Rather than separate male and female issues, we consider the tasks as common to both sexes. Thus, adolescent pregnancy prevention becomes a responsibility for both boys and girls.

Acceptance of Physical Maturation

Physical maturation provides incontrovertible evidence of impending adulthood; an acceptance of this process is required early in adolescent development. *Pubescence* encompasses the biologic changes leading to the development of reproductive capacity. During pubescence, the hypothalamic-pituitary-gonadal axis is activated by a decreased sensitivity of the hypothalamus to the negative feedback of sex steroid hormones.[3] The gonads, as well as the adrenal glands, then increase the production of these hormones, effecting the characteristic physical changes noted during this stage of life. In addition to the changes in the genital system, there is a gain of 25 percent of the final height, a gain of 50 percent of the ideal body weight, and the maturation of many organ systems.[4]

Adolescence encompasses the psychological and social development associated with puberty, leading to adulthood. Important in this process are the tasks of ego (identity) development, the achievement of personal independence, and the attainment of more sophisticated cognitive skills. Home and school constitute the major environments in which these changes evolve, a fact of monumental importance when one considers the degree to which discussion about adolescent sexuality is often excluded from these environments.

Because the two processes of pubescence and adolescence generally proceed concurrently, they are often assumed to be identical. There is no evidence, however, that early sexual development is necessarily accompanied by early ego development, early achievement of independence, or early attainment of adult thinking skills.[5] In fact, females who undergo puberty at an earlier age appear to be at a disadvantage in many respects. The Oakland Growth Study found that, in contrast to boys, the physically early maturing females were below average in prestige, popularity, sociability, leadership, cheerfulness, poise, and expressiveness.[6] This study found that the early maturers had a significantly higher need for recognition than the late maturing females.

Nevertheless, it is common for health care professionals to expect a Tanner stage V, 14-year-old to "act like an adult." This expectation is usually counterproductive since it does not take into account the fact that physically mature adolescents may not be emotionally mature. A therapeutic relationship with an adolescent requires attention to the psychosocial as well as the physical development.

For females, visible evidence of sexual physical development precedes menstruation by at least 1 year. Menarche, however, represents the "definite dividing line between childhood and adulthood."[7] With respect to menarche, the *secular trend* is the gradual decrease in the average age at which this event has been noted to occur over the past several generations. Although recent evidence brings into question a trend over several centuries,[8] there is good evidence that the onset of menses in industrialized countries now occurs, on the average, about 4 years younger than it did 100 years ago.[4] Despite an average age of menarche of 12.5 years, there is wide individual variation in the normal timing of this event, from age 9 years to 16 years. The work of several investigators, most notably Marshall and Tanner,[9] has shown such chronological variability to be true for all aspects of physical development.

These points concerning puberty and adolescence lead to several important considerations. Because of the wide variability of physical development, services and programs should not be directed toward a specific age group: need, not age, should be the entry criterion. Services and programs need to be available for those who begin sexual maturation, sexual activity, or both at an early age. One study reported that over one-half of the sexually active boys at a senior high school had sexual intercourse while in junior high, but their sex education course was not offered until senior high.[10] If adolescents establish reproductive capacity before attaining sufficient maturity to integrate this change into their developing self, there is a biologic risk for premature parenthood.[11]

Finally, when dealing with the individual teenager one must evaluate the adolescence and the pubescence of each individual separately. The patient needs to be approached in a manner appropriate for the psychosocial, not physical, stage of development. For further information regarding adolescent developmental assessment the reader is referred to Daniel's excellent text.[12]

Cognitive Transition

The teenager often functions cognitively at some level between the concrete operational stage of thinking characteristic of the preadolescent, and the formal operational stage of thinking characteristic of the adult as described by Piaget.[13] Adults familiar with the thinking style of the child may find the emerging adolescent cognitive skills refreshing. On the other hand, those more familiar with the thinking style of the adult may find the adolescent thinking style frustrating.

In the *concrete operational* mode, thinking is limited to the "here and now"; directly experienced events are the main focus of thought. The cognitive repertoire does not include considering the future, the consequences of behavior, or the alternatives of behavior. Only one option for behavior exists: that which one *does*. Thus, the teenager who is concrete operational may have difficulty responding appropriately to questions that require formal operational skills.

Formal operational thinking is characterized by the ability to make abstractions, to see the long-range consequences of behavior, to plan for the future, and to "think about thinking." Classical Piagetian theory marks the beginning of formal operations at age 11 or 12 years; however, the emergence of a formal operational thought structure is not characteristic of all people.[14] Dale noted that less than 75 percent of the 15-year-olds that he tested had reached a conventional stage of formal thought.[15]

For those who do reach formal operations, the transition from concrete to formal operations is not an "off–on" phenomenon, but is attained gradually. Typically, the cognitively transitional youth may be able to earn money for a pair of designer jeans (something concrete), but at the same time not be able to study toward a college education (something abstract).

Cognitively, pregnancy and parenthood are also abstractions. As such they may represent concepts that are distant, intangible, and therefore inaccessible with respect to the adolescent's thought processes. Thus, decision making around issues related to childbearing, even for the pregnant adolescent, may be an extremely difficult task. Queries regarding the plans of the mother-to-be for child care may be met with a puzzled "Huh?". She may lack not the intelligence but the reasoning ability to analyze and process the relevant issues realistically.

As formal operations develop, normal adolescent cognition exhibits three additional interrelated dimensions, best described by Elkind:[16] egocentrism, the imaginary audience, and the personal fable. Awareness of these dimensions leads to a more complete appreciation of how adolescents may think with respect to sexual issues.

Egocentrism refers to the normal narcissism of adolescence. Self-centeredness is an important prerequisite for a stable adult identity; only by focusing on his or her self can a boy or girl come to know who he or she is. Hence, egocentric adolescents may feel temporarily that the world revolves around them, and that to some degree they should not be influenced by possible consequences of their behavior. With respect to sexual behavior, this is often interpreted by others as selfish and hedonistic.

Normal adolescents also often act as if "all eyes are on them." This transitory phenomenon, called the perception of an *imaginary audience,* grows out of emerging formal operational thought processes. Thinking about one's own thoughts is tied inextricably to thinking about the thoughts of other people. The adolescent feels "on stage" when she assumes that other people are thinking about her thoughts. If this process causes her to fell vulnerable, she may mask, deny, or hide any evidence that might disclose her thoughts. The self-consciousness and guilt surrounding the use of a "visible" contraceptive, such as a diaphragm, undoubtedly are related to this phenomenon. [17] To use a diaphragm is to admit to thinking about and planning for sexual activity. Contrariwise, the imaginary audience may provide the adolescent male the opportunity to disclose his "machismo" as he proudly displays his recently purchased condoms to his friends.

With respect to pregnancy, the *personal fable* is an extremely important aspect of adolescent cognitive development. In the magical thinking of this phenomenon an adolescent views himself or herself as idealized and special; feelings of invulnerability and immortality characterize the personal fable. Established sexual facts that apply to others do not apply to the individual because he or she is unique. In this context, a sexually active adolescent does not need contraception because pregnancy "couldn't happen to me." An attitude such as this does not necessarily reflect a lack of sexual responsibility. It may exemplify a normal developmental cognitive immaturity in which undesirable outcomes cannot even be considered. This often carries over into pregnancy, so that the adolescent mother-to-be fantasizes the course and outcome of her pregnancy: she will be an ideal mother, her baby will be an ideal child. [18]

Additional examples of the influence of the cognitive transition on adolescent pregnancy abound. Some youth may not be aware of the cause-and-effect relationship of sexual intercourse and pregnancy. Others believe that infrequent or one's initial intercourse cannot lead to pregnancy. Still others, classically concrete operational, may place their birth control pills intravaginally, or cut holes in their diaphragms so that they will "look just like the ones in clinic."

Obviously, the adolescent's ability to "reason about" pregnancy is related to the "reasons for" adolescent pregnancy. Teenagers have reported a multitude of reasons for becoming pregnant. [19] Researchers have also focused on developmental or psychoanalytical interpretations of the causal factors for adolescent pregnancy. [20] Semmens and Lammers[21] combined many stated and inferred reasons for adolescent pregnancy and proposed the following clinically useful, cognitive-based classification:

• *Intentional.* The adolescent is clearly motivated with a "conscious intent to become pregnant" for a wide variety of reasons to be discussed later. Although the element of planning may be important in this category, these adolescents often operate concretely and from an elaborate personal fable. It is important to note that "intentional" or "planned" does not necessarily mean "desired" or "wanted." Likewise, what was intended at the time of conception may bear no relation to what was intended in the second trimester of pregnancy. The vacillating emotions characteristic of normal adolescent ambivalence often make the provision of services to this group of adolescents difficult. The intentionally pregnant group constitutes a much larger proportion of pregnant adolescents than had previously been thought.[22]

• *Accidental.* These adolescents are engaged in sexual behavior in which the "conscious participation is minimal."[23] Some of these adolescents may be characterized as risk takers, or they may be reflecting familial or cultural behavior patterns. Also included in this category are those who use their sexuality to "satisfy teenage goals: identity, independence conflict . . . , or rebellion towards a society that seems to move too slowly or in the wrong direction."[21] True contraceptive failure accounts for a small proportion of the accidentally pregnant group.

• *Misinformed or uninformed.* This is the group in which pregnancy could be avoided if the proper information or services were available and utilized. Many of the early programs to prevent adolescent pregnancy stressed fertility education and easy access to services, under the assumption that sexual ignorance or unavailability of services led to a large number of teenage conceptions.[23] Clearly, those who wait to have intercourse until 1 week after their period has ended are not effective contraceptors and need to become aware of their fertile days. We now realize, however, that the provision of sex education in the school and contraceptives in the community does not immunize the youth against pregnancy.[22,24]

It is obvious that the cognitive influence on sexual decision making relates to the process as well as the input; that is, sexual behavior seems to be influenced not only by information or knowledge, but also by the context in which sexual decision making occurs. According to the National Health Survey, from 1966 to 1970 the median amount of time that 15-year-olds spent watching television was more than 800 hr/yr,[25] and there is no evidence that adolescents spend any less time viewing television in the 1980s. A large proportion of their present viewing includes popular daytime "soaps" and nighttime "adventures" or "comedies" that portray sexual behavior almost as a hobby, with unrealistic or no consequences. This survey also found that those youths interviewed listened to radio an additional 700 hr/yr. Popular music, which was being listened to most of that time, has an increasingly explicit sexual theme. Hence, although the cognitive apparatus of the adolescent may be exposed to a modicum of sexual facts, it is generally immersed in sexual fantasy. Any attempt to improve adolescent sexual decision making must take these realities into account.

Achievement of Independence

Emergence from dependence upon the parents and family to self-sufficient independence is another important task of normal adolescence that can be directly related to sexuality and childbearing. For some girls there seems to be no more certain means to attain personal, social, and legal independence than to become pregnant; they can be catapulted from minor status to adult status upon giving birth to a child. In this context, sexual behavior leading to pregnancy may be "viewed as a means of escaping from one's life situation."[26]

Closely related to sexual activity intended to provide an escape is sexual activity that represents a manifestation of adolescent rebellion against, or hostility toward, parental values. As noted by Cohen and Friedman, "parents who are uneasy, anxious, and threatened when confronted with sexual matters are the most vulnerable to the potent weapon of (adolescent) sexual activity."[26]

It is important to note that when sexual activity or pregnancy is used in the attainment of independence, it is usually for "negative" reasons; that is, the adolescent is not so much approaching an ideal situation as avoiding an intolerable one, usually at home or school. In subcultures where adolescent pregnancy represents a "rite of passage" this may not be true; here, pregnancy demonstrates a coming of age; however, these subcultures generally offer the adolescent less than optimal home or school environments.[27] The point is that with respect to the struggle for independence, adolescent pregnancy often reflects familial or societal values, or value conflict. Individual health care providers must be aware of how such issues influence their individual clients or patients.

Identity Development

Although the integration of physical, cognitive, and social change is important, the essence of adolescence is the emergence of a stable identity, a sense of self. In moving toward an identity, the youth often wonders "Am I normal?" in the early phases of adolescence. The normalcy of the multitudinous changes that he or she may be experiencing can only be judged with reference to other people who are undergoing similar changes—the peer group. Paradoxically, then, the first phase of identity attainment is often a forfeiture of one's personal identity to the peer group identity. In this respect, sexual activity may reflect a need to "be like other kids."

The need to be identical to his or her peers gradually lessens, however, as the youth begins to wonder "Who am I?" The normal youth may begin to seek ways in which he or she is different from most of the peer group.

If sexual behavior is a means by which this question is answered, either an increase or a decrease in sexual activity might be noted.

An additional question for the individual later in adolescence becomes "Where am I going?" with respect to education, vocation, and marriage. Thus, the youth may not be able to plan realistically for the future from the base of a stable identity until late adolescence. Likewise, sexual behavior cannot be truly self-motivated until late adolescence.

An inconsistent self-image or an unstable role identity lead to identity confusion.[28] According to Erikson's developmental theory, the most important result of identity confusion, as far as this discussion is concerned, is the difficulty encountered in establishing intimate relationships. Intimate relationships need not be sexual, and sexual relationships need not be intimate. In fact, the youth who is not sure of her identity often "shies away from interpersonal intimacy and throws (herself) into acts of intimacy which are promiscuous."[28] Hence, those adolescents who often appear to be sexually most sure of themselves may in fact be quite confused. Even normal adolescents often go through a period of identity confusion. During such times, they too may be "vulnerable to perform sexually for nonsexual reasons."[26] Sexual activity arising from nonsexual motivation is an issue of crucial importance. Searching for intimacy or the release of a powerful sex drive are adult sexual motivations, which adults characteristically ascribe to sexually active adolescents. Neither of these forces appears to be very common in adolescence, however.[29]

The influence of the peer group is important with respect to sexual activity in identity formation. As discussed above, the peer group is the benchmark against which many behaviors are measured. Parental and familial values are sometimes rejected to attain peer approval and acceptance. Sexual activity may be a means to attain both, "either because it allows the adolescent to compete with peers by showing a willingness to engage in sex or because the behavior is modeled after an emulated and accepted peer who is sexually active."[26] Intercourse as a means of "keeping a boyfriend," or because one's boyfriend "expects it" are additional examples of peer-related, nonsexually motivated sexual activity.

In concluding this section on adolescent development, it is important to discuss one final problem associated with identity formation: *identity foreclosure*. This concept refers to the acceptance of an identity, the formation of which did not actively involve the adolescent. Foreclosure of identity is especially troublesome with regard to adolescent childbearing since it limits the young mother's options and influences all aspects of her being. Ryan described it best:

> If the greatest thing a teenage girl can achieve in her life is to have a place of her own, someone to love her, and a baby, and if she can do that at age

16 and there is nothing else to look forward to in life, there is not much I can do to get her to wait until age 22.*

Clearly, not all cases of adolescent pregnancy are conceived under such circumstances; but the extent to which this foreclosure is true, the extent to which a person sees herself as being capable of being a mother *only*, in part determines the extent to which she is likely to begin childbearing early in life.

HISTORICAL PERSPECTIVE OF ADOLESCENT PREGNANCY

Programs to prevent adolescent pregnancy are in their own adolescence. The majority are less than 20 years old, are striving for independence from the fiscal restraints of funding sources, and are seeking a distinctive identity. The development of these programs reflects the development over time of various concepts about adolescent sexuality and childbearing.

In the first half of this century, an unmarried, pregnant adolescent was treated as an outcast. The result of moral turpitude, lack of good sense, or an "accident," her obvious loss of virginity left her with deflated social status. She had limited options available to her. She could arrange a precipitous marriage, an illegal abortion, an admission to a maternity home, or a "visit" to a relative in a distant city. The latter two options generally resulted in the adoption of her offspring. Her education and peer-related activities were also greatly curtailed.

From a public health point of view, each occurrence of adolescent pregnancy in that era was seen as an isolated, sporadic case. As such, there was little need for an organized approach to prevention, and little was written about the pregnant teenager in the obstetric or preventive health literature.[30,31] Even the prevention of an individual case of pregnancy in a sexually active girl was an elusive objective, in part because effective birth control methods were yet to be developed.

In the second half of this century drastic changes in American society were accompanied by drastic changes in the thinking about adolescent sexuality, pregnancy, and childbearing. The "baby boom" after World War II resulted in a massive cohort of teenagers from the early 1960s through the mid-1970s. Major scientific breakthroughs also occurred during this time, especially in the field of medicine. Important events included the Federal Drug Administration approval of oral contraceptives in 1960, and of intra-

---

*From Ryan GM: Attitudes of adolescents toward pregnancy and contraception. Editorial reply. Am J Obstet Gynecol 137:366, 1980. With permission.

uterine devices in 1964. Prior to the availability of these methods of birth control, a strong sense of fertility awareness and a strong motivation not to conceive were required of any sexually active adolescent who did not want to become a parent.

In addition to these changes in demography and contraceptive technology, dramatic cultural changes were also taking place in the 1960s. In 1964, war was declared on poverty in the name of the Great Society by President Johnson. The prevention of adolescent pregnancy was an important objective in that war because adolescent childbearing represented an important component of the vicious "cycle of poverty."[32] Cultural change was not limited to the poor adolescent, however. Some of the middle-class members of the baby boom developed into the "love generation" with the motto "If it feels good . . . do it!" They too contributed to the so-called epidemic of adolescent sexual expression and pregnancy which was felt to be occurring at that time.

Concerns about adolescent pregnancy as a national problem grew as the number of births to teenagers grew. Between 1950 and 1970, births to women less than 19 years of age increased from 425,221 to 656,460, an increase of 54 percent. No longer isolated and sporadic, each occurrence of adolescent pregnancy became evidence of an epidemic (despite the fact that the birth rate for adolescents had been gradually increasing over several decades).[33] Hence, as noted by Howard, the federal government became involved when it became obvious that adolescent pregnancy was adversely affecting the health (maternal and neonatal), education (high school dropouts), and welfare (government assistance) of a large number of young Americans.[34] As a result of the attention attracted by this problem, numerous research projects were conducted during the late 1960s and early 1970s to determine the extent, determinants, and consequences of adolescent pregnancy. Both governmental and private agencies were involved in these endeavors.[35]

The federal government became more involved in adolescent pregnancy in 1973, when the U.S. Supreme Court granted a mother the right to obtain an abortion. Abortion has become the most controversial issue relating to childbearing for both adolescents and adults; however, political decisions regarding abortion have relatively greater impact on adolescents because they experience the highest abortion to pregnancy ratio of any age group.

The research projects mentioned earlier were followed by numerous demonstration and pilot studies that examined various outcome variables in relation to adolescent pregnancy. Those studies sometimes yielded conflicting results; their findings are discussed elsewhere in this book and need not be chronicled here. The recurrent theme that emerged from such studies, however, was that sexual intercourse leading to early reproduction is associated with numerous contemporary disadvantages for both mother and child.

Certain important points have emerged from this research: (1) young age alone need not significantly increase the risk of obstetric or neonatal complications;[36] (2) a large proportion of those pregnancies that are carried to term are intended;[37] (3) fertility awareness and contraceptive availability often do not have the desired effects with respect to prevention of pregnancy;[38] and (4) the evaluation of preventive services is very difficult because it is difficult to identify events that do not occur (it is much easier to identify a pregnancy that occurs than it is to identify one that is avoided). Therefore, abortion and delivery rates "before" and "after" intervention services are established, although crude, are the main outcome variables used to measure preventive effectiveness. It is only recently that the "milieu" of adolescent pregnancy has been studied;[39] that is, the familial and cultural context, as well as the age, race and socioeconomic status, of teenaged mothers are being examined.

Given the dynamic nature of the past presented in this section, it is important to be able to adapt to the various exigencies that may arise, both on an individual and a societal level, in the future. Uncertainty regarding the direction change will take permeates any plans for the future. Abortion could return to being an illegal activity or could become more readily available. Birth control might become more safe and accessible or might become more restricted in use. Society might return to family units or might become further atomized. Medical information concerning adolescent childbearing that was held as dogma in the past decade may become debatable this decade. Whatever direction change takes, we need to be able to respond to the needs of our youth.

ADOLESCENT PREGNANCY PREVENTION PROGRAMS

In this section various preventive programs are examined generically rather than specifically, following the classification described by Brann et al.[40] Maintaining a developmental perspective, we explore possible pitfalls in each of these strategies and suggest key elements for successful programs.

Broadcast Approach

The broadcast strategy focuses on providing information to groups of individuals rather than to individuals per se. It can operate in a school system, a youth organization, a juvenile detention center, or a health center. Use is also made of television, radio, and newspapers to disseminate information. As previously noted, the media tend to provide a one-sided, casual approach to sexuality; the broadcast approach can attempt to counteract the dominant "sex without consequences" message.

Community education is directed toward teachers, staffs of local youth organizations, health department employees, and anyone who has contact with a large number of adolescents. Parents can also effectively be included in this approach, as was shown in San Bernardino, California, where a family life education project was developed to "reinforce and increase the support of family life education among parents and other adults in the community."[41]

Information alone does not necessarily influence teenage behavior, however. The personal fable can have a strong influence in convincing an adolescent that certain things "can't happen to them." Likewise, a friend telling an adolescent that she should not use contraceptives may bear more credence than an adult telling her that she should. This "get the facts straight" approach is an important, but not sufficient, overture in adolescent pregnancy prevention.

In favor of this approach is the fact that it is relatively inexpensive and makes common sense use of existing community services. Cobliner et al. found that a study group of never pregnant girls relied on books and pamphlets for birth control information, whereas their ever pregnant counterparts relied on hearsay and speculation.[42]

Standard Outreach

Family planning programs that have some special activities directed toward teenagers utilize what is called standard outreach, which represents more focused preventive activity than the broadcast approach. Included are "rap sessions for teenagers in the clinic, formal or informal speakers' bureaus, advertising the availability of services through the various media, . . . in-clinic counseling sessions for those who use contraceptives and those who seek pregnancy tests or abortions, and information telephone lines."[40] This approach allows for some individualization of care, especially as it relates to the provision of medical services.

The major drawback to this type of preventive approach, which includes many "teen clinics" based in hospitals, is that it requires the adolescent to enter the health care system, which is sometimes a formidable task. Furthermore, it requires the adolescent seeking contraception to admit to sexual activity. As noted by Brann et al., "before she can admit this to a doctor, clinician, or pharmacy clerk, she first must admit it to herself."[40]

Providing Everything at One Site

The "provide everything at one site" approach evolved as an alternative to the standard medical model of pregnancy prevention. This strategy is utilized by The Door in New York City and Threshold in Rochester, New York, among other programs, and approaches the youth from a more personal, intensive viewpoint. Medical, vocational, educational, counseling, and recreational services are provided in addition to family planning services. Confidential, low-cost, comprehensive services make programs with this approach attractive to adolescents.

Developmentally this strategy is also attractive. Rather than isolate sexuality from other adolescent developmental concerns, this model of care includes sexuality as an integral part of maturation. In such facilities a youth seeking a high school equivalency diploma can also find information about venereal disease, or a youth seeking treatment for venereal disease can also obtain counseling on drug abuse. Naturally, such programs are expensive to operate; but for those individuals who are reached, these programs often represent the single most substantial source of support on which a troubled adolescent can rely.

Intensive, One-on-One, "Find Them Where They Are" Approach

Numerous projects of this genre have been attempted, but the one that most clearly demonstrates effectiveness is operated by the St. Paul (Minnesota) Maternal and Infant Care Project. The details of this project are available elsewhere.[43] For the purposes of this discussion, the key points are as follows: (1) a comprehensive (not family planning) clinic operates on school premises; (2) confidentiality is ensured because the clinic is administratively totally separate from the school; (3) services such as dispensing oral contraceptives are provided by the same staff as at the school clinic, but at a community clinic after school hours; (4) students who miss appointments are called to the clinic, and patients using contraceptives are followed monthly. Under this format, this program demonstrated a 56 percent reduction in student fertility rates without reliance on abortion.

This program and others like it appear to be able to accomplish the impossible—to change the childbearing intentions of unmarried teenagers. In the words of Brann et al.:

> Students previously ambivalent about contraception and childbearing are now effectively using contraceptives . . . by bringing the program to the students, by becoming the best friends in the adult world that many of these students have ever had, and by acknowledging that contraception is both permissible and necessary if the student has made a decision to be sexually active. They have lowered both the initial hurdle that a teenager must face in admitting sexual activity and approaching the health-care establishment for contraceptives, and the succeeding hurdles by maintaining close personal contact with the students.*

*With permission. Excerpta Medica. *Advances in Planned Parenthood*, Vol. 14 (1979). Princeton, N.J.

Such programs appear to be very effective but are very expensive to operate. Money allocated to their operating budgets must be balanced against alternative uses for that money. Money used in the operation of a comprehensive clinic cannot be used in the operation of an immunization program, a lead screening program, or a water purification program. However, it is specious to compare the budget of an adolescent pregnancy prevention program to the budget of a water purification program.

What must be considered in the evaluation of any prevention program is not only the operating cost to run the program but also the opportunity cost incurred when it is decided to forego such a program. Brann et al. caution,

> We must decide whether it is better to spend $200 on preventing a pregnancy and/or birth to a 15-year-old girl, or $2000 and more on supporting that teenage mother and her child with prenatal care, delivery services, infant health care, and remedial educational services . . . and still wonder if the $2000 really did any good.*

ADOLESCENT SEXUAL DECISION MAKING: KEY TO INDIVIDUAL PREVENTION

Despite the protests of some adolescents to the contrary, sexual intercourse leading to pregnancy does not "just happen." Decisions are made at each of the various steps between chastity and parenthood, whether or not the youth is aware of them. Responsible sexual behavior requires responsible decisions on the part of the individual. There is evidence that the process of adolescent sexual decision making can be modified with appropriate input from concerned adults.[44]

As noted by Juhasz and Sonnenschein-Schneider, responsible sexual decision making requires certain skills that adolescents often lack.[45] First, in the area of cognition, they need to understand factual information that applies to them; however, the various influences of evolving formal operational thought process may adversely affect this skill. Second, in the area of socialization, they need to be able to incorporate their sexual identity into their evolving value structure. Peer pressure may make this difficult. Third, with respect to situation-specific behavior, they need to be able to evaluate the numerous variables that impinge on them on a day-to-day basis and change from day to day.

In addition to these skills, a certain process needs to occur. From a sense of self-awareness, one needs to communicate with others, relaying and

---

*With permission. Excerpta Medica. *Advances in Planned Parenthood*, Vol. 14 (1979). Princeton, N.J.

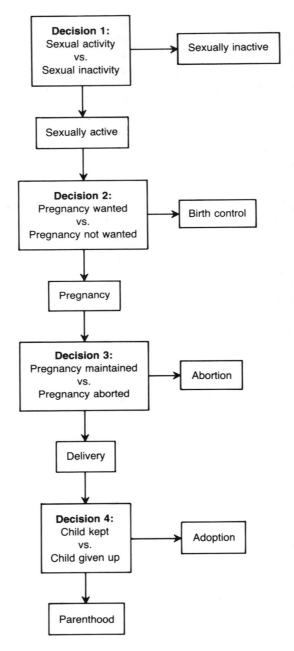

Figure 3-1. Decision tree for adolescent sexual decision making.

reflecting feelings and ideas. Values become clarified as one communicates with others, and from this personal base of self-awareness and awareness of others the adolescent can become ready for problem solving and decisions. Without this process, sexual activity is mechanistic and devoid of meaning.

The decision tree shown in Figure 3-1 may help bring all these elements into better focus. By realizing the decisions that are made, either actively or passively, the adolescent may be better able to deal with the relevant issues maturely.

Decision 1: Sexual Inactivity Versus Sexual Activity

At some point in the process of heterosexual differentiation, a decision opting for heterosexual activity that includes intercourse may be made. It often occurs "in an atmosphere of play acting,"[24] but it should be obvious that this decision is important with respect to pregnancy prevention. It is frequently overlooked, however, when one is dealing with the individual adolescent who is "assumed" to be having intercourse on a regular basis. In Zelnik and Kantner's 1979 study 12 percent of the premaritally "sexually active" young women had had intercourse only *once*.[46]

Especially among younger adolescents, virginity may still be valued. Because virginity once lost cannot be retrieved, some adolescents feel that once they have had intercourse, they have nothing more to lose. These youths need to realize that continued sexual activity does not necessarily follow the initial experience. Chastity can be of value for virgins and nonvirgins alike.

For those who do continue to have sexual intercourse after their initial experience, responsible sexual activity implies the adolescent has the ability to evaluate the relationship in which it occurs, not merely the ability to prevent conception. As previously noted, this process requires effective communication, a skill which many sexually active adolescents lack.[47] This should not deter the health care provider; individual sexual responsibility is an issue that needs to be addressed in a nonjudgmental manner if one is to foster mature behavior.

It is especially important to support the decision of those who choose to remain sexually inactive. If one-half of the unmarried female population is sexually active by age 19 years, one-half of that population is sexually inactive. It seems, however, that positive reinforcement for abstinence comes slowly and in small measure, not only from the peer group but from society at large.

Concerns are often voiced that discussing sexuality with teens only encourages sexual activity. The evidence used to support this contention is the increase in sexual activity that has occurred among adolescents over the past several years.[46] Most sex education research has shown that increasing an adolescent's sexual knowledge does not increase his or her sexual activity,[48] and that adolescents obtain very little information regarding sexuality from reliable sources.[49] It is not surprising that the myths that tend to characterize adolescent sexual awareness are perpetuated. We proscribe sex education in the home and school, and by default sanction sex education on street corners, in movie houses, and on television.

The influence of the family on adolescent sexual activity has been studied infrequently. Lewis did examine this area and found that "rather than stimulate coital experimentation, sex information given primarily by parents seems to contribute to more restrictive premarital sexual behavior."[50] As pointed out by Fox, "it may well be that such discussion is important not so much for the factual information imparted as because such discussion can make explicit . . . sexual behavior."[51] Some efforts are being made to include parents more integrally in the sexualization process, but these efforts need to begin early in the child's life and need to be expanded to include the schools.[52]

Decision 2: Pregnancy Wanted Versus Pregnancy Not Wanted

For the adolescent female who chooses to be sexually active, the next decision that needs to be addressed is whether or not she wants to become pregnant. For the ambivalent adolescent, this is frequently a difficult decision. Brann et al. pointed out that for some teenagers, "one day they want to get pregnant; the next day it is the last thing in the world they want to do."[40] The female is not the only person to whom this question should be addressed, however. The male also needs to decide whether or not he wants his coital partner to become pregnant. Clarification of the issues surrounding this decision, a time-consuming endeavor, may help the youth resolve this dilemma. The issues that need to be clarified are usually related to the developmental tasks that were discussed earlier.

Frequently, the adolescent wants to be sexually active and does not want to become pregnant, but does not want to use birth control. She can sometimes be made aware of the illogic of this line of thinking. By making the decision "concrete" (by the use of a decision tree) and by illustrating the consequences of sexual activity without birth control (abortion, adoption, or parenthood), the health care provider may be able to remove an important barrier to realistic decision making. Clarification of the issues influencing the youth's decision can then be explored. She may truly wish not to be sexually active, she may have a subconscious desire to become pregnant, or she may have medical or religious objections to birth control.

Incongruous as it may seem, it is not unusual for an unmarried teenager to be sexually active but object to contraception on religious grounds. For this person, the decision to use the rhythm method or the Billings method of ovulatory timing may be acceptable (although not optimal). Those who decide to be sexually active but do not want to become pregnant, and are willing to use birth control should be provided with a method (see Chapter 4).

Decision 3: Pregnancy Maintained Versus Pregnancy Aborted

Once conception occurs, the adolescent must decide whether she will maintain or abort her pregnancy. This is the first decision to be made at the secondary level of prevention—the level of prevention of disability. Some pregnant adolescents will "bypass" this decision by delaying definitive diagnosis until abortion is nullified as an option. Others may have their pregnancy diagnosed at 8 weeks' gestation but "miss appointments" or "not be able to decide" about abortion for long enough, in effect, to make the decision to maintain their pregnancy. Recent trends, however, show that the majority of younger adolescents and a large proportion of older adolescents who become pregnant decide in favor of abortion.[53]

If the adolescent seeks health care early in gestation (less than 14 weeks), both options should be discussed with her in a factual, unbiased manner, even if she seems to have decided in favor of one or the other option. An informed decision requires an awareness of the pertinent facts. To withhold or distort information so that it conforms to one's own value system is to deny the youth her freedom of choice and is professionally unethical.

Another ethical dilemma arises if the younger adolescent requests an abortion, but also requests that no one else know about it. This request often grows out of her fear of negative parental response to the pregnancy. In such a case it might be an error to provide an abortion based on the principles of confidentiality or legal justification; rather, an in-depth examination of the issues influencing her decision is called for, prior to accepting or rejecting any requests. With gentle guidance, and the health care provider acting as a "buffer," the adolescent may be able to include certain family members in the decision-making process.

Decision 4: Child Kept Versus Child Adopted

If the pregnancy is maintained, there are only two options available to the mother: either to keep the child or place the child for adoption. The clarification of the issues influencing the adolescent's decision at this juncture is of paramount importance. Decisions are often couched in terms of "my mother would kill me if I put my baby up for adoption" or "I just want a baby to love me." Such statements need to be explored with the mother-to-be with respect to underlying values and possible ramifications. The purpose of such exploration is not to alter the decision, but to ensure that it has been made with adequate information.

The present trend is for very few teenage mothers to place their babies for adoption; the overwhelming majority of them now raise their babies, with varying levels of support from family and friends.[54] The consequences of this phenomenon are discussed in Chapters 10 and 16.

Rehabilitation, the tertiary level of prevention, should come into effect whenever there is evidence that adolescent growth or development has been adversely affected because of pregnancy. This is most likely to occur with childbearing. Counseling, job training, formal education, and parenting support, as well as renewed primary prevention efforts, are all important aspects of "rehabilitating" the premature parent.

CONCLUSIONS

Addressing the prevention of adolescent pregnancy is a challenging enterprise, especially if the reader is seeking definitive answers. The emphasis of this chapter is not so much on preventing pregnancy as it is on fostering and shaping responsible adolescent behavior, taking into account the developmental forces that may be operating. Underlying this emphasis is the premise that the assumption of sexual responsibility by adolescents, more than the prescription of contraceptives or the proscription of sexual activity by adults, will eventually lead to fewer teenage pregnancies.

This is not to say that we should endorse teenage sexual activity. On the other hand, adolescents rarely seek our consent to be sexually active. When they seek contraception, it is likely that they have already been sexually active for at least six months.[55] It has been noted that "current family-planning program activities, which focus on those teenagers who are already sexually active and seeking services, are not likely to have a large impact on national childbearing and abortion patterns for teenagers."[53] We must therefore enhance the awareness of adolescents regarding their own sexuality.

Although the adolescent is ultimately responsible for his or her own behavior, an awareness of the developmental influences on adolescents may enable the professional to provide more effective preventive care. Only by working in concert with adolescents can we hope to prevent teenage pregnancy. The physically mature but psychosocially immature youth may have difficulty establishing control over an emergent reproductive capacity. Developmentally appropriate nonsexual activities need to be available for these as well as other youths; recreational facilities, sports teams, and community organizations all need to be provided and supported.

The 15-year-old who believes that pregnancy could never happen to her needs to become aware of the consequences of this belief. This might be accomplished through a variety of approaches discussed earlier in this chapter, each with various developmental advantages and disadvantages. Controlling the sexual atmosphere that surrounds our adolescents should also aid in the prevention of premature teenage sexual activity, but this would require a major shift in the dominant mores of our society. It appears that many adults in our society are not willing to expect of themselves what they expect of adolescents in regard to restricting their "sexual expression."

With the cooperation of parents, schools, and other interested adults, perhaps we can do something to help solve this "problem that hasn't gone away." An old saying goes: "If you give someone food, you feed him for a day; but if you teach him how to grow his own, he can feed himself for life."

REFERENCES

1. Havighurst RJ: Developmental tasks and education. New York, Longmans, 1972
2. Erikson EH: Childhood and Society (ed 2). New York, Norton, 1963, pp 261–263
3. Sizonenko P: Hormones in puberty. Am J Dis Child 132:704–712, 1978
4. Tanner JM: Growth at Adolescence (ed 2). London, Blackwell, 1962, pp 1–27
5. Money J, Clopper RR: Psychosocial and psychosexual aspects of errors of pubertal onset and development. Hum Biol 46:173–181, 1974
6. Gross RT, Duke PM: The effect of early versus late physical maturation on adolescent behavior. Pediatr Clin North Am 27:71–77, 1980
7. Muuss RE: Puberty rites in primitive and modern societies. Adolescence 5:109–128, 1970
8. Bullough VL: Age at menarche: A misunderstanding. Science 213:365–366, 1981
9. Marshall WA, Tanner JM: Variations in the pattern of pubertal changes in girls. Arch Dis Child 44:291–303, 1969
10. Finkel ML, Finkel DJ: Sexual and contraceptive knowledge, attitudes and behavior of male adolescents. Fam Plann Perspect 7:256–260, 1975
11. Elster AB, McAnarney ER: Medical and psychosocial risks of pregnancy and childbearing during adolescence. Pediatr Ann 9:11–20, 1980
12. Daniel WA: The Adolescent Patient. St. Louis, Mosby, 1970, pp 3–36
13. Melnick SD: Piaget and the pediatrician: Guiding intellectual development. Clin Pediatr 13:913–918, 1974
14. Lerner RM, Spanier GB. Adolescent Development: A Life-span Perspective. New York, McGraw-Hill, 1980, p 248
15. Dale LG: The growth of systematic thinking: Replication and analysis of Piaget's first clinical experiment. Aust J Psychol 22:277–286, 1970
16. Elkind D: Children and Adolescents. New York, Oxford University Press, 1970, pp 90–95
17. Notman MT: Teenage pregnancy: The nonuse of contraception. Psychiatr Opinion 12:23–27, 1975
18. Phipps-Yonas S: Teenage pregnancy and motherhood: A review of the literature. Am J Orthopsychiatry 50:403–431, 1980

19. Panzarine S, Kubis J, Elster AB, et al: Motivated adolescent pregnancy. J Curr Adolesc Med 1:57–59, 1979

20. Nadelson CC: The pregnant teenager: Problems of choice in a developmental framework. Psychiatr Opinion 12:6–12, 1975

21. Semmens J, Lammers W: Teenage Pregnancy. Springfield, Ill, Thomas, 1968

22. Ryan GM, Sweeney PJ: Attitudes of adolescents toward pregnancy and contraception. Am J Obstet Gynecol 137:358–362, 1980

23. Gordis L, Finkelstein R, Fassett JD, et al: Evaluation of a program for preventing adolescent pregnancy. N Engl J Med 282:1078–1081, 1970

24. Nadelson CC, Notman MT, Gillon JW: Sexual knowledge and attitudes of adolescents: Relationship to contraceptive use. Obstet Gynecol 55:340–345, 1980

25. National Center for Health Statistics: Self-reported health behavior and attitudes of youths 12–17 years, Series 11, no 147, 1975 (DHEW Publ No (HRA) 75-1629)

26. Cohen MW, Friedman SB: Nonsexual motivation of adolescent sexual behavior. Med Aspects Hum Sexuality 9:8–31, 1975

27. Gabriel A, McAnarney ER: Pregnancy and parenthood in two subcultures: A comparison of white middle-class couples and black low-income class couples. Adolescence (in press)

28. Erikson E: Identity: Youth and Crisis. New York, Norton, 1968, pp 91–93

29. Schaffer C, Pine F: Pregnancy, abortion, and the developmental tasks of adolescence. J Am Acad Child Psychiatry 11:511–536, 1972

30. Eastman NJ, Hellman LM: Obstetrics (ed 13). New York, Appleton-Century-Crofts, 1950, pp 352–353

31. Maxcy KF: Preventive medicine and hygiene (ed 7). New York, Appleton-Century-Crofts, 1951, pp 639–653

32. Harrington M: The other America: Poverty in the United States. New York, MacMillan, 1962

33. National Center for Health Statistics: Fertility Tables for Birth Cohorts by Color: United States, 1917–1973 (DHEW Publ No (HRA) 76-1152). Washington, DC, US Government Printing Office, 1976

34. Howard M: Bringing about change: A national overview with respect to early childbearing and childrearing, in Zackler J, Brandstadt WE (eds): The Teenage Pregnant Girl. Springfield, Ill, Thomas, 1975, pp 248–249

35. Klerman LV: Adolescent pregnancy. A new look at a continuing problem. Am J Public Health 70:776–778, 1980

36. McAnarney ER, Roghmann KJ, Adams BN, et al: Obstetric, neonatal, and psychosocial outcome of pregnancy in adolescents. Pediatrics 61:199–206, 1978

37. Davis K: A theory of teenage pregnancy in the United States, in Chilman CS (ed): Adolescent Pregnancy and Childbearing: Findings from Research (DHHS Publ No (NIH) 81-2077). Washington, DC, US Government Printing Office, 1980, pp 309–336

38. Freeman EW, Rickels K, Huggins GR, et al: Adolescent contraceptive use: Comparisons of male and female attitudes and information. Am J Public Health 70:790–797, 1980

39. Cobliner WG: Prevention of adolescent pregnancy: A developmental perspective, in McAnarney ER, Stickle G (eds): Pregnancy and Childbearing During Adolescence: Research Priorities for the 1980s. March of Dimes Birth Defects Foundation, Birth Defects: Original Article Series vol 17, no 3. New York, Liss, 1981, pp 35–49

40. Brann EA, Edwards L, Callicott, T, et al: Strategies for the prevention of pregnancy in adolescents. Adv Plann Parent 14:68–76, 1979

41. Yates GL: Parent education and community support: Key factors for success. Transitions 4:3–6, 1981

42. Cobliner WG, Schulman H, Smith V: Patterns of contraceptive failure. J Biosoc Sci 7:307–328, 1975

43. Edwards LE, Steinman ME, Arnold KA, et al: Adolescent contraceptive use: Experience in 1,762 teenagers. Am J Obstet Gynecol 137:583–587, 1980

44. Edwards LE, Steinman ME, Arnold KA, et al: Adolescent pregnancy prevention services in high school clinics. Fam Plann Perspect 12:6–14, 1980

45. Juhasz AM, Sonnenshein-Schneider M: Adolescent sexual decision-making: Components and skills. Adolescence 15:743–750, 1980

46. Zelnik M, Kantner JF: Sexual activity, contraceptive use and pregnancy among metropolitan-area teenagers: 1971–1979. Fam Plann Perspect 12:230–237, 1980

47. Cvetkovich G, Grote B: Psychosocial development and the social problem of teenage illegitimacy, In Chilman CS (ed): Adolescent Pregnancy and Childbearing: Findings from Research (DHHS Publ No (NIH) 81-2077). Washington, DC, US Government Printing Office, 1980, pp 15–41

48. Spanier GB: Sources of sex information and premarital sexual behavior. J Sex Res 13:73–88, 1977

49. Zelnik M: Sex education and knowledge of pregnancy risk among U.S. teenage women. Fam Plann Perspect 11:355–357, 1979

50. Lewis RA: Parents and peers: Socialization agents in the coital behavior of young adults. J Sex Res 9:156–190, 1973

51. Fox GL: The family's influence on adolescent sexual behavior. Child Today 8:21–25, 1979

52. Hawkins RO: The Uppsala connection: The development of principles basic to education of sexuality. SIECUS Report 8:11–16, 1980

53. U.S. Department of Health and Human Services: Childbearing and abortion patterns among teenagers—U.S., 1978, Morbidity and Mortality Weekly Report 30:611–617, 1981 (DHHS Publ. No. (CDC) 81-8017)

54. Alan Guttmacher Institute: Teenage pregnancy: The problem that hasn't gone away. New York, Author, 1981, p 27

55. Zabin LS, Kantner JF, Zelnik M: The risk of adolescent pregnancy in the first months of intercourse. Fam Plann Perspect 11:215–222, 1979

4

Alternatives to Adolescent Pregnancy: Review of Contraceptive Literature

Donald E. Greydanus

Adolescence is the bridge between childhood and adulthood. It is a time of rapid development, of growing to sexual maturity, discovering one's real self, defining personal values, and finding one's vocational and social directions.[1] It is also a time of testing, of pushing against one's capabilities and limitations to reach new personal dimensions. It is the "period in life when the individual is in the process of transfer from the dependent 'irresponsible' age of childhood to the self-reliant, responsible age of adulthood [when] the maturing child seeks new freedom and in finding it, becomes accountable to society."[2]

More attention has been directed over the past decade to the phenomenon of increased sexual activity by teenagers[3] with its resultant growth in pregnancy and sexually transmitted diseases.[4,5] Attempts to deal with such complicated adolescent issues as pregnancy or contraception must be rooted in an understanding of the process of adolescence. It is important to note that psychological growth during adolescence is divided into three substages: early, middle and late adolescence.[6]

Early adolescence occurs between ages 10–14 years and is characterized by rapid physical growth and development. During this period the youth

Presented in part at the American Medical Association Conference on Adolescent Sexuality and Factors Influencing Pregnancy, Chicago, September 4–6, 1980.

becomes preoccupied with his or her developing body and begins symbolically to move away from the parents and establish a peer group. The ability for abstract or formal thought also begins.

Middle adolescence is usually the most difficult phase for the youth and his or her family. During ages 14–17 the youth has completed much of the growth process and now becomes invested in major emancipation conflicts, peaking peer group influences, sexuality explorations, maximal intellectualization, and other intense processes. The maturation of cognitive skills allows the youth to develop "formal abstract thinking abilities that permit him (her) to engage in scientific and philosophical thinking, to plan realistically for the future and to understand the historical past."[7]

Late adolescence (ages 17–20) is characterized by final pubertal development, procurement of emancipation, and establishment of a secure body image and gender role definition. The goals of adolescence should climax now with successful emancipation and identity formation (intellectual, sexual, and functional).[8]

These issues of adolescent growth and development are critical ones, and a psychosocial profile must be developed for an individual youth who is seeking health care. Likewise, it is important to develop a pubertal assessment (Tanner staging)[9] for a youth and apply it to the psychosocial evaluation.[10] Providing contraception for some sexually active teenagers is a difficult task because of the particular conscious or unconscious factors contributing to pregnancy in adolescence.

The young adolescent is often not developmentally prepared to understand the concept of pregnancy.[11,12] Thus the pregnancy may be used to create a close relationship with the mother or even to see if pregnancy is possible, as if one could become only a "little" pregnant. Failure to acknowledge the consequences of sexual activity is a major cause of adolescent pregnancy. Domination by an older teenage or adult male, rape, incest, and other factors are also operational in some youth. Application of effective contraception in this group may be quite difficult. Some middle adolescents may present as very problematic individuals for contraception. A youth who is in the middle of critical adolescent issues may use her sexual activity and consequent pregnancy as a means to obtain various goals, such as to compete with the mother for her father, to acquire a new autonomy, or even to change specific aspects of her life. The older adolescent often, but not invariably, has more adultlike motivation and may be more capable of avoiding pregnancy than her younger counterpart.

There are other reasons adolescents fail to use contraception. "Magical thinking" may play a role: the young or middle adolescents may feel they are special and somehow will be protected from pregnancy despite coital activity. Some may equate the use of contraception with a keen and unacceptable desire for sex, or refuse to have their "free spirit" burdened or limited by thoughts of sex preparation. Some methods require unacceptable self-intimacy (e.g., a diaphragm) or carry the risk of being detected by parents (e.g., birth control pill packets). There may be no or minimal support from her partner, leaving her developmentally unwilling to abstain from coitus and incapable of assuming the sole contraceptive responsibility.

There are many other factors that are not understood. Those sexually active individuals who are at high risk for contraceptive failure or refusal require identification and further study. Education on sexual matters should be presented to teenagers (including young adolescents) without fear that it will encourage more promiscuous sexual attitudes. Various formats for education can be used, including classrooms, office visits, walk-in clinics, and even the mass media.[13,14] The clinician can choose an appropriate time to discuss contraception—during a school physical examination in early adolescence, at menarche in middle adolescence, or during evaluation of sexual dysfunction in late adolescence. Education about sexuality is important for both male and female adolescents.

Since 90 percent or more of couples will conceive within 1 year with regular coitus,[15] it is not surprising that the number of pregnancies among sexually active teenagers—over 1 million annually in the United States—is so high. Because there is no one contraceptive method ideal for all individuals, many variations of contraception must be offered, even in a "cafeteria" or "supermarket" manner. Thus it is critical that health care providers (general practitioners, pediatricians, internists, gynecologists, nurse practitioners, etc.) who deal with teenagers be capable of providing counseling on sexual matters and specific contraception to those wishing it.[16,17] Adequate motivation and training of these health care providers is very important.[18]

Indeed, the physician can actually impede the interested adolescent's use of contraception by not offering contraception with assurance of adequate confidentiality and with sufficient expertise. Some young people seek contraceptive counseling and information without their parents' or guardians' knowledge or permission. If the physician cannot ensure this confidentiality or has moral objections to providing contraception, he or she should refer the patient to local resources where such care can be provided. Certainly the physician's personal attitudes in this area will influence the patient. Issues of morality and legal rights of minors should also be considered in this context, but will not be reviewed in this manuscript.

The adolescent patient–parent–physician relationship is critical. A primary physician–adolescent patient relationship should be developed in which the youth feels his or her needs are being addressed by the health care provider in a mutually acceptable setting. Counseling on sexual matters and specific contraception can then be provided to the interested youth. Clearly, those individuals who are intent on avoidance of pregnancy will do a much better contraceptive job than those who are unsure of their contraceptive aims.

Reassurance by the health care professional that abstinence from coital activity is physiologically and psychologically healthy may be helpful to some youths who are under peer pressure to become or remain sexually active. Many teenagers are *not* coitally active and some wish to remain so. It is also important that professionals who work with youth avoid judgmental views. We can allow the patient to question all aspects of contraception, but if we tell our patient what to do or what not to do based on our own moral viewpoint, we are not helping the youth in a constructive manner. If the patient wishes abstinence, however, we certainly can encourage this. If the patient wishes to become or remain sexually active, contraceptive advice then becomes critical.

A thorough history and physical examination should precede the recommendation or prescription of contraception. Pelvic examination should be performed and cervical culture for *Neisseria gonorrhoeae* obtained. Screening tests, such as a hematocrit, urinalysis, syphilis serology, and others, are recommended by some.[17] Other tests or evaluations depend on the particular situation and clinical judgment. Counseling regarding sexually transmitted disease should be included in this overall plan. The youth should be made

Table 4-1. Sexually Transmitted Disease Agents

Neisseria gonorrhoeae

Treponema pallidum

Haemophilus ducreyi

Donovania granulomatis

Trichomonas vaginalis

Monilia albicans

Herpes simplex

Chlamydia trachomatis

Ureaplasma urealyticum

Mycoplasma hominis

Molluscum contagiosum

Genital wart (condyloma accuminata) virus

Sarcoptes scabiei var. *hominis*

Phthirus pubis

Hepatitis viruses (A and B)

Haemophilus (Gardnerella) vaginalis

Cytomegalovirus (?)

Cause(s) of Reiter's syndrome (?)

Cause of Bechçet's disease (?)

Others (*Entamoeba histolytica, Giardia lamblia, Shigella, Campylobacter fetus,* and others)

aware of the many types of veneral diseases for which the unwary individual may be at risk (Table 4-1).[4,5]

The increasing extent of coital activity among teenagers was reviewed by Zelnik and Kantner.[3] It seems clear that whatever *safe* measures exist that can effectively lessen this problem would be welcomed by many. Thus prevention of an unwanted pregnancy is the goal of the clinician caring for adolescents. Methods of contraception are outlined in Table 4-2; some of these are very effective, but some do not work very well and thus are not

Table 4-2. Contraceptive Methods for Adolescents

Oral contraceptives (estrogen and a progestin)

Low-estrogen oral contraceptives (estrogen and a progestin)

Minipill (progesterone-only pill)

Intrauterine contraceptive devices

Barrier methods
    Diaphragm
    Condom
    Cervical cap
    Vaginal contraceptives (creams, foams, jellies, powders, pastes, suppositories, tablets, other)

Postcoital contraceptives
    Diethylstilbestrol
    Other estrogens (ethinyl estradiol or conjugated estrogens)
    Minipill
    Estrogen and progesterone combination
    Intrauterine contraceptive device

Injectable contraceptives

Abstinence

Periodic abstinence
    Basal body temperature
    Calendar method
    Fertility awareness or Billing's ovulation method
    Others
    Combinations

Miscellaneous methods
    Coitus interruptus ("strategic withdrawal")
    Postcoital douche
    Lactation
    Noncoital sexual activity (petting, hand-holding, kissing, anogenital sex, masturbation, others)
    Sterilization
    Abortion

recommended for teenagers.[19,20] The most effective methods are the combined birth control pill (estrogen and a synthetic progesterone) and intramuscular medroxyprogesterone acetate (Depo-Provera), both with pregnancy rates under 1/100 woman-years of use. Others (IUD and the condom or diaphragm with foam) have higher pregnancy rates but are potentially very effective contraceptive methods.[21]

Concern over the side effects of various contraceptive methods must be carefully discussed. It should be remembered, however, that the mortality rate from pregnancy and childbirth far exceed the mortality rate for any contraceptive method.[22,23] A careful matching of the individual patient and an appropriate contraceptive method will reduce associated morbidity. Frequent follow-up of any teenager given contraception is important to improve compliance and monitor possible complications of the method chosen by the patient with her physician's guidance. Adolescent pregnancy rates can be reduced with the help of concerned health care professionals.

HISTORICAL OVERVIEW

Pregnancy prevention and management of sexually transmitted diseases has been of concern to individuals for centuries.[1] Progress was slow for a long time, but the association of these phenomena with coital activity has always stimulated the quest for new contraceptive and venereal disease information. Advances in our knowledge during the past century (and indeed the past 20 years) far exceeds the knowledge of the past 6000 or so years of recorded human history. Some of the significant events in this area[24-26] are chronicled in Table 4-3.

The ancient Egyptians relied on prolonged lactation and various vaginal occlusive agents, while the Greeks and Romans utilized coitus interruptus and vaginal occlusives, with abortion as a backup measure. Coitus interruptus has remained a popular method in many parts of the world. Gabriel Fallopius (1564), an Italian anatomist, developed the idea of using a damp linen cloth to protect the adverturesome male from syphilis.[24] The condom (from a French word for "concealment") then emerged in the 16th and 17th centuries from attempts to prevent venereal disease. The condom is a classic example of the historical intertwining of contraceptive and disease prevention principles. When the process of rubber vulcanization was developed by Charles Goodyear in the mid-1800s, a method for mass production of commercial condoms was initiated. It was not until the middle of this century, however, that quality-controlled, effective prophylactics became available to everyone. In the past 100 years several effective contraceptive methods have been developed. The diaphragm was invented by Dr. Fredrick Wilde in 1838, and then introduced by Wilhelm Mensinga in Europe in the 1880s. Sexuality

Table 4-3. Historical Outline of Developments in Contraception and Sexuality

Date	Event
2637 B.C.	Huang-Ti describes gonococcal infection in China.
1900 B.C.	Prolonged lactation and barrier methods (placing various substances in the vagina: wine, garlic, gums, honey, and even crocodile dung) are recommended in Egypt
1500 B.C.	Genesis 38:8,9 mentions and condemns coitus interruptus; Leviticus XV discusses douching (probably for hygienic reasons) and various public health measures to prevent or deal with probable sexually transmitted diseases
400 B.C.	Hippocrates uses the term "stranguary" to describe the gonococcal infection
350 B.C.	Aristotle discusses abortion as a contraceptive technique
131 A.D.	Galen coins the the term "gonorrhea"—meaning a flowing forth after sexual contact
150 A.D.	Soranus recommends occlusion of the cervix with a pessary, utilizing various acidic ingredients
1564	Fallopius recommends a damp linen cloth as a protection from syphilis
Late 1700s	Condom is advocated in London and elsewhere as a venereal disease prophylactic
1831	Ricord discusses the distinction between gonorrhea and syphilis
1838	Wilde advocates the use of a rubber cervical cap
1850	Knowlton recommends contraception with a postcoital douch using alum and other ingredients
1880	Lungren performs a tubal sterilization and initiates the modern era of sterilization as a means of permanent contraception
1882	Mensinga, using the pseudonym Hasse, develops an early prototype of a diaphragm
1879–1855	*N. gonorrhoeae* organism is described (Neisser, 1879), identified via staining (Gram, 1884), and cultured (von Bumm, 1885)
1897	Beard postulates that the ovarian corpus luteum of pregnancy is responsible for inhibition of ovulation
1909	Richter uses a silk-worm gut type of intrauterine device
1920s	Sanger introduces the diaphragm to the United States
1929	Graefenberg advocates the use of an intrauterine device as a safe and effective contraceptive method
1930	Mayer demonstrates in vitro the possible contraceptive effect of estrogens on the ovary

(continued)

Table 4-3. (continued)

Date	Event
1943	Mahoney introduces 160,000 units penicillin sodium (intramuscularly) as effective treatment for gonorrhea
1949	Eastman and Seidelo discuss the effectiveness of a vaginal suppository or jelly as a sole contraceptive method
1956	Pincus advocates the development of oral contraceptives due to the production of synthetic progesterone
1956	Vaginal contraceptives with surface-active agents (e.g., nonoxynol-9) are developed
1959	Oppenheimer advocates the use of the Graefenberg ring
1960	Envoid, the first oral contraceptive, becomes commercially available; modern era of effective contraception now is underway
1961	First commercially available aerosol vaginal contraceptive is introduced
1963	Siegel discusses the use of periodic progesterone injections
1964	Thayer-Martin media is developed for the growth of *N. gonorrhoeae*
Late 1960s	Progesterone-only pills (minipill) are developed with the hope of providing effective contraception without combined pill side effects
1972	Male contraceptive pill is developed in China
1973	Contraceptive film (C-film) becomes commercially available
1975	β-lactamase strain of *N. gonorrhoeae* is isolated in the United States
1980s	Possible development of other medical contraceptive methods: various release vehicles for progesterone contraceptive vaccines (male or female); male contraceptive pills; postcoital contraceptive-type pills for more frequent use; prostaglandin tampons; etc.

From Greydanus DE: Alternatives to adolescent pregnancy: A discussion of the contraception literature from 1960–1980. Semin Perinatol 5:53–90, 1981. With permission.

was a delicate subject, leading Mensinga (a German physician) to introduce his technique in a country different from his own (the Netherlands) and with a false name (Hasse) to hide his real identity. Through the courage and determination of Margaret Sanger, the diaphragm (or "Dutch cap") was introduced in the United States in the 1920s and was being widely used by the 1930s, along with postcoital douching, coitus interruptus, and the rhythm method (periodic abstinence). In the 20th century the development of an IUD was furthered by many individuals, including Richter (1909), Graefenberg (1929) and Oppenheimer (1959).[26] This method, however, remains tainted by its association with pelvic infection (noted since its introduction), which convinces many clinicians not to use it, especially with respect to promiscuous individuals. Its present-day utilization by the teenager remains controversial.

The modern era of contraceptive technology began in the early 1960s with the commercial availability of the birth control pill (combined oral contraceptive) and vaginal contraceptives, along with renewed interest in the intrauterine device. As noted by Drill, the introduction of an available, effective oral contraceptive in 1960 is one of the most significant developments of the 20th century[25]—especially in a crowded world which is becoming dangerously overpopulated. Other medical contraceptive means have been produced since then, including various medicated IUDs (copper 7, copper T, and its various modifications, Progestasert IUD, etc.), various vaginal contraceptives, the progesterone-only pill ("mini-pill"), and others. In 1972, the Chinese introduced a male contraceptive pill made from cottonwood seed, called Gossypol. If it proves truly effective and safe, it will be classified as another major development of the 20th century, since the only currently available male contraceptives are coitus interruptus, abstinence, and vasectomy. It may, however, traverse the same course as the minipill, introduced with great expectation but finalized with many limitations.

What about the 1980s? It is hoped that this decade will witness the availability of still other contraceptive measures, such as various progesterone-releasing vehicles (intravaginal rings, subdermal implants, or even bracelets), immunologic methods (male or female contraceptive vaccine), prostaglandin tampons, chemicals to selectively inhibit follicle-stimulating hormone (FSH) secretion (inhibin) or epididymal functioning, intranasal steroid sprays, vaginal sponges impregnated with spermicides, "paper pills" (steroids absorbed onto special paper), intracervical devices, thyrotropin-releasing hormone (to inhibit ovulation and extend the amenorrheic state of lactation), and many others.

A discussion of currently available methods is now presented, with special note of their applicability to the adolescent, and the literature of the past 20 years is reviewed, with special emphasis on oral contraceptives.

COMBINATION ORAL CONTRACEPTIVES

The combination of estrogen (ethinyl estradiol or mestranol) and a synthetic progestogen (in decreasing order of potency—norgestrel, ethynodiol diacetate, norethindrone acetate, norethindrone, or norethynodrel) has become the most popular medical contraceptive method among teenagers and adults alike.[27] The oral contraceptive remains one of the most effective methods, since it prevents pregnancy in many ways: prevention of ovulation by inhibition of FSH and luteinizing hormone (LH), inhibition of implantation by endometrial atrophy, and alteration of cervical mucus so sperm does not penetrate as readily. FSH inhibition is due to the estrogen content of the pill, while the progesterone component causes the LH inhibition and the local endometrial and cervical changes.

Traditional pill side effects are classically described as estrogen or progesterone related (Table 4-4). In addition, ethinyl estradiol is considered more potent than mestranol, which is converted to ethinyl estradiol in the liver. The side effects of the five progestogens listed above may vary also. Further classification of these agents includes their relative estrogenic, androgenic, anabolic, and antiestrogen potencies. Thus, on the basis of what symptoms are classified as due to estrogen or progesterone, brands of oral contraceptives are interchanged if certain symptoms (Table 4-4) are noted for 2–3 months. This type of brand switching may not be valid, however. The relative potencies of these hormones are controversial. Progestin potency is difficult to measure accurately, making potency comparisons potentially invalid. The hepatic demethylation of mestranol to ethinyl estradiol is variable, and the former has been shown to have greater strength than the latter in some cases. Reliably predicting which problems are estrogen or progesterone related is an uncertain task. Finally, the recommendation that pills contain no more than 50 μg of estrogen restricts the actual degree of brand switching possible.

The results of many laboratory tests are altered by use of a combined

Table 4-4. Oral Contraceptive Side Effects

Progesterone induced
  Fatigue
  Increased appetite
  Shortened menses and reduced vaginal secretion
  Reduced libido
  Acne
  Hirsutism
  Leg cramps
  Alopecia
  Depression (?)
  Others

Estrogen induced
  Nausea and/or emesis
  Dysmenorrhea and/or premenstrual tension (with or without edema)
  Cervical erosion and mucoid vaginal discharge
  Fibrocystic breast disease or tender breasts
  Elevated blood pressure
  Vascular headaches
  Chloasma
  Others

oral contraceptive (Table 4-5).[28-31] Many of these changes in laboratory test results are not of clinical importance (an increase in vitamin A level, for instance). Many results are quite variable (changes in cholesterol, albumin, or immunoglobulin levels). Some present a false picture of an altered metabolic or endocrine state, such as an increase in total cortisol or thyroxine (due to increases in binding proteins) although there is normal thyroid and

Table 4-5. Laboratory Tests Affected by Oral Contraceptives

Values increased (serum values, unless otherwise stated)
  Erythrocyte sedimentation rate (sometimes the hematocrit, white blood count, and platelets)
  Serum iron and iron-binding capacity
  Sulfobromophthalein and sometimes bilirubin
  SGOT, SGPT, and serum glutamyl transpeptidase
  Alkaline phosphatase
  Clotting factors I, II, VII, VIII, IX, X, and XII; also, increased antiplasmins and antiactivators of fibrinolysis
  Triglycerides, phospholipids, and high-density lipoproteins (sometimes serum cholesterol)
  Serum copper and ceruloplasmin
  Increase in various binding proteins (transferrin, transcortin, thyroxine-binding globulin)
  Renin, angiotensin, and aldosterone
  Insulin, growth hormone, and blood glucose
  C-reactive protein
  Globulins (α-1 and α-2)
  α-1 Antitrypsin
  Total estrogens (urine)
  Coproporphyrin (feces and urine) and porphobilinogen (urine)
  Vitamin A
  Xanthuric acid (urine)
  Positive antinuclear antibody test and LE preparation
  Others
Values decreased
  Antithrombin III
  LH and FSH
  Pregnanediol and 17-ketosteroids
  Folate and vitamin B_{12}
  Glucose tolerance
  Ascorbic acid
  Zinc and magnesium
  Triiodothyronine (T-3) resin uptake
  Fibrinolytic activity
  Haptoglobulin
  Cholinesterase
  Others

Table 4-6. Contraindications to Oral Contraceptives

Absolute contraindications
    History of thromboembolism or thrombotic disease
    Active acute or chronic liver disease
    Pregnancy
    Undiagnosed uterine bleeding
    Breast cancer
    Estrogen-dependent neoplasia

Relative contraindications
    Pituitary dysfunction
    Lactation
    Fibrocystic breast disease
    Potential drug interactions
    Heavy cigarette smoking (over 20/day)
    Hypertension
    Hyperlipidemia
    Diabetes mellitus
    Epilepsy
    Sickle cell anemia (other hemoglobinopathies)
    Uterine leiomyomatas
    Cholelithiasis or cholecystitis
    History of jaundice of pregnancy
    Migraine headaches
    Raynaud's disease
    Collagen vascular disorder (e.g., rheumatoid arthritis or systemic lupus
        erythematosus)
    Oligomenorrhea
    Pseudotumor cerebri
    Chorea
    Porphyria
    Bleeding diatheses
    Major organ disease (heart, lungs, renal)
    Retinal disorders
    Depression
    Severe, chronic monilial vaginitis
    Various dermatologic problems (erythema nodosum, melasma, others)
    Otosclerosis
    Hemolytic-uremic syndrome
    Inflammatory bowel disease
    Varicose veins
    Elective surgery
    Age over 35 years

adrenal status.[28] Some are of enormous clinical importance, such as those indicating a tendency toward hypercoaguability, diabetogenic status, or a hypertensive state. Some of these results change within 3 months (e.g., bilirubin), while others change within 3–9 months of oral contraceptive use (other liver function tests).

Rather than concentrate on estrogen- or progesterone-related effects, or on the myriad altered laboratory tests results, it is more useful to reflect on what this all means for the particular patient who wishes to take the birth control pill. The American College of Obstetricians and Gynecologists lists six absolute contraindications for the pill;[31] under many other conditions (relative contraindications) the pill places the individual at increased morbidity risk, but it may be less than the risk of morbidity or mortality from a pregnancy (Table 4-6).[19,20]

In the following discussion of side effects and contraindications specific emphasis is given to cardiovascular conditions, cardiopulmonary conditions, hypertension, migraine headaches, epilepsy, oligomenorrhea, diabetes mellitus, sickle cell disease, hepatic disorders, and cancer, and various other conditions are summarized.

Cardiovascular Conditions

The suspicion that oral contraceptives increase the risk for thromboembolism or thrombotic disease began early in the 1960s with Jordan's report of pulmonary embolism in 1961,[32] Lorentz' observation of a patient with cerebrovascular accident in 1962,[33] and Tyler's discussion of the pill and venous thrombosis in 1963.[34] Although in the late 1960s a few investigators questioned this relationship,[35,36] the evidence of the past 20 years clearly indicates that such a cause-and-effect relationship does exist. Women who are on combined oral contraceptives do develop more thrombophlebitis, vascular thrombosis (venous and arterial), and pulmonary embolism. Cerebral and vertebral ischemia can occur, with increased risk for thrombotic and hemorrhagic stroke, including subarachnoid hemorrhage. Blood type A may constitute a greater risk factor than others, especially blood type O. Even teenagers have died from vascular lesions while on the pill. Measurement of releasable plasminogen activator and antithrombin III activity in the blood may serve as a screening method to detect women at risk for thromboembolism while on the pill.

What about the risk factor for the teenager? Although women who are over age 30 have a five times greater mortality rate if on the pill, even this risk seems to be reduced (but not eliminated) by low-dose pills (50 μg estrogen or less).[37] It is important to note that the mortality rate for women aged 15–19 is 1.2 deaths per 100,000 pill users who do not smoke, and 1.4 for those who do smoke. This is sharply contrasted with the mortality rate for women aged 15–19 from pregnancy and childbirth: 11.1 deaths per 100,000 live births.

The teenager who wishes to be placed on the birth control pill should be screened for risk factors that increase the threat of cerebrovascular accidents and/or thrombophlebitis (Table 4-7). These factors do not necessarily prohibit the use of the pill; careful follow-up, however, is critical. Two of these factors, smoking and surgery, are discussed below; others are discussed in later sections.

The teenager should be encouraged to refrain from cigarette smoking[38] since it combines with the risk factor of the pill to worsen the odds for developing subarachnoid hemorrhage, coronary artery disease, hyperlipidemia, and thromboembolic phenomena in general. The risk of developing these complications is already increased by the pill alone, and then worsened by smoking. Thus, many classify smoking as a contraindication to pill use.[39] The risk is low with adolescents, however, and it is very difficult to have many of these individuals stop such a very common addiction. It should not be considered a strong contraindication unless other risks are also present. The clinician, as always, must weigh the risk factors against the pregnancy

Table 4-7. Risk Factors for Cerebrovascular Accidents and Thrombophlebitis

Cerebrovascular accidents
   Hypertension
   Coronary artery disease
   Carotid bruits
   Transient ischemic attacks
   Diabetes mellitus
   Heavy cigarette smoking
   Hyperlipidemia
   Hemoglobinopathies
   Polycythemia
   Oral contraceptives
   Migraine headaches (?)
   Age factors (whether chronological or just "biologic," such as progeria)

Thrombophlebitis
   Heavy cigarette smoking
   Postoperative period
   Prolonged immobilization (i.e., a leg or back cast)
   Pregnancy
   Postpartum period
   Oral contraceptives
   Obesity
   Neoplasms (e.g., pancreatic or lung)

risks. Indeed, smoking and pregnancy cause problems also, such as increased spontaneous abortions and postpartum hemorrhage, as well as lowered infant birth weight.[38,39]

An increased incidence of thromboembolism is noted in individuals on the pill shortly after surgical procedures.[40-42] Since the hypercoaguability state induced by the pill can last a few weeks or more, it is recommended to stop the pill 4–6 weeks prior to elective surgery and/or administer anticoagulation therapy (e.g., heparin) during the postoperative period.[41]

In conclusion, there is a slight risk factor for the teenager to develop thromboembolic disorders while on the oral contraceptive. Screening for risk factors is important and alternatives to the pill can be used, such as the minipill or medroxyprogesterone acetate.[43]

Cardiopulmonary Conditions

It has been well documented that the pill increases the risk for coronary artery thrombosis and myocardial infarction.[44] Myocardial infarction is more likely in individuals with hypertension, hyperlipidemia, diabetes mellitus, obesity, preeclamptic toxemia, or a strong family history of cardiac disease, among other conditions. Heavy cigarette smoking also raises the possibility for such an event in the female on the pill. It is of interest to note that noncontraceptive estrogen preparations do not pose such a risk.[45] More importantly, the risk to the adolescent is quite small for the individual without serious underlying cardiac disease. The effect of the pill on the individual with normal cardiopulmonary function should be minimal. Ventricular and spirometric studies have been normal.

However, marked deterioration in cardiopulmonary status has been observed in individuals with congenital cardiac defects and rheumatic heart disease. The problem of pulmonary embolism has been mentioned previously, and hypertension is covered in the next section.

The pill should not be given to the teenager with cyanotic cardiac disease, rheumatic heart disease with valve defects or damage (as aortic stenosis or pulmonary stenosis), bacterial endocarditis, or pulmonary hypertension (whether primary or secondary). Such patients are often prone to strokes, pulmonary embolism, thrombophlebitis, hypertension, and water retention associated with congestive heart failure. Even the patient with acute severe chest pain should be withheld from the pill until the exact nature of the pain is determined. Medroxyprogesterone acetate may be a suitable contraceptive alternative for such patients when the pill is contraindicated. Teenagers with small left to right shunts, rheumatic heart disease without valvular disease, or mild asthma without severe, chronic pulmonary complications may be placed on the pill.

Hypertension

A reversible, mildly elevated blood pressure is noted in 5–18 percent of women on oral contraceptives.[1] Usually an increase of 5–7 mm Hg is noted with the systolic blood pressure and 1–2 mm Hg with the diastolic pressure in susceptible individuals. The mechanism of this hypertensive reaction may include hypervolemia due to sodium and fluid retention, activation of the renin-angiotensin aldosterone system, and possibly increased adrenergic or catecholamine activation.[46] Whether this occurs in individuals who would spontaneously develop hypertension at some point is unclear. A few, often unpredictable patients are very susceptible and develop severe or malignant hypertension, and even irreversible renal damage or failure.

Thus teenagers should be screened and monitored for hypertension. The presence of mild hypertension is not necessarily a contraindication or side effect of oral contraceptive use. Other causes should be sought, including essential hypertension, renal disorders (pyelonephritis, glomerulonephritis, etc.), cardiovascular disorders (renal artery stenosis, fibromuscular dysplasia of the renal artery, coarctation of the aorta, etc.), endocrine disorders, central nervous system disorders, drug-induced or anxiety-induced hypertension, and many others. A careful evaluation is necessary in such cases. If the work-up is negative, and the blood pressure drops after the pill is discontinued, one can probably assume a relationship between the pill and the hypertension. All factors should be weighed before restarting the pill. The patient should be carefully monitored and the pill stopped if the diastolic pressure exceeds 102–104 mm Hg or if there is evidence of hypertensive complications (as fundi changes, cardiac hypertrophy or renal damages) or other risk factors for cardiac disease. A history of pregnancy-related hypertension or strong family history of hypertension or cardiac disease may be significant risk factors. Less effect on the blood pressure may be noted with a lower estrogen pill and virtually no effect is observed with the minipill.

Migraine Headaches

Although some women do not have any change in headache symptomatology on the pill, the overwhelming body of literature from the past 20 years indicates that oral contraceptives may initiate or worsen migraine headaches. Of even more concern are many anecdotal reports and published implications that cerebrovascular accidents and neuro-ophthalmic sequelae (e.g., retinal vessel spasm or occlusion) occur in women on the pill who also had migraine headaches.[47,48] Although surveys may not have proven a definite association between strokes and migrainoid women on the pill, reports such as those by Ask-Upmark et al. are worrisome: they reported that a 17-year-old female with frequent vascular (migrainoid) headaches developed a cerebrovascular accident after 18 months of pill usage; she developed hemiplegia and died.[47] Some authors note that the appearance of migraine headaches may serve as a warning of an impending stroke; thus many have concluded that migraines are a contraindication to oral contraceptive use.[49]

Faced with such reports, what is the clinician to do with a migrainoid teenager who wishes to take the pill? Certainly a very careful history is important. In taking the history one should attempt to distinguish a tension type of headache from a migraine type, in which there is an aura, automonic dysfunctioning, and a unilateral or bilateral throbbing lasting a variable amount of time. There are many types of migraines, including classic, common, cluster, hemiplegic, ophthalmoplegic, basilar artery, and atypical. Common migraine characteristics are listed in Table 4-8. A history of "mild" migraines does not necessarily serve as an absolute contraindication to pill use, but efforts should be undertaken to find another contraceptive method. A history of worsening vascular headaches should prompt a *careful* search for precipitating factors (Table 4-9). Very careful monitoring of the patient is necessary. Unfortunately, there is no proven way to predict which patients will develop headaches or experience worsening of their previous pattern. One should avoid or discontinue the pill if the teenage patient has severe migraines, prolonged aura (especially of the ophthalmoplegic or hemiplegic type), a varying migraine pattern, or additional risk factors for vascular phenomena.

Table 4-8. Common Migraine Characteristics

Aura
  Visual (scintillating scotomas, flashing lights, visual field defects, others)
  Auditory
  Gastrointestinal
  Motor
  Psychological (including mood changes, confusion)
  Other: pallor, syncope, hyperhidrosis
  Combinations

Vascular headache with evidence of autonomic dysfunctioning
  Nausea alone or with emesis
  Anorexia
  Photophobia
  Diarrhea
  Diuresis
  Constipation
  Edema
  Fever
  Blood pressure changes
  Pallor

Table 4-9. Migraine Precipitating Factors

Fatigue

Poststress situations

Stress

Menses and/or ovulation

Flickering lights (including harsh sunlight)

Birth control pills

Barometric or humidity changes

Alcohol (especially with antihistamine medications)

Drugs (reserpine, vasodilator drugs, ergotamine withdrawal, analgesic abuse, others)

Missed meals

Caffeine

Specific foods
    Tyramine (old cheese, red wine)
    Nitrates or nitrites (as in sausage, pastrami, canned ham, corned beef, smoked fish, bologna, hot dogs, salami, pepperoni, bacon, others)
    β-phenylethylamine in chocolate
    Citrus fruits
    Monosodium glutamate ("Chinese restaurant syndrome": oriental style foods, nuts, TV dinners, instant gravies, canned soup, gourmet seasonings, some potato chip products, some dry roasted nuts, others)
    Other foods

Change in sleep patterns

Hypertension

Allergens (?)

Exercise

Coitus ("orgasmic headaches")

Others

Epilepsy

Seizure disorders are not necessarily a contraindication to oral contraceptive use. Some individuals do experience more difficulty in seizure control, but many can do quite well with appropriate adjustment of their antiepileptic medications. Certainly the patient with severe or poorly controlled epilepsy is not a candidate for this form of contraception. In addition, some authors have felt there is an increase in the incidence of epilepsy among women on the pill; however, this is difficult to verify. It is of interest to note that hormonal agents (such as the oral contraceptive progesterone-only pill, or medroxyprogesterone acetate) may actually improve some forms of epilepsy—especially the catamanial type which worsens with menstruation or the premenstrual syndrome.

The real problem with epileptics on the pill may be a high pregnancy rate despite good compliance and motivation to avoid failures.[50] A possible mechanism is drug-induced microsomal enzyme induction in the liver, with resultant increased oral contraceptive metabolism. Interference with enterohepatic recirculation is another possible mechanism. Drugs that cause such pill interactions include antiseizure medications such as barbiturates, phenyltoin, primidone, ethosuccimide, and possibly others. Thus these patients should be on additional or alternative contraceptive methods. More study is needed in this area.

Finally, it should be noted that there are other drugs that produce such interactions with the pill, including rifampicin, tetracycline, chloramphenicol, nitrofurantoin, sulphamethoxypyridazine, amidopyrine, chlordiazepoxide, chlorpromazine, meprobamate, cyclophosphamide, phenylbutazone, dihydroergotamine, and others.[51,52] Thus potential drug interactions should be considered as a possible contraindication to pill usage. More study is needed, since it is not always clear which medications are involved. Ampicillin, for example, has been implicated in some reports but not in others.

Oligomenorrhea

Most gynecologists recommend not to start the teenager on the pill unless she has had 1–2 years of regular menstruation.[53] This rule is based on the concern that starting a teenager on the pill before regular menses occurs might oversuppress the hypothalamic-pituitary-ovarian axis and produce postpill amenorrhea and possibly subsequent infertility. However, some feel that there is no evidence that the pill can really permanently suppress this axis and that oral contraception should not be withheld from the sexually active female solely because of irregular periods.[54]

The whole problem of postpill amenorrhea remains controversial. Studies show that amenorrhea lasting 6 or more months after discontinuation of the pill occurs in 0.7–2.2 percent of women. A delay in conception has been reported in some pill users after stopping the pill.[55] It does not correlate with parity, previous menstrual irregularity, or duration of pill usage. Most of these women will or can be induced to ovulate eventually. An extensive evaluation should be done after 6 months, including looking for pituitary prolactinomas, especially in patients with amenorrhea, hyperprolactinemia, and galactorrhea. Although the pill can induce elevated prolactin levels, there is no evidence it induces pituitary adenomas per se,[56] and no actual evidence it really induces amenorrhea after its discontinuation.[57]

How does the clinician decide what to do with the teenager who presents with irregular periods? This can be a complex process, requiring a thorough diagnostic assessment before consideration of a prescription. The type of bleeding should be ascertained, whether menorrhagia, metrorrhagia, menometrorrhagia, polymenorrhea, oligomenorrhea, intermenstrual bleeding, or dysfunctional uterine bleeding. Many possible causes must be considered, and a complete history and physical examination must be done. Some of the causes include physiologic anovulation, pregnancy complications (such as a spontaneous or induced incomplete abortion, ectopic pregnancy, or hydatidiform mole), weight changes (due to anorexia nervosa, dieting, exercise, etc.), pelvic inflammatory disease or sexually transmitted diseases (due to *N. gonorrhoeae, Trichomonas vaginalis,* or *Chlamydia trachomatis*), blood dyscrasias (severe iron deficiency anemia, factor VIII deficiency, von Willebrand's disease, idiopathic thrombocytopenic purpura, leukemia, etc.), endocrinopathies (such as hypothyroidism or congenital adrenal hyperplasia), neoplasms (such as pituitary adenoma or vaginal sarcoma botryoides), ovarian disorders (such as the Stein-Leventhal syndrome, persistent corpus luteum cyst or tumor), endometriosis, diabetes mellitus, trauma, emotion, and medications (such as the phenothiazines).

Although oligomenorrhea need not be an *absolute* contraindication to pill use, prescription without a careful search for underlying causes would be a contraindication. The pill should *not* be used to mask underlying fertility problems. It should be noted again that many continue not to recommend the pill for teenagers with oligomenorrhea, regardless of the cause.

Finally, there is one type of irregular menstruation or bleeding which should be mentioned in this context. It is common for some "breakthrough" bleeding to occur in the first few months of oral contraceptive use. It is usually mild and resolves over time without specific treatment. It is more common with 20-μg estrogen tablets than with the 30–50 μg estrogen brands. If it does not improve over a few cycles, ethinyl estradiol supplements (10–20 μg/day) can be given for 7–10 days, or a higher estrogen pill chosen (up to 50 μg). Breakthrough bleeding occurring after several months or more of pill usage may be due to a progesterone effect on the endometrium and often responds to a pill brand with a more potent progestogen. A clinician should seek to ensure that the patient is taking the pill each day.

Diabetes Mellitus

The decade of the 1960s made it clear that many women developed abnormal or reduced glucose tolerance while on the pill. The mechanisms of this diabetogenic tendency may include elevated cortisol and growth hormone levels, liver function changes, alteration of peripheral glucose utilization, and alteration of gastrointestinal factors.[58] Those individuals with a positive family history for diabetes may have greater glucose elevations on the pill. Identification of individuals who develop this tendency is often difficult prior to pill prescription, but HLA typing may eventually become a useful screening tool in this regard. Although the pill does not increase the incidence of diabetes in "healthy" individuals, women with subclinical or gestational diabetes may develop overt disease while on the pill.

What about the youth with diagnosed disease who wishes to use the pill as a contraceptive method? Many regard diabetes as a strong relative contraindication to pill use, due to the fear of worsening the complications of diabetes—especially since the triglyceride level is often increased while on the pill.

The presence of hyperlipidemia prior to pill usage is a strong contraindication to its prescription. However, the risks of the overt diabetic becoming pregnant must also be considered, and adequate contraception must be provided for the sexually active teenager if it is desired or will be accepted. Although diabetics are more difficult to control while on the pill, some can remain in adequate metabolic control with careful physician monitoring and patient motivation. Nevertheless, oral contraceptives are not the first choice for these patients. Recent studies by Steel and Duncan indicated that some women with type I diabetes mellitus (insulin-requiring) develop more vascular phenomena, including cerebrovascular accidents, as well as more progressive retinopathy and nephropathy while on the combined oral contraceptive; this increased risk may even include teenagers and young adult women in good metabolic control.[59-61]

Alternative contraceptives include barrier methods either alone or with the minipill as well as medroxyprogesterone acetate. The IUD is not an alternative due to the risk of increased pelvic infections and possible high failure rate from metabolic interaction with the diabetic endometrium. Sterilization is strongly considered for some adult women.

Sickle Cell Disease

It is clear that oral contraception should be avoided in patients with sickle cell anemia or sickle cell C disease due to the increased risk of sickling crisis and vascular phenomena. The female with the sickle cell trait, however, is usually asymptomatic and presents with no unusual hematologic picture unless a screening sickling test or hemoglobin electrophoresis is done. These individuals are heterozygous for sickle cell disease and the sickle cell tests (sodium metabisulfide or solubility tests) are positive and the hemoglobin electrophoresis demonstrates 20–25 percent hemoglobin S and 55–75 percent hemoglobin A.[1] Many difficulties have been reported in patients with sickle cell trait (Table 4-10). The individual is at risk for a severe sickling crisis under certain conditions. Sudden death in an otherwise healthy individual

Table 4-10. Potential Complications of Sickle Cell Trait

Sickling during situations involving prolonged hypoxia (PaO_2 under 20 mm Hg)
    Prolonged anesthesia (especially during postoperative period)
    Prolonged underwater swimming
    Flying in an unpressurized airplane
    Unusual duration of tourniquet constriction
    Severe congenital heart disease or severe pulmonary disease

Renal phenomena
    Hematuria (can be massive)
    Renal infarctions (with renal papillary necrosis, renal medullary necrosis, renal
        failure)
    Hyposthenuria (noted in adults)
    Others

Other organ infarctions (hepatic, splenic, pulmonary, others)

Retinopathy

Priapism

Avascular necrosis of the femoral head

Pregnancy complications
    Increased toxemia
    Increased urinary tract infection or pyelonephritis

Increased fetal morbidity and mortality, especially if the father has sickle cell trait

Difficulty if heterozygous sickling diseases are present

Reduced fetal weight

Neurologic disorders (?)

Complicated migraine complex (?)

Abnormal growth and development

Others

---

with sickle cell trait has been reported, as well as various neurologic complications. Increased anesthetic risks, superior longitudinal sinus thrombosis (postoperatively in a 12-year-old boy), possible impaired growth and development, proliferative retinopathy, pulmonary infarction, renal difficulties, and other phenomena have been reported in "healthy" individuals with sickle cell trait.

It is not clear whether oral contraceptives worsen the potential risks of sickle cell trait.[62] Anecdotal reports of stroke or pulmonary embolism in women on the oral contraceptive who have sickle cell trait do not necessarily imply a significant risk. A recent major review did not note much proven association between sickle cell trait and general morbidity.[63] Furthermore, in a recent survey of certain practicing physicians in Rochester, New York, the majority of gynecologists contacted felt that oral contraceptives were the first choice of contraception for a normal teenager with sickle cell trait.[64]

The oral contraceptive *may* increase potential difficulties of sickle cell trait in certain situations, such as with anesthesia, severe dehydration, strenuous exercise, high-altitude flying in an unpressurized airplane, prolonged tourniquet use, and possibly others; for example, the possibly increased risk of postoperative thrombosis noted in patients on oral contraceptives may augment the potential anesthetic risks implicated in sickle cell trait. It is not clear whether increased hemoglobin S is a factor in sickle cell trait and these complications. The potential problems are really unknown.

In summary, there is at present no convincing reason to withhold oral contraceptives from the normal youth with sickle cell trait. This trait does constitute a relative contraindication, especially if the teenager is placed in situations that augment the chances of sickle cell crisis. Another contraceptive method should be considered if additional relative contraindications are noted in the patient with sickle cell trait. A thorough history and examination are important and the choice of contraception is up to the physician and the patient.

What about an alternative for the patient with sickle cell anemia? The increased fetal and maternal morbidity associated with this disorder suggests that pregnancy be avoided. An IUD is considered by some but may pose additional risks of infection. The barrier methods alone or with the minipill may be a suitable alternative. Medroxyprogesterone acetate has also been recommended. Sterilization is often recommended for adult women.

Hepatic Disorders

Oral contraceptives are fully contraindicated in the presence of active, acute, or chronic liver disease; they have been shown to cause or worsen such conditions as hepatitis, cholestatic jaundice of pregnancy, and primary biliary cirrhosis. The pill-induced hepatitis (with abnormal sulfobromphthalein retention, and elevated SGOT, SGPT, alkaline phosphate, and bilirubin) is usually mild and self-limited but can produce considerable morbidity in some cases. Once liver function has returned to normal after viral hepatitis, the pill can be restarted without sequelae.[65] Careful monitoring of the liver status in any patient, however, is important. Gilbert's disease is a relative contraindication to pill usage.

The decade of the 1960s established the potential hepatotoxic effect of the pill, while the 1970s demonstrated its association with the development of benign hepatic adenomas in a small but significant number of pill users.

Since the report, Baum et al. in 1973,[66] many more cases have been added to the literature. Hepatic cell adenoma or focal nodular hyperplasia can develop while a patient is taking the pill, and may resolve after the pill is stopped. Pills with mestranol have been implicated most often, possibly due to its demethylation to ethinyl estradiol in the liver. Although often asymptomatic, these lesions may be quite vascular and can rupture into the liver or peritoneum, producing a syndrome of abdominal pain, right shoulder pain, abdominal mass in the right upper quadrant, and shock. Menses may precipitate tumor hemorrhaging, and long-term use of the pill may encourage the development of these lesions. A liver scan and arteriogram aid in this diagnosis, but a liver biopsy is contraindicated. Thus, patients on the pill should be periodically monitored for right upper quadrant masses; the onset of upper abdominal pain, with or without evidence of shock, should bring this entity to mind. The number of patients involved is small, but the morbidity and mortality can be considerable.

Cancer

Despite extensive investigation and observation of oral contraceptive use in millions of women over the past 20 years, there is no evidence that they cause cancer.[67] The only association shown is with benign hepatic adenomas, as previously discussed. There is no current evidence that women on the pill have an increased risk for breast tumors,[68] pituitary tumors, or cervical cancer. More studies are needed, however, especially with regard to cancer of the cervix. This is a disorder with many underlying factors, including frequency of coitus and number of coital partners. Abnormal cervical Papanicolaou smears have been reported in sexually active teenagers and young women; thus the eventual risk for the teenager who is on the pill and has risk factors such as frequent or promiscuous coital patterns is still unknown. Careful monitoring is needed, with regular examinations and Papanicolaou smears. Whether the pill is a potential risk factor for cervical cancer is not yet clear. Remember that the possible association between the sequential contraceptives and endometrial carcinoma resulted in their being withdrawn from commercial use. The pill seems to worsen choriocarcinoma, while its relationship to endometrial carcinoma in adult women remains to be clarified.

Miscellaneous Effects

There are many disorders that have developed in individuals on the pill, although a cause-and-effect relationship is not always possible to establish.

Ocular Disorders

In addition to retinal vessel spasm and/or occlusion, as discussed previously, pill users have been reported to develop initial or worsening episodes of optic neuritis, retrobulbar neuritis, retinal edema, corneal edema (with contact lens irritation), and worsening myopia. Although a direct association has been questioned by some clinicians, the pill is contraindicated for those with retinal or optic nerve disorders. Careful eye examinations are necessary for patients on the pill, especially if ocular symptomatology arises. Problems in teenagers have been reported.

Ear Disorders

Eustachian tube dysfunction has been noted in some individuals on the pill, as well as worsening of otosclerosis. The mechanism of these effects is unclear, but otosclerosis should be considered a contraindication for oral contraceptive use.[69]

Gastrointestinal Disorders

Liver disorders have been discussed. Other gastrointestinal problems include cholelithiasis, pancreatitis, and mesenteric vascular disease. There has been an increase in gallstones reported in women using the pill, and thus this form of contraception should be added to the list of risk factors for cholelithiasis and cholecystitis, even in teenagers. Such a list would include obesity, blood dyscrasias, and recent dieting and weight loss, among other factors. The mechanism is unclear since studies have not revealed a pill-induced change in gall bladder kinetics.

Women have also developed pancreatitis while on oral contraceptives. Individuals with hyperlipidemia (especially types IV and V) who are placed on the pill can develop marked elevations in lipid levels and subsequent severe pancreatitis. This complication may also develop in diabetics. Thus the pill should not be given to patients with hyperlipidemia (type IV, V), especially if they have diabetes mellitus.

Mesenteric vascular disease has also been reported in a few patients on the pill, although a direct association is difficult to prove. Finally, there have been reports of possible pill-induced hepatic vein obstruction (Budd-Chiari syndrome) and even ulcerative colitis. The latter is of unknown clinical importance, especially in view of the significant morbidity and mortality associated with inflammatory bowel disease in adolescence. The pill should not be given to an individual with unusual or atypical abdominal pain until its etiology is ascertained and then a further decision is made about the possibility of pill use.

Gynecologic (Including Breast) Disorders

Various pill effects on the breast tissue have been reported, but there is no evidence of increased breast cancer or tumors in pill users.[70] In fact, pill users have less benign breast disease than nonusers. Galactorrhea has been rarely reported in association with the pill. Although the effect of oral contraceptives on lactation is not clear,[71] a reduction is noted in the amount of breast milk, with less protein and less lipid content. The hormonal content does appear in the breast milk, and there have been reports of subsequent vaginal cornification of nursing female infants and gynecomastia in nursing infants. Thus lactation is considered by some as a contraindication for oral contraceptives.

Some individuals on oral contraceptives experience an increase in vaginitis due to *Candida albicans*. The mechanism includes pill-induced increased glycogen content of the vaginal epithelium, favoring growth of the fungus. The patient can usually be effectively treated with standard antifungal medications (e.g., nystatin, miconazole nitrate, or clotrimazole) without discontinuation of the pill. Treatment of the associated male partner's candidal balanoposthitis is also important. A few cases, however, become very resistant and the pill must be stopped. Attention to the many precipitating factors for monilial vaginitis is important in planning a therapeutic regimen for chronic candidal vaginitis.

Other potential gynecologic effects of the pill include benign cervical polyps or polypoid hyperplasia of the endocervical glands, worsening leiomyomas (a relative contraindication to pill usage), and perhaps less pelvic inflammatory disease.[72]

Genitourinary Disorders

An increase in urinary tract infections and bacteriuria is noted in women on the pill; they may be related to pill-induced urinary bladder trabeculations and/or increased or more promiscuous coital activity of some pill takers. Whether such mechanisms produce an increase in the acute urethral syndrome (the pyuria–dysuria syndrome)[73] remains to be investigated.

The pill is contraindicated in the presence of renal disease, especially glomerulonephritis or hypertension (essential, renovascular, or other types). These patients should receive other contraceptives, such as the minipill, barrier methods, injectable progesterone, etc. The hemolytic-uremic syndrome may be precipitated or worsened with oral contraceptives.

Neurologic Disorders

Various neurologic problems have been reported in women on the pill.[1] The unsettled situation concerning migraine headaches has been discussed previously. In addition, dizziness, pseudotumor cerebri, chorea,[74] rheumatoid symptomatology, systemic lupus erythematosus, and Raynaud's disease have developed or worsened in patients on oral contraceptives. Such reports emphasize the importance of carefully screening and monitoring patients placed on the pill. A pill-induced effect has not been noted in patients with multiple sclerosis.[75]

Dermatologic Disorders

Melasma (chloasma) is one of the most common skin reactions to the pill. It occurs in as many as 5–8 percent of individuals, especially those with dark complexions. It may fade slowly after pill discontinuation, or remain permanently despite dermatologic treatment (with cosmetics, sun screens, hydroquinones, etc.) Acne vulgaris may be improved or worsened by the pill. Often the low-estrogen contraceptive worsens the condition, while the higher dose causes improvement. Thus the teenager may expect worsening of her acne condition while on the recommended lower dose pill. Treatment, however, is easily available and pill discontinuation should not be necessary.

Porphyria should be considered a contraindication to pill use, since there are many reports of its development or worsening in women taking the oral contraceptive. Other dermatologic conditions evoked by pill use include[76] erythema nodosum, angioneurotic edema, alopecia, spider nevi, progesterone dermatitis,[77] and acanthosis nigricans. In addition, the pill may worsen telangiectasias and malignant melanomas and thus is contraindicated with these conditions.

Endocrine Functioning

Thyroid function remains normal on the pill despite an increase in thyroxine (due to an increase in binding protein) and protein-bound iodine levels. If a question arises regarding thyroid functioning, the pill can be discontinued and thyroid status evaluated in 2–3 months without pill effects on the laboratory tests. Other means of contraception should then be provided. Adrenal functioning remains normal, despite an increase in the cortisol-binding globulin level and an increase in plasma cortisol level. Some authors have reported a reduced adrenocorticotropin (ACTH) reserve and a lowered pituitary reserve, and the pill should probably be avoided in cases of hypopituitarism or ACTH deficiency.

Depression

There have been reports that the pill causes depression in some women due to a deficiency in pyridoxine and a resultant disturbance in tryptophan metabolism; however, this relationship is not yet clear.[78] Some authors feel it occurs in women with a previous history of depression, while others feel a link has not been established. Others contend that there is an increased sadness in some women on the pill because the chance for pregnancy has been removed. Other studies have attempted to look at the resultant coital frequency and sex drive as influenced by the pill; however, the influence of the pill on an individual is complex and difficult to compare in this regard.

Fetal Anomalies

Women who become pregnant while on the pill and then continue to take it subject the fetus to increased morbidity risk. The resultant congenital anomalies include vertebral, anal, cardiac, limb reduction, and other defects. The pill is not considered a major teratogen. There is no observable effect in the sex or intelligence of the offspring of contraceptive users. An important requirement of women on oral contraceptives is the ability and motivation to take the pill *each day*. If they skip the pill, irregular bleeding may occur. This may be the early sign of poor compliance by the teenager. Continued poor compliance may result in pregnancy and subsequent increased risk of fetal morbidity.

Other Problems

Other problems have been described in pill users, including increased gingivitis, influenza, allergic rhinitis, and chicken pox, increased twinning in women who conceive shortly after discontinuing the pill, and pill failure after gastroenteritis because of absorbtion failure.

Combined Oral Contraceptives and the Teenager

Many sexually active adolescents wish to and can use contraceptive methods to avoid pregnancy. A careful history and physical examination should precede prescription or recommendation of a method which the patient can choose, with the guidance of her health care professional. A pelvic examination with sexually transmitted disease screening (including a cervical culture for N. gonorrhoeae) and a Papanicolaou smear is mandatory. Counseling in areas of sexuality, including providing information on venereal disease is also important. Although a barrier method or even abstinence are the first choices of many clinicians, many teenagers wish to take the pill. Specific laboratory procedures, such as syphilis serology, lipid screening, or liver function testing, depend on the clinician's judgment in view of each patient's presentation. The teenager should be informed of any relative contraindications that may exist, as well as possible common side effects, including acne vulgaris, monilial vaginitis, weight gain (about 5 lb or so), edema, and others. Some of these situations can be treated and the pill continued.

It is very important that the patient, regardless of her chronological age, understand what methods of contraception are available; if she chooses the pill she must be willing and motivated to take the pill every day and to return for frequent follow-up visits. She should not necessarily be withheld from the pill if there is an acute or chronic medical condition. The risk of pregnancy and its associated morbidity (or mortality) may be great enough to place her on the pill if no other method is available, or acceptable, despite the presence of certain relative contraindications.

Often a patient can be placed on the pill for a brief time, until she is psychologically mature enough to accept another alternative such as a barrier method. It is important to view the use of the pill in these situations as a brief, acceptable alternative to pregnancy, and as a means to "hold her over" until other, safer methods are chosen. Thus the oral contraceptive may be necessary for the individual with irregular periods, controlled diabetes mellitus, mild migraine headaches, or cigarette addiction at a specific time in her life. Other methods can be offered at various times. A major contribution the clinician can make is to advise the teenage patient of the risks and help her arrive at a decision. This assumes that the health care professional (obstetrician-gynecologist, pediatrician, internist, family practitioner, or other) has developed a sound data base in adolescent sexuality and contraception. This also assumes that the patient will follow medical advice appropriately and allow for close monitoring. This doctor–patient relationship requires mutual responsibility to ensure safe and effective birth control.

LOW-ESTROGEN ORAL CONTRACEPTIVES

Pills that contain more than 50 μg estrogen are not recommended for teenage or adult women. Use of a low-dose pill (with 35–50 μg estrogen) or a micropill (with 20–35 μg estrogen) seems to reduce the risk of throm-

Table 4-11. Oral Contraceptives with 50 μg or Less Estrogen

Brand	Amount (μg) of Ethinyl Estradiol
Ovral	50
Demulen	50
Loestrin 1/20	20
Loestrin 1.5/30	30
Lo/Ovral	30
Zorane 1.5/30	30
Zorane 1/20	20
Brevicon (Modicon)	35
Norinyl 1/50	50*
Norlestrin 1/50	50

*Mestranol.

boembolic phenomona and produce fewer metabolic effects. Perhaps there is less pituitary suppression and thus a lower incidence of postpill amenorrhea. The risks for vascular and other phenomona still exist, however, and more breakthrough bleeding may be noted—especially with the 20-μg tablets. Some of the low-dose pills are listed in Table 4-11. The full protection afforded by these low-estrogen pills is not yet established. Many of the side effects described in the literature of the 1960s resulted from the larger dose estrogen pills (75–100 μg). Low-dose estrogen pills are as effective as the combined oral contraceptive pill, and their careful use should produce less morbidity.

TRIPHASIC ORAL CONTRACEPTIVES

In order to reduce the pill side effects attributable to estrogen and progesterone, there have been continued efforts to reduce both hormonal agents to their lowest levels. A new type of pill developed along this line is the triphasic oral contraceptive.[79-81] A current formulation consists of ethinyl estradiol and levonorgestrel in a "triphasic" arrangement: for the first 6 days the pill contains 30 μg estrogen and 50 μg progestogen; then from day 7 to 11 there is 40 μg estrogen and 75 μg progestogen; finally, from day 12 to 21 the pill contains 30 μg estrogen and 125 μg progestogen.[82] This formulation reduces these hormones to low levels and simulates the varying concentrations noted in a normal menstrual cycle. Researchers have found this pill to be effective and yet cause fewer menstrual bleeding difficulties than the traditional pill.[83] There is also less acne vulgaris noted in women on the triphasic pill.[84] There is some increase in breast tenderness, dysmenorrhea, and serum triglycerides in comparison to the fixed-dose pill. The triphasic pill has become popular in Europe and may be introduced in the United States within the next several years.

MINIPILL

Pills that contain only progesterone are called minipills and were introduced in the mid-1960s with the hope of providing effective contraceptive action without the many side effects of the estrogen-containing pills. The contraceptive action is based on cervical mucus alteration (causing interference with sperm migration), endometrial lining alteration (preventing blastocyst implantation), increased ovum transport through the oviduct, and alteration of corpus luteum function. Ovulation is usually not inhibited. Three pills are commercially available: Micronor (0.35 mg norethindrone), Nor-Q.D. (0.35 mg norethindrone) and Ovrette (0.075 mg norgestrel).

Advantages of minipill use include a significantly reduced risk for thromboembolism, hypertension, and metabolic changes. There is no effect on lactation and there may be an improvement in premenstrual tension and dysmenorrhea. Disadvantages include an increased pregnancy rate (1–3 or more/100 woman-years versus a rate of under 1/100 woman-years for the combined oral contraceptive), frequent menstrual irregularity or amenorrhea (resulting in more women stopping the pill), increased tubal pregnancies, and some weight gain (3–5 lb in some). The minipill has not lived up to its earlier expectations and currently its role with teenagers needs further study. It is recommended, however, in some situations in which the combined pill is contraindicated, such as lactation, hypertension, diabetes mellitus, a history of thromboembolism, and others. It has been used to treat menstrual-induced or catamanial epilepsy.

INTRAUTERINE CONTRACEPTIVE DEVICES

The placement of a plastic and/or metallic device within the uterus to prevent pregnancy has been controversial since the introduction of this method by Richter and Graefenberg.[85–87] It can be an effective method, although in large series a failure rate two or more times that for oral contraceptives has been reported.[85–87] The mechanism of action is to prevent blastocyst implantation and not to inhibit actual conception per se. The addition of copper increases the spermicidal activity of the IUD. Although many types of IUDs have been developed, the copper IUD is the main one being used in nulliparous adolescents. The copper 7 or copper T devices are popular currently, but other modifications (such as the T Cu 200, T Cu 300 or T Cu 380A) are becoming available. An IUD with progesterone, the Progestasert IUD, is also available.

Contraindications to IUD use include pelvic infection, high risk for sexually transmitted disease, cervical or uterine hypoplasia, uterine malignancy, severe dysmenorrhea, severe menorrhagia, coagulation disorders, severe anemia, high risk for bacterial endocarditis, recent septic abortion, recent postpartum endometritis, acute cervicitis, and history of ectopic pregnancy. Complications of IUD use include pain during insertion, increased dysmenorrhea, menstrual bleeding with iron deficiency anemia, inability to find the IUD string, IUD expulsion, uterine perforation with peritonitis, small or large bowel perforation, accidental pregnancy with increased maternal and fetal morbidity, ectopic pregnancy, spontaneous abortion, embedding of IUD into the endometrium with resultant necrosis, appendicitis, bacterial endocarditis, and pelvic infections.[88] A recent study has challenged the traditional view that the IUD increases the overall risk for ectopic pregnancy.[89] A major objection to IUDs raised by clinicians is the significant increase in pelvic inflammatory disease noted in patients using these devices. These pelvic infections include gonococcal salpingitis, pelvic actinomycosis, ovarian abscesses, and others. The three- to ninefold increase in pelvic infections and other IUD complications has prompted some clinicians not to recommend the IUD for teenagers. Individuals at greatest risk are those with multiple partners or with one promiscuous partner. In addition, some youths will not accept this method of contraception since they do not like the idea of any type of device within their bodies.

It is the opinion of this author that the IUD has a definite role in a limited number of adolescent women who are carefully screened for contraindications, who have limited risk for sexually transmitted diseases, who choose this method, and who will allow careful follow-up.[90] There are serious risks, but failure to prevent pregnancy in the youth who will accept no other method may have greater risks.

BARRIER METHODS

Diaphragm

The diaphragm is a rubber cap whose rim contains a metal spring.[91] This cap and a contraceptive cream or jelly are placed into the vagina prior to coitus. The cap is held in place by the spring tension of the rim, the vaginal muscle tone, and the pubic bone. Anatomically, the firm nulliparous perineum of the adolescent or young adult female retains the diaphragm better than that in older individuals. By this means the sperm is blocked from entering the external cervical os and is killed by the spermicidal jelly or cream. Although the failure rates with diaphragm use can be unacceptably high (2.4–29.0/100 woman-years), the properly motivated adolescent or adult female *can* use this method very effectively.[92,93]

Unfortunately, the preparation, skill, and self-intimacy needed with each use prevents many teenagers from effectively utilizing the diaphragm.[94] Although currently unpopular with teenagers, it is a method that clinicians should encourage for their teenage patients. It can provide adequate contraception, has minimal side effects, is very safe to use, may protect women from cervical cancer, and is ideal for the patient who has infrequent coitus or is in need of an interim contraceptive method when switching methods (e.g., stopping the oral contraceptive and getting an IUD). Perhaps, with strong clinician support, the recently reported rise in diaphragm use will continue. Physicians who learn how to fit diaphragms can continue to encourage this trend. There has also been some interest in the cervical cap as a contraceptive method for some adult women, but its use in teenagers is even more limited than the diaphragm. Its real effectiveness has recently been questioned.[95] Toxic shock syndrome has been rarely reported in association with the diaphragm, but not with the cervical cap.

Condoms

Although the condom has long been a neglected contraceptive method, recent articles in the medical literature have urged its renewed encouragement and application.[19,20] It has about the same failure range as a diaphragm, 2.6–30/100 woman-years. With proper use and motivation, however, the condom can be a very effective method. It is probably the most common method used world wide today and clearly deserves a major role among individuals wishing contraception.

There is, however, a tendency for the teenager to avoid using the condom. The male adolescent may have various partners and not wish to take any role in contraception. If the female partner is not motivated to use personal contraception or is not capable of urging her male partner to be responsible, a high risk of adolescent pregnancy ensues. Reasons for not using condoms include fear of decreased sexual pleasure, need for its use with each act of intercourse (with possible disruption of foreplay), failure of health professionals to advocate this method, cost, and unwillingness to accept contraceptive roles. Advantages of the condom include partial protection from sexually transmitted diseases, effective contraception, limited side effects, reliable quality, possible reduced risk for cervical cancer, no prescription necessary, possible improvement of sexual dysfunction (as premature ejaculation), effective prophylaxis of allergic seminal vulvovaginitis, effective relief of dyspareunia, and others. Counseling the teenage couple together may be helpful, so that mutual sharing of contraceptive responsibility can be openly discussed. Effective birth control for women often means open dialogue with the male partner also. It can be pointed out to the female partner that refusal by the male to use contraception may be a sign of his refusal to accept mature sexual responsibility. Education of the public to the importance of the condom is necessary.

Finally, since serious study into male contraception only began recently, the condom is likely to remain the major male contraceptive method, at least for the near future. Condoms can be used by some teenagers, especially if they are made available; thus physicians should encourage their distribution to sexually active youths. Current research in male contraceptive technology is focusing on a male pill (gossypol), injectable testosterone, antiepididymal drugs, agents that selectively inhibit FSH secretion (inhibin), LH-releasing hormone analogs, and various immunologic drugs. These methods will probably not be available for adolescent males in the near future.

Vaginal Contraceptives

Since the work of Baker and Eastman, many types of vaginal contraceptives have become available, including jellies, creams, pastes, powders, suppositories, foaming powders, tablets, and contraceptive film. Contraceptive action is based on the presence of surface-active agents or bactericidal chemicals (e.g., Nonoxynol-9, Octoxynol, etc.) which kill the sperm. Al-

Table 4-12. Vaginal Contraceptives

Name	Active Ingredient	How Supplied
Delfen Cream	Nonoxynol-9	2.46-oz tube with applicator
Delfen Foam	Nonoxynol-9	0.70-oz can with applicator
Emko Foam	8.0 Nonylphenoxypoly-ethoxyethanol + 0.2% benzethonium chloride	45-g aerosol with applicator
Koromex Contraceptive Cream	Nonoxynol-9	22-g can with applicator
Koromex II Contraceptive Cream	Octoxynol	2.65-oz tube with applicator
Koromex II Contraceptive Jelly	Octoxynol	2.85-oz tube with applicator
Koromex II-A Contraceptive Jelly	Nonoxynol-9	4.76-oz tube with applicator
OrthoCreme Contraceptive Cream	Nonoxynol-9	2.46-oz tube with applicator
OrthoGynol Contraceptive Jelly	p-Diisobutyl phenoxy polyethoxyethanol	2.85-oz tube with applicator
Ramses 10-hour Vaginal Jelly	Dodecaethyleneglycol monolaurate	3-oz tube with applicator
Encare Oval Vaginal Suppositories	Nonoxynol-9	Box of 12 inserts
Because Birth Control Foam	8.9% Nonylphenoxypoly-ethoxyethanol + 0.2% benzethonium chloride	10-g tube with applicator
Conceptrol Birth Control Cream	Nonoxynol-9	Premeasured package of 6 applications

though a wide range of failure rates (1.3–38/100 woman-years) is reported, effective contraception is possible if these agents are used by a motivated individual in combination with a diaphragm or condom.[96] The use of vaginal contraceptives is probably most valuable for the individual having sporadic coital activity.

Some teenagers are not developmentally capable of using vaginal contraceptives, whether alone or in combination with other agents. Some are concerned with the increased pregnancy risk or are discouraged from using this method by their physician's advice. It is worthwhile for the clinician to find those willing to contracept who are not overly bothered by the inherent messiness of self-intimacy required. Indeed, the advantages are many: relatively inexpensive but effective contraception is available without a prescription and with few side effects. Allergic reaction is possible, as is a cystitis if a suppository is placed in the urethra. Dyspareunia may be relieved, some protection from sexually transmitted diseases may occur, and the couple may share in the contraceptive responsibility if a condom and vaginal contraceptives are used. There is recent evidence that the use of these spermicidal agents may be mildly teratogenic;[97] however, this is a very controversial topic, and more study is needed.[1]

Available brands of vaginal contraceptives are listed in Table 4-12. Foam seems to be the best vehicle and cream the second best. A new vaginal suppository, Encare Oval, has recently been introduced with claims of superiority over the other types of vaginal contraceptives; however, studies indicate it is about equal to the other vaginal contraceptives. Finally, a new intravaginal contraceptive method has been developed, an intravaginal collagen sponge, with vaginal contraceptives added to or impregnated onto the sponge material.[98] Its contraceptive role among adolescent women remains to be determined.

Barrier Methods and the Teenager

Barrier methods (condoms, diaphragm, and vaginal contraceptives) should be the first methods recommended by clinicians when their teenage patients desire contraception. The condom with or without vaginal contraceptives and the diaphragm with vaginal contraceptives can be very effective, safe methods. Encouragement by the knowledgeable physician may result in their more widespread use. Although developmental factors inhibit their utilization, as the individual proceeds through adolescence, gaining maturity, he or she often reaches a level at which barrier methods can be offered and accepted. The health care professional should continuously probe for this point in the teenager's development.

POSTCOITAL CONTRACEPTIVES

The postovulatory use of estrogen to prevent pregnancy beyond implantation has been studied for many years.[1] Such a regimen is based on implantation inhibition and is thus ineffective after conception and uterine implantation have occurred. Diethylstilbestrol (DES) is the main postcoital contraceptive in current use. DES is given in a dose of 25 mg orally, twice per day for 5 days, commencing within 72 hours of coitus. Its use as an emergency treatment, such as after rape, is approved by the Federal Drug Administration, and its accepted use in college health services has been noted. Due the the the development of urinary tract anomalies in male offspring (cryptorchidism, hypoplastic testis, epididymal cyst, reduced sperm count, etc.) as well as vaginal adenosis and other anomalies (such as clear cell vaginal carcinoma or fertility difficulty) in female offspring due to DES, pregnancy should be ruled out before this treatment is given. Thus, some clinicians recommend obtaining signed consent before giving this postcoital contraceptive, and abortion is usually recommended if pregnancy has occurred. Although some do not recommend the use of DES as a postcoital agent, it does have a role in the prevention of pregnancy after rape in teenagers.

The main side effect of this high-dose estrogen therapy is nausea and emesis in as many as 50 percent of the patients. Giving the DES with meals, giving enteric-coated DES, or adding an antiemetic medication may relieve this considerably. A possible increase in ectopic pregnancy may be associated with DES, and one case of acute pulmonary edema has been reported. Some women develop menorrhagia with the next menstrual period. The risk to the fetus if pregnancy has occurred is unknown.

Other postcoital methods that seem to work (although they are not

Table 4-13. Postcoital Methods of Contraception*

Ethinyl estradiol 5 mg orally, once a day for 5 days
Conjugated estrogens 30 or 50 mg orally, once a day for 5 days
Premarin 30 mg orally, once a day for 5 days
Premarin 50 mg intravenously for 2 days
Conjugated estrogens 20 or 25 mg intramuscularly for 30 days
Estradiol benzoate 30 mg intramuscularly for 5 days
d-Norgestrel
Quingestanol acetate
Estrogen and progestogen combination
Copper IUD

*Other than DES.

FDA approved) are listed in Table 4-13. Although some patients try postcoital douching (e.g., with water or even a cola drink) or postcoital use of topical spermicidal agents, these are ineffective methods.

INJECTABLE CONTRACEPTIVES

The use of intramuscular, long-acting progesterone compounds as contraceptive agents was first noted in the 1960s.[1] It is now evident that 150 mg medroxyprogesterone acetate (Depo-Provera) given intramuscularly every 3 months is as effective a contraceptive as the combined birth control pill—both have pregnancy failure rates of under 1/100 woman-years.

Its mechanism of action includes inhibition of ovulation by preventing the midcycle LH surge, reduced volume with increased viscosity of cervical mucus, and establishment of a thin, inactive endometrium. It has minimal effect on lactation and blood pressure. Although it is a major form of contraception in many countries around the world, and is considered safe by many, the FDA has not approved of its use for contraception, because of three major concerns: (1) a possible increased risk of congenital malformation; (2) a possible increased risk of breast nodules and carcinoma; and (3) the high rate of menstrual irregularities associated with its use (amenorrhea in 23 percent of patients at 1 month, 69 percent at 24 months). Other side effects are abnormal glucose tolerance tests (in 15 percent of patients), intermenstrual spotting, weight gain, nausea and emesis, headaches, and nervousness.

This remains an attractive method, however, for individuals in whom the combined oral contraceptive is contraindicated (e.g., those with sickle cell anemia, heart disease, or a history of thromboembolism) and for certain intellectually impaired or mentally ill teenagers. Although the need for repeated injections and resultant menstrual irregularity (with return of ovulation, sometimes at uncertain times) are limiting factors for general population use, it should be considered a good alternative in selected teenagers. In addition, there are other long-acting injectable contraceptives, such as norethisterone enanthate and lynestrenol.

PERIODIC ABSTINENCE (RHYTHM METHOD)

Periodic abstinence is an old method of birth control which is based on avoidance of coital activity near or at the time of suspected ovulation.[1] Traditionally, this has not been a popular or successful method with teenagers due to their often irregular menses, ignorance of their own physiology, their failure to accept self-intimacy, and other reasons. This method is generally not recommended by clinicians.

Current methods of periodic abstinence that are under study involve the ovulation method or symptothermal method. In 1932, Latz stimulated interest in the "rhythm method." Then the calendar method (Ogino-Knaus method) was developed on three basic concepts: (1) the fertile life span of the oocyte is only 24 hours after ovulation; (2) the viability of sperm in the female genital tract is 4 days or less; and (3) ovulation occurs 14 days after menstruation.

Calculation of the "nonsafe" days is based on these principles; the accuracy of the last two is in doubt, however. The temperature method (basal body temperature) is based on detecting a temperature rise of 0.3°–0.5°C (0.5°–1.0°F) at ovulation. Its accuracy has been questioned, and many women find it difficult to do this *every* month.

The change in cervical mucus during the menstrual cycle has been noted since 1855, and recently there has been much interest in utilizing it as a contraceptive technique. This Billings, or ovulation, method is based on a specific cycle of cervical mucus changes: menses is followed by a number of days without discharge ("dry days"). Then a period of "mucus symptoms" occurs, in which there is an increase in cloudy and sticky secretions over several days. During the immediate periovulatory period, mucus becomes clear, slippery, and copious. Ferning and spinnbarkeit ("raw egg white" appearance) are described. This is the time to avoid coitus. Then the mucus becomes thick, opaque, and scanty, indicating a "safe" period has begun again. Some authors recommend combining this with the basal body temperature method (symptothermal method) or with the use of a diaphragm.

Some investigators feel this is a predictable and reliable method of contraception for many women; however, some feel its reliability has yet to be shown. It is my own feeling that a few carefully selected adolescents with considerable motivation may be able to use this method well, but it has not been shown to be of value for many teenagers. Most recent studies have applied this method to adults, not adolescents. In one study only 8 percent of the population was adolescent and an age breakdown was not reported. As noted with barrier methods, many teenagers do not accept self-intimacy. Thus, rhythm in general is often not advocated for most teenagers. It may be an acceptable method for a *limited* number of well-motivated adolescents and adults.

Finally, the possibility that rhythm methods increase the chances of abnormal implantation or fetal anomalies due to aged gametes has been raised. There are no current data to support this hypothesis.

MISCELLANEOUS METHODS

Coitus Interruptus

Coitus interruptus, or withdrawing the penis from the vagina prior to ejaculation, has been a key male contraceptive method for centuries.[1] It has other names, including the withdrawal method, strategic withdrawal, the French method, the sin of Onan (Genesis 38:8,9), and others. It is still very popular, and is a major male method, along with abstinence and the condom. Although it may be used by certain males with some success, many clinicians do not recommend reliance on it as a good contraceptive method. Part of the difficulty with coitus interruptus is the need to overcome the natural male urge for greater penetration prior to ejaculation, and the possibility of sperm existing in preejaculate fluid. Most teenage males would not possess such control. Variations of coitus interruptus include coitus reservatus (coitus for an extended time until detumescence occurs without ejaculation) and coitus obstructivus (retrograde ejaculation due to pressure placed on or around the penis at ejaculation). Neither would be recommended for male youths.

Finally, as previously noted, there is a need for a safe and effective male contraceptive pill to add to the few male methods available now. There are males eager for such a method so that they can share in mutual contraception with their partners. Some older adolescent males would certainly be in this category.

Postcoital Douche

Although postcoital douche is a time-honored method of contraception, it is currently not recommended due to its very high pregnancy rate. The sperm can reach the cervical mucus in 90 seconds and the fallopian tubes within 5 minutes. Thus such a method cannot be recommended to teenagers under any circumstances. Douching is, however, part of normal female hygiene and can be encouraged as such. Douching with water is not harmful, but deaths from carbonated beverage douches have been reported.

Lactation

Although lactation prolongs amenorrhea, it cannot be relied on for effective contraception. Many women ovulate before menses returns, and the longer amenorrhea is prolonged, the more likely it is that the first cycle will be ovulatory. The average amenorrheic state is about 7 months, and nearly all women ovulate within the first year after delivery. Since 3−10 percent of lactating women who use no contraceptive become pregnant even before menses returns, the act of breastfeeding is not an effective contraceptive method in itself. The recent birth of an infant is a good time to offer contraception to the nursing mother.

Noncoital Sexual Activity

Discussion of sexual activity and contraception may even lead to consideration of the role of noncoital sex (petting, hand-holding, kissing, anogenital sex, masturbation,[99] etc.). The recent societal changes regarding sexuality should be recognized by clinician and patient alike, and certainly each may have different views regarding this subject. For example, current lay teenager literature often refers to masturbation as a harmless and even physiologically beneficial aspect of human sexuality. The physician's counseling in such areas often reflects his or her own views; some of this is certainly unavoidable.

Sterilization

The application of sterilization techniques to a selected group of adolescents is a very emotional subject. Sterilization as a permanent and effective contraceptive technique is certainly technically possible, but the associated legal and moral issues are such that it is difficult to sterilize a particular youth except in very special circumstances. Over the past 20 years, much progress has been made in the definition of the legal rights of minors.[100] Recent court decisions have upheld the concept that minors (those under 21 years) do have some rights to seek and accept health care. However, more precise rulings are needed regarding *who* can decide to sterilize a mentally impaired teenager or youth with severe illness.

CONCLUSIONS

It is the premise of this discussion that there are contraceptive methods available to the adolescent and that the knowledgeable clinician can help the patient choose the most suitable method.[1,19,20] Although the oral contraceptive remains the most popular effective method among teenagers, the clinician should stress the safety and efficacy of barrier methods for the motivated teenager. An understanding of these issues of adolescent contraception and pregnancy is rooted in an understanding of the very process of adolescence itself.

Finally, the health care professional should remember that he or she is often providing information for the teenage patient for only part of her reproductive years. A method (such as the birth control pill) that the patient chooses at a particular time in her life may be replaced by other methods (such as the mucus method of Billings, diaphragm, condom and foam, or others) as the dynamics of her life change. The patient's physicians often change—sometimes at a blurring speed as the patient gets older. The patient chooses for herself while we only provide information and advice; this often changes depending on whom she consults. *Primum non nocere.*

REFERENCES

1. Greydanus DE: Alternatives to adolescent pregnancy: A discussion of the contraceptive literature from 1960–1980. Semin Perinatol 5:53–90, 1981
2. Landis PH: Adolescence and Youth. New York, McGraw-Hill, 1975, p 23
3. Zelnik M, Kantner JF: Contraceptive patterns and premarital pregnancy among women aged 15–19 in 1976. Fam Plann Perspect 10:135–142, 1978
4. Handsfield HH: Sexually transmitted diseases. Hosp Pract 17:99–116, 1982
5. Greydanus DE, McAnarney ER: Vulvovaginitis in adolescents. J Curr Adolesc Med 1(1):56–63, 1(2):52–56; 1(4):40–47, 1979
6. Daniel WA Jr: An approach to the adolescent patient. Med Clin North Am 59:1281–1287, 1975
7. Elkind D: A Sympathetic Understanding of the Child Six to Sixteen. Boston, Allyn & Bacon, 1971, p 93
8. Committee on Adolescence: Normal adolescence: Its dynamics and impact. Group Adv Psychiatry (New York) 6:830, 1968
9. Tanner JM: Growth and Adolescence (ed 2). Oxford, Blackwell, 1962
10. Greydanus DE, McAnarney ER: The value of the Tanner staging. J Curr Adolesc Med 2(2):21–25, 1980
11. Hatcher S: Understanding pregnancy and abortion. Primary Care 3:407, 1976
12. McAnarney ER, Greydanus DE: Adolescent pregnancy—A multifaceted problem. Pediatr Rev 1(4):123–126, 1979
13. Sweeney WO: Media communications in population/family planning programs: A review. Popul Rep 6:289–305, 1977
14. Greydanus DE: Should the media advertise contraceptives? Am J Dis Child 135:687–688, 1981
15. Tietze C, Guttmacher AF, Rubin S: Time required for contraception in 1727 planned pregnancies. Fertil Steril 1:338–342, 1950
16. Committee on Adolescence, American Academy of Pediatrics: Statement on teenage pregnancy. Pediatrics 63:795–797, 1979
17. Task Force on Adolescent Pregnancy, The American College of Obstetricians and Gynecologists: Adolescent Perinatal Health. St. Louis, Ames College of Obstetrics and Gynecology, 1979, p 40
18. Calderone MS: Childhood sexuality and the pediatrician. Am J Dis Child 133:685–686, 1979
19. Greydanus DE, McAnarney ER: Contraception in the adolescent: Current concepts for the pediatrician. Pediatrics 65:1–12, 1980

20. Greydanus DE: Contraception in adolescence: An overview for the pediatrician. Pediatr Ann 9:52–66, 1980

21. Jaffe FS: The pill: A perspective for assessing risks and benefits. N Engl J Med 297:612–614, 1977

22. Tietze C, Bongaarts J, Schearer B: Mortality associated with the control of fertility. Fam Plann Perspect 8:6–14, 1976

23. Tietze C: New estimates of mortality associated with fertility control. Fam Plann Perspect 9:74–76, 1977

24. Tatum HJ, Connell-Tatum EB: Barrier contraception: A comprehensive review. Fertil Steril 36:1–12, 1981

25. Drill VA: History of the first oral contraceptive. J Toxicol Environ Health 3:133–138, 1977

26. Harper MJK: Contraception: Retrospect and prospect. Prog Drug Res 21:293–407, 1977

27. Ford K: Contraceptive utilization in the United States: 1973 and 1976. Advancedata (DHEW) 36:1, 1978

28. Elgee NJ: Medical aspects of oral contraceptives. Ann Intern Med 72:409–418, 1970

29. Miale JB, Kent JW: The effects of oral contraceptives on the results of lab tests. Am J Obstet Gynecol 120:264–270, 1976

30. Poller L: Oral contraceptives, blood clotting and thrombosis. Br Med Bull 34:151–156, 1978

31. Tyrer LB, Josimovich J: Contraception in teenagers. Clin Obstet Gynecol 20:651–666, 1977

32. Jordan WM: Pulmonary embolism. Lancet 2:1146–1147, 1961

33. Lorentz IT: Parietal lesion and "Enovid." Br Med J 2:1191, 1962

34. Tyler ET: Oral contraception and venous thrombosis. JAMA 185:131–132, 1963

35. Drill VA, Calhoun DW: Oral contraceptives and thromboembolic disease. JAMA 206:77–84, 1968

36. Markush RE, Seigel DC: Oral contraceptives and mortality trends from thromboembolism in the United States. Am J Public Health 59:418–434, 1969

37. Zador G: Estrogens and thromboembolic diseases. Present conception of a controversial issue. Acta Obstet Gynecol Scand [Suppl] 54:13–28, 1976

38. Kretzschmar RM: Smoking and health: The role of the obstetrician and gynecologist. Obstet Gynecol 55:403–405, 1980

39. Ory HW, Rosenfield A, Landmark C: The pill at 20: An assessment. Fam Plann Perspect 12:278–283, 1980

40. Liebermann EJ: Teenage sex and birth control. JAMA 240:275–276, 1978

41. Elective surgery and the pill (editorial). Br Med J 2:546, 1976

42. Beck WW: Complications and contraindications of oral contraceptives. Clin Obstet Gynecol 24:893–901, 1981

43. Perkins RP: Contraception for sicklers. N Engl J Med 285:296, 1971

44. Stadel BV: Oral contraceptives and cardiovascular disease. N Engl J Med 305:607–611, 672–677, 1981

45. Rosenberg L, Slone D, Shapiro S, et al: Non-contraceptive estrogens and myocardial infarction in young women. JAMA 244:339–342, 1980

46. Finnerty FA Jr: Contraception and pregnancy in the young female hypertensive patient. Pediatr Clin North Am 25:119–126, 1978

47. Ask-Upmark E, Glas JE, Stenram U: Oral contraceptives and cerebral arterial thrombosis. Acta Med Scand 185:479–481, 1969

48. Radnot M, Folimann P: Ocular side effects of oral contraceptives. Am Clin Res 5:197–204, 1973
49. Dalen JE, Hickler RB: Oral contraceptives and cardiovascular disease. Am Heart J 101:626–629, 1981
50. Coulam CB, Annegers JF: Do anticonvulsants reduce the efficacy of oral contraceptives? Epilepsia 20:519–526, 1979
51. Drug interaction with oral contraceptive steroids (editorial). Br Med J 281:93–94, 1981
52. Khov SK, Correy JF: Contraception and the "high-risk women." Med J Aust 1:60–68, 1981
53. Tyrer LB, Granzig WA: Contraceptives for the teenager: Things to know before prescribing. Consultant 15:170–179, 1975
54. Speroff L: Which birth control pill should be prescribed? Fertil Steril 27:997–1008, 1976
55. Linn S, Schoenbaum SC, Monson RR, et al: Delay in conception in former "pill" users. JAMA 247:629–632, 1982
56. Coulam CB, Annegers JF, Abboud CP, et al: Pituitary adenoma and oral contraceptives: A case control study. Fertil Steril 31:25–28, 1979
57. Rey-Stocker I, Aufferey MM, Lemarcharnd MT, et al: The sensibility of the hypophysis, the gonads and the thyroid of adolescents before and after the administration of oral contraceptives: A resume. Pediatr Ann 10:15–20, 1981
58. Sondheimer S: Metabolic effects of the birth control pill. Clin Obstet Gynecol 24:927–941, 1981
59. Steel JM, Duncan LJP: The effect of oral contraceptives on insulin requirements in diabetics. Br J Fam Plann 3:77–78, 1978
60. Steel JM, Duncan LJP: Serious complications of oral contraceptives in insulin-dependent diabetics. Contraception 17:291–295, 1978
61. Steel JM, Duncan LJP: Contraception for the insulin-dependent diabetic woman: The view from one clinic. Diabetes Care 3:557–560, 1980
62. Greydanus DE: Contraindications to the pill—Sickle cell anemia. Pediatrics 66:643–644, 1980
63. Sears DA: The morbidity of sickle cell trait. A review of the literature. Am J Med 64:1021–1036, 1978
64. Schaff EA, Greydanus DE: Questionnaire data. Contraceptive attitudes and practices for adolescents by Rochester, New York, physicians. Unpublished data, 1979
65. Esialo A, Konttiner A, Hetala O: Oral contraceptives after liver disease. Br Med J 3:561–562, 1977
66. Baum JK, Bookstein JJ, Holtz F, et al: Possible association between benign hepatomas and oral contraceptives. Lancet 2:926–928, 1973
67. Kretzschmar RM: Oral contraceptives and cancer. CA 28:118–123, 1978
68. Ramcharan S, Pellegrin FA, Ray RM, et al: The Walnut Creek Contraceptive Drug Study. A prospective study of the side effects of oral contraceptives. J Reprod Med [Suppl] 25(6):345–372, 1980
69. Haller J: A review of the long-term effects of hormonal contraceptives. Contraception 1:233–251, 1970
70. Huggins GR, Giuntoli RL: Oral contraceptives and neoplasia. Fertil Steril 32:1–23, 1979
71. Committee on Drugs, American Academy of Pediatrics: Breast feeding and contraception. Pediatrics 68:138–140, 1981

72. Senanayake P, Kramer DG: Contraception and the etiology of pelvic inflammatory disease: New perspectives. Am J Obstet Gynecol 138:852–860, 1981

73. Komaroff AL, Friedland G: The dysuria–pyuria syndrome. N Engl J Med 303:452–453, 1980

74. Wadlington WB, Erlendson IW, Burr IM: Chorea associated with the use of oral contraceptives. Report of a case and review of the literature. Clin Pediatr 20:804–806, 1981

75. Poser S, Raun NE, Wikstrom J, et al: Pregnancy, oral contraceptives and multiple sclerosis. ACTA Neurol Scand 59:108–118, 1979

76. Nelson JH: Selecting the optimum oral contraceptive. J Reprod Med 11(4):135–141, 1973

77. Stone J, Downham T: Autoimmune progesterone dermatitis. Int J Dermatol 20:50–51, 1981

78. Slap GB: Oral contraceptives and depression. Impact, prevalence and cause. J Adolesc Health Care 2:53–54, 1981

79. A triphasic oral contraceptive: Logynon and Trinordiol. Drug Ther Bull 18(25):98–100, 1980

80. Larrange A, Sartoretto JW, Winterholter J, et al: Clinical evaluation of two biphasic and one triphasic norgestrel/ethinyl estradiol regimens. Int J Fertil 23:193–199, 1978

81. Schneider WHF, Spona J, Schmid R, et al: Efficacy of three phase oral contraceptives. International Symposium on Hormonal Contraception. Utrecht, Sep 10, 1977. Amsterdam, Excerpta Medica, 1978, p 123

82. Zador G: Fertility regulation using "triphasic" administration of ethinyl estradiol and levonorgestrel in comparison with the 30 plus 150 mcg fixed dose regime. Acta Obstet Gynecol Scand [Suppl] 88:43–48, 1979

83. Lachnit-Fixson U: Clinical investigation with a new triphasic oral contraceptive, in Greenblatt RB (ed): The Development of a New Triphasic Oral Contraceptive. Proceedings of a Special Symposium at the 10th World Congress on Fertility and Sterility, Geneva, July 1980. International Medical, 1980, pp 99–107

84. Triphasic oral contraceptive (editorial). Lancet 1:1191–1192, 1981

85. Huber SC, Piotrow PT, Orlans B, et al: IUD's reassessed: A decade of experience. Popul Rep B(2):21–48, 1975

86. Chaudhury RR: Current status of research on intrauterine devices. Obstet Gynecol Sur 35:333–338, 1980

87. IUD's: Update on safety, effectiveness and research. Popul Rep B(3):49–58, 1979

88. Christian CD: What price contraception. South Med J 74:523–524, 1981

89. Ory HW: Women's health study. Ectopic pregnancy and intrauterine contraceptive devices: New perspectives. Obstet Gynecol 57:137–144, 1981

90. Bolton GC: Adolescent contraception. Clin Obstet Gynecol 24:977–986, 1981

91. Bernstein GS: Conventional methods of contraception: Condom, diaphragm and vaginal foam. Clin Obstet Gynecol 17:21–33, 1974

92. Tatum HJ, Connell-Tatum EB. Barrier contraception: A comprehensive overview. J Reprod Med 36(1):1–12, 1981

93. Liebermann DJ: Teenage sex and birth control. JAMA 240:275–276, 1978

94. Hunt WB: Adolescent fertility—Risks and consequences. Popul Rep J(10):157–175, 1976

95. Smith GG: The use of cervical caps at the University of California/Berkeley. J Am Coll Health Assoc 29:93–94, 1980

96. Speidel JJ, Kessel E, Berger GS, et al: Recent developments in technology for the control of female fertility. Obstet Gynecol Annu 7:397–454, 1978

97. Jick H, Walker AM, Rothman KJ, et al: Vaginal spermicides and congenital disorders. JAMA 245:1329–1332, 1981
98. Chvapil M, Droegemueller W: Collagen sponge in gynecologic use. Obstet Gynecol 10:363–374, 1981
99. Greydanus DE, Geller B: Masturbation: An historical perspective. NY State J Med 80:1892–1896, 1980
100. Stepan J, Kellogg EH, Piotrow PT: Legal trends and issues in sterilization. Popul Rep E(6):73–102, 1981

Part III

BIOLOGY OF ADOLESCENT PREGNANCY AND CHILDBEARING

5

Adolescent Age and Obstetric Risk

William Baldwin Carey, Thurma McCann-Sanford,
and Ezra C. Davidson, Jr.

Early childbearing has serious demographic and socioeconomic consequences for the young parent as well as for society as a whole. The
obstetric risks that are likely to be more pronounced at a younger maternal
age than at an older one are examined in this chapter.

Current data indicate that the risk of maternal death is 60 percent
higher for pregnant girls under 15 years than for women in their early 20s.
Some complications of pregnancy are accentuated in this young age group.
The most important complications are pregnancy-induced hypertension (PIH),
cephalopelvic disproportion, iron deficiency anemia, and low birth weight
infants. Other problems are alcohol, tobacco, and drug abuse and sexually
transmitted diseases. The presence of these conditions does not imply inherent health problems in younger women; it is more likely to be an indication of a lifestyle that may negatively affect pregnancy outcome. It is now
recognized, however, that early antenatal care improves the outcome of
teenage pregnancy.[1,2]

Unfortunately, it is only recently that a major effort is being made to
provide special attention to the pregnant adolescent. Data from more recent
studies show a pregnancy outcome comparable to the adult populations of
similar background when antenatal care takes into consideration the special
needs of the young gravida. It should be emphasized that there are adverse
outcomes of teenage pregnancy that are not so readily affected by improved
prenatal care or are not easily explained by physiologic or anatomic differ-

ences. These outcomes are probably the result of the combined effects of biologic and psychosocial factors related to the adolescents' age, developmental stage, and living environment.

As early as the 1920s, physicians were concerned that pregnancy in teenagers carried additional risks related specifically to age. In 1922 Harris published the results of his study of 500 pregnant girls, aged 12–16 years.[3] This group was 68 percent black. He concluded that the most significant risk was toxemia, a conclusion which has been confirmed by many authors since. A review of the literature reveals an incidence of toxemia usually in the range of 7–23 percent (extremes are 1 percent and 34 percent). The incidence of toxemia for the general population is 5 percent.[4]

Premature childbirth has also been reported to have a higher incidence among adolescents, particularly the very young. The definition of prematurity includes births between the 20th and 37th weeks of gestation and birth weights between 500 g and 2500 g. Analysis of data from the Obstetrical Statistical Cooperative indicates that the highest incidence of prematurity is in girls under 15 years of age,[5] a finding which has been confirmed in other studies.

GROWTH AND DEVELOPMENT

An understanding of the relationship between adolescent age and obstetric risk requires consideration of the developmental changes that occur at adolescence. There is a spurt of rapid linear growth when the adolescent is reaching his or her maximum height. Girls usually begin this growth spurt at age $10\frac{1}{2}$ years and reach their peak by age 14 years; 98 percent of adult height is usually attained by age 18 years in the female. Weight gain is dependent on the size of the skeleton, muscular enlargement, growth of internal organs, and subcutaneous fat. Velocity curves for weight gain are very similar to those curves for skeletal growth in terms of age at onset and age at peak. Since muscular enlargement is a major contribution to weight gain, male adult weight is greater than female adult weight. Sex hormone changes are responsible for the initiation and cessation of skeletal growth and normal weight gain. The hormonal influences include closure of the epiphyses and redistribution of subcutaneous fat.

There are other changes in secondary sex characteristics that affect the outward appearance of an adolescent. Tanner organized these secondary sex characteristics and utilized them as measures of the various stages of puberty and maturity (Tanner stages or sex maturity ratings) ranging from 1 (prepubertal) to 5 (adult).[6] In the female, the gradual elevation of LH and FSH from stage 1 to stage 5 is the stimulus for uterine and ovarian enlargement. This occurrence is regulated by an intricate hypothalamic-pituitary-gonadal axis in the prepubertal child and organizes pubertal events. Elevation of the estrogen 17β-estradiol is the stimulus for breast development and increase of fat deposition about the hips. Widening of the pelvic girdle and epiphyseal closure also occur at this time. As the girl approaches the sexual maturity of midadolescence (Tanner stage 3), fluctuations in levels of LH and FSH begin a cyclical pattern. These cyclical changes occur for as long as 2–3 months prior to the menarche, although the luteal phase of the cycle is very short during this early period. Adolescents are frequently under the mistaken impression that this irregular cycling phase is a nonfertile time,[7] and this ignorance may contribute to the risk of pregnancy.

PREGNANCY-INDUCED HYPERTENSION (PREECLAMPSIA AND ECLAMPSIA)

According to the standards adopted by the American College of Obstetricians and Gynecologists and the American Committee on Maternal Welfare, PIH is divided into two types: preeclampsia and eclampsia. The disease(s) may arise after the 20th week of gestation or may complicate the pregnancy in a patient known to be hypertensive prior to pregnancy.[8,9] Preeclampsia is almost always a disease of the primigravida and is particularly prevalent among socioeconomically depressed adolescents regardless of ethnic background.[9]

The diagnosis of PIH is considered when a randomly obtained blood pressure is 140/90 mm Hg or when either the systolic blood pressure has increased 30 mm Hg or the diastolic pressure has increased 15 mm Hg over baseline values. These blood pressure changes should be documented on two occasions at least 6 hours apart. Traditionally, the concomitant finding of 2+ proteinuria is needed to support the diagnosis of preeclampsia since many young patients demonstrate a labile form of hypertension without proteinuria which responds quickly to bed rest. The combination of hypertension and proteinuria is particularly ominous. Other signs, such as edema and oliguria as well as complaints of headache, visual disturbances, and abdominal pain, may also be noted; these are usually manifestations of more advanced disease. Eclampsia is diagnosed when the patient manifests a convulsive disorder with hypertension. Nonetheless, the hypertension may not be particularly severe. The genesis of the convulsive disorder is uncertain, but its presence suggests a dysfunctional cerebrovascular condition that must be addressed immediately, since the probability of intrauterine fetal demise is greatly enhanced with an eclamptic convulsion.

Recent evidence suggests that the value 140/90 mm Hg is not an acceptable criterion for making the diagnosis of PIH in the young primigravida.[10] Patients aged 14–20 years without evidence of antecedent hypertension or vasculorenal disease usually manifest diastolic arterial blood pressures between 50 and 60 mm Hg. Such values are commonly found with the patient in the lateral recumbent position. Gradual increases in the diastolic arterial blood pressure along with excessive weight gain often presage the development of PIH. Thus, some authors believe that PIH is a covert pathophysiologic process which begins 3–4 months before hypertension is evident.[11] Although identification of these patients at risk of developing PIH is imprecise, prenatal care and periodic assessment of blood pressure are most important.[12]

Once the diagnosis of PIH is made, the patient is generally hospitalized and fully evaluated. Termination of pregnancy is suggested if (1) the fetus is mature, as determined by ultrasound studies and amniocentesis, (2) the fetus is in jeopardy, as determined by so-called stress testing (nonstress test, oxytocin challenge test) and low assays of plasma free estriol, and (3) hypertension is not responding. Recently, reports on the outpatient management of mild preeclampsia (diastolic arterial blood pressure less than or equal to 110 mm Hg) have appeared.[13] Most clinicians terminate pregnancy by vaginal delivery or by cesarean section when the diastolic pressure cannot be reduced to the arbitrary value of 90 mm Hg or if proteinuria is persistent. The emphasis is on maternal health rather than fetal well-being. This philosophical attitude is related to questionable evidence of progressive fetal growth and development once the disease complex is manifest. While the genesis of PIH is uncertain, the fundamental pathophysiologic defect is unquestionably a generalized arteriolar vasoconstriction which affects all organs, in particular, the kidney, uterus, and central nervous system.[9] Termination of pregnancy results in the rapid relief of signs and symptoms so that even the most acutely ill antepartum patient demonstrates no stigmata of hypertension 2 weeks post partum. Future pregnancies may well be uncomplicated.[9]

The management of PIH includes bed rest, observation, and stabilization with pharmacologic intervention if necessary. Anticonvulsant medications are used with parenteral magnesium sulfate to prevent an eclamptic convulsion. The recent literature emphasizes the concomitant use of antihypertensive therapy sufficient to reduce and/or maintain the diastolic blood pressure at less than 90 mm Hg.[14,15] The choice as to which antihypertensive medication best serves the patient depends, in part, on the severity of the process and the experience of the attending physician. Complementary therapy with diuretics and intravenous fluid is likewise variable and inconsistent. Recent efforts at assessing proper fluid and antihypertensive therapy by monitoring cardiac function (measured with a Swan-Ganz balloon catheter floated into the pulmonary artery) have been encouraging.[16] Such invasive monitoring methods are best reserved for those with severe PIH who undergo cesarean section.

In summary, PIH is apparent in 15–40 percent of teenage pregnancies and represents the most prevalent medical complication of pregnancy. Rarely is the disease of such severity that there is a need to supplement conventional management (bed rest, magnesium sulfate, and delivery) with more potent pharmacologic measures. No significant preventive measures other than prenatal care have been validated. All teenage pregnancies are potentially at risk of PIH and careful attention must be given to seemingly trivial increases in arterial blood pressure.

PREMATURITY

Traditionally, prematurity has been defined as birth weight under 2500 g. In the past there was a tendency to include infants of low birth weight due to early delivery as well as infants of low birth weight due to retarded growth. Clearly, these are dissimilar problems. Maturity has a definite effect on mortality rate, regardless of weight. The current World Health Organization recommendation is that infants delivered earlier than 37 weeks (less than 259 days) from the first day of the last menstrual period should be defined as preterm, whereas infants weighing less than 2500 g at term delivery are designated as low birth weight.[17] There will be errors associated with such a classification since length of gestation is more difficult to ascertain than is birth weight. For the purposes of this discussion, prematurity is a birth gestational age greater than 20 weeks but less than 37 completed weeks and a birth weight of greater than 500 g but less than 2500 g.[18] The highest incidence of preterm delivery for both white and nonwhite groups occurs in the 15-year-old and under age group.[11] There are factors other than age and race that can be ascribed to groups of women with higher rates; those factors that apparently contribute to low birth weight are more common in pregnant adolescents than in pregnant adults. The interrelationship of these factors and the significance of each have not been fully characterized; they often occur in combinations that may result in a poor pregnancy outcome. The following factors have been found to be associated with premature births in adolescent patients:

- Low prepregnancy weight[17]
- Ethnic origin (nonwhite pregnant teenagers have a higher incidence than whites, 7.0 versus 3.4 percent[5])
- Adverse social conditions such as urban living, lower income, poor prenatal care, lower social class ("ward" patients have a 67–84 percent increase over "private" patients[5])
- Unmarried status (particularly significant among white unmarried gravidas, with a 90 percent higher risk[5])

- Smoking (risk of premature infants is related to number of cigarettes smoked[19])
- Narcotic use[20]
- Anemia (hemoglobin level less than 11 g/100 ml
- Primigravida
- Inadequate prenatal care

Although the rate of cesarean section has been quoted as higher in adolescent deliveries, this assertion has not been corroborated by a thorough review of the literature.

CHANGES IN PHYSICAL APPEARANCE

It is important for a young adolescent to accept her physical appearance during pregnancy. Particularly in the early phase of psychological development, an adolescent is very concerned with body changes. Exaggeration of sweat and sebaceous gland function make it uncomfortable to be in a crowded environment. Nausea and malaise may be an annoying and frequent complaint. Body fat deposition appears in the lower regions of the body, particularly the hips and buttocks. Pigmentation patterns vary during pregnancy, probably due to estrogen production; a betamelanocyte-stimulating hormone has recently been described. The classic "cloasma" or mask of pregnancy and the changing pattern of hyperpigmentation around the areola of the breast are two examples of this pigmentation pattern. Striae are another manifestation of pregnancy. They are caused by alterations in the ground substance of the connective tissue of the skin. These lines may leave an indelible mark on the abdomen and hips.

DRUG ABUSE AND ALCOHOLISM

The most profound effect of substance abuse on the outcome of adolescent pregnancy may be associated with the lifestyle of drug abuse: this lifestyle often includes inadequate nutrition, poor hygiene, and inattentiveness to basic health needs. Use and abuse of stimulant or depressant substances can alter the outcome of adolescent pregnancy. Apparent effects vary according to substance and intensity and duration of use. Limited data suggest that heavy use of amphetamines has been associated with cardiac anomalies. The use of lysergic acid diethylamide (LSD) has been associated with limb bud anomalies in a limited number of cases. No direct association can be made between the use of opiates or barbiturates and teratogenicity.

Poor fetal outcome can be associated with two commonly used substances—tobacco and alcohol. Birth weight is an average of 400 g less if the mother smokes one pack of cigarettes per day than if she does not smoke. Similarly, chronic consumption of 2 oz or more of alcohol per day or repeated episodes of drinking 6 oz or more of alcohol at any one time during pregnancy may be associated with intrauterine and postnatal growth retardation, mental retardation, and various skeletal abnormalities in the offspring. The *fetal alcohol syndrome* continues to be defined and documented in the literature. The hallmarks of this syndrome are fetal malformation and developmental delay.[21]

Drug addiction in the pregnant adolescent means addiction in the fetus as well. Switching a heroin-addicted mother to methadone does not reduce the newborn's drug withdrawal problem, but does reduce the risk of hepatitis: methadone is a known quantity, whereas street drugs can contain quantifiable and even lethal impurities. Narcotic addiction in any form can lead to critical problems in the newborn with regard to withdrawal effects.

Cannabis (marijuana) usage is very common among young adolescents. There has been national concern regarding its use among those under 12 years of age. Animal studies are currently being conducted to determine the effects of cannabis on the fetus. At present the data indicate that there is a teratogenic potential but this effect has not been demonstrated in humans. The drug is transferred via the placenta but its effect on the fetus is not yet known.[22] Phencyclidine (PCP, angel dust) is a popular drug among adolescents and is the most popular drug in the Los Angeles community. Its effects on the fetus are unknown but are currently being researched.

VENEREAL DISEASE

Physicians are concerned not only with classical venereal diseases—gonorrhea, syphilis, chancroid, granuloma inguinale, and lymphogranuloma venereum—but also with other sexually transmissible diseases, such as trichimonas vaginitis, monilial vaginitis, and herpes progenitalis. Five venereal diseases are reported at epidemic levels in the United States at the present time: gonorrhea, trichomonas vaginitis, monilial vaginitis, herpes progenitalis, and condyloma accuminata. Three additional diseases threaten to reach epidemic proportions: nongonococcal urethritis, pediculosis pubis, and scabies. Young adults 20–24 years of age have a higher incidence of gonorrhea than do other age groups, and they are followed by adolescents 15–19 years of age. Gonorrhea ranks first among the reported communicable diseases in the United States. The overt manifestations of the disease (endometritis/salpingitis, peritonitis) are readily recognized, but the impact of the gonococcus in obstetric patients is much more subtle: there is a risk of fetal or neonatal infection.

Once the patient goes into labor and the fetal membranes are ruptured the barrier to ascending infection has been removed. With prolonged rupture, chorioamnionitis and/or postpartum endometritis may ensue. If the process involves the fetal vasculature, the potential is introduced for neonatal septicemia or congenital arthritis.

Gonococcal ophthalmia neonatorum may involve the mucous membranes of the eye of the infant. Before the introduction of silver nitrate, *N. gonorrheae* reportedly was responsible for 12 percent of all blindness in the world. Today this should only occur in the absence of medical care.

In women who have untreated syphilis, the unborn fetus is at risk of infection. This in utero infection can result in stillbirth, neonatal death, or developmental anomalies in the live born infant. The fetus may become infected at any stage during gestation. The risk of disease is greatly diminished when diagnosis is early and treatment is adequate. It is our recommendation that each gravida be screened by cervical culture for *N. gonorrheae* at the time of the initial visit and again at 36 weeks. Follow-up cultures should be obtained from women 3–5 days after completion of treatment. All patients should have a serologic test for syphilis at the time of the initial visit and during the third trimester.

Genital herpes is an increasingly common infection in the young and can have severe effects on the newborn if it becomes infected: 50 percent mortality and significant morbidity of survivors. Young patients, especially in the third trimester, should be carefully examined and questioned about signs and symptoms of herpes. These are generally small, often coalescing vesicles/ulcers which are tender if located on the external genitalia. Examination of these local and cervical lesions by cytology and cultures assists in diagnosis. Active infection in the mother 4–6 weeks before delivery should be managed by cesarean section to avoid neonatal infection. In the presence of maternal genital herpes and with ruptured membranes, immediate cesarean section should be done.

SPECIAL PRENATAL CARE SERVICES

Pregnant adolescents need a wide range of quality prenatal health care services. Risks such as PIH and low birth weight are more common among adolescents who are poor, nonwhite, and/or noncompliant. There is a need for increased medical antepartum and intrapartum surveillance which would allow an earlier assessment of developing obstetrical problems and consequently more effective management. Through the use of modern obstetrical methods, such as antepartum fetal heart rate monitoring, ultrasound examination, and biochemical tests of fetal well-being and maturity, any of the conditions previously cited could become less frequent for this group of patients. These specialized tests can be made available to adolescent's who regularly use prenatal services. The adolescent pregnancy clinic at the Martin Luther King, Jr., General Hospital in Los Angeles is designated to provide prenatal care and support services to pregnant teenagers $11–15\frac{1}{2}$ years of age. The statistics generated from this clinic give an indication of the needs of a sample of pregnant teenagers in Los Angeles.

In the period from October 1978 through December 1979 this project accepted 124 pregnant teenagers for prenatal care: 72 were black, 49 had Spanish surnames, and 3 were white. The problems frequently encountered in these pregnant adolescents included age, anemia, vaginitis, unsure dates, size–date discrepancy, and late entry to prenatal care. During the study period a total of 97 patients were delivered: 78 has spontaneous vaginal deliveries, 12 deliveries by low forceps, and 7 deliveries by cesarean section. An additional 15 patients were undelivered by the end of the study and 12 were lost to follow-up. The most frequent justification for induction of labor was PIH. The primary indication for cesarean section was cephalopelvic disproportion. Complications of delivery consisted of endometritis in 4 percent and vaginal/perineal lacerations in 13 percent. Fetal loss occurred in 1 case with premature delivery at 24 weeks' gestation. Two other premature births occurred, at 34 weeks' and 36 weeks' gestation, without subsequent neonatal problems.

From the psychosocial assessments, several problem areas were identified. The pregnant girls expressed serious concerns about schooling, and home (parental) conflicts increased. Socialization on the whole was poor and serious conflicts over identity problems were evident. As a result, a large proportion of the girls demonstrated repeated episodes of depression and/or anxiety. Other problems—economic difficulties, illegitimacy, and "shotgun" marriage—were evident in this group, and 93 percent had little or no knowledge about parenting.

The emphasis of the educational services at the clinic is not didactic. The aim is to have an effective interchange among the instructors and students so that ideas and cultural beliefs can be clarified to encourage acceptable methods of parenting. The prenatal classes include feeding and bathing, layette composition, and home economics. Maternal nutrition and tips on health and hygiene of mother and infant are shared. These classes are well attended by teenage mothers.

REFERENCES

1. Briggs RM: Pregnancy in the young adolescent. Am J Obstet Gynecol 84:436–441, 1962
2. Baldwin W, Cain VS: The children of teenage parents. Fam Plann Perspect 12:34–43, 1980

3. Harris JW: Pregnancy and labor in the young primapara. Bull Johns Hopkins Hosp 33:12–16, 1922
4. Pritchard JA, MacDonald PC: Hypertensive disorders in pregnancy, in Pritchard JA, MacDonald PC (eds): Williams Obstetrics (ed 15). New York, Appleton-Century-Crofts, 1976, p 551
5. Kaltreider DF, Kohl S: Epidemiology of pre-term delivery. Clin Obstet Gynecol 23:17–31, 1980
6. Tanner JM: Growth at Adolescence. London, Blackwell, 1962
7. Odell W, Moyer DL: Physiology of Reproduction in Puberty. St. Louis, Mosby, 1971
8. Hellmann LM, Pritchard JA: Hypertensive disorders of pregnancy, in Pritchard JA, MacDonald PC (eds): Williams Obstetrics (ed 14). New York, Appleton-Century-Crofts, 1971, p 685
9. Chesley LC: Hypertensive Disorders in Pregnancy. New York, Appleton-Century-Crofts, 1978
10. Friedman EA: Hypertensive disease in pregnancy: Blood pressure and edema, in de Alvarez RR (ed): The Kidney in Pregnancy. New York, Wiley, 1976, pp 97–111
11. Gant NF, Warley RJ: Hypertension in Pregnancy, Concepts and Management. New York, Appleton-Century-Crofts, 1980
12. Morris JA, O'Grady JP, Hamilton OJ: Vascular reactivity to antigiotensin II infusion during gestation. Am J Obstet Gynecol 130:379–384, 1978
13. Schneider JM: Outpatient management of diabetes mellitus and pregnancy induced hypertension, in Ryan GM (ed): Ambulatory Obstetrics and Gynecology. New York, Grune & Stratton, 1980, pp 91–116
14. Ferris TF: Toxemia and hypertension, in Burrow GN, Fessir TF (eds): Medical Complications During Pregnancy. Philadelphia, Saunders, 1975, pp 53–104
15. Morris JA: The acute hypertensive disorders complicating pregnancy. Hosp Formulary 13:445–456, 1978
16. Strauss RG, Keefer JR, Burke T, et al: Hemodynamic monitoring of cardiogenic pulmonary edema complicating toxemia of pregnancy. Obstet Gynecol 55:170–174, 1980
17. Baird D: Epidemiology patterns over time, in Reed DM, Stanley FJ (eds): The Epidemiology of Prematurity. Baltimore, Urban and Schwarzenberg, 1977, p 3
18. Pritchard JA, MacDonald PC: Prematurity, post maturity and fetal growth retardation, in Pritchard JA, MacDonald PC (eds): Williams Obstetrics (ed 15). New York, Appleton-Century-Crofts, 1976, p 784
19. Meyer MB: Effects of maternal smoking and attitudes on birth weight and gestation, in Reed DM, Stanley FJ (eds): The Epidemiology of Prematurity. Baltimore, Urban and Schwarzenberg, 1977, p 81
20. D'Angelo L, Sokol RJ: Prematurity: Recognizing patient at risk. Perinatal Care 2:16, 1978
21. Jones KL, Smith DW: The fetal alcohol syndrome. Teratology 12:1–10, 1975
22. American Academy of Pediatrics, Committee on Drugs: Effects of marijuana on man. Pediatrics 56:134–143, 1975
23. Butler NR, Alberman ED, Schatt WH: The congenital malformations, in Butler NR, Alberman ED (eds): Perinatal Problems. London, Livingston, 1969
24. Strauss MB: Etiology and treatment of anemia in pregnancy. JAMA 102:281–283, 1934
25. American College of Obstetricians and Gynecologists, Task Force on Adolescent Pregnancy: Adolescent Perinatal Health: A Guide Book for Services. Chicago, American College of Obstetricians and Gynecologists, 1979

6

Nutritional Risks of Adolescent Pregnancy and Their Management

Marc S. Jacobson and Felix P. Heald

Nutritional care of the pregnant adolescent must focus on the health of both mother and infant and requires knowledge of the role of nutrients in physiologic processes as well as basic principles of adolescent growth and development. In this chapter we synthesize what is known about prenatal nutritional care from the disciplines of adolescent medicine, obstetrics, and nutrition into a system adaptable to the prenatal care of pregnant adolescents. Nutritional assessment and intervention should be an integral part of prenatal care for the adolescent. [1–5]

It is somewhat surprising that the relationship between nutrition and perinatal outcome is still inferential. Common sense dictates that such a relationship should exist, yet only in animal models and in a relatively few studies of nutritional supplementation in undernourished populations has an adverse effect of undernutrition been shown. [6] A considerable amount of data developed during the past decade point to the specific parameters to be monitored[4,5,7–10] (e.g., prepregnancy weight, prenatal weight gain, and acetonuria). Classically, the effect of nutrition in pregnancy had been judged by the birth weight of the infant; now it is important to look at a broader

This work was supported in part by Adolescent Health Care Training Grant MCT-000980. The authors wish to thank Cheryl McKeen and Valerie Walker for their help in preparing this manuscript.

spectrum of nutritional measures both for infant and mother such as detailed anthropometrics and gestational age.

Requirements for a particular nutrient can be experimentally determined in five basic ways reviewed by Sanstead.[11] The more methods applied to a particular nutrient the more confidence can be placed in the recommended level of intake. Few nutrients have been studied by more than one method in normal or pregnant adolescents. Much information currently thought to be correct may need to be altered as new data become available. A patient who is doing well despite not meeting recommended intakes should be advised to alter her intake only after careful observation and reassessment.

The adolescent is at increased nutritional risk for physiologic, psychosocial, and demographic reasons. The physiologic risk presented in pubertal growth is well documented.[12] Puberty is the only postnatal period when the rate of growth is accelerating: 50 percent of adult weight and 15 percent of adult height are gained during the pubertal growth spurt. This anabolic process accounts for a significant portion of the adolescent's increased need for nutrients. Individual variability is great, but the majority of growth occurs prior to menarche in most females. Gynecologic age (i.e., difference between chronological age and age at menarche) can give a rough guide to the importance of pubertal growth in setting nutrient needs for any particular individual and should be part of the initial assessment, as should dietary intake and anthropometrics. The younger the adolescent is and the less her gynecologic age, the higher are her nutrient requirements.[13]

Peer and family pressure may result in diet restriction in order to retain the highly valued slender body habitus. Hueneman found that the majority of teenage girls surveyed in a secondary school wanted to lose weight and practiced dietary restriction.[14] The need to conceal pregnancy from family or peers may exacerbate this problem.

Adolescents were found to have the highest prevalence of dietary deficiencies of any age group in the Ten State Nutrition Survey focusing on low-income groups of all ages in the United States.[15] Energy, iron, vitamin A, and riboflavin intakes were noted to be the most frequent problem areas in this study. School lunches were reported to be particularly important to the low-income adolescents, providing one-third of dietary intake of calories, iron, and vitamin A, and as much as one-half of calcium intake.

Pregnancy puts the adolescent and her offspring at increased nutritional risk. Prior nutritional status, reflected grossly in the prepregnancy weight and height, and intrapartum status, measured as weight gain, have both been shown to be risk factors predicting the percentage of low birth weight infants.[5,7-9] Hence prepregnancy nutritional status should be assessed and intrapartum weight gain should be closely monitored using a standard grid such as that provided by the Food and Nutrition Board of the National Research Council[16] (Fig. 6-1).

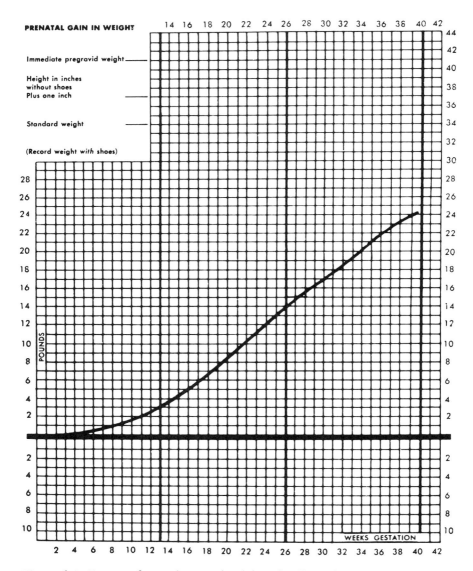

Figure 6-1. Pattern of normal prenatal weight gain. (From Committee on Maternal Nutrition, Food and Nutrition Board, National Research Council.[16])

121

The nutritional role of fast foods, junk foods, and erratic or unconventional food habits among teenagers remains controversial. Truswell and Darnton-Hill, in an extensive review of the world literature, concluded that widely variant nutrient requirements are smoothed over by cross-sectional population studies and that many of the maligned food habits of adolescents provide the necessary high caloric intakes that support rapid growth.[17] Before restrictions are attempted in food habits for the pregnant adolescent, adequate assessment is necessary.

The energy, protein, vitamin, and mineral needs of pregnant adolescents are discussed below. An overview of the data on nutritional supplementation follows.

ENERGY

For many years nutritionists concentrated on protein metabolism and the need for dietary protein in preventing and treating malnutrition. This was particularly true in the 1950s and 1960s when the focus was on malnutrition in the developing world. In 1970, McLaren called attention to the fact that during the intensive study of protein metabolism in malnourished, ill-fed infants and children, the critical component, energy, had been overlooked.[18] It has been known for a long time that energy is a crucial factor in malnutrition and that no amount of protein can result in an anabolic state if calories are inadequate; since pregnancy is an anabolic event, in all prob-

Table 6-1. Recommended Dietary Allowances for Pregnant and Lactating Adolescents

Group	Energy (kcal)	Protein (g)	Minerals (mg)		
			Iron	Calcium	Zinc
Nonpregnant girls					
11–14 years	2200	46	18	1200	15
15–18 years	2100	46	18	1200	15
Additional allowance					
Pregnancy	+300	+30	+30–60‡	+400	+5
Lactation	+500	+20	+30–60‡	+400	+10

From Food and Nutrition Board, National Research Council.[21]
*Retinol equivalents.
†Milligrams α-tocopherol equivalents.
‡Cannot be provided by diet (see text).

ability the same thing holds true. More recent work tends to support this thesis.

The United States is blessed with an agricultural industry that supplies this country with huge surpluses. Any malnutrition detected in this country is usually mild and socially or psychologically determined. Therefore, many studies attempting to link better pregnancy outcome with improved nutrition have been conducted developing countries. In Bogota, Colombia, a nutritional supplement was added to the diet of pregnant women with a history of a prior malnourished child.[19] It was estimated that these women had been consuming 1600 kcal and 35.5 g protein a day. The supplement consisted of 133 kcal and 20 g protein daily for each woman. The women gave birth to infants an average of 77 g heavier (males 100 g, females 12 g) if they were supplemented for one trimester or more. The subjects with an enriched diet also had a greater maternal weight gain. In contrast, a study of pregnant women in New York City in the 1970s yielded a different result.[6] These lower socioeconomic status urban women were identified as being at high risk for low birth weight infants upon entrance into a public prenatal clinic. The controls in this study had an energy intake of 2065 kcal and 79 g protein per day. There were two supplements under study. The first contained 470 kcal and 40 g protein (high-protein supplement), and the second contained 322 kcal plus 6 g protein (balanced supplement), plus vitamins and minerals in an appropriate amount. The result with the balanced supplement was that infants weighed on the average 41 g *more* than the controls. The high-protein supplement was associated with infants weighing 42 g *less* than the controls. Both the balanced supplement and the high-protein supplement

Fat-Soluble Vitamins			Water-Soluble Vitamins						
A (μg*)	D (μg)	E (mg†)	C (mg)	Thiamin (mg)	Riboflavin (mg)	Niacin (mg)	B_6 (mg)	B_{12} (μg)	Folacin (μg)
800	10	8	50	1.1	1.3	15	1.8	3.0	400
800	10	8	60	1.1	1.3	14	2.0	3.0	400
+ 200	+ 5	+ 2	+ 20	+ 0.4	+ 0.3	+ 2	+ 0.6	+ 1.0	+ 400‡
+ 400	+ 5	+ 3	+ 40	+ 0.5	+ 0.5	+ 5	+ 0.5	+ 1.0	+ 100‡

prevented the decreased birth weight associated with heavy smoking. The effect of high-protein feeding on neonatal outcome is discussed later.

The few studies that have focused on the energy needs of pregnant teenagers generally report that the teenagers frequently do not achieve the National Research Council's recommendations for caloric intake. It has recently been suggested that optimal pregnancy weight gains for mothers who are underweight in the beginning of pregnancy are larger than previously considered normal. Naeye raised the possibility that optimal weight gains for fetal survival may be higher in young teenagers since both mother and infant compete for the same nutrient source.[10] This may be particularly true in the very young teenager 10–14 years of age. Furthermore, he observed that the young teenager has more acetonuria (5 percent) than 17 to 32-year-olds (2 percent). These young mothers had a higher fetal or neonatal death rate than mothers with no acetonuria. This fact needs to be kept in mind when considering the energy needs of the poor, for whom a sustained and adequate amount of energy yielding foods may not always be available. The clinician should be particularly careful about monitoring the urine for acetonuria and the dietary intake for energy. The presence of acetonuria requires prompt evaluation and intervention.

Table 6-1 can be used to calculate the daily energy needs of pregnant teenagers. Pregnant adolescents 11–14 years of age need 2500 kcal and pregnant teenagers 15–18 years old need 2400 kcal. On a weight basis, 40 kcal/kg body weight/day is recommended. This is 5 kcal/kg in excess of the energy considered adequate to support positive nitrogen balance of pregnancy. However, data are not now available to determine whether this is entirely adequate in the very young adolescent; therefore, it is unwise to restrict energy intake in a young pregnant adolescent, and careful evaluation of acetonuria and weight gain should be carried out at each prenatal visit.

PROTEIN

The issue of the proper protein requirement for the pregnant adolescent is a complex one. Protein is needed for formation of maternal and fetal tissue. Cellular growth, function, and structure require the turnover and metabolism of the component amino acids. Different methods of determining protein needs results in different figures for recommended protein intake. Calculating needs from the amount required for nonpregnant teenagers and adding the amount in fetal and maternal tissues at term results in a figure only one-half as large as that found in balance studies. King et al., who performed careful nitrogen balance studies on pregnant teenagers, presented the best experimental data on which to base protein recommendations.[20] They suggested an intake of 85 g total protein/day (based on 30 percent net nitrogen utilization = dietary nitrogen × biologic value/100). The Food and Nutrition Board of the National Research Council recommends a slightly lower value of 76 g/day based on calculated, survey, and experimental data. For the lactating teenager 66 g/day is the recommended dietary allowance (RDA). Alternatively, requirements can be calculated as 1.0 g/kg/day for girls aged 10–14 years or 0.9 g/kg/day for those aged 14–18 years with 30 g/day additional for pregnancy and 20 g/day for lactation.

Most studies of the diets of pregnant teenagers in the United States indicate that protein intake is usually adequate. Of considerable importance is the work of Rush et al., who noted the adverse effect on fetal growth of the high-protein supplement given to pregnant women in their study.[6] There

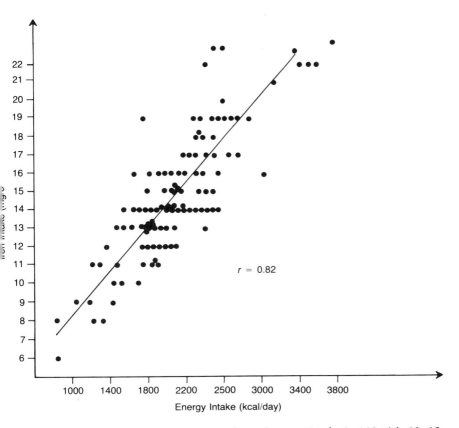

Figure 6-2. Correlations between iron intake and energy intake in 110 girls 13–15 years of age. (Redrawn from Elsborg L, Rosenquist A, Helms P: Iron intake by teenage girls and by pregnant women. Int J Vitam Nutr Res 49:211–214, 1979. With permission.)

were a large number of premature deliveries, excessive neonatal deaths, depressed birth weight, and retarded growth among the premature. This observation has been confirmed in experimental studies in primates. Thus, much to everyone's surprise, a high-protein supplement not properly balanced with calories has an adverse effect on the fetus. Although the mechanism for this undesirable effect is not clear, caution should be urged in the feeding of pregnant women so that an appropriate calorie/protein ratio is maintained.

Finally, in discussing calories and protein it is of considerable importance to note that—particularly in the United States, where there is an abundance and variety of foods—the caloric level is a rough guide to the adequacy of other nutrients. The best example of this is shown by the data presented in Figure 6-2, in which the total caloric intake correlates highly with the amount of iron consumed in the diet; that is, low caloric intake is associated with low iron intake and vice versa. There are obvious exceptions to this rule related to ethnicity, socioeconomic status, and dietary fads but, in general, if caloric intake is adequate then there is a better chance of there being adequate supplies of other nutrients.

VITAMINS

The material in this section and the following one on minerals is primarily taken from the *1980 Recommended Dietary Allowances* of the National Research Council of the National Academy of Sciences.[21] This volume contains the most current data available on nutrient needs and should be part of the reference library of any prenatal clinic for adolescents. A few caveats are necessary when using the RDAs for a particular patient. An RDA is that level of intake of a particular nutrient considered adequate to meet the needs of practically all healthy persons and thus is population based. An RDA is set at a particular level such that practically all individuals in a population consuming that level will have sufficient intake; by definition, this exceeds the level needed by many individuals in that population. Calories are an exception—as discussed above, there is no safety factor included in the RDA of energy needs. Furthermore, RDAs are meant to be met by a diet of a wide variety of foods, not by supplementation. Therefore, individual intakes should be assessed before supplementation is begun. The RDAs for pregnant adolescents of the nutrients of most common concern are summarized in Table 6-1.

In mixed U.S. diets of adequate caloric intake, vitamin supplements are unnecessary for the nonpregnant adolescent. But it is difficult for the health care provider to ensure that a varied diet is eaten and that it contains adequate calories. Dietary surveys of adolescents have shown caloric restriction to be commonplace, and in pregnant adolescents other nutrient intakes have been shown to be low as well.[22,23]

During pregnancy the daily requirement for many nutrients is increased. Two nutrients—iron and folacin (discussed in detail below)—cannot be adequately supplied by diet and should be supplemented; the remaining ones may be low in certain diets and need individual assessment. The RDAs of many nutrients are higher for adolescents than for children or adults. These nutrients are discussed individually to emphasize their metabolic role, signs of deficiency, dietary sources, and RDAs.

Fat-Soluble Vitamins

Vitamin A

Two forms of vitamin A activity are found in the diet: preformed (retinol) and provitamin (carotenoids). Retinol has six times the biologic activity of β-carotene on a weight basis. Vitamin A needs are now generally expressed in retinol equivalents rather than the previous International Units.[22] Vitamin A is important in the maintenance of mucus membranes and in vision. Clinical signs of mild vitamin A deficiency include impaired visual adaptation to darkness and follicular hyperkeratosis. More severe deficiency results in xerophthalmia and eventually blindness. Good dietary sources are butter, milk, fortified margarine, liver, and green or yellow vegetables. Pregnancy requires that 200 retinol equivalents be added to the RDA to account for fetal needs and 400 are added for lactation to supply adequate levels for secretion into milk.

Vitamin D

Vitamin D is the general term for a group of sterols that have activity in regulating calcium and phosphorous metabolism through intestinal absorption and bone mineralization. Vitamin D is produced by ultraviolet irradiation of the plant sterol ergocalciferol or the naturally occurring animal sterol 7-dehydrocholesterol to form D_2 or D_3, respectively. Vitamin D_3 is further metabolized in the liver and then in the kidney, resulting in the biologically most active form, 1,25-dihydroxycholecalciferol. The fact that D_3 is also formed in skin exposed to sunlight adds complexity to the determination of dietary need. In winter and in areas of air pollution, skin exposure to ultraviolet irradiation is reduced and dietary intake may be more important in meeting metabolic needs. Widespread vitamin D fortification of milk and other foods has resulted in a high probability of adequate or elevated intake such that supplementation is not advisable without prior assessment of dietary intake. During adolescence an increased intake of 5 μg/day over the 5-μg/day RDA for adults is recommended to account for bone growth and mineralization. Adolescent pregnancy or lactation should be accompanied by a further 5-μg increase for a total of 15 μg/day. Because of potential toxicity increase of intake above recommended levels should be discouraged, as should supplementation.

Vitamin E

No clinical symptoms of vitamin E deficiency have been found in adolescent or adult humans but laboratory findings of increased red blood cell fragility and elevated urinary creatinine excretion in deficiency states underscore the necessity of adequate intake. Dietary sources in the United States are generally felt to provide sufficient amounts for the needs of all but the individual with fat malabsorption. Therefore, although RDAs are increased for adolescents and during pregnancy, supplementation is not indicated.

Vitamin K

Vitamin K is necessary for liver synthesis of prothrombin and other clotting factors; deficiency can result in bleeding abnormalities. Newborns are generally given intramuscular vitamin K to supply their needs until intestinal flora can be established. Green leafy vegetables are the best dietary source of vitamin. Bacterial synthesis of vitamin K is sufficient in normal human intestine, so that no daily allowance is recommended. The patient with fat malabsorption or prolonged antibiotic use may need assessment, but both inadequate intake and insufficient synthesis are probably necessary to cause deficiency, which is uncommon.

Water-Soluble Vitamins

Vitamin C

Adequate vitamin C (ascorbic acid) is needed to prevent the development of scurvy, which is manifested by petechiae, ecchymoses, follicular hyperkeratosis, and gingival hemorrhage, as well as eventual profound fatigue, lethargy, arthralgia, effusions, and pitting edema. Although vitamin C is clearly involved in wound healing and connective tissue formation generally, the exact mechanism of action is not known. It is widely available in the diet in citrus and other fruits, tomatoes, potatoes, peppers, and other vegetables. Cereal grains have no vitamin C, and meat and dairy products are relatively poor sources. Adolescents tend not to prefer the vitamin C–rich foods.

The RDA for ascorbate is 60 mg/day for adolescents, and pregnancy requires an added 20 mg/day. The added lactation allowance is 40 mg/day. These allowances are generous. With normal body stores, 45 days with no intake would be needed to develop scurvy. With adequate diet supplementation is unnecessary: 1–3 oz of the abovementioned fruits and vegetables should provide more than the allowance. Pharmacologic doses (1 gm or more) have not been shown to be of any advantage in controlled studies.[21]

Thiamin

Thiamin (B_1) is responsible for several reactions in energy metabolism; therefore, the recommended intake level is linked to caloric intake. Prolonged deficiency leads to the clinical disease beriberi, which is rare in the United States; alcoholics are at greatest risk. Red meat and whole or enriched grains are the main dietary sources. Thiamin is one of the few nutrients for which there are data on adolescent needs. The recommended dietary allowance is 0.5 mg/1000 kcal or 1.1 mg/day for females 11–22 years of age. An added 0.4 mg/day is recommended during pregnancy and 0.5 mg/day during lactation. A balanced diet can readily provide these amounts.

Riboflavin

Riboflavin (B_2) is important in both energy and protein metabolic pathways, functioning as the reactive portion of flavoproteins. Ariboflavinosis produces cheilosis, angular stomatitis, and seborrheic dermatitis. Dietary sources include milk, liver, and enriched grains. Riboflavin has not been well studied in adolescence; therefore, the dietary allowance is extrapolated from data on adults. A safe margin of 0.6 mg/1000 kcal is recommended, with a minimum of 1.2 mg/day for those consuming less than 2000 kcal/day. Since pregnancy is accompanied by lowered riboflavin excretion and biochemical signs of deficiency, an additional 0.3 mg/day is called for. The lactation increment is 0.5 mg/day.

Niacin

Niacin is a component of two key coenzymes that participate in energy production and storage and are present in all body cells, nicotinamide adenine dinucleotide (NAD) and its phosphate (NADP). Deficiency results in the classic nutritional disorder pellagra, presenting as dermatitis and diarrhea, and in severe cases dementia. Niacin is present in meat, eggs, beans, peas, and enriched grains and can be synthesized from dietary tryptophan. Average U.S. diets contain three to five times the recommended allowance of 6.6 niacin equivalents/1000 kcal, hence supplementation is normally unnecessary.

Vitamin B_6

Three pyridines—pyridoxine, pyridoxal, and pyridoxamine—constitute the group of compounds known as vitamin B_6. They appear to be interchangeable in terms of activity and are considered here collectively. They participate in many metabolic processes, including glycolysis, transamination, and serotonin synthesis. Deficiency states have a variety of clinical signs and symptoms, including seizures in infants, depression, mood changes, weight loss, peripheral neuropathy, and dermatitis in adults. Vitamin B_6 is available in such foods as meats, cereals, fruits, and vegetables. The allowances are based on studies of biochemical abnormalities in adults following depletion diets or administration of antagonists. High-protein diets seem to increase the requirement for B_6. The RDA for adolescents aged 11–14 years is 1.8 mg/day, and 2.0 mg/day for age 15 and above. For pregnancy an additional 0.6 mg/day is recommended and for lactation 0.5 mg/day.

A recent study of 58 pregnant or lactating women in Indiana showed mean unsupplemented intakes of B_6 to be less than two-thirds of the RDA.[23] Serum and milk levels correlated with intake. This suggests that some individuals in the United States may be at risk. At this time evidence for routine B_6 supplementation is lacking. Issues related to B_6 and oral contraceptive use in adolescents have recently been reviewed.[24]

Vitamin B_{12}

Vitamin B_{12} consists of a group of cobalt-containing compounds that function as parts of coenzymes in amino acid, lipid, and nucleic acid metabolism. For absorption from foods they require a binding glycoprotein, intrinsic factor, which is secreted in the stomach and interacts with a specific receptor site in the ileum. Deficiency results in macrocytic anemia. In the absence of gastrointestinal disease or strict adherence to a vegan (vegetable only) diet, deficiency is rare. Generally, U.S. diet intakes exceed the RDA. The allowance for the adolescent is 3.0 mg/day with an addition of 1.0 mg for pregnancy or lactation.

Folacin

Folacin and folate are interchangeable terms for compounds with the biologic activities of pteroylglutamic acid (folic acid) that participate in nucleic acid synthesis and amino acid metabolism. Deficiency results in megaloblastic anemia and disorders of other cells with rapid turnover. Good dietary sources are liver, leafy vegetables, fruit, and legumes. Two recent reports of low folacin intake among pregnant women and adolescents underscore the need for supplementation of this vitamin.[25,26] The recommended allowance is 800 mg/day for pregnant adolescents and 500 mg/day for lactation. Supplementation of 200–400 mg/day should be sufficient to bring daily intake near these levels and should be prescribed routinely.

MINERALS

Mineral requirements for pregnant adolescents are listed in Table 6-1. Those of special relevance, i.e., iron, calcium, and sodium are discussed in detail.

Iron

Iron is an essential component of hemoglobin, myoglobin, and enzymes such as succinate dehydrogenase. Its presence is necessary for both maternal and fetal normal red blood cell formation. Maternal blood expansion occurs in the second trimester, and fetal blood formation occurs primarily in the third.[2] Deficiency results in microcytic hypochromic anemia for the mother and increased risk of iron deficiency in the infant.[27] Iron is present in many foods, including liver, meat, eggs, whole or enriched grain, leafy vegetables, nuts, legumes, and dried fruit. Its bioavailability ranges from 3 to 23 percent in any given meal depending on whether or not heme iron is consumed, whether vitamin C is present or absent, and whether meats, poultry, or fish are present in the meal. Heme iron is best absorbed and ascorbate and flesh foods enhance absorbability.

Iron is one of the best studied nutrients in pregnancy and in adolescents and the need for dietary supplementation rests on firm data. The fetus requires 250 mg elemental iron, and this is obtained at maternal expense. At term the placenta contains 150 mg and the increase in maternal erythrocyte mass (20–30 percent) requires another 500 mg; therefore, the total amount of iron needed is 900 mg, or 6 mg/day for the second half of pregnancy. Dietary sources can provide 1–2 mg absorbed iron a day and supplementation is necessary for the remainder. Clinical experience suggests that 325 mg ferrous sulfate (60 mg elemental iron) once a day throughout pregnancy is well tolerated by most adolescents. In those who are already iron deficient (i.e., low serum ferritin), a regimen of 325 mg ferrous sulfate three times a day is usually prescribed in addition to dietary counseling. Serum ferritin is highly correlated with stainable iron in bone marrow and is the screening method of choice for iron deficiency. It will be low before any other measure has changed.[24] Furthermore, recent studies suggest a strong correlation between maternal and infant ferritin at birth and at 6 months of age.[28,29]

Calcium

Calcium is needed for the bone growth of the adolescent and her fetus as well as for a variety of cellular processes such as cardiac and skeletal muscle contraction. Calcification of the fetal skeleton and dentition require 30 g calcium. This is less than 5 percent of maternal stores, so the effects of a deficient diet are not immediately seen even if maternal intakes are well below needs. The long-term effect of low calcium consumption during pregnancy on the maternal skeleton is not known; therefore, an increment of 400 mg/day for pregnancy above the allowance of 1200 mg/day for the adolescent is recommended. Milk is an excellent source of dietary calcium. A quart of milk contains 1.2 g calcium as well as 10 mg vitamin D and 35 g complete protein. Many consider milk to be the perfect food for the pregnant teenager.[30] Adolescents who do not tolerate milk or milk products well (whether on the basis of lactose deficiency or not) may need calcium supplements during pregnancy and lactation.

Sodium

In the past decade much has been learned about the role of sodium in pregnancy. Glomerular filtration increases during pregnancy by 50 percent, resulting in an increased filtered sodium load. Progesterone, which is elevated in pregnancy, acts to decrease tubular resorption of sodium and further increase sodium loss. The renin-angiotensin system acts to counterbalance these forces, resulting in high circulating levels of aldosterone. As pregnancy proceeds, plasma volume expands, osmotic pressure decreases, and further increases in renin and aldosterone result, leading to a further increase in tubular sodium resorption. If sodium intake is inadequate and diuretics are prescribed in an attempt to prevent preeclampsia, the system is further strained. It may be argued that the old practice of sodium restriction during pregnancy caused no noticeable harm, but clearly with present concepts the burden of proof is on those that advocate restriction in normal pregnancy.[31] Furthermore, King and her colleagues showed that for pregnant teenagers prescription of salt-restricted diets results in decreased caloric intake.[22]

NUTRITIONAL SUPPLEMENTATION

In 1980 Rush et al. reviewed the effects of prenatal nutrition on pregnancy outcome.[6] The studies summarized were from Bogota[19], Guatemala[32], New York City, and Taiwan.[6] The diet modifications varied from select foods for the entire family to liquid supplements nutritionally balanced or a high-protein supplement.

Although all the supplemental programs resulted in an average increase in birth weight of 50–797 g, none of the results achieved statistical significance. The effect on maternal weight gain varied from no effect to greater maternal weight gain. No consistent trend emerged from these studies. The only adverse effect was with the high-protein supplement in the New York study. As previously noted, there were a larger number of very premature births, excess neonatal deaths, and depressed birth weights (among prematures only).

A positive effect of supplementation on infant morbidity and mortality was not demonstrated in the New York study, but reduced perinatal mortality (not statistically significant) was observed in the Bogota study. The other two studies either had equivocal results (Guatemala) or did not examine this issue (Taiwan).

The effect of nutritional supplementation on behavior has been difficult to establish. In the Bogota study there was more rapid habituation (visual fixation) at 15 days. The Guatemala study noted advanced psychomotor performance in pre- and postnatal supplemented children to age 4 years, and only 1 significant effect among 22 subtests on the Bayley scale. The New York City study noted rapid habituation in the supplement group at 1 year; also playtime was increased. The usual developmental indices showed no changes. Although the overall results were not clear-cut and disappointing to some, the role of nutrition in pregnancy is being clarified enough to allow further and more definitive research.

CONCLUSIONS

Prenatal care for the adolescent should include careful nutritional assessment, including previous growth factors, dietary intake, and prior use of supplements. Supplements of iron and folacin as well as other nutrients assessed and found to be lacking should be prescribed. Ongoing care should include frequent reassessment of diet, weight gain, and compliance with iron, folacin, and other indicated supplements. Compliance has been shown to be an important problem in pregnancies with presenting iron problems because of associated symptoms.[33] When significantly lower than expected weight gain (Fig. 6-1) is noted, it is advisable to hospitalize the pregnant adolescent in order to assess what factor or factors are responsible. Infection, depression, inadequate parental supervision, unavailability of food at home and desire not to gain weight are among the problems that may account for poor weight gain.

Proper intervention can reverse the weight loss or inadequate gain if provided in a timely fashion.[1,34] An established method for this intervention begins with a thorough medical, nutritional, and psychosocial assessment in the hospital utilizing principles familiar to all pediatricians in the failure to thrive work-up. Particular attention is paid to ruling out infections of the genitourinary tract, including cystitis, pyelonephritis, and cervicitis. Food intake by recall and direct observation in the hospital is calculated. When problem areas are found their underlying causes are sought, for example: (1) Is enrollment in the Federal Food Supplementation Program for Women, Infants and Children completed? (2) Are the foods being delivered? (3) Who is competing for food at home? It is especially important to know if the patient is attending school, as school lunch may be a major source of nutrients. Psychosocial assessment should include current functioning in school, in the family, and with peers, including the baby's father. Depression during pregnancy may result in loss of appetite and weight loss or inadequate gain and should always be ruled out. The syndrome of depression, anorexia, and weight loss should be treated aggressively by hospitalization in an adolescent inpatient facility. Usually the causes of depression can be clarified, resulting in improved intake and weight gain in the hospital and continued appropriate weight gain following discharge. A number of cases of inadequate weight gain have been successfully treated in this manner at University of Maryland Hospital with improved weight gain and good fetal outcome.[1,34]

REFERENCES

1. Heald FP, Jacobson MS: Nutritional needs of the pregnant adolescent. Pediatr Ann 9:21–31, 1980.
2. Pitkin RM: Nutritional influences during pregnancy. Med Clin North Am 61:3–15, 1977
3. Osofsky HJ, Risk PT, Fox M, et al: Nutritional status of low income pregnant teenagers. J Reprod Med 6:29–33, 1971
4. Kaminetzky HA, Langer A, Baker H, et al: The effect of nutrion in teen-age gravidas on pregnancy and the status of the neonate. Am J Obstet Gynecol 115:639–646, 1973
5. Simpson JW, Lawless RW, Mitchell AC: Responsibility of the obstetrician to the fetus. II. Influence of prepregnancy weight and pregnancy weight gain on birthweight. J Obstet Gynecol 45:481–487, 1975
6. Rush D, Stein Z, Susser M: Diet in Pregnancy. A Randomized Controlled Trial of Nutritional Supplements. New York, Liss, 1980
7. Keeping JD, Chang A, Morrison J: Birth weight: Analysis of variance and the linear additive model. Br J Obstet Gynecol 86:437–442, 1979
8. Edwards LE, Alton IR, Barrada MI, et al: Pregnancy in the underweight woman. Am J Obstet Gynecol 135:297–302, 1979
9. Gaziano EP, Freeman DW, Allen TE: Antenatal prediction of women at increased risk for infants with low birthweight. Am J Obstet Gynecol 140:99–107, 1981
10. Naeye RL: Teenaged and pre-teenaged pregnancies: Consequences of the fetal–maternal competition for nutrients. Pediatrics 67:146–150, 1981
11. Sandstead HH: Methods for determining nutrient requirements in pregnancy. Am J Clin Nutr 34:697–704, 1981
12. Tanner JM: Growth at Adolescence (ed 2). Philadelphia, Lippincott, 1962
13. Wait B, Blair R, Roberts L: Energy intake of well-nourished children and adolescents. Am J Clin Nutr 22:1383–1390, 1969
14. Huenemann R, Shapiro LR, Hampton MC, et al: A longitudinal study of gross body composition and body conformation. Am J Clin Nutr 18:325, 1966
15. Anonymous: Highlights from the Ten State Nutrition Survey. Nutr Today July/Aug:4–11, 1972

16. Committee on Maternal Nutrition, Food and Nutrition Board, National Research Council: Maternal Nutrition and the Outcome of Pregnancy. Washington, DC, National Academy of Sciences, 1970
17. Truswell AS, Darnton-Hill I: Food habits of adolescents. Nutr Rev 39:73–88, 1981
18. McLaren DS: The great protein fiasco. Lancet 2:93–96, 1974
19. Mora JO, de Paredes B, Wagner M, et al: Nutritional supplementation and the outcome of pregnancy. Am J Clin Nutr 32:455–462, 1979
20. King JC, Calloway DH, Margen S: Nitrogen retention, total body ^{40}K and weight gain in teenage pregnant girls. J Nutr 103:772–785, 1973
21. Food and Nutrition Board, National Research Council: Recommended Dietary Allowances (ed 9). Washington, DC, National Academy of Sciences, 1980
22. King JC, Cohenour SH, Calloway DH, et al: Assessment of nutritional status of teenage pregnant girls. I. Nutrient intake and pregnancy. Am J Clin Nutr 25:916–925, 1972
23. Roepke JLB, Kirksey A: Vitamin B6 nutriture during pregnancy and lactation. I. Vitamin B6 intake, levels of the vitamin in biological fluids, and condition of the infant at birth. Am J Clin Nutr 32:2249–2256, 1979
24. Heald FP, Roseborough R, Jacobson MS: Nutrition and the adolescent. J Adolesc Health Care 1:142–151, 1980
25. Elsborg L, Rosenquist A: Folate intake by teenage girls and by pregnant women. Int J Vitam Nutr Res 49:70–76, 1979
26. Bailey LB, Mahan CS, Dimperio D: Folacin and iron status in low-income pregnant adolescents and mature women. Am J Clin Nutr 33:1997–2001, 1980
27. Elsborg L, Rosenquist A, Helms P: Iron intake by teenage girls and by pregnant women. Int J Vitam Nutr Res 49:211–214, 1979
28. Puolakka J, Janne O, Vihko R: Evaluation by serum ferritin assay of the influence of maternal iron stores on the iron status of newborns and infants. Acta Obstet Gynecol Scand [Suppl] 95:53–56, 1980
29. Kaneshige E: Serum ferritin as an assessment of iron stores and other hematologic parameters during pregnancy. Obstet Gynecol 57:238–242, 1981
30. Worthington BS, Vermeersch J, Williams SR: Nutrition in Pregnancy and Lactation. St. Louis, Mosby, 1977
31. Linheimer MD, Katz AI: Pathophysiology of preeclampsia. Ann Rev Med 32:273–289, 1980
32. Lechtig A, Habicht, J-P, Delgado, H: Effect of food supplementation during pregnancy on birthweight. Pediatrics 56:508–520, 1975
33. Orr RD, Simmons JJ: Nutritional care in pregnancy: The patient's view. J Am Diet Assoc 75:131–135, 1979
34. Howard R, Jacobson MS, Heald FP, et al: Reversal of prenatal weight loss in the young adolescent. (manuscript in preparation, 1982)

7

Immune Status of Adolescents and the Prevention of Infectious Diseases

Keith R. Powell

The epidemiology of several childhood diseases has been dramatically changed by immunization practices.[1,2] The combination of the availability of vaccines that effectively prevent poliomyelitis, measles, rubella, and mumps and the enforcement of laws requiring immunization for entry into school, has significantly reduced the incidence of these diseases among infants and children. With the exception of poliomyelitis, however, the number of adolescents susceptible to these dieases has not been noticeably changed by the introduction of effective vaccines. In this chapter epidemiologic concepts about infectious diseases in adolescents are discussed with an emphasis on some of the shortcomings of preventive medicine as it is currently practiced that have left large numbers of adolescents susceptible; of particular interest are pregnant adolescents.

Adolescence is generally defined in terms of secondary sex characteristics and somatic growth. For epidemiologic purposes, however, it is necessary to talk about age. The two adolescent age groups commonly used in reporting incidence figures for infectious diseases are 10–14 and 15–19 years; for ease of discussion, therefore, all individuals 10–19 years old will be considered adolescents.

EPIDEMIOLOGY OF ADOLESCENTS

In order to concentrate on infectious diseases as they relate to the pregnant adolescent, the epidemiologic variables unique to this subpopulation must be identified. Epidemiologic variables such as race, socioeconomic status, nutritional status, and stress do not place adolescents at greater risk for infection than the general population. Likewise, adolescents are not at increased risk for infections spread by nonhuman vectors (Rocky Mountain spotted fever, yellow fever, tularemia, etc.) or environmental contact (brucellosis, salmonellosis, giardiasis, etc.). Adolescence is, however, a unique age in relation to diseases transmitted from person to person. This uniqueness relates to previous exposures to infectious agents or vaccines, changes in the number and types of interpersonal contacts, and the relative immunity of the "herds" with which adolescents interact.

The concepts of immunity and herd immunity are important to understand. *Immunity* is the exemption from a penalty of some kind. The penalties associated with infectious agents range from subclinical infection to overt disease. In the pregnant adolescent the penalties associated with infection might affect the mother, the fetus, or both. Humans are innately immune to a large number of infectious agents found in the environment that infect other primates or lower animals. Infection or medical immunization can result in immunity to diseases to which humans are susceptible by stimulating the production of antibodies and/or cellular immunity against specific infectious agents.

Herd immunity is a situation in which a large percentage of individuals are immune to an infectious agent, making it less likely for someone susceptible to the disease to come in contact with someone who is infected. The major misconception about herd immunity is the definition of the "herd." People talk about a magic percentage of persons with immunity to a certain agent being necessary to prevent the transmission of the disease, but if 90 percent of the population in the United States is immune to rubella, it does not help in evaluating the risk of a certain pregnant woman acquiring the disease. Herd immunity applies only to a randomly mixing population, which in reality occurs only in well-defined, usually small, closed populations. Therefore, when analyzing disease prevention in adolescents, the total percentage of immune adolescents in the country, state, or county is of less importance than the level of immunity found in local families, junior high and high schools, colleges, church groups, street gangs, military bases, etc. where adolescents are likely to have most of their interpersonal contacts.

Once the herd has been defined, the likelihood of disease transmission depends on two individuals having adequate contact to allow transmission of the infecting agent, and the probability that *any* two persons (herd immunity depends on random mixing) in the herd will make adequate contact within a certain time. Thus, both the infectivity of an agent as well as the social habits of the population are implied by the term *contact rate*. (For a more complete development of the concept of herd immunity see Fox et al.[3]

With adolescence comes major changes in social behavior. Less time is spent with the family and more time with peers. Junior high and high school students change classrooms for different subjects, so that the number of peers they come in contact with is increased. In boarding schools, camps, and the military large numbers of adolescents from different parts of the community or country live and interact in close quarters. The net effect of all of these changes in social habits is to include more susceptible individuals in varied subpopulations and effectively increase the contact rate.

The type of socialization also changes in adolescence. Sexual activities expose a highly susceptible population to infectious agents transmitted primarily or exclusively via sexual contact. Thus the high incidence of sexually transmitted diseases among adolescents is related to immunologic virginity rather than immunodeficiency. Since these diseases receive considerable attention in the literature and elsewhere, emphasis is placed on vaccine-preventable diseases.

In general, through natural infection and by immunization, the adolescent has a fair immunologic armamentarium against most of the so-called childhood diseases. There always will be, however, some who are susceptible: children who were not immunized at all, who were vaccine failures, or whose immunity did not persist from childhood into adolescence. Thus, although the number of individuals immune to a given infectious agent increases with age, a number of susceptible persons will still exist; and the social activities of adolescents are likely to bring the susceptible ones together.

PREGNANCY AND INFECTION

Many interactions between host(s) and microbes are possible during pregnancy. Pregnant women seem to have more susceptibility to or more severe manifestations of some infections. For example, they are more likely to excrete cytomegalovirus (especially in the second and third trimesters),[4] contract urinary tract infections, and develop tuberculosis than nonpregnant women.

Either overt or subclinical infection during pregnancy can lead to an increase in fetal mortality, prematurity, and perinatal death.[5] Increased fetal mortality has been associated with rubella and mumps during the first 12 weeks of pregnancy and with hepatitis in the later weeks of pregnancy.[6] Prematurity occurs with increased frequency with maternal hepatitis, measles, and rubella infections; this association has not been observed with mumps or chicken pox infections.[7] Clinically severe infection of almost any type may result in fetal death without necessarily infecting the fetus. The exact mechanism leading to fetal death is not known, but fever, increased basal metabolic rate, increased oxygen consumption, and disturbance of body chemistry probably all contribute.[8] Infection of the placenta or fetus also may result in fetal death.

Occult or overt maternal infection with agents as diverse as rubella, cytomegalovirus, *Toxoplasma gondii,* and *Treponema pallidum* can cause fetal infection with teratogenic results. Live-born infants who are severely affected at birth frequently die in infancy. Others with mild or occult infections at birth later are found to be blind, deaf, or mentally retarded.

Finally, maternal infections late in pregnancy can result in transmission of the disease to the neonate during passage through the birth canal. Infections caused by herpes simplex virus or enterovirus tend to be of relatively little consequence to the adolescent but can result in systemic disease and death of the neonate.

Childhood diseases can adversely affect the outcome of a pregnancy. Immunization against many of the childhood diseases has resulted in a dramatic decrease in the incidence in North America. The tremendous decrease in the total number of cases, however, is attributable to a reduction of disease in infants and children; due to this changing epidemiology, adolescents have become the largest group susceptible.

CHANGING EPIDEMIOLOGY

In order to estimate the risk of infection in the pregnant adolescent, we must evaluate the immune status of the adolescent. Remember that in order for a pregnant adolescent to acquire one of the childhood diseases, she must be susceptible and have sufficient contact with the infectious agent to become infected.

Rubella

Since a vaccine is available that could potentially eliminate congenital rubella syndrome, rubella provides an excellent example of changing epidemiology in the vaccine era and the implications for the pregnant adolescent. The purpose of rubella immunization is to prevent congenital rubella syndrome, not rubella. Since only women susceptible to rubella and capable of becoming pregnant are at risk for bearing a child with congenital rubella syndrome, preventive measures should be directed at reducing the chance of infection in this group.

Prior to the licensing of rubella vaccines in 1969, epidemiologic surveys showed that 80–85 percent of women of childbearing age had antibody against rubella.[2] Two different strategies to reduce the incidence of congenital rubella were implemented at about the same time in the United States and England. In the United States the approach was to immunize preschoolers over 1 year of age and school children 5–9 years of age. It was reasoned that the chance of an exposure adequate for a susceptible woman to contract rubella from a casual contact was much lower than the chance of such an exposure at home. Therefore, if a woman had reached the childbearing age without immunity to rubella she was most likely to acquire the infection from her children or younger siblings. By vaccinating children, it was thought that transmission to susceptible mothers would be prevented.

The other strategy, used in England, was to vaccinate 11- to 14-year-old girls. A serologic survey in 1980 showed that 93–96 percent of the women born after 1956 (i.e., those included in the rubella vaccination effort) had protective antibody against rubella.[2] This is quite different from the situation in the United States, where about 15–20 percent of women over 10 years of age are susceptible.

Since the introduction of rubella vaccine in 1969, the number of cases in the United States has decreased by over 70 percent (Fig. 7-1).[9,10] As Figure 7-1 illustrates, however, the decrease in the prevalence of congenital rubella syndrome has been much less dramatic. Furthermore, the number of reported cases may represent less than one-third of actual incidence and does not take into account spontaneous or therapeutic abortions.[11] In fact, the number of cases in women of childbearing age (age-specific prevalence) has not changed. From 1966 to 1968, before rubella vaccine was introduced, most cases occurred in children less than 10 years old,[9] whereas from 1978 to 1980, the prevalence was greatest in adolescents[10] (Fig. 7-2).

The effectiveness of rubella immunization should be discussed in terms of whether congenital rubella is being prevented. Consider, instead of national statistics, the experiences in three geographically separate communities. Shortly after a rubella vaccination campaign in Casper, Wyoming, wherein 83 percent of elementary school children and 52 percent of preschoolers were immunized, a rubella epidemic occurred.[12] During the outbreak, 84 percent of the cases of rubella occurred in adolescents. Despite a high level of herd immunity, at least 8 women had rubella during pregnancy. Of the 3 women who were infected during the first trimester, 2 aborted— a teenager spontaneously and another woman therapeutically. The third infant had no clinical or serologic evidence of congenital rubella. Of the 830 pregnant women in Casper during the study period, 602 had prenatal rubella serology performed and about 20 percent had no detectable antibody. Thus a minimum of 8 of 166 susceptibles had documented rubella during their pregnancy. It is significant that 20 percent of the pregnant women in Casper were susceptible and 84 percent of the cases of rubella occurred in adolescents,

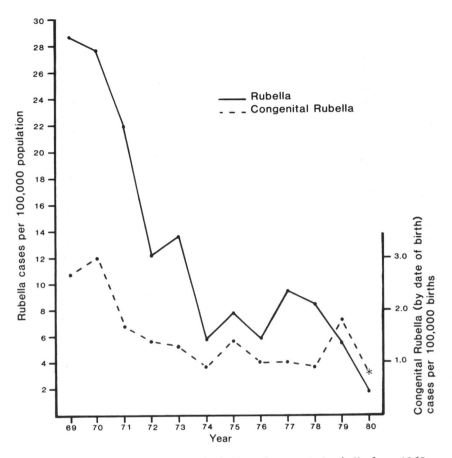

Figure 7-1. Changes in incidence of rubella and congenital rubella from 1969 to 1980 (*reporting in 1980 not complete). (Data from references 9 and 10.)

about one-half of whom were female. Thus, the potential for infants being born with congenital rubella was not much changed by the extensive vaccination of children.

Late in 1979 and early in 1980, an outbreak of congenital rubella occurred in the San Francisco Bay area counties.[13] In a large rubella outbreak between February and May 1979, 45 percent of the reported cases occurred in 15 to 19-year-olds, 23 percent in elementary or intermediate school-aged children, 17 percent in persons over 20, and the remaining 15 percent in preschoolers or the elderly. The following year, at least 13 infants were born with congenital rubella syndrome. The mean age of the mothers was 21.4 years. The number of spontaneous or therapeutic abortions related to maternal rubella viral infection was not mentioned.

A similar rubella epidemic occurred in Chicago in 1978, and a survey of Chicago hospitals and physicians identified 30 infants born late in 1978 or early in 1979 with congenital rubella syndrome.[11] About 40 cases are reported annually in tbe United States. (Only 8 of the cases in Chicago had been reported to the Chicago Board of Health.) The disease occurs when women reach the childbearing age without immunity to rubella; in the Chicago experience, this was about 13 percent of the pregnant women tested. None of the 30 mothers who gave birth to infants with congenital rubella syndrome had been immunized. Premarital screening would have been ineffective, as 20 of the 30 women were not married. Postpartum immunization would have been no help to two-thirds of these women as the affected infant was their first.

These statistics clearly demonstrate that congenital rubella syndrome continues to occur despite widespread immunization of children. Since the percentage of susceptible women of childbearing age has not changed from the prevaccine era, something more immediate must be done to prevent rubella from occurring in pregnant adolescents.

Ideally, this would mean testing all 10- to 12-year-old girls and immunizing those found to have no antibody. Many arguments, including cost ineffectiveness and impracticality, oppose this practice, and it is unlikely to

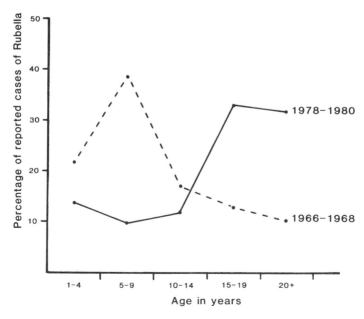

Figure 7-2. Age-specific prevalence of rubella before introduction of rubella vaccine (1966–1968) and in recent years (1978–1980). (Data from references 9 and 10.)

be put into effect on a large scale. The major objection to immunization of adolescents is the possibility that the adolescent is pregnant or will become pregnant while infected with the vaccine virus. Although no recognized teratogenicity has been associated with rubella immunization, virus has been isolated from aborted fetuses and normal infants with serologic evidence of intrauterine infection have been born to mothers immunized during pregnancy.[14] Nonetheless, it seems safe to say that if rubella vaccine is teratogenic, the rate is considerably lower than the 25 percent incidence observed after natural rubella infection during the first trimester. Since the incidence of pregnancy is low in 12-year-olds, perhaps laws should make immunization mandatory for girls entering the sixth grade.

What can the physician caring for adolescents do? Find out whether female patients have been immunized. If they have, it is probably not necessary to perform antibody tests, as evidence is accumulating that even if no antibody is detected, immunized patients will have an anamnestic response to reimmunization.[15] If previous rubella immunization cannot be documented, a decision must be made whether to check for antibody. If antibody is checked, susceptible patients may be immunized selectively; if antibody is not measured, all should be immunized. The former practice is ideal, but congenital rubella might be prevented more effectively by vaccinating all adolescents not previously vaccinated.

The possibility of vaccinating a female patient who is pregnant or becomes pregnant shortly after vaccination poses a difficult problem. In a study performed among adolescent girls in Cincinnati, seronegative girls attending an upper middle-class junior and senior high school, and their parents were informed of the side effects of rubella vaccination and the serious risk of pregnancy.[16] After consent was obtained, girls were immunized if they were within 5 weeks of their last menses. A group of sexually active girls attending an adolescent clinic also were studied. These seronegative girls were informed of the risks but were vaccinated only during menses; if adequate birth control was questioned, a single dose of 150 mg medroxyprogesterone was given at the time of vaccination. There were no pregnancies in either group.

The risk of pregnancy must be weighed and a decision made as to the necessary steps to prevent pregnancy. Since risk of teratogenicity is low, in situations where follow-up is poor and the risk of adolescent pregnancy is great, the potential risk of vaccinating a pregnant adolescent is probably much less than the risk of natural rubella. In fact, the most recent recommendations of the Advisory Committee on Immunization Practices (ACIP) include the following statement:

> Therefore, the ACIP believes that rubella vaccination during pregnancy should not be a reason to routinely recommend interruption of pregnancy. Although

a final decision must rest with the individual patient and her physician, the ACIP believes that the risk of vaccine-/associated malformations is so small as to be negligible.[17]

Measles

The epidemiology of measles has been changed drastically by the introduction of effective vaccines. Before the licensing of vaccine in 1963, clinical surveys demonstrated that at least 95 percent of the population had had measles before the age of 15. As the general prevalence of measles decreased, the age-specific prevalence shifted dramatically (Fig. 7-3). Before the introduction of measles vaccine, only 13 percent of cases occurred in persons over 10 years of age.[18] From 1977 to 1980, however, 60 percent of cases occurred in persons over 10.[19]

Another epidemiologic change important in the care of adolescents is the occurrence of atypical measles. Atypical measles is seen in adolescents and young adults who received killed measles vaccine at sometime in the past. Since killed virus vaccine has not been available since 1967, this disease

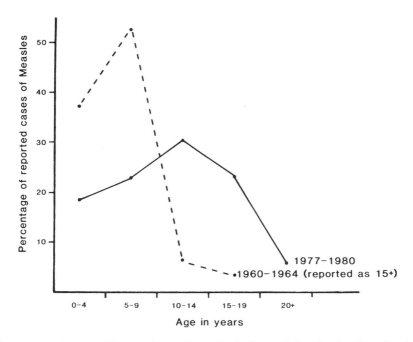

Figure 7-3. Age-specific prevalence of measles before and shortly after introduction of measles vaccine (1960–1964) and in recent years (1977–1980). (Data from references 18 and 19.)

should become increasingly rare. For the next few years, however, the diagnosis of atypical measles should be considered in the differential diagnosis of an ill adolescent with an exanthem and pulmonary disease.

Fetal mortality does not seem to increase with maternal measles, and congenital measles does not seem to be a problem.[6,20] Since morbidity and mortality associated with measles in adolescents is quite low, the major concern is that adolescents now constitute the largest population susceptible to measles. This is of considerable importance in plans to eradicate endemic measles from the United States.

If the elimination of measles in the United States is truly a goal, great efforts must be taken to identify susceptible adolescents and young adults. This might be done in conjunction with efforts to find those susceptible to rubella; individuals could be simultaneously immunized against both diseases. Because measles vaccines have been available since 1963, large numbers of adolescents have already been immunized, and with enforced school entry laws requiring immunization, protection will be even greater in the future. For now, however, the most practical approach for increasing immunity among adolescents is to identify and vaccinate those who cannot provide documentation of previous vaccination. Although serologic screening followed by immunization of those without antibody is ideal,[2] the success of such an approach in a country with such a large, diverse, and mobile population as the United States is doubtful.

Mumps

Although a live-attenuated mumps vaccine was licensed for use in 1967, the number of doses of mumps vaccine given has risen slowly. Immunization practices are going to effect very little change in the immune status of the adolescent for years to come. As of 1978, 31 percent of the cases of mumps occurred in the 10- to 19-year-old age group.[21]

Arguments for the necessity of a mumps vaccine have addressed primarily mumps meningoencephalitis and associated morbidity. The question of congenital mumps syndrome remains controversial, and the possibility of increased fetal death associated with mumps during the first 12 weeks of pregnancy has not been pursued.

Since the incidence of mumps does not seem to be decreasing in adolescents, while the incidence of mumps encephalitis increases with age, strategies to improve the immune status of adolescents and young adults should include immunization against mumps. Likewise, since the incidence of mumps in women of childbearing age has not changed, the type and magnitude of problems associated with mumps during pregnancy need to be better defined.

ADOLESCENT ADVOCACY

Childhood vaccination programs against measles, mumps, and rubella have done little to alter the incidence of these diseases in adolescents. This fact should motivate practitioners to prevent the same situation when new vaccines become available. A vaccine to prevent chicken pox is currently being tested. If and when it becomes licensed, initial efforts should include not only immunizing preschool-aged children, but also identifying adolescents who have not had the disease, testing for antibody, and immunizing those susceptible.

Data on the susceptibility of adolescent girls to toxoplasmosis and cytomegalovirus need to be evaluated. These two microbes are responsible for the largest numbers of congenital infections and both present major problems in vaccine development. *Toxoplasma gondii* is a parasite, and immunization against parasitic diseases has met with little success.

Candidate vaccines have been developed against cytomegalovirus, but some serious concerns exist. Cytomegalovirus may become latent, that is, people can shed the virus intermittently for years without knowing they are infected. Furthermore, maternal antibody to cytomegalovirus does not prevent transmission of the virus to the fetus.

Many diseases, such as gonorrhea, syphilis, *Ureaplasma urealiticum,* and *Chlamydia trachomatis* infections, can be diagnosed and treated in both mothers and infants. Other diseases can only be prevented or diagnosed. As it becomes possible to prevent these diseases, the epidemiology of the diseases must be studied and measures taken so that adolescents are not once again left susceptible longer than is necessary.

REFERENCES

1. Horstman DM: Viral vaccines and their ways. Rev Infect Dis 1:502–516, 1979
2. Cherry JD: The "new" epidemiology of measles and rubella. Hosp Practice 15:49–57, 1980.
3. Fox JP, Elveback L, Scott W, et al: Herd immunity: Basic concept and relevance to public health immunization practices. Am J Epidemiol 94:179–189, 1971.
4. Gehrz RC, Christianson WR, Linner KM, et al: Cytomegalovirus-specific humoral and cellular immune responses in human pregnancy. J Infect Dis 143:391–395, 1981
5. Hardy JB: Fetal consequences of maternal viral infections in pregnancy. Arch Otolaryngol 98:218–227, 1973
6. Siegel M, Fuerst HT, Peress NS: Comparative fetal mortality in maternal virus diseases. A prospective study on rubella, measles, mumps, chicken pox and hepatitis. N Engl J Med 274:768–771, 1966
7. Siegel M, Fuerst HT. Low birth weight and maternal virus diseases. A prospective study of rubella, measles, mumps, chicken pox and hepatitis. JAMA 197:88–92, 1966

8. Hardy JB: Viral infection in pregnancy: A review. Am J Obstet Gynecol 93:1052–1065, 1965
9. Centers for Disease Control: Rubella Surveillance, Jan 1976–Dec 1978. (DHHS Publ No (CDC) 80-8023). Washington, DC, US Government Printing Office, 1980
10. Rubella—United States, 1978–1981. Morbid Mortal Weekly Rep 30:513–515, 1981.
11. Check WA: Pregnant women still vulnerable to rubella. JAMA 245:325–326, 1981
12. Rachelefsky GS, Herrmann KL: Congenital rubella surveillance following epidemic rubella in a partially vaccinated community. J Pediatr 84:474–478, 1974
13. Dales LG, Chin J: An outbreak of congenital rubella. West J Med 135:266–270, 1981
14. Hayden GF, Herrmann KL, Buimovici-Klein E, et al: Subclinical congenital rubella infection associated with maternal rubella vaccination in early pregnancy. J Pediatr 96:869–872, 1980
15. Butler AB, Scott R McN, Schydlower M, et al: The immunoglobulin response to reimmunization with rubella vaccine. J Pediatr 99:531–534, 1981
16. Rauh JL, Schiff GM, Johnson LB: Rubella surveillance and immunization among adolescent girls in Cincinnati. Am J Dis Child 124:71–75, 1972
17. Rubella prevention. Morbid Mortal Weekly Rep 30:38–42, 1981
18. Measles—United States. Morbid Mortal Weekly Rep 26:109–111, 1977
19. Age characteristics of measles cases—United States, 1977–1980. Morbid Mortal Weekly Rep 30:502–503, 1981
20. Siegel M: Congenital malformations following chicken pox, measles, mumps and hepatitis. Results of a cohort study. JAMA 226:1521–1524, 1973
21. Mumps—United States, 1978–1979. Morbid Mortal Weekly Rep 28:422–424, 1979

8

Infants of Adolescent Mothers: Perinatal, Neonatal, and Infancy Outcome

Ruth A. Lawrence and T. Allen Merritt

The critical analysis of the impact of adolescent pregnancy has historically directed attention to the outcome of the young mother and her personal lifestyle potential. A highly important aspect of pregnancy, however, is the resulting offspring and his or her potential for a meaningful and productive life. It is appropriate, therefore, to address the outcome of the infants of adolescent mothers in relation to the infants of more mature mothers. Most reviews that discuss the significance of adolescent pregnancy in our society today generalize by saying that adolescent childbearing leads to increased obstetrical risk, increased risk of prematurity, and increased risk of perinatal morbidity and mortality. It is usually concluded that child abuse and neglect are predominantly the result of adolescent childbearing. Initially, studies of the children of young mothers were not controlled for factors such as socio-economic status and access to medical care. Studies conducted during the 1970s that provided good medical care for pregnant adolescents have shown outcome comparable to that for older mothers of similar socioeconomic status. It is yet to be determined whether biologic or social inadequacies best explain the apparent reproductive disadvantage of U.S. teenagers and the impaired

The authors extend appreciation to Klaus J. Roghmann, Ph.D. Associate Professor of Sociology, Pediatrics, Preventive Medicine and Community Health, University of Rochester Medical Center, for his advice and suggestions in the biostatistical analysis.

149

well-being of their babies. A critical analysis of both the short- and the long-term consequences of adolescent childbearing requires further study.

The incidence of adolescent pregnancy has been termed "epidemic" by many, including the Select Committee on Population of the 95th Congress.[1] The report suggests that "very young women . . . are biologically too immature for effective childbearing."[2] The age of menarche has declined from 14.0 years in 1900 to 12.5 years in 1970,[3] suggesting earlier maturation, but little data are available relating menarche to medical outcome of the pregnancy or the infant.

The social and medical consequences of adolescent parenting, although substantial, have not received systematic analysis. The discussion here focuses on perinatal, neonatal, postnatal, and infant health. The physical and developmental outcome of children born to adolescent mothers is examined as it relates to other biologic and social factors.

The data discussed in this chapter have been derived from several sources. We previously discussed data from two extensive studies:[4] (1) neonatal data on 55,711 pregnancies collected by the Collaborative Perinatal Project of the National Institute of Neurological and Communicative Disorders and Stroke, which have been extensively analyzed by Naeye,[5] and (2) neonatal data on 4000 pregnancies (770 of teenage mothers) from the University of Kansas Medical Center, Kansas City, Kansas, reported on by Miller and Merritt.[6] In addition, a preliminary review was made of the obstetric, perinatal, and neonatal data concerning 6087 pregnancies in 1976–1978 at the Regional Perinatal Center at the University of Rochester, New York. Since that time, we have reviewed an additional 9000 patients who gave birth in Monroe County (the county where the Regional Perinatal Center is located) in 1979. We have also considered the relationship of outcome of the infant to the gynecologic age of the mother.

BIRTH WEIGHT AND GESTATIONAL AGE

Several authors have reported that infants of adolescent mothers are more likely to be born prematurely and have a low birth weight (under 2500 g),[7] and numerous reports have suggested a significant correlation between young age of mother and poor outcome. Little attention has been paid, however, to the many other factors identified as significant in reproductive outcome in general. The data have not been controlled for prenatal care patterns, maternal weight and weight gain, complicating medical conditions, or maternal smoking. The relationship between gynecologic age and fetal growth patterns has not been reported. In a long-range study, Hardy and Mellits found that young black women had a high frequency of low birth weight infants.[8] First-born infants were lighter, however, than subsequent infants up to a maternal age of 35 years. This is an illustration of the influence of parity on birth weight. Little significant difference was seen in birth weight and birth length based on age of the mother in a study of Nashville General Hospital from 1974 to 1977 (Table 8-1).[7]

In an extensive national review, Hoffman et al. found a relationship between maternal age and the weight and gestational age of the fetus.[9] Mothers under 18 years of age had shorter mean gestational ages (i.e., less than full term) but their infants were appropriate weights for gestational age. The mothers over 35 years of age tended to have infants who were smaller than those born to 14- to 24-year-olds, and they were more frequently premature. In other words, younger mothers had more premature births, but their infants were not growth retarded.

The data from Monroe County, New York (University of Rochester–Strong Memorial Hospital) showed that the risk of giving birth to an infant weighing less than 2500 g was six times greater for those 14 years old or younger. The distribution of infant birth weight for three maternal age categories is shown in Figure 8-1.

Black adolescents account for a disproportionate number of pregnant adolescents in the population in Monroe County, New York, which parallels findings in other study populations.[10–13] The distribution by race in the 1979 data paralleled the previously reported[4] (Fig. 8-2). The adult group of mothers had a racial distribution proportional to that of the general community. The Hispanic population was represented consistently throughout all three age groups in proportion to community representation.

Black adolescent mothers consistently had a higher frequency of very low birth weight infants (under 1500 g) and had significantly fewer infants 4000 g or over than 20- to 29-year-old blacks (Table 8-2). Adolescent white

Table 8-1. Mean Physiologic Characteristics of Infants, by Age of Mother: Nashville, Tennessee, 1974–1977

Age of Mother	Birth Weight (kg)	Birth Length (cm)	Apgar Score	
			1 Minute	5 Minutes
13–14	3.05	49.33	7.00	8.33
15–16	3.19	50.52	8.07	9.62
17–18	3.10	49.47	8.12	9.45
19–20	3.11	49.29	8.43	9.48
21–24	3.19	50.26	7.77	9.49
25–39	3.01	49.71	9.50	10.00

From Baldwin W, Cain VS: The children of teenage parents. Fam Plann Perspect 12:34–43, 1980. With permission.

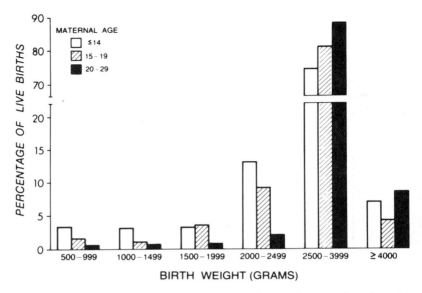

Figure 8-1. Birth weight versus percentage live births, by age of mother. (From Merritt TA, Lawrence RA, Naeye RL: The infants of adolescent mothers. Pediatr Ann 9:100–107, 1980. With permission.)

mothers had a greater number of infants under 2500 g than the older white mothers, but the number of adolescent white mothers delivering very low birth weight infants was too small for meaningful comparisons. A greater number of preterm infants (less than 37 weeks) were born to young black mothers than to white adolescent mothers or adult mothers of either race (Table 8-3 and Fig. 8-3).

There is evidence that behavioral patterns and specific medical complications are more powerful determinants of infant birth weight less than 2500 g than the age of the mother alone. The weights of infants born to white teenagers in Kansas City, Kansas, were similar to the weights of infants born to white mothers in all age groups.[6] The incidence of medical complications of pregnancy (acute or chronic hypertension, preeclampsia, third trimester vaginal bleeding, chronic medical disease, etc.) was 15 percent for all white mothers and 15.4 percent for white mothers under 19 years of age. The incidence of complicating behavioral conditions (low prepregnancy weight, poor weight gain in pregnancy, lack of prenatal care, heavy smoking, drug addiction, and alcoholism) was 47.3 percent in the adolescent mothers who gave birth to infants with complications. Similarly, 45 percent of all white mothers who gave birth to infants with complications had complicating behavioral conditions. The incidence of complicating be-

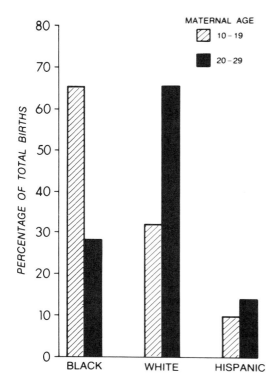

Figure 8-2. Distribution of births to younger and older mothers, by race (mother). (From Merritt TA, Lawrence RA, Naeye RL: The infants of adolescent mothers. Pediatr Ann 9:100–107, 1980. With permission.)

Table 8-2. Distribution (in Percentages) of Birth Weight, by Race and Age of Mother: Monroe County, New York, 1976–1979

Birth Weight (g)	Black 10–19 Years	Black 20–29 Years	White 10–19 Years	White 20–29 Years
0–499	0.27	0.08	0	0.24
500–999	3.50*	1.95	0	1.54
1000–1499	2.15*	1.40	0.86*	2.23
1500–2499	13.20	11.10	12.10*	7.29
2500–3999	78.70	80.30	81.90	78.40
Over 4000	2.18*	5.17	5.14*	10.30

From Lawrence RA, Merritt TA: Infants of adolescent mothers. Sem Perinatol 5:19–32, 1981. With permission.
*$p < 0.05$.

Table 8-3. Distribution (in Percentages) of Gestational Age (Dubowitz), by Race and Age of Mother: Monroe County, New York, 1976–1979

Gestation (weeks)	Black		White	
	10–19 Years	20–29 Years	10–19 Years	20–29 Years
Under 28	3.81*	1.41	0	1.24
28–29	0.82	0.66	0.86	1.24
30–31	1.36	0.99	0.86	1.09
32–33	2.18†	1.66	1.72	2.33
34–36	7.08	5.63	9.48*	5.12
37–41	83.90	88.10	86.21	87.22
Over 41	0.85	1.65	0.87	1.76
Under 37	15.25*	12.06	10.35	11.03
37 or more	84.75	87.94	89.65	88.97

From Lawrence RA, Merritt TA: Infants of adolescent mothers. Sem Perinatol 5:19–32, 1981. With permission.
*$p < 0.01$.
†$p < 0.05$.

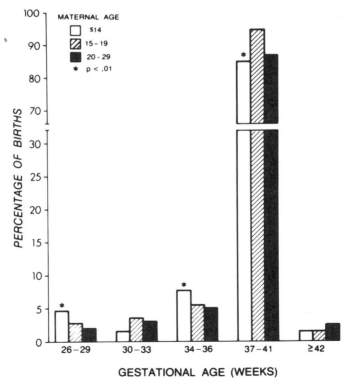

Figure 8-3. Distribution of gestational age, by age of mother. (From Merritt TA, Lawrence RA, Naeye RL: The infants of adolescent mothers. Pediatr Ann 9:100–107, 1980. With permission.)

154

Table 8-4. Low Birth Weight Infants Born to 770 Teenage Mothers: University of Kansas Medical Center, Kansas City, Kansas

Age of Mother	Mothers with No Complicating Conditions		Mothers with Complicating Behavioral Conditions*		Mothers with Medical Complications of Pregnancy†	
	Mothers	Low Birth Weight Infants	Mothers	Low Birth Weight Infants	Mothers	Low Birth Weight Infants
Adolescents						
14 or less	2	1 (50.0)	6	2 (33.3)	5	0 (0)
15–16	51	3 (5.9)	76	6 (7.8)	30	8 (26.4)
17–19	171	4 (2.3)‡	214	21 (9.8)	70	9 (12.8)
Total	224	8 (3.6)	296	29 (9.8)	105	17 (16.2)
20–34	384	8 (2.3)	248	26 (10.5)	NA§	NA

From Miller HC, Merritt TA: Fetal Growth in Humans. Chicago, Year Book, 1979. With permission.
*Abnormally low prepregnancy weight for height; low maternal weight gain in pregnancy; lack of any prenatal casre; cigarette smoking during pregnancy; use of addicting drugs or consumption of large amounts of ethanol during pregnancy.
†Acute chronic hypertension; preeclampsia; severe vaginal bleeding (third trimester); chronic disease involving heart, liver, lungs, kidney, gastrointestinal tract, thyroid, or adrenal glands; disseminated lupus erythematosus; sarcoidosis; severe chronic infections; anemia (hemoglobin below 10 g/100 ml); leukemia; malignant solid tumors; large ovarian cysts; continuous medication with steroids or immunosuppressive, teratogenic, or growth-retarding drugs; polyhydramnios; oligohydramnios.
‡Percentages are shown in parentheses.
§NA: not available.

havioral patterns was distinctly higher in the group under 15-years of age than in the adult group (Table 8-4). Among mothers with no medical or behavioral complicating factors, the incidence of low birth weight infants did not differ significantly between teenagers (3.6 percent) and adult mothers (2.3 percent).

In summary, adolescent women in the Kansas City study showed a disproportionate number of both medical and behavioral complicating factors. When these factors were excluded from the statistics, the incidence of low birth weight infants was the same for mothers under 19 years of age and those 20 years and older. In other words, when maternal and fetal growth retarding factors are taken into consideration, no biologic disadvantage appears to be unique to adolescent mothers.

PERINATAL MORTALITY

In order to determine the influence of the mother's age on the incidence of perinatal mortality, a study was conducted of autopsy material based on standardized postmortem examination of infants and their placentas.[6] Primary and secondary diagnoses were assigned to each death. Primary diagnoses alone were used to determine perinatal mortality rates. The excess antenatal and neonatal mortality among the infants born to adolescent mothers was related to an increased incidence of preeclampsia and low birth weight. The lowest perinatal mortality of all groups by maternal age, however, was achieved by those in the group 16–19 years of age (38 deaths/10,000 live births). The highest rate was seen in the group 10–15 years old (52/10,000). An increased incidence of amniotic fluid infection, abruptio placentae, and placental growth retardation was found in these very young mothers.

When the data were controlled for race, the difference in the incidence of amniotic fluid infection by age was muted. When the data were controlled for socioeconomic status, the outcome for the nonpoor but young was not significantly different from that for the older mother.

These findings fail to support the traditional position that biologic immaturity is the main factor in poor outcome of infants of adolescent mothers. The data do suggest that amniotic fluid infections[14] are correlated with the excessive preterm deliveries recorded in the youngest mothers in Rochester. The majority of very young mothers, as noted previously, are black.

Table 8-5. Distribution (in Percentages) of Apgar Scores, by Race and Age of Mother: University of Rochester–Strong Memorial Hospital, 1976–1979

	Black		White	
Apgar	10–19 Years	20–29 Years	10–19 Years	20–29 Years
1 minute				
Under 3	8.8*	5.1	6.0*	3.5
4–7	19.9	22.8	21.5	20.9
8–10	71.3	72.1	72.5	75.6
5 minutes				
Under 3	3.7	5.1	0.8	1.9
4–7	9.7	5.6	5.2	3.3
8–10	86.6	89.3	94.0	94.8

From Lawrence RA, Merritt TA: Infants of adolescent mothers. Sem Perinatol 5:19–32, 1981. With permission.
*$p < 0.05$.

Table 8-6. Acidosis* at Birth per 1000 Births, by Age of Mother: University of Rochester–Strong Memorial Hospital, 1976–1979

pH	10–19 Years	20–29 Years
7.10–7.27	27.0	24.7
Under 7.10	8.1	10.2

From Lawrence RA, Merritt TA: Infants of adolescent mothers. Sem Perinatol 5:19–32, 1981. With permission.
*Cord blood pH.

NEONATAL AND INFANT HEALTH

Apgar Scores

When the relationship between the mother's age and the baby's health and behavior was determined by Sandler in an analysis of birth data from Nashville General Hospital, 1974–1977, it suggested a linear relationship between increases in Apgar score and increases in maternal age (Table 8-1).[7] The Apgar scores, however, were reported as a mean for the age group, which may indeed average out the incidence of significantly low scores. When the Apgar scores are grouped, rather than averaged, the significance at 5 minutes may be negligible.

Grouped Apgar scores from the Rochester study were used to compare the neonatal health of nearly 1500 infants born to primigravida adolescents with that of 4668 first-born infants of women 20–29 years old. Infants born to adolescent mothers had significantly more Apgar scores of less than 3 at 1 minute than the infants of the 20- to 29-year-old mothers (Table 8-5). The difference was not present, however, at 5 minutes. There were no differences between the groups with regard to cord blood pH or first arterial pH (Table 8-6).

Nursery Admission

More infants born to adolescent mothers were admitted to the intensive care or special care nurseries at the University of Rochester Medical Center than were infants born to mothers 20–29 years of age (15.7 versus 13.9 percent). The infants of adolescents, however, were sometimes admitted for observation because of the added risk factor often automatically associated with an adolescent mother.

Complications

Frequent neonatal complications and causes of significant infant mortality and morbidity are listed in Table 8-7. In the Rochester study, infants born to black adolescent mothers had significantly more hypoglycemia, Respiratory Distress Syndrome, pneumonia, seizures/apnea, and necrotizing enterocolitis than those of older black women. Except for neonatal pneumonia, infants of adolescent white mothers experienced either no differences or only a few more neonatal complications when compared to infants of white mothers 20–24 years old. Congenital malformations detected by routine physical examination were grouped according to the organ system most severely affected for ease of analysis. Many anomalies involved dysmorphic patterns of multiple systems. Cardiac, genitourinary, and renal malformations oc-

Table 8-7. Percentage Neonatal Complications, by Race and Age of Mother: University of Rochester–Strong Memorial Hospital, 1976–1979

Complication	Black		White	
	10–19 Years	20–29 Years	10–19 Years	20–29 Years
Birth trauma	3.8	2.8	2.6	2.5
Sepsis (suspected or proven)	11.5	9.2	8.6	8.2
Meningitis	0.29	0.17	0	0.36
Necrotizing enterocolitis (suspected and proven)	1.46*	0.24	0	0.54
Glucose under 30 mg/dl	5.67*	3.31	0	3.27
Bilirubin (indirect) over 15 mg/dl	1.11	2.77*	4.30	3.20
Anemia (hematocrit under 40%)	1.13	1.20	1.01	0.83
Respiratory Distress Syndrome	4.85*	2.05	1.72	3.47*
Meconium aspiration syndrome	0.57	1.02	0.17	0.67*
Pulmonary airleaks	0.57	0.42	0	0.94
Pneumonia	0.59*	0.25	0.88*	0.31
Seizures/apnea	4.13*	2.07	0.89	2.47*

From Lawrence RA, Merritt TA: Infants of adolescent mothers. Sem Perinatol 5:19–32, 1981. With permission.
*$p < 0.01$.

curred significantly less frequently in infants of adolescent mothers. There were fewer documented chromosomal abnormalities among babies of adolescent mothers, although the difference was not statistically significant.[6]

The total duration of hospitalization was slightly longer in infants of adolescent mothers. Although adolescent mothers visited and telephoned the intensive care nursery less than older mothers did, greater financial and transportation problems among adolescent mothers make this fact difficult to interpret. We have yet to confirm follow-up data regarding long-range outcomes in this group of high-risk babies born to mothers less than 19 years of age.

Mortality

Although the incidence of late fetal death in the Rochester study was nearly the same for infants of both adolescent mothers and older mothers, more infants of black adolescent mothers died in the delivery room or within the first 24 hours of life. Neonatal mortality from the first to the seventh day of life was similar for infants of adolescent and adult mothers (Table 8-8); however, a significant increase in the rate of infant death among babies of adolescent mothers occurred by their second birthday. Similar observations were reported by Shapiro et al.[15]

In addition to being at risk for the causes of infant morbidity and mortality (Table 8-7), infants born to adolescent mothers were at an increased risk of dying of sudden infant death syndrome. The risk was significantly increased in the second- or third-born child of a mother under 20 years of age. This finding was obtained by using multifactorial analysis to control for other variables; no biologic cause can be implicated, and the reason for the increased risk remains unexplained.[16-19]

Table 8-8. Newborn Mortality per 1000 Births, by Age of Mother: Monroe County, New York, 1976–1979

Life Span	Black		White	
	10–19 Years	20–29 Years	10–19 Years	20–29 Years
Live birth, death within 24 hours	17.09*	7.32	8.62	6.94
24 hours–7 days	5.70	4.88	0	8.43

From Lawrence RA, Merritt TA: Infants of adolescent mothers. Sem Perinatol 5:19–32, 1981. With permission.
*$p < 0.03$.

GYNECOLOGIC AGE

Chronological age has traditionally been used in studies of the outcome of pregnancy in adolescent women. Montagu suggested that successful pregnancy becomes possible when prolactin secreted by the anterior pituitary causes the corpus luteum to produce progesterone and not the menarche itself.[20] He correlated poor reproductive outcome with the high number of anovulatory cycles and the irregular pattern of menstrual cycles of the pubertal female and theorized that the period of reproductive maturity is at its optimum for the 5 years from 23 to 28 years of age. It is not known whether the biologic maturation of the mother is an important variable in the perinatal growth of the fetus. In a retrospective study of 12- to 15-year-old black unmarried girls who delivered during 1957–1967 in Maryland, Erkan et al. found that the 124 mothers who were 24 months or less post menarche at the time of conception had more low birth weight infants (31.4 percent) than the 137 mothers who were more than 24 months post menarche at the time of conception (16 percent). Zlatnik and Burmeister also reported a significant increase in low birth weight babies born to mothers who were 24 months or less post menarche.[22] When the population was further divided by age, it was found that those patients who were less than 15 years old and more than 24 months post menarche had fewer low birth weight infants than the mothers over 15 years old but less than 24 months post menarche. These data support the conclusion that post menarche age is a significant independent variable.

In an effort to evaluate the relationship of the gynecologic age of the mother to the outcome of the infant, the records of all adolescent mothers delivered at the University of Rochester Medical Center in 1979 were reviewed. Gynecologic age was defined as the age of the mother at the time

Table 8-9. Gynecologic and Chronological Age Compared to Birth Weight, by Race of Mother: University of Rochester–Strong Memorial Hospital, 1979

Birth Weight (g)	Mean Gynecologic Age (months)		Mean (±SD) Chronological Age (years)	
	Blacks	Whites	Blacks	Whites
1499 or less	59.7	73.7	16.8 ± 4.8	19.5 ± 0.5
1500–2499	65.4	67.1	17.8 ± 2.1	17.7 ± 1.4
2500–3999	72.3	67.6	17.6 ± 3.4	19.1 ± 3.1
4000 or more	62.3	57.7	17.9 ± 1.1	19.0 ± 1.7

From Lawrence RA, Merritt TA: Infants of adolescent mothers. Sem Perinatol 5:19–32, 1981. With permission.

of the birth of her infant minus the age of the mother at menarche. The gynecologic age was considered in relation to birth weight and birth length of the infant. Similar analyses were also performed by chronological age for comparison. The groups were divided by race. Among white adolescents the birth weight did not vary significantly in relation to gynecologic age (Table 8-9), although the very young mother was more likely to have a very large infant (4000 g or more). Among black adolescents there was a more distinct trend for mothers of younger gynecologic age to have smaller infants. In contrast, birth weight did not vary in relation to the mother's chronological age for either white or black adolescents (Table 8-9).

LONG-RANGE PROSPECTS FOR INFANTS BORN TO ADOLESCENT MOTHERS

Infants born to adolescent mothers are said to be more likely to weigh less when they reach school age, to have poorer grades, and to be subject to more child abuse and neglect than those born to older mothers. Any analysis of the data, however, should consider maternal race and socioeconomic status as well as age.

Morbidity, Abuse, and Neglect

When children are followed longitudinally, the health status of the child shows a relationship not only to the mother's age at the time of the birth, but also to the marital status of the mother and basic family structure. A study conducted in Denmark from 1959 to 1961 revealed that the children of mothers less than 20 years old who were raising their children alone were clearly worse off with respect to physical health compared to those raised by adolescent mothers and fathers or by adolescent mothers and grandmothers.[7] LaBarre reported that the infant death rates due to respiratory infections and accidents were more than twice as high among infants born out of wedlock than among infants born to married mothers.[23]

Card reported no adverse effects on the infant's physical health associated with young maternal age if high-quality medical care had been provided throughout pregnancy and into infancy.[24] The data analyzed by Card came from Project Talent, which began with a national sample of high school youth in 1960 and followed them at 1, 5, and 11 years after graduation. The study group consisted of children whose mothers had been less than 15 years old, 16–17 years old, and 18–19 years old when they were born. The data were controlled for race, sex of child, and socioeconomic status. The health of the offspring in this study was more dependent on the presence of two rather than one adult in the home.

In a 7-year, prospective, longitudinal study of adolescents in the Collaborative Perinatal Project of the National Institute of Neurological Disorders and Stroke, Broman found battered child syndrome to be a rare diagnosis.[25] The frequency decreased with increasing age of the mother at birth. Among whites the frequency was 0.9 percent in the youngest, 0.3 percent among older adolescents, and 0.1 percent in the adult group ($p <$ 0.005). The white mothers were middle income on a 3-point scale. Among blacks the frequency was 0.1 percent in adolescent mothers and 0.01 percent in adults, all of lower socioeconomic status.

In a study of inflicted burns in children, it was noted that 75 percent of the injured children had single parents who were, in most cases, young or adolescent at the time of birth.[26] The personality characteristics of abusive parents were described by Spinetta and Rigler as less mature, less intelligent, and more aggressive, impulsive, self-centered, tense, and self-critical than nonabusive parents.[27] This portrayal indicates only that abusive parents, who may also be young, are members of multiproblem families with a complete spectrum of personal and social pathology. Although reviews of adolescent pregnancy frequently include abuse and neglect as one of the significant features demonstrating poor outcome, there are no carefully controlled studies to substantiate this claim. The temperament of the child is thought to contribute to the abusing tendency of the parent.[28]

Brazelton Scores

Because the early interaction skills of the infant may affect the mother's behavior toward the infant, assessment of the behavior of the infants of adolescents may be significant. The Brazelton Neonatal Assessment Scale has been found to be a good predictor of later functioning; it is sensitive to mild dysfunction of the central nervous system and to cultural/racial group differences.[29,30] When the infants of adolescent mothers are evaluated with the Brazelton scale and compared with the infants of adult mothers, differences in arousal state are noted by some observers.[7] This social and neurologic assessment was done on the infants of adolescents at 2 days of age and significant differences were noted when compared to infants of adults. The former were more likely to be underaroused or overaroused, and it was suggested that, over time, this could influence how the adolescent interacts with her child. In this study, however, when obstetric risk factors, race, and socioeconomic group were considered, age was not an independent determinant on the Brazelton score.

Thompson et al. administered the Brazelton scale to 30 infants of adolescent mothers (less than 18 years old at delivery) and to 30 infants of older mothers, at 2–5 days of age).[31] They found the infants of adolescent mothers "were significantly less capable of responding to social stimuli, less alert, and less able to control motor behavior and to perform integrated motor activities."

The effects of Brazelton scale demonstrations on early interactions of preterm infants and their teenage mothers were investigated by Widmayer and Field.[32] They did not find a significant difference in the performance of the infant in relation to maternal age. The mother's observation of the Brazelton scale being administered to the infant and weekly completion of the home assessment scale during the first month appeared to facilitate more optimal feeding and face-to-face interactions than were experienced by mothers who had not seen the Brazelton performed. The study mothers became more sensitive to the unique capabilities of their infants than the control mothers. This observation may have a practical application in teaching adolescents to care for their infants.

Growth

Oppel and Royston reported that infants born to adolescent mothers are more likely to be underweight and shorter in the first years of life than matched controls born to adult mothers.[33] In the Johns Hopkins Development Center in Baltimore, Maryland, Hardy et al. found no differences between physical growth of children born to adolescent mothers and those of older mothers by the time the children reached the age of 7 years.[34] In the 7-year follow-up of the Collaborative Perinatal Project reported by Broman, nine indices of physical status were selected, and four of these were found to correlate with maternal age.[25] Children of adolescents had a slight increase in cerebral palsy and severe anemia (whites only). The children of the youngest mothers were slightly taller. The incidence of epilepsy, failure to thrive, chronic infections, and burns was not related to maternal age.

Cognitive Development

The intellectual function of the children of adolescents was followed over an 8-year period by Lobl et al.[35] The children were compared by maternal age at the time of birth, with race, sex of infant, birth weight, and birth order controlled. The older the mother, the higher the intellectual function in both blacks and whites, regardless of birth weight. Racial differences were minimal. The authors concluded that children of mothers 15 years old or younger and the first-born children of mothers 35 years old or older are at a disadvantage in later cognitive development.

The Moray House Picture Test was used to measure the IQ of 11,280 seven-year-old children in Aberdeen, Scotland. Illsley reported that IQ increased with maternal age when parity and social class were controlled.[36]

The Stanford-Binet administered to 12-year-olds showed barely perceptible differences (2.98 mean IQ points) between children of mothers 17 and younger when they were born and matched pairs of mothers 18 and older.[33] The Wechsler Intelligence Scale for Children (WISC) showed similar results. The Bender Gestalt Test for Young Children, however, showed differences in results depending on degree of deprivation, ethnic group, and sex of the child.[37] The deprived black children did poorly compared to the deprived white children. The difference between advantaged and disadvantaged whites was minimal, whereas black advantaged children scored significantly higher than black disadvantaged children.

The long-range outcome of the children born to adolescents was also examined by Hardy et al. as part of the Johns Hopkins study.[34] When given the Stanford-Binet tests at the age of 4, children who had been born to adolescent black mothers tended to cluster in the low IQ group; few were in the above average group. The scores of the 4-year-olds increased with maternal age at birth.

Babies of black, urban, adolescent mothers scored less well than those of black urban adult mothers on the Bayley developmental examination at 8 months of age, the Stanford-Binet test at 4 years of age, and the WISC and the Wide Range Achievement Tests at age 7.[7] A longitudinal study of 404 unmarried, primiparous, young teenage mothers who were predominantly black and poor included evaluations at 1, 3, and 5 years post partum. Furstenberg assessed preparation for school, as determined by the Preschool Inventory, among children aged 42–60 months.[38] The children's scores, standardized for age, were lower than the scores of children of a matched sample of older adolescents and significantly lower than scores obtained by the children of middle-class black and white children. Furstenberg found an inverse relationship between the time spent with a child by the young mother and the child's score: when the mother was young and unemployed and the sole caretaker of the infant, the infant scored less well than when there were other adult caregivers because the mother worked or went to school.

The relationship of maternal age to other variables known to affect development has yet to be studied. It has been suggested, for instance, that male children born to adolescents are at increased risk for poor cognitive outcome.[38] In view of the data on the effect of race and socioeconomic status on IQ scores, any relationship of maternal age to the intelligence of offspring requires further controlled analysis. It has been stressed by Sameroff and Chandler that the data from various longitudinal studies of prenatal and perinatal complications have yet to produce a single predictive variable more potent than the familial and socioeconomic characteristics of the caretaking environment.[39] The predictive influence of the socioeconomic status is especially accurate at the low end of the intelligence scales. These authors also noted that the organization of intelligence in children changes with age. As children age, they move from a sensorimotor mode of functioning to a conceptual mode, and early deficits tend to disappear. Parental attitudes and social status seem to influence this tendency: early stimulation and special efforts with high-risk infants have some positive effects on long-range outcome. Of particular note among long-range studies is the work by Werner et al., who followed 670 children born on the island of Kauai, Hawaii, in 1955.[40] This study included the entire population and ample controls for race and socioeconomic status were inherent in the geographic setting. The distribution of perinatal complications was related to later physical and psychological disabilities in lower income families but did not influence outcome in stable upper class families.

Data collected from the Social Psychiatry Study Center's longitudinal community-wide study in Chicago included a group of 500 adolescent mothers.[7] The children of these mothers were evaluated on admission to school and for several years thereafter. Failure to adapt to school at age 6 years was strongly related to maternal age; however, 10 years later, the psychiatric scores of the same offspring did not demonstrate such a relationship. On the other hand, failure to adapt to school at age 6 was associated with intense psychiatric symptoms as a teenager.

These studies and those of Kellam et al. showed a correlation among the sex of the child, maternal age, and outcome.[41] Male children of adolescent mothers were more apt to adapt poorly to school than male children of adult mothers. Separate analysis of verbal and performance scores of 7-year-old black children indicated that the age of the mother was related to both verbal and performance scores in boys, but only verbal scores in girls.[7]

Hardy et al. used academic achievement as a measure of outcome at both 7 and 12 years of age.[34] They found that children of adolescent mothers performed less well in school and repeated a grade more often than did the children of older women. Self-concept, as determined by the Coopersmith and Piers-Harris tests, did not differ in the children of the two groups. Maternal education achievement differed significantly. Only 35 percent of the younger mothers had completed high school at the end of the study, compared to 77 percent of the older women. In addition, postgraduate education, skills, training, job levels, and income were significantly lower in the adolescent mothers even when the data were corrected for age.

Oppel and Royston found that the children of young mothers were, on the average, 0.38 years below the reading level of children of older mothers in their match-control study of adolescent mothers.[33] At age 10, 29 percent of the children of adolescent mothers had achieved third-grade reading level, whereas 55 percent of the children of older mothers had achieved third-grade level. Their analysis of behavioral traits of the two groups of children at ages 8 and 10 showed the offspring of young mothers to be more dependent and distractable. There were no differences in other personality traits studied by Oppel and Royston; however, Kellam et al. reported the children of adolescent mothers were less likely to adapt to school.[41] This finding was particularly significant for male children.

CONCLUSIONS

Although adolescent pregnancy has been associated with increased medical risk, a review of the collective data that takes into consideration the race and socioeconomic status of the maternal nuclear family indicates that age is not the critical factor in adolescent pregnancy unless the mother is 14 years of age or younger. The ideal time to give birth, from a medical perspective, appears to be between the ages of 16 and 19 years, provided the mother is given adequate prenatal care and rears the child in a stable environment.

The data on the psychosocial outcome of premature parenting are sparse and inconclusive. The intellectual, developmental, and educational expectations for children of adolescents have been lower than the expectations for those of older mothers. These children, however, are disproportionately poor, black, and living in extended, often disrupted families with multiple caregivers. The major studies have been of adolescents who bore infants between 1950 and 1960. The present data suggest that the mothering skills and child-rearing practices of adolescent women have yet to be evaluated adequately. Parenting skills and maternal readiness may well be the critical determinants in the long-range outcome of the infants born to adolescent mothers.

REFERENCES

1. Lincoln R: Is pregnancy good for teenagers? Testimony before the Select Committee on Population, 95th Congress, 1979, p 318
2. Lowe CU: Fertility and contraception in America. Adolescent and Pre-Adolescent Pregnancy Hearings before the Select Committee on Population, 95th Congress, second session, 1979, p 570
3. Tanner JM: Foetus into Man—Physical Growth from Conception to Maturity. London, Open Books, 1978
4. Merritt TA, Lawrence RA, Naeye RL: The infants of adolescent mothers. Pediatr Ann 9:100–107, 1980
5. Naeye RL: Teenage and pre-teenage pregnancies: Consequences of the fetal–maternal competition for nutrients. Pediatrics 67:146–150, 1981
6. Miller HC, Merritt TA: Fetal Growth in Humans. Chicago, Year Book, 1979
7. Baldwin W, Cain VS: The children of teenage parents. Fam Plann Perspect 12:34–43, 1980
8. Hardy JB, Mellits ED: Relationship of low birthweight to maternal characteristics of age, parity, education and body size, in Reed DM, Stanley FJ (eds): The Epidemiology of Prematurity. Baltimore, Urban and Schwarenberg, 1977, pp 1–174

9. Hoffman HJ, Lundin FE, Bakketeig LS, et al: Classification of births by weight and gestational age for future studies of prematurity, in Reed DM, Stanley FJ (eds): The Epidemiology of Prematurity. Baltimore, Urban and Schwarenberg, 1977, pp 297–325

10. Dott AB, Fort AT: Medical and social factors affecting early teenage pregnancy. Am J Obstet Gynecol 125:532–535, 1976

11. Dwyer JF: Teenage pregnancy. Am J Obstet Gynecol 118:373–376, 1974

12. Niswander NR, Gordon M: The Women and Their Pregnancies. Philadelphia, Saunders, 1972

13. Spellacy WN, Mahan CS, Cruz A: The adolescent's first pregnancy: A controlled study. South Med J 71:768–771, 1978

14. Edwards LE, Barrada MI, Hamann AA, et al: Gonorrhea in pregnancy. Am J Obstet Gynecol 132:637–640, 1978

15. Shapiro S, McCormick BH, Starfield JP, et al: Relevance of correlates of infant mortality for significant morbidity at one year of age. Am J Obstet Gynecol 136:363–373, 1980

16. Bergman AB, Ray CG, Pomeroy MA, et al: Studies of the sudden infant death syndrome in King County, Washington. III: Epidemiology. Pediatrics 49:860–870, 1972

17. Frogatt P, Lynas MA, Marshall TK: Sudden unexpected death in infants (cot death): Report of a collaborative study in Northern Ireland. Ulster Med J 40:116–135, 1971

18. Kraus JF, Borhani NO: Post-neonatal sudden unexpected death in California: A cohort study. Am J Epidemiol 95:497–510, 1972

19. Kraus JF, Franti CE, Borhani NO: Discriminatory risk factors in post-neonatal sudden unexplained death. Am J Epidemiol 96:328–333, 1972

20. Montagu A: The adolescent's unreadiness for pregnancy and motherhood. Pediatr Ann 10:52–56, 1981

21. Erkan KA, Rimer BA, Stine OC: Juvenile pregnancy: Role of physiologic maturity. Md State Med J 20:50–52, 1971

22. Zlatnik FJ, Burmeister LF: Low "gynecologic age": An obstetric risk factor. Am J Obstet Gynecol 128:183–186, 1977

23. LaBarre M: Emotional crises of school-age girls during pregnancy and early motherhood, in Schwartz JL, Schwartz LH (eds): Vulnerable Infants: A Psychological Dilemma. New York, McGraw-Hill, 1977, pp 30–47

24. Card J: Long-term consequences for children born to adolescent mothers. Palo Alto, Calif, American Institute of Research, 1978

25. Broman SH: Longterm development of children born to teenagers, in Scott KG, Field T, Robertson E (eds): Teenage Parents and Their Offspring. New York, Grune & Stratton, 1981, pp 195–224

26. Hight DW, Bakalra HR, Lloyd JR: Inflicted burns in children, recognition and treatment. JAMA 242:517–520, 1979

27. Spinetta JJ, Rigler D: The child-abusing parent: A psychological review. Psychol Bull 77:296–304, 1972

28. Grow LJ: Early Childrearing by Young Mothers: A Research Study. New York, Child Welfare League of America, 1979

29. Brazelton TB: Neonatal Behavioral Assessment Scale: Clinics in Developmental Medicine, no 50. Philadelphia, Lippincott, 1973

30. Brazelton TB, Tronick E, Adamson L, et al: Early mother–infant reciprocity, in Porter R, O'Connor M (eds): Parent–Infant Interaction, Ciba Foundation Symposium 33. Amsterdam, Elsevier, 1975

31. Thompson RJ, Cappleman MA, Zeitshel KA: Neonatal behavior of infants of adolescent mothers. Dev Med Child Neurol 21:474–482, 1979

32. Widmayer SM, Field TM: Effects of Brazelton demonstration on early interactions of preterm infants and their teenage mothers. Infant Behav Dev 3:79–89, 1980

33. Oppel WC, Royston AB: Teenage births: Some social, psychological and physical sequelae. Am J Public Health 61:751–756, 1971

34. Hardy JB, Welcher DW, Stanley J, et al: Long term outcome of adolescent pregnancy. Clin Obstet Gynaecol 21:1215–1232, 1978

35. Lobl M, Welcher WD, Mellits ED: Maternal age and intellectual functioning of offspring. Johns Hopkins Med J 128:347–360, 1971

36. Illsley R: Family growth and its effect on the relationship between obstetric factors and child functioning, in Platt R, Parkes S (eds): Social and Genetic Influences on Life and Death. London, Oliver and Boyd, 1967, pp 29–42

37. Koppitz EM: The Bender Gestalt Test for Young Children, vol 1: Research and Application 1963–1973. New York, Grune & Stratton, 1975

38. Furstenberg FF Jr: Unplanned Parenthood: The Social Consequences of Teenage Childbearing. New York, Macmillan, 1976

39. Sameroff AJ, Chandler M: Reproductive risk and the continuum of caretaking casualty, in Horowitz FD, (ed): Review of Child Development Research, vol 4. Chicago, University of Chicago Press, 1975

40. Werner EE, Bierman JM, French RE: The Children of Kauai. Honolulu, University of Hawaii Press, 1971

41. Kellam SG, Ensminger ME, Turner RJ: Family structure and the mental health of children. Arch Gen Psychiatry 34:1012–1022, 1977

9

Impact of Gynecologic Age on Outcome of Adolescent Pregnancy

Dorothy R. Hollingsworth, Jane Morley Kotchen, and Marianne E. Felice

The role of chronological age in the outcome of pregnancy in adolescents has been examined in varied settings for more than half a century. The assessment of obstetric problems has been complicated because of differences in socioeconomic and racial characteristics among the groups who were reported. Many earlier (before 1970) accounts of outcome of pregnancy in patients who were under 16 years of age addressed adolescents who were severely deprived both economically and medically. [1-9] In most of these reports of predominantly black teenagers (72–100 percent) from inner cities there was a high prevalence of complications of pregnancy at a young age, particularly anemia, pregnancy-induced hypertension, and prematurity. However, in three early descriptions of more economically advantaged young white adolescents, [10-12] a low chronological age did not appear to have adverse effects on the course of pregnancy or neonatal outcome.

The view that pregnancy at a young age is necessarily a high-risk medical problem has been modified since 1970. There has been a revolution in obstetric and newborn infant care with the development of the fields of perinatology and neonatology and the concept of regionalized perinatal care for complicated pregnancies. Several investigators have proposed in retrospective studies that some measure of physiologic maturity rather than chronological age might correlate better with the outcome of teenage pregnancies. Erkan et al. described physiologic maturity as the postmenarcheal age of the

169

mother until the last menstrual period before pregnancy.[13] Zlatnik and Burmeister coined the term *gynecologic age* to indicate the chronological age minus the age at menarche and used it to assess pregnancy risks in adolescents.[14]

It is difficult to dissociate the effects of a low gynecologic age from those of a low chronological age in the literature on teenage pregnancy. The problem is complicated further by the confounding variables of poor socioeconomic environment, low maternal prepregnancy weight, and poor nutrition.[15] In this chapter we describe and compare the impact of low gynecologic and chronological ages on outcome of pregnancy in retrospective and prospective reports published since 1970.

EFFECT OF AGE ON COMPLICATIONS OF PREGNANCY

Williams, in 1917, was the first to challenge the prevalent view of early obstetricians that pregnancy and labor were accompanied by a greater danger in young girls than in older women.[1] He stated that labor in those age 16 years or less was no more serious than in women of mature years. Harris reexamined this hypothesis in 1922 by reviewing the pregnancy and labor experience of 500 young primiparae (68 percent black, 32 percent white) who were followed at Johns Hopkins Hospital in Baltimore.[2] Premature labor occurred in 58 (11.6 percent). Among the 442 women who delivered at term, the duration of labor was actually shorter and the mean weight of infants (3181g) was not different from that of older women. Abnormal pelves were the same in both groups. All maternal deaths were due to infections (preantibiotic era). Harris concluded from a purely obstetric point of view that the ages under consideration, 12–16 years, appeared to be the optimum time for first labor.

Erkan et al. retrospectively assessed the role of gynecologic age in 261 patients ranging in age from 12 to 15 years (94 percent black, 6 percent white); 124 women had a low gynecologic age (24 months or less). They found that 31.4 percent of the infants born to the latter group had low birth weights (under 2500 g), compared with 16 percent of infants born to mothers who were more physiologically mature ($p < 0.01$). There was no significant difference in the frequency of preeclampsia. No comparison data were given for older adolescents with a low gynecologic age, or for mature women (over 20 years of age) from the same clinic. No information was given concerning maternal nutritional status, prepregnancy weight, or weight gain during pregnancy.

Zlatnik and Burmeister reported a retrospective review of the charts of 1114 patients under 17 years and under who were delivered at the University of Iowa Hospitals from 1972 to 1974.[14] Age at menarche was obtained historically from the records of 1005 patients. A subset of 15-year-old patients was segregated by gynecologic age. Chi square tests were utilized to compare proportions of low birth weight infants among mothers of various chronological and gynecologic ages. Of the 46 subjects of low gynecologic age, only 8 had low birth weight infants. Gynecologic age had no predictive effect for toxemia or other pregnancy complications. The trend toward increased prevalence of low birth weight infants among mothers of low gynecologic age was not statistically significant for 15-year-olds and was even less apparent when gynecologic age was assessed at ages 16 and 17 years. There were too few 13- and 14-year-old patients with delivery of low birth weight infants to draw conclusions. The birth weight distribution of 282 infants delivered of 15-year-old mothers from 1970 to 1975 was also reviewed. Of the infants born to women of low gynecologic age, 17 percent had low birth weights, compared with 7 percent of those born to women of older gynecologic age ($p < 0.05$). No data were available concerning prepregnancy weight or weight gain during pregnancy.

In 1978 Perkins et al. reported the results of the first 2 years of an intensive and individual approach to pregnant women less than 17 years of age.[16] In their study at the University of Colorado, Denver, 135 13- to 16-year-olds in an intensive prenatal program (group A) were compared with 100 controls of similar age treated routinely (group B), and 100 women of more nearly "ideal" childbearing age (19–24 years; group C). Their findings are summarized in Table 9-1. In these three groups of patients hypertension appeared to have racial associations, but no other clear correlates. Eclampsia occurred only in the young. There was no clinically significant increase in small pelvic inlet as determined by labor performance in the younger women. Cesarean section for fetopelvic disproportion was actually lower in group A than in group C (ages 19–24 years).

There were slightly more low birth weight infants among the younger groups, corresponding to prematurity rates. This difference was significant ($p < 0.05$) only when indigent, mostly Chicano patients receiving care at local health stations (group B) were compared with older women, and did not apply to the 135 women ages 13–16 years cared for by the intensive prenatal approach. Fetal loss was small and no different in the three groups (1.0–2.2 percent). These excellent results may represent the combined effects of excellent perinatal care in a western setting, where indigency (in contrast to other urban settings) implies a greater degree of socioeconomic privilege.[16]

Lawrence and Merritt examined the records of all mothers 19 years old or less delivered at the University of Rochester Medical Center, Rochester, New York, in 1979. They found no relationship between birth weight and gynecologic age in white adolescents. In blacks, there was a trend for mothers with a lower gynecologic age to have smaller infants. No differences in birth

Table 9-1. Complications of Pregnancy (Percentages) in Adolescents (13–17 Years of Age) and Older Women (19–24 Years of Age): Denver, Colorado, 1974–1976

Group and Chronological Age (years)	Low Gynecologic Age	Hypertension	Cephalopelvic Disproportion		Low Birth Weight Infants		Fetal Loss
			Total	Cesarean Section	Total	Under 38 weeks*	
A, 13–16 (N = 135)	34.8	21.9	5.2	3.7	11.6	11.1	2.2
B, 14–17 (N = 100)	23.1	24.0	4.0	6.0	14.0	19.0	2.0
C, 19–24 (N = 100)	0	25.0	9.0	7.0	8.0	8.0	1.0

Adapted from Perkins RP et al.[16]
*Groups B and C differ ($p < 0.05$).

weight were noted between racial groups when evaluated by chronological age. The mothers in this retrospective study were disproportionately poor, black, and living in extended often disrupted families with multiple caregivers.

In other reports of pregnancy in women 15 years of age or younger the complications of pregnancy and fetal outcome have varied. Coates compared black patients under the age of 15 with older controls and found an increase in toxemia, uterine dysfunction, 1-day fever, and congenital heart disease in the younger women.[18] Klerman and Jekel observed a 14 percent prevalence of toxemia, 3 percent cesarean section rate, and 0.1 percent prenatal loss in their study of predominantly black, indigent adolescents.[19] They also detected a very high prematurity and perinatal loss rate in the same women during subsequent pregnancies. Klein studied a mostly black and clearly indigent group and found that premature birth, fetal death, neonatal death, and perinatal death were all increased in adolescents.[20]

Duenhoelter et al. compared patients under 15 years of age with controls ages 19–25. They found an increase in preeclampsia (34 versus 25 percent), small pelvic inlet, and early sexual maturation in their mostly black, single, young patients.[21] They did not find a difference between the two groups in clinic attendance, anemia, duration of pregnancy, operative delivery, infant weight, or perinatal mortality. This study supported the findings of a number of other investigators who also failed to show an increased prevalence of prematurity in adolescent pregnancy.[7,10,11,22-24]

Dott and Fort reviewed 414 births to women under 15 years of age in New Orleans.[25] Infant mortality was high (6–50/1000 live births), depending on medical and social circumstances. Prenatal care was generally less in teenagers, and prematurity, stillbirth, perinatal, and infant mortality rates were generally higher than those in older women.

Spellacy et al. retrospectively reviewed the records of 1021 primigravid women who delivered single infants from 1973 to 1976. In a comparison of 115 black adolescents 10–15 years old with mature women 20–24 years old (324 black, 553 white), they found the adolescent group was more often unmarried and received less prenatal care. The high frequency of hypertensive disorders was related to race. Their most important findings in adolescents were an increase in prematurity (20 percent versus 8 percent in mature blacks and 7.2 percent in mature whites) and postpartum endometritis (17.4 percent versus 3.4 percent in mature blacks and 6.5 percent in mature whites). There was no significant difference in fetal, neonatal, or perinatal mortality.

Felice et al. evaluated the impact of comprehensive prenatal care on the incidence of low birth weight infants.[27] They reported that only 9.0 percent of infants born to 67 mothers under 15 years of age in a special program weighed under 2500 g, compared with 20.9 percent of infants born to 67 mothers who were matched for age, race, socioeconomic status, and parity but were followed in a regular obstetric clinic.

UNIVERSITY OF KENTUCKY YOUNG MOTHER'S PROGRAM

In a prospective study of 417 primiparous teenagers 12–18 years of age, Hollingsworth and Kotchen evaluated both low gynecologic age (under 2 years) and young chronological age (under 16 years) at conception.[15] This University of Kentucky Young Mother's Program, in Lexington, located in a midwestern border state, had a racial distribution of 54 percent black and 46 percent white adolescents who were all from a comparable lower socioeconomic background. Gynecologic age was calculated for 398 adolescents in whom age at menarche was recorded; 14 percent were of low gynecologic age. Although many of these adolescents did not come under medical supervision until late second or third trimester, extensive medical, social, and attitudinal information was obtained on the entire population prenatally, as well as at the time of delivery and at postpartum visits to the clinic.

Gynecologically older and younger adolescents were similar with regard to race and indicators of socioeconomic background. There was a significant age difference between the two groups ($p < 0.0001$). The mean ($\pm$ SD) chronological age of the gynecologically older group was 16.3 $\pm$ 0.1 years at the time of conception, whereas in the younger group it was 15.0 $\pm$ 0.2 years. On the average the older group had a mean gynecologic age of 4.2 $\pm$ 0.1 years compared to 1.4 $\pm$ 0.1 years in the younger group ($p < 0.0001$).

In Table 9-2 characteristics of the mothers and infants in the two groups are compared. No statistically significant differences were found between the gynecologically older and younger adolescents with regard to history of prepregnancy weight, height measured at the first clinic visit, or weight gain during pregnancy. Adolescents with a low gynecologic age were significantly older at menarache ($p < 0.0001$) and significantly younger when they first engaged in sexual intercourse ($p < 0.0003$). On the average, gynecologically young adolescents first engaged in intercourse 9 months after menarche, compared with an average interval of 2 years 11 months for the gynecologically older group.

There were no differences between groups in their infants' birth weight, length, head circumference, gestational age, or weight of the placenta (Table 9-2). In addition, no group differences were found for antecedent health problems, amount of prenatal care, complications of pregnancy or delivery, the condition of infant at delivery, or the number or severity of neonatal problems (data for the entire study group are shown in Fig. 9-1).

Table 9-2. Mean Values for Younger and Older Groups of Mothers and Their Infants

Characteristics	Gynecologic Age		Chronological Age at Conception	
	2 Years or More (N = 343)	Under 2 Years (N = 55)	16 Years or More (N = 227)	Under 16 Years (N = 173)
Mothers				
Prepregnancy weight (lb)	125.6	119.9	125.6	123.8
Height (in.)	63.6	63.4	63.6	63.4
Age at menarche (years)	12.2	13.6*	12.6	12.0‡
Age at first intercourse (years)	15.1	14.3†	15.9	13.9‡
Pregnancy weight gain (lb)	27.2	24.3	26.9	26.8
Infants				
Weight (g)	3126.1	3052.4	3116.8	3114.1
Length (cm)	49.6	48.8	49.5	49.5
Placental weight (g)	629.9	598.2	626.1	625.0
Gestational age (weeks)	39.1	39.4	39.2	39.0
Head circumference (cm)	34.3	34.3	34.3	34.3
Age of infant's Father (years)	19.3	19.0	19.7	18.7§

From Hollingsworth DR, Kotchen JM: Gynecologic age and its relation to neonatal outcome, in McAnarney ER, Stickle G (eds): Pregnancy and Childbearing during Adolescence: Research Priorities for the 1980's. New York, Alan R. Liss, 1981, pp 91–105. With permission.
*$p < 0.0001$.   ‡$p < 0.001$.
†$p < 0.0003$.   §$p < 0.004$.

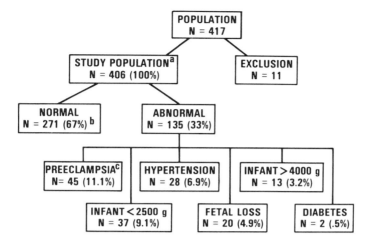

a The study population contained 219 black (54%) and 187 white (46%) patients
b All percentages based on study population
c Abnormal subgroups are not always mutally exclusive

Figure 9-1. Outcome of pregnancy in Kentucky Young Mother's Program for primiparous adolescents, 1971–1974. (From Hollingsworth DR, Kreutner AKK: Outcome of adolescent pregnancy, in Kreutner AKK, Hollingsworth DR (eds): Adolescent Obstetrics and Gynecology. Copyright © 1978 by Year Book Medical Publishers, Inc., Chicago. With permission.)

Because adequacy of dietary intake has been associated with pregnancy outcome, the dietary intake of all adolescents participating in the Young Mother's Program was determined. Dietary adequacy was assessed by a grading system based on detailed questioning of adolescents prenatally. Diets were classified as excellent, good, fair, or poor based on dietary history. The distribution of dietary ratings was significantly different for the two groups (Fig. 9-2). A greater proportion of the older group had excellent to good dietary intakes in comparison with the younger group ($p < 0.03$). The relatively large proportion of women in both groups with "poor" dietary ratings suggests that dietary counseling is of special concern in prenatal care of both older and younger adolescents.

Attitudinal responses to pregnancy were assessed. The proportions of gynecologically older and younger teenagers who expressed "happy," "mixed up," "afraid," "depressed" or other feelings about pregnancy are shown in Figure 9-3. Gynecologically younger adolescents more often expressed replies of either "happy" or "afraid" and less often described "mixed up" or "depressed" feelings than did gynecologically older adolescents. Surprisingly few teenagers in either group voiced "other" feelings, a category which included expressions of "disbelief," "guilt," or "anger."

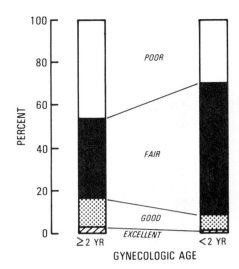

Figure 9-2. Prenatal dietary ratings for gynecologically older and younger adolescents.

A major concern with regard to early childbearing is the impact it will have on final educational attainment. Educational level at first pregnancy was assessed by determining the last grade in school completed at the time of the first clinic visit (Fig. 9-4). Gynecologically young adolescents had a lower educational status at the time of first pregnancy: 78 percent had a ninth grade education or less compared with 47 percent of the older group. Only 10 percent of the older group, and none of the younger group, had completed high school. Gynecologically immature pregnant adolescents and almost one-half of more physiologically mature pregnant teenagers were concentrated at the junior high school level. These findings suggest that

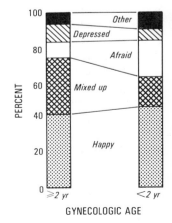

Figure 9-3. Attitudinal response to pregnancy expressed by gynecologically older and younger adolescents.

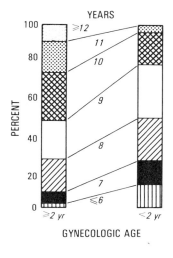

Figure 9-4. Educational grade completed by gynecologically older and younger adolescents at time of first pregnancy.

major interventions designed to prevent or address the social, economic, and educational problems experienced by early childbearing women must occur before high school.

Because the actual age at which pregnancy occurs may be closely related both to the experience of being pregnant and to the medical, social, and economic outcomes of pregnancy, the data from the Kentucky Young Mother's Program were also analyzed by chronological age of the mother at the time of conception. Age at conception was calculated by determining the difference between the mother's age at the time of delivery and the estimated length of the infant's gestation based on physical examinations during pregnancy and on the reported date of the last menstrual period. Mothers were arbitrarily categorized as being "older" adolescent mothers if their age at conception was 16 years or more. "Young" adolescent mothers were those who were under 16 years at conception. The mean (± SD) age at conception of the older adolescent group was 17.2 ± 0.05 years; in the younger group it was 14.9 ± 0.06 years. Gynecologic ages of these two groups were 4.5 ± 0.1 and 2.8 ± 0.1 years, respectively ($p < 0.0001$).

No differences between the older and younger groups were found for prepregnancy weight, height measured at the first clinic visit, or weight gained during pregnancy (Table 9-2). The older adolescents were significantly older at menarche ($p < 0.0001$) and when they first engaged in sexual intercourse ($p < 0.0001$). On the average, 3.3 years elapsed between menarche and the initiation of sexual activity in the older group, compared with 1.9 years in the younger group.

No group differences were found between older and younger adolescents for antecedent health problems, number of prenatal visits, complications of pregnancy, labor, or delivery, the condition of the infant at delivery, or the number or severity of neonatal problems. No group differences were found in infant birth weight, length, placental weight, gestational age, or head circumference (Table 9-2). Fathers of infants born to older adolescents were significantly older than the fathers of infants born to younger mothers ($p <$ 0.0004).

There was a striking difference in the racial composition of chronologically older and younger mothers. In those over 16 years of age there was an equal racial distribution (46.5 percent black). In sharp contrast, chronologically younger mothers were predominantly (63.6 percent) black ($p <$ 0.0006). Despite significant racial differences between age groups, selected socioeconomic indicators suggested that the groups were comparable with regard to socioeconomic status. There were no group differences in annual family income, type of residence (i.e., public housing, single family homes, apartments, etc.), number of occupants in the household, home ownership, or number of siblings. However, a significantly greater proportion of adolescents who were under 16 years at the time of conception were recipients of food stamps, medicaid coverage, and aid to dependent children.

Most teenagers in the younger age group (65 percent) had completed the eighth or ninth grades in school at the time of conception, whereas a majority of the older group (59 percent) had completed either the tenth or eleventh grades in school. Less than 10 percent of the older adolescents and none of the younger group had completed high school at the time of conception. Among those who had not completed high school, a significantly greater proportion ($p < 0.001$) of the younger adolescents (61 percent) than older adolescents (47 percent) were students at the time of their first clinic visit (Fig. 9-5). Of those who dropped out, 75 percent of the younger school

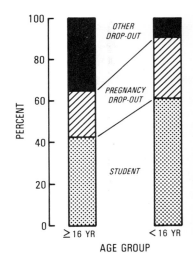

Figure 9-5. School status of older and younger adolescents at time of first prenatal clinic visit.

dropouts had quit school specifically because of their pregnancy, while most of the older school dropouts (62 percent) had quit for unrelated reasons which often antedated their pregnancies.

Each adolescent was asked what plans she had for herself after the arrival of her baby. Postpartum plans for older and younger adolescents differed. As indicated in Figure 9-6, 89 percent of young adolescents planned to return to school following their pregnancies, compared with 60 percent of older adolescents ($p < 0.0001$). Very few young adolescents contemplated working and only 9 percent planned to stay at home. Comparable values for older adolescents who planned to work or stay at home were 22 percent and 18 percent, respectively.

Almost all young women participating in the Kentucky program planned to keep their babies. Prenatally, all teenagers were asked whom they perceived as caretaker of the infant. The response of older and younger groups were quite different. Almost 70 percent of the younger group saw their own mothers playing a significant role in care of the baby ($p < 0.0001$), and only 4 percent perceived themselves alone as primary caretaker (Fig. 9-7). In contrast, the older group was relatively equally divided between those who saw themselves as caretakers, those who saw the baby's father playing a role, and those who perceived their own mothers as participating significantly in the care of the baby.

As part of the comprehensive prenatal assessment for the purpose of providing appropriate individual counseling, all adolescents were interviewed to determine the extent of their knowledge regarding sex and the adequacy of their information on contraceptive methods. Younger adolescents were less well informed than those in the older age group (Fig. 9-8). Among

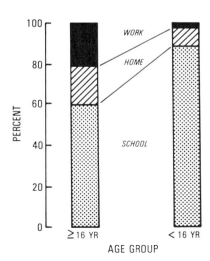

Figure 9-6. Postpartum plans of older and younger adolescents expressed at prenatal evaluation. A significantly greater number of young teenagers planned to return to school ($p < 0.0001$).

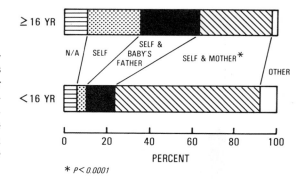

Figure 9-7. Perceived caretakers for the infant as planned by older and younger adolescents. Younger teenagers perceived their mothers and themselves to be the infant caretakers more often than did older teenagers (*p* < 0.0001).

those under 16 years of age, 15 percent had no knowledge or information about sex, compared to 3 percent uninformed among older adolescents. Twice as many younger adolescents (41 percent) had little knowledge of sex, as those in the older group (20 percent), and 77 percent of older adolescents had some or extensive information about sex compared to 45 percent of the younger group. Similar group differences were found with regard to the adequacy of knowledge concerning contraceptive methods. A greater percentage of older adolescents had an adequate knowledge of contraception compared to the younger group (Fig. 9-9).

This experience with a large population of pregnant adolescents at the time of first pregnancy suggests the following:

- Adolescents with a gynecologic age of less than 2 years at the time of their first pregnancies, or adolescents less than 16 years of age at conception, do not differ from older groups with respect to antecedent

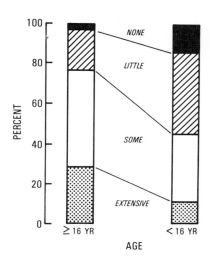

Figure 9-8. Assessment of knowledge of sex in older and younger adolescents.

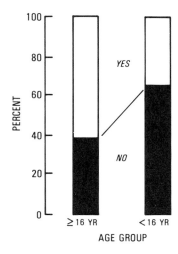

Figure 9-9. Adequacy of knowledge concerning methods of contraception in older and younger adolescents.

medical problems, complications of pregnancy, and pregnancy outcome at delivery.

- Gynecologically and chronologically younger adolescents differ significantly from gynecologically more mature or chronologically older adolescents with regard to age at menarche and age at which sexual activity is initiated.
- Younger and older adolescents are primarily distinguished by racial distribution, levels of educational attainment, prenatal school status, knowledge of sex and contraceptive methods, attitudes toward the pregnancy, and postpartum plans for themselves and their infants.

We concluded from our review of the Kentucky Young Mother's Program that neither a low gynecologic age nor a low chronological age could be shown to distinguish adolescents with respect to medical complications of pregnancy or neonatal outcome.

FOLLOW-UP OF KENTUCKY PROGRAM TEENAGERS 6 AND 9 YEARS AFTER FIRST PREGNANCY

The true measure of outcome of pregnancy lies in the long-term effects of early childbearing. In 1977 and 1980 Kotchen examined a subset of 121 (28 percent) of the women in the original Kentucky study. For all variables examined (age, race, socioeconomic status, and education), no differences were found between those observed at follow-up and in the original study. The mothers in the older and younger groups now had mean ages of 25 and

22 years, respectively. Almost all mothers had elected to keep their infants; the relatively few adolescents who decided to place their babies for adoption were excluded from follow-up. All mothers and their first children were interviewed in their homes and were also seen in the clinic for physical examination and selected medical tests. During the second follow-up (1980) information was obtained on three generations: the young mother, the child, and the young mother's mother. Because only a small number of women in the follow-up group had had a gynecologic age of less than 2 years at conception, most analyses were restricted to comparisons between women who conceived before 16 years of age and those who conceived at 16 years or older. On the average 7 years had elapsed since these women had experienced their first pregnancy.

In Table 9-3 selected characteristics of adolescents who were less than 16 years old at the time of conception are compared with those of adolescents who were 16 years or more. Heights and weights were measured at the time of the first prenatal visit and at home during both follow-up visits in order to determine whether adolescents had reached their full stature at the time of their first pregnancy. No differences were found between the mean heights of older and younger adolescents either at the time of pregnancy or at 6–9 year follow-up. Neither group of young mothers had grown during the interval between, suggesting that even young adolescents have cessation of linear growth which antedates or is associated with first pregnancy. This may reflect epiphyseal closure following the marked increase in estrogens and androgens during gestation. Weight, however, was found to increase substantially and consistently between the time antedating first pregnancy and the first follow-up, and between the first and second follow-up studies. By 1980, the older and younger groups had gained 22 and 27 lb, respectively.

Table 9-3. Mean Values for Younger and Older Groups of Mothers at 6–9 Year Follow-up

| | Mother's Age at Conception | |
| | 16 Years or More ($N = 70$) | Under 16 Years ($N = 51$) |
Characteristic		
Age in 1980 (years)	25.0	22.4*
Years post partum	7.2	6.9
Height during pregnancy (in.)	63.4	63.3
Height at follow-up (in.)	63.5	63.3
Prepregnancy weight (lb)	128.5	122.2
Weight at follow-up (lb)	146.6	149.2

From Hollingsworth DR, Kotchen JM: Gynecologic age and its relation to neonatal outcome, in McAnarney ER, Stickle G (eds): Pregnancy and Childbearing during Adolescence: Research Piriorities for the 1980's. New York, Alan R. Liss, 1981, pp 91–105. With permission.
*$p < 0.001$.

Clinical assessment of the young mothers revealed that the major health problem was inactivity and continued weight gain, with frank obesity apparent in many members of the group.

A significant group difference in education continued to exist at follow-up. The younger group had completed 9.9 years of schooling, which was significantly less ($p < 0.03$) than the 10.7 years completed by the older group.

The cumulative percentage distribution of educational attainment for both groups of young mothers is shown in Figure 9-10. The entire distribution of educational attainment for the younger mothers was shifted to lower grade levels than the distribution for older adolescents. These findings suggest that early adolescent childbearing is associated not only with relatively low educational status, but also with lower subsequent educational status.

The cumulative distribution for the total number of pregnancies experienced by each age group is shown in Figure 9-11. The younger group experienced slightly more pregnancies than the older group (mean 2.8 versus 2.4). In 1980 the younger and older groups had an average of 2.5 and 2.2 living children, respectively (no significant difference).

At 6–9 year follow-up, 59 percent of the adolescent mothers had never married, and marital status did not differ for the older and younger groups. All of the women remained sexually active and it was of interest to compare methods of contraception. The findings were quite surprising (Table 9-4). Bitubal ligations had been performed in 36.7 percent of the women and an additional 5.1 percent had had a hysterectomy. Thus, 41.8 percent had completed their childbearing while still in their early 20s. Oral contraceptives were used by only 22.4 percent of the group. At the time of the follow-up

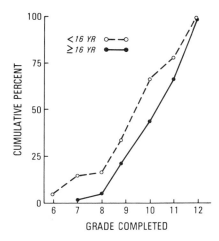

Figure 9-10. Cumulative distribution of educational attainment in 1980 by mothers who were older and younger adolescents at time of first pregnancy.

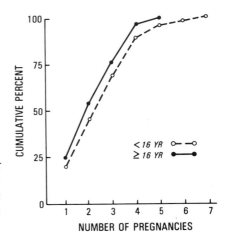

Figure 9-11. Cumulative distribution of the total number of pregnancies in 1980 experienced by mothers who were older and younger adolescents at the time of first conception.

visit 10 percent were pregnant and an additional 13 percent reported that they were not using any contraceptive method; 63 percent of the women using no contraceptive method had experienced only 1 pregnancy since the first and had had an average of 1.6 children, which was substantially fewer than the group as a whole.

The findings in this study concerning contraceptive practices in teenagers following delivery indicate that it is unrealistic for health planners to rely only on oral contraceptives for postpartum birth control in adolescents since only a small percentage will select this option for a prolonged period

Table 9-4. Contraceptive Methods Used by Young Mothers 6–9 Years Following Their First Pregnancy ($N = 121$)

Method	Percentage
Tubal ligation	36.7
Hysterectomy	5.1
Oral contraceptive	22.4
Foam/jelly	5.1
IUD	4.1
Partner uses contraceptive	2.0
Rhythm method	1.0
Pregnant	10.2
No method	13.3

From Hollingsworth DR, Kotchen JM: Gynecologic age and its relation to neonatal outcome, in McAnarney ER, Stickle G (eds): Pregnancy and Childbearing during Adolescence: Research Priorities for the 1980's. New York, Alan R. Liss, 1981, pp 91–105. With permission.

of time. The long-term emotional and psychological consequences of early permanent sterilization and/or abortion as the most common forms of birth control for young women of low socioeconomic status are unknown. Jekel et al. examined the extent to which women who become mothers while of school age use surgical means to control fertility.[28] They followed four cohorts of women who delivered a child before reaching age 18 for 6–12 years and found that 40 percent relied on abortion or sterilization. This outcome was not anticipated, particularly in the follow-up of the comprehensive Yale Young Mothers Program, which had emphasized contraception through counseling and education. These follow-up studies clearly indicate that existing methods of contraception are not adequate to meet the needs of at least 70 percent of sexually active adolescents who have experienced one or more pregnancies.

The first children of teenage mothers in the Kentucky program had an average age of 7 years in 1980 and almost all were attending school. In Figure 9-12 the pattern of child care is shown, as reflected by the persons who had assumed direct responsibility for the children. Most children (83 percent) lived with and were cared for by their natural mothers. No significant differences in living arrangements were found between the older and younger groups of mothers. Those children living with a relative other than their own mother, in general, lived with their maternal grandmother. A few of the children had been placed in foster homes ("other"). Four children had died of accidental causes.

All children were seen at both follow-up visits. Growth for the two groups of children was similar. In 1980 mothers and teachers were requested to respond to a questionnaire regarding the child's behavior and activity

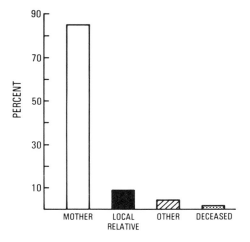

Figure 9-12. Caretakers in 1980 of the children who had been born to adolescent mothers.

level. No differences were found between the children born to the two groups of mothers.

In 1980, the maternal grandmothers of the children were visited at home and interviewed concerning their health status and pregnancy history. Sixty-seven percent of the young mother's mothers lived in the same general area as their daughters and 25 percent lived at considerable distances; 10 percent were deceased (average age at death 49.8 years). The cause of death was cancer or cardiovascular disease in 50 percent, trauma in 20 percent, and miscellaneous in 30 percent. Most of the maternal grandmothers who were alive in 1980 had completed their childbearing and were an average age of 51 years.

In a single generation there had been a striking change in reproductive patterns in this population. The cumulative frequency of pregnancies in the mothers of teenage mothers is shown Figure 9-13. The range is 2–17 pregnancies, and 50 percent had had 7 or more pregnancies. There were no differences in the number of pregnancies of women whose daughters had conceived early in adolescence compared to those who conceived later. This reproductive pattern is in marked contrast to that of their daughters: The younger group had a mean of only 2.5 and the older group 2.2 children by 1980.

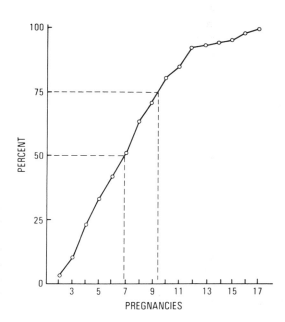

Figure 9-13. Cumulative frequency of pregnancies for mothers of teenage mothers. Inner broken line indicates that 50 percent had had 7 or more pregnancies. Almost 25 percent had had 10 or more pregnancies.

SIGNIFICANCE OF GYNECOLOGIC AGE

Childbirth at a low gynecologic age or early chronological age does not appear to have adverse medical effects when prepregnancy health and nutrition are good and excellent prenatal care is readily available.

The concept of gynecologic age has little if any practical significance since age at menarche is not a good marker for physiologic maturity.[29] More important physiologic milestones might be bone age, childhood and prepregnancy growth curves, and age at at adrenarche (increased production of adrenocortical androgens with the consequent appearance of pubic and axillary hair). It is not known whether women who conceive at early ages and have greater fecundity have earlier adrenarche and earlier onset of regular ovulatory cycles. It is also possible that behavioral correlates exist between early adrenarche and time of first coitus. These are difficult variables to assess without epidemiologic data, and no information is at hand to distinguish the role of physiology versus peer pressure and environmental pressures that lead to early reproductive behavior.

The formula for computing gynecologic age requires age at menarche as a fixed data point. This may not be historically accurate nor physiologically meaningful, as shown by the list of possible variables in Table 9-5. Since age at menarche does not imply hypothalamic-pituitary-ovarian maturity and regular ovulatory cycles at a predictable time, this index is not useful in correlating pregnancy risks after confounding variables have been eliminated. The study at the University of Colorado[16] shows that neonatal outcome is not adversely affected by low gynecologic age when good prenatal care and a regional perinatal center are available (Table 9-1). No reports have been

Table 9-5. Menarche as an Unreliable Data Point in Calculating Physiologic Maturity

Inaccurate memory and margin of error (i.e., retrospective chart review does not distinguish between 12 years and 12 years 11 months)

Menarcheal time of occurrence and physiologic significance are variable

Menarche does not imply physiologic maturity of the hypothalamic-pituitary-ovarian axis

Skeletal maturation may be a better "timekeeper" (the skeletally mature child arrives at physiologic maturity earlier)

Early maturing girls with early establishment of normal ovulatory cycles are taller and heavier than late maturing girls (weight to height ratio is also greater)

Chronological age at menarche and skeletal age at menarche are frequently not correlated (chronological age is twice as variable)

published that compare immediate or long-term pregnancy outcome in older (16–18 years) versus younger (12–15 years) adolescents of low gynecologic age.

We have been unable to find any follow-up studies on the long-term outcome of infants of mothers of low gynecologic age. Neonatal data are limited to a few reports that have recorded only birth weight and perinatal mortality. For the infant, the important questions lie in the months and years after birth.

Rothenberg and Varga investigated the relationship between maternal age at birth and children's health and development at approximately 3 years of age.[30] In their population of black and Hispanic women who delivered in New York City in 1975 they found no differences between children of teenage and older mothers in terms of prematurity or birth weight. In this analysis of long-term follow-up, 13.8 percent of the mothers were between the ages of 13 and 17 years at the time of first birth. Children of these younger mothers had higher Apgar scores than those of older mothers, even after control for a variety of independent variables was assessed. Children of young mothers scored significantly higher on measures of child development. In this study there was no support for the view that children of teenaged mothers were disadvantaged in terms of health and development compared to those of older mothers with similar poor socioeconomic levels. Infants of teenage mothers appear to be at greater risk for health and developmental problems related to economic deprivation rather than the mother's age at conception.[31]

CONCLUSIONS

During the 1970s teenage pregnancy came to be considered primarily a sociological problem with medical consequences. It has become apparent that teenage pregnancy is common in all social, economic, and racial groups in all parts of the nation. High obstetric risk has been found to be associated with poverty, inadequate nutrition, and poor prepregnancy health rather than low maternal chronological or gynecologic age. The higher rates of pregnancy-induced hypertension, anemia, prematurity, and perinatal mortality in teenagers with a low gynecologic or chronological age were documented in reports from urban clinics with 72–100 percent black patients. In sharp contrast, reports from more economically advantaged clinics with 67–91 percent white teenagers[10,11,24] did not show an increase in medical complications in teenagers age 16 years or less or their newborn infants.

In our health planning for prevention of teenage pregnancy in the future we will need a better understanding of the interaction of biologic and psychosocial factors that increase the risk of early and unplanned pregnancies. Zabin et al. noted that some adolescents have a high fertility risk factor (early age at first coitus plus conception within 1–6 months) and that this group contributes disproportionately to the pool of teenage pregnancies. More effective contraceptive counseling and implementation should be focused on those young women at high risk for repeat pregnancies and their sexual partners. Early age at menarche, early initiation of coitus, and intense peer pressure for sexual activity in junior and senior high school are powerful forces that result in pregnancy at a young age. It seems highly unlikely that simple distribution of contraceptives or poorly prepared courses in sex education can effectively combat the impetus of peer pressure and group acceptance of early sexual activity. Our problems of pregnancy in teenagers stem not so much from low gynecologic or chronological age at conception as from the sociological implications of foreclosure of personal, educational, occupational, and developmental goals.

REFERENCES

1. Williams JW: Textbook of Obstetrics. Appleton, 1917, p 250
2. Harris JW: Pregnancy and labor in young primiparae. Johns Hopkins Hosp Bull 33:12–21, 1922
3. Marchetti AA, Menaker JS: Pregnancy and the adolescent. Am J Obstet Gynecol 59:1013–1020, 1950
4. Mussio TJ: Primagravidas under age 14. Am J Obstet Gynecol 84:442–444, 1962
5. Israel SL, Woutersz TB: Teenage obstetrics: A cooperative study. Am J Obstet Gynecol 85:659–668, 1963
6. Battaglia FC, Frazer TM, Hellegers AE: Obstetrical and pediatric complications of juvenile pregnancy. Pediatrics 32:902–910, 1963
7. Hulka JF, Schaaf JT: Obstetrics in adolescents: A controlled study of deliveries by mothers 15 years of age and under. Obstet Gynecol 23:678–685, 1964
8. Sarrel PM, Davis C: The young unwed primipara: A study of 100 cases with 5 year follow-up. Am J Obstet Gynecol 95:722–725, 1966
9. Osofsky HJ, Hagen JH, Wood PW: A program for pregnant school girls. Am J Obstet Gynecol 100:1020–1027, 1968
10. Briggs RM, Herren RR, Thompson WB: Pregnancy in the young adolescent. Am J Obstet Gynecol 84:436–441, 1962
11. Claman A, Bell HM: Pregnancy in the very young teenager. Am J Obstet Gynecol 10:350–354, 1964
12. Semmens JP, Lamers WM: Teenage Pregnancy. Springfield, Ill, Thomas, 1968
13. Erkan KA, Rimer BA, Stine OC: Juvenile pregnancy. Role of physiologic maturity. Md State Med J 20:50–52, 1971
14. Zlatnik FJ, Burmeister LF: Low "gynecologic age": An obstetric risk factor. Am J Obstet Gynecol 128:183–186, 1977
15. Hollingsworth DR, Kotchen JM: Gynecologic age and its relation to neonatal outcome. Birth Defects 17:91–105, 1981

16. Perkins RP, Nakashima II, Mullin M, et al: Intensive care in adolescent pregnancy. Obstet Gynecol 52:179–188, 1978
17. Lawrence RA, Merritt TA: Infants of adolescent mothers: Perinatal, neonatal and infancy outcome. Semin Perinatol 5:19–32, 1981
18. Coates JB III: Obstetrics in the very young adolescent. Am J Obstet Gynecol 108:68–72, 1970
19. Klerman L, Jekel L: School-age Mothers: Problems, Programs and Policy. Hamden, Conn, Shoestring Press, 1973
20. Klein L: Early teenage pregnancy, contraception and repeat pregnancy. Am J Obstet Gynecol 120:249–256, 1974
21. Duenhoelter JH, Jimenez JM, Baumann G: Pregnancy performance of patients under fifteen years of age. Obstet Gynecol 46:49–52, 1975
22. Morrison JH: The adolescent primagravida. Obstet Gynecol 2:297–301, 1953
23. McGanity WV, Little HM, Fogelman H, et al: Pregnancy in the adolescent. I. Preliminary summary of health status. Am J Obstet Gynecol 103:773–788, 1969
24. Mellor S, Wright JD: Adolescent pregnancy. Practitioner 215:77–82, 1975
25. Dott AB, Fort AT: Medical and social factors affecting early teenage pregnancy. Am J Obstet Gynecol 125:532–536, 1976
26. Spellacy WN, Mahan CS, Cruz AC: The adolescent's first pregnancy: A controlled study. South Med J 71:768–771, 1978
27. Felice ME, Grandados JL, Ances IG, et al: The young pregnant teenager. J Adolesc Health Care 1:193–197, 1981
28. Jekel JF, Tyler NC, Klerman LV: Induced abortion and sterilization among women who became mothers as adolescents. Am J Public Health 67:621–625, 1977
29. Simmons K, Greulich WW: Menarcheal age and the height, weight and skeletal age of girls age 7–17. J Pediatr 22:518–548, 1943
30. Rothenberg PB, Varga PE: The relationship between age of mother and child health and development. Am J Public Health 71:810–817, 1981
31. Osofsky HJ, Kendall N: Poverty as a criterion of risk. Clin Obstet Gynecol 16:103–119, 1973
32. Zabin LS, Kantner JF, Zelnik M: The risk of adolescent pregnancy in the first months of intercourse. Fam Plann Perspect 11:215–222, 1979

Part IV

PSYCHOSOCIAL ASPECTS OF ADOLESCENT PREGNANCY AND PARENTHOOD

10

Adolescent Adaptation to Pregnancy and Parenthood

Howard J. Osofsky and Joy D. Osofsky

During pregnancy and new parenthood, the expectant and new parents are required to make major adjustments. The disequilibrium and new responsibilities that occur during this time can significantly affect the individuals' level of functioning, the relationship of the couple, and the patterns and adequacy of interaction with the new child. In our experience as well as that of others, pregnancy and the impact of the responsibilities of new parenthood can contribute to individual difficulties, family dysfunction, and, at times, increasing disagreements and estrangement of the couple.

Pregnancy has been variously described as a crisis, a developmental phase, or a developmental process. In general, the focus of the literature has been more on the mother than on the father or the couple and the resultant changes in their relationship. Where the father has been studied, much of the available research has focused either on difficulties in adjusting to, or emotional disturbances during or following, the pregnancy.

PSYCHOLOGICAL ADJUSTMENT OF THE MOTHER

Pregnancy and Psychological Stress

Many investigators have viewed pregnancy as a biologically determined period of psychological stress. Benedek suggested that pregnancy represents a developmental phase, one that is profoundly influenced by concurrent metabolic and hormonal shifts.[1] She further suggested that pregnancy results in a continuation of previous developmental processes and that it brings up earlier conflictual feelings that need to be worked through and resolved within the individual and between the couple in order to reach a new level of maturation. According to Benedek, the maturational potential is influenced both by the level of evolved psychic structural development and by psychobiologic factors in interaction with the new reality experiences of the period.

Bibring and colleagues described pregnancy for the woman, like puberty or menopause, as a period of crisis involving profound psychological as well as somatic changes.[2-4] On the basis of their work, primarily with women whom they followed longitudinally with psychoanalytically oriented interviews, social work interviews, and psychological testing, they postulated that the disturbance in equilibrium that occurs at this time may seem to be a more severe disintegration; however, the outcome of the crisis most often leads to healthy solutions. They stated that the more severe the psychological disturbances before pregnancy, the more likely it is that dramatic problems will emerge during this period. At other times, depending on the inner conflicts, the pregnancy may relieve the difficulties and promote solutions of the neurotic tensions.

Caplan described pregnancy as a "crisis" for the woman—a term that he modified in subsequent writings.[5] He suggested that the woman's emotional state varies at different stages during pregnancy depending on her adjustment to the physiologic and psychological changes. He suggested that the woman's emotional status during pregnancy is influenced by her reactions to the sexual aspects of the reproductive process; these are associated with the details of her personality structure and the vicissitudes of her sexual development. Her emotional status also reflects her psychological development during the course of pregnancy into the role of the mother; this process is influenced by her relationship with her own mother and women who serve as important models.

Caplan also noted that in pregnancy, as in all human crises, the outcome is dependent not only on the long-standing personality patterns of the participants, but also on their current life situations.[5] Thus, the outcome may be influenced by helping figures in the family and environment and services in the community. Caplan stated that preventative intervention has a potentially greater effect during this period than it would during a period of stability. He also stressed that minimal intervention during pregnancy is often remarkably effective in promoting and safeguarding not only the relationship of the mother to her future child but other relationships among family members as well.

A review of the studies of normative psychological adjustment as well as emotional disturbance and pregnancy is available in other sources.[6] In general the studies on normative adjustment indicate that while reactions may differ for an individual woman or couple during pregnancy, other factors, including age of the parents, available support systems, previous adjustment, and parenting experience, play significant roles in the process. Emotional disturbances during pregnancy seem to be related to maturational and psychological readiness for the process, emotional stability and instability at the time of pregnancy, early life experiences, the overall social situation, and probably the very significant hormonal shifts that occur.

In the course of our combined clinical and research efforts focusing on adaptation to pregnancy and new parenthood[6,7] we have also found that women experience profound psychological changes during the course of pregnancy and following the birth of their new baby. Struggles seem to be most profound with a first pregnancy.

Women's Fears about Pregnancy

In spite of, and perhaps related to, initial enthusiasm about being pregnant and a desire for the baby, many women experience fears and concerns about themselves and the unborn baby. A common worry is whether the baby will be normal. Women especially worry if there are realistic concerns, but even if there are no medical problems women still worry. They may be afraid that they will be denied the opportunity to have a healthy baby and to experience the pleasures of motherhood. They worry about whether they will or have hurt their baby. With the issues raised by modern magazines, radio, and television, mothers are especially concerned about the effects of alcohol, smoking, pills, over- and undereating, using additives, consuming artificial sweeteners, and even worrying itself.

Women also worry about themselves. They wonder whether they will die during pregnancy or especially during childbirth. Quite frequently a woman may express concern about how the infant will get out, whether she will be injured in the process, whether her body will be distorted or mutilated. Especially with a first pregnancy, the woman may ponder how she will know when labor has begun, whether she will get to the hospital on time, what will labor and delivery be like, how much will it hurt, and whether she will lose control.

The Effect of Body Changes on Women's Feelings

All women have concerns about the changes in their bodies during pregnancy. These feelings vary considerably, depending on the woman, the support she receives, and the attitudes that she has acquired from her mother and other important people in her life. For many women, pregnancy and motherhood represent truly becoming a woman; some women describe feeling like a woman for the first time only after the onset of a pregnancy. Especially with the first pregnancy, women may enjoy the early signs of pregnancy and the beginnings of looking pregnant, wearing maternity clothes, and the stares and changed attitudes of people around them. However, not all of the feelings about their looks are happy ones. Many women feel awkward and ugly—some from the beginning of the pregnancy. As the pregnancy progresses, women may describe themselves as fat, looking like balloons, or being distorted. Women who have prided themselves on being young, attractive, and slim may find it difficult to adjust to the changes in their weight and figures. They often wonder whether they will regain their figures after pregnancy.

Physical symptoms may be especially disconcerting to the woman. Increased breast fullness and breast sensitivity may cause discomfort and even pain. Women may worry about the frequency of urination, constipation, and periodic fatigue that frequently accompany pregnancy. Various smells may become offensive to them. They may have problems eating or engaging in intercourse because of negative reactions to normal odors.

Emotional Changes Due to Pregnancy

Pregnant women experience various psychological shifts. Especially after they feel quickening, women frequently become preoccupied with themselves and their coming babies. At times, it may seem as though pregnant women have room for no one else. They frequently experience mood swings that are dramatic and more extreme than they have experienced previously. For many women, the changes in mood seem relatively unprovoked and difficult to control.

The Effect of Emotional Changes on Relationships

There are frequently alterations in relationships with husbands or boyfriends. Some but not all of the changes relate to growing concerns with the coming baby. The mother-to-be may become progressively aware of the changes in her life that are going to follow the birth of the baby. She may worry about the necessary adjustments in her education, work, and social life. She may begin to resent her husband or boyfriend because of the required changes in her life that he does not have to make. These feelings may alternate with warm desires for motherhood and the coming baby. At the same time the woman may be aware of a growing feeling of dependence upon her husband, or if unmarried but in a stable relationship, upon her boyfriend. She may develop more concerns about his job, his earning capacity, and his overall providing abilities. She may express comfort over this growing sense of dependence, or she may feel resentful and wish to maintain independence at all costs. She may describe, perhaps for the first time, a growing concern about the marriage or relationship. Whereas her husband or boyfriend may have been a fine spouse or lover, the mother-to-be may wonder, and at times with a realistic basis, whether he has the capacity or desire to be a responsible father and provide the emotional security necessary for themselves and their future children.

Feelings after Childbirth

Following the birth of the baby, a new mother may experience confusing feelings. While in the hospital she may feel alone and isolated. Some women have also described missing the feeling of being pregnant and of not having the baby still within the uterus. In addition, women describe an awareness of the very real changes that are going on in their lives. More than they had expected, they feel confronted with the responsibilities of parenthood. When they go home from the hospital and are confronted by fatigue and by the baby's demands, frequently they question when this will end. It takes a considerable time for people to realize that the old sense of what was normal will not return, but that a different and hopefully comfortable kind of normalcy will occur. The problems and adjustments are often more intense and complicated for adolescent mothers.

PSYCHOLOGICAL ADJUSTMENT OF THE FATHER

In comparison with the literature on expectant motherhood, considerably less work has been carried out on expectant fatherhood, and very little has dealt with the experiences of adolescent fathers.[8] Some authors have described the male's developmental progression toward fatherhood from a psychoanalytical perspective.[9-15] However, the available clinical studies concerning adjustment to expectant and new fatherhood have focused on emotional difficulties that men experience during their wives' pregnancies or new parenthood rather than on the process itself as a developmental phase. Since 1970, there has been some increase in the number of studies, although they have addressed primarily somewhat related areas such as the role of the father during labor and delivery and a reconsideration of the role of the father in child development.[16] Fundamental developmental considerations of mechanisms of the coping process have continued to receive relatively little emphasis, and there has been a tendency to continue to minimize the adjustments that normal males make in response to pregnancy and new parenthood. Parke et al. suggested that the "mother-centered" bias in our culture is particularly acute for adolescent parents, but that available evidence indicates that adolescent fathers may be actively involved in the early development of their infants and children.[17]

Psychological Stress

As with the reports of others, we have observed men who have experienced gross psychiatric disturbance apparently precipitated by expectant or new fatherhood.[18] We have been struck by the finding that men who had no histories of overt psychiatric symptoms preceding the pregnancy experienced considerable lability and feelings of being unsettled during the pregnancy and following the birth of the baby.[6,7] As with the more disturbed individuals, the choice and timing of symptoms—and the degree of adequacy of solutions—seems to be related to unresolved conflicts and developmental difficulties. Life circumstances, including age, degree of economic stability, religious background and patterns, family and community support, and the strength and flexibility of the relationship all seem to be important for the father's adjustment to parenthood.

Most of the studies focusing on the male's development of emotional symptoms in response to his wife's pregnancy or the birth of the baby have approached the topic utilizing the case history method with intensive study of a few men.[19-23] In general, the findings of available studies indicate that pregnancy is a crucial time that may contribute to emotional difficulties in men who may be predisposed because of a variety of developmental and personal circumstances. Often the men who develop symptoms had unfulfilled dependency needs and became extremely demanding, which placed additional stress on their wives. On the basis of these studies, it appears that more attention should be given to the adjustment processes of the prospective father. Defining and identifying significant changes that occur, the necessary adjustments that are required, and strategies for intervention and support seem to be very much needed. In one of the few studies on adolescent fathers, Hendricks found that many of the young fathers expressed interest in attending a teenage parenting agency if it offered services for unwed adolescent fathers.[24] Parke et al. also described the nature of support systems that may help adolescent fathers with their parental role and provided empirical evidence of one type of supportive intervention.[17]

Emotional Reactions

In our clinical and research efforts concerning the adaptation to fatherhood, we have found that most married men experience an initial sense of excitement and pride when they find out that their wives are pregnant. There are obviously exceptions, for example, men who have been forced into a marriage because of the pregnancy or men who have felt tricked or pressured into the pregnancy. Frequently the pregnancy has made the men feel more manly, thus helping to settle doubts about their virility and potency and concerns about whether their wives might leave them for other men. Although our experience with single and adolescent fathers has been less systematic, we have been impressed that feelings of virility and manliness are important components of the initial complex reaction to the pregnancy.

Following the initial sense of excitement and pride, other feelings frequently emerge. Husbands describe feeling strange—not totally themselves. Some have talked worriedly about the current and anticipated changes in their lives and in their relationships with their wives. A considerable number in various ways have spoken about their feelings of neediness and rivalry toward the baby. Most men have described a greater sense of responsibility for which they may not feel ready and which at times seems overwhelming. Some unmarried men, at times with less commitment to the relationship or parenthood, may respond to these feelings b disclaiming responsibility and ending the relationship. Because the mother-to-be is preoccupied with the coming baby, men frequently feel alone and sense a loss of intimacy and difficulty in communicating. At times they are frightened by the changes that are occurring and are concerned that their partner may die during childbirth and leave them alone.

Some men have described feelings of envy of the woman's ability to reproduce and have a baby growing within her body. They feel like bystanders, unable to experience directly the changes in fetal growth, the beginning feelings of life, and the patterns of fetal movement. In order to compensate for these feelings, a number of men have found themselves engaging in other areas of interest at work or in creative efforts.

At times men have expressed other worries about becoming fathers. They wonder generally what kind of fathers will they be. Will they be like their fathers or, as many men desire, be able to do things differently? Will they be adequate parents and role models for their children?

Men who are married or in stable relationships frequently experience new feelings about their partners. For example, married men often describe being more comfortable with their wives, feeling greater warmth and tenderness, and seeing them as being more beautiful during the pregnancy. Yet at the same time men, at least intermittently, may also view their wives as ugly and clumsy. They may take the mood shifts and frustrations that their wives experience as personal criticisms. Thus, men often find themselves reacting irritably toward their wives, with these mixed feelings evoking a sense of confusion and guilt.

Because of men's conflicts about neediness and taking on the parental role, pregnancy is a time when they frequently engage in fantasies about other women. A small number of married men have affairs during this time. A larger number have described their intermittent wishes to be out of the relationship or marriage—with subsequent feelings of confusion and guilt. They may worry whether this woman, whom they have loved as a companion and/or a spouse, is the woman whom they wish to be the mother of their children—they wonder whether she will measure up to their own mothers. They may also experience a sense of panic, a feeling of being trapped, of wondering whether they are ready to settle down, have children, and accept the responsibilities of parenthood. Although feeling guilty, a number of men, whether married or unmarried, have on occasion voiced the question, "Is the child really mine? You can be sure of the mother but not the father."[25]

SPECIAL TASKS AND CONCERNS OF ADOLESCENT PARENTS

When one considers the stresses and disequilibrium that individuals experience in the process of becoming parents and the resultant impact on the family, the age of the parents would appear to assume extreme importance. As we have indicated, the process of becoming parents is difficult in general; the task for adolescents appears even harder. The pregnancy and new baby may bring up important developmental considerations for young parents. In addition to the struggles already mentioned, they may have to cope with difficult psychological and realistic situations. If single, the young mothers are confronted by their family's attitude—and frequently their parents' disappointment, their changing role within the family, educational and job considerations, and restrictions in their still adolescent social lives. After a period of idealistic enthusiasm about the possibilities of marrying the father-to-be, they may also be confronted by the realities of a male who may wish for no responsibility and possibly no further commitment. If married, or if they marry, they need to cope with the adjustments to marriage and the responsibilities of parenthood at a time when they may not have resolved important developmental tasks.[26,27] At least in part related to their changing roles and responsibilities, they are less likely to complete as many years of schooling as their classmates, and they are more likely to have less satisfying and lower-paying jobs than their peers.[28] Although the discrepancies are somewhat less for adolescent fathers, they too tend to achieve less education and are more likely to become blue-collar workers than their peers.[28] Because adolescent marriages are frequently preceded by conception,[29,30] the couple may also have to struggle with consolidating their marriage with a limited courtship and the burdens accompanying the care of a child.[31-33] When pregnancy precedes marriage, couples tend to fare less well financially than their peers.[34] A combination of factors, including age, economic instability, family pressure, individual problems, and inadequate social supports, contributes to a much higher incidence of divorce in these couples than in the population at large.[26,28,31,35,36]

A recent issue of the *Journal of Social Issues* was devoted to adolescent pregnancy.[37] Several themes appeared consistently in many of the papers: (1)

the crucial role played by the teenage mother's mother; (2) the importance of a variety of social support systems; (3) the set of events leading to positive as well as negative consequences for the woman and her family; and (4) the idea of increased choices. The overall issues being explored in the papers in this special volume were the consequences, both positive and negative, for the teenage mother and those involved with her of her bearing a child and undertaking the role of teenage parent.

A recent issue of the *American Journal of Orthpsychiatry* also focused on teenage pregnancy in an attempt to understand issues including social and psychological correlates of pregnancy resolution, psychological factors involved in earlier attachment and interaction, concerns of adolescent fathers, and issues of child abuse and maltreatment.[38] The conclusions emanating from the reviews and research in the area are that there are many complicated issues involved that have yet to be better understood. It is not possible to make overall assumptions or to generalize.

Support Systems

An important factor contributing to pressure on adolescent parents is the changes in support systems that have occurred in recent decades. Available support, particularly on a long-term basis from family, society, and religion, is in general more limited than it was at a time with less geographic mobility and different values. The adolescent couple, if married, often does not experience much support from professionals, peers, or an informed community and religious network. They may receive little help from their parents, who may indeed perceive of the marriage as pulling them away from the family network.[35] Community services are often fragmented and crisis oriented and do not fill the void created by the decline in traditional supports. Other forms of support, such as welfare programs, have results that are complex and difficult to interpret. For example, while there are obvious benefits from welfare programs, there have been discrepant findings concerning whether there is an association between payment level and marital breakup.[39-41] Sawhill et al. found a lower frequency of remarriage among divorced women who were welfare recipients, an association that may have multiple explanations.[42] Recently, we helped develop and evaluate an intervention program in Kansas City, Kansas, in which all new mothers received hospital visits, support, and education. Also, as necessary or desired, mothers received follow-up home visits.[43] Mothers at greatest risk, especially young mothers, frequently experienced relatively little support from spouses, boyfriends, families, or community resources. Of some note, relatively small increases in professional and community support appear to be of considerable help to the parents and their infants. Economic considerations interacting with the usual stresses of new parenthood likely contribute to difficulties in parenting and the high incidence of separation and divorce in young economically disadvantaged couples.

CONCLUSIONS

Even psychologically normal women experience considerable psychological upheavals during pregnancy and the adjustment to a new baby. Women must be able to integrate the maturational changes and adjustments that come with this period in order to achieve a new equilibrium. Under optimal conditions, the process may result in an opportunity for further growth. At other times, the experience may lead to long-lasting difficulty or poor adjustment.

It is our belief that all men, especially when they become fathers for the first time, undergo considerable shifts and internal disequilibrium when a spouse or girlfriend is pregnant, and a few if any are the same afterward. Some men may experience conscious severe upheavals. Most men experience profound changes in their sense of responsibility, in their relationship with their spouse, and in their feelings about themselves.

Many factors stress the relationship of expectant parents. Although there may be meaningful and growth-related considerations for some adolescents in undertaking a pregnancy, adolescent parents have important age-related developmental tasks of their own. Their educational and economic opportunities may be compromised. They may feel—and may be—unready for the responsibilities of marriage. The family, religious, and community supports may be fragmentary and inadequate.

It is important to understand the increased difficulties that often occur at this time as part of a normative process. Erikson described major steps in human growth and stressed the reactions and upheavals that occur as part of the growth process.[11,44] Considerable disequilibrium and crisis can herald the beginning of a new growth process. However, in adolescence, a major developmental task to be accomplished has to do with identity formation. An adolescent at some point must deal with issues of "Who am I?" and "Who do I want to be?" Having to go through the struggle of finding a direction for one's life at the same time as accepting the responsibilities of parenting can create major problems and conflicts. Such a situation can be disruptive to both the parent and the child. The adjustments and conflicts that result may depend on the individual's personality and life circumstances at the beginning of and during the process. The outcome for adolescent parents and their offspring will depend both on inner resources and support from family, community, and environment. Under optimal circumstances and with appropriate support and intervention, pregnancy and parenthood may offer the opportunity for an enhancement of the maturational process and a positive outcome for the adolescent parents and their offspring.

REFERENCES

1. Benedek T: Parenthood as a developmental phase: A contribution to the libido theory. J Am Psychoanal Assoc 7:389–417, 1959
2. Bibring GL: Some considerations of the psychological processes in pregnancy. Psychoanal Study Child 14:113–121, 1959
3. Bibring GL, Dwyer TF, Huntington DS, et al: A study of the psychological processes in pregnancy and of the earliest mother–child relationship. I. Some propositions and comments. Psychoanal Study Child, 16:9–24, 1961
4. Bibring GL, Dwyer TF, Huntington DS, et al: A study of the psychological processes in pregnancy and the earliest mother–child relationship. II. Methodological con sid- erations. Psychoanal Study Child, 16:25–72, 1961
5. Caplan G: Psychological aspects of maternity care. Am J Public Health, 47:25–31, 1957
6. Osofsky HJ, Osofsky JD: Normal adaptation to pregnancy and new parenthood, in Taylor PM (ed): Parent–Infant Relationships. New York, Grune & Stratton, 1980
7. Osofsky JD, Osofsky HJ: Psychological and developmental perspectives on expectant and new parenthood, in Parke RD (ed): Review of Child Development Research. Chicago, University of Chicago Press, 1982 (in press)
8. Earls F, Siegel B: Precocious fathers. Am J Orthopsychiatry 50:469–480, 1980
9. Jacobson E: Development of the wish for a child in boys. Psychoanal Study Child 5:139–152, 1950
10. Brunswick RM: The preoedipal phase of libido development. Psychoanal Q 9:293–319, 1940
11. Erikson E: Childhood and Society. New York, Norton, 1950
12. Parens H: Parenthood as a developmental phase. J Am Psychoanal Assoc 23:154–165, 1975
13. Ross JM: The development of paternal identity: A critical review of the literature of nurturance and generativity in boys and men. J Am Psychoanal Assoc 23:783–817, 1975
14. Ross JM: Towards fatherhood: The epigenesis of paternal identity during a boy's first decade. Int Rev Psychoanal 4:327–349, 1977
15. Ross JM: Fathering: A review of some psychoanalytic contributions on paternity. Int J Psychoanal 60:317–327, 1979
16. Parke R: Perspectives on father–infant interaction, in Osofsky JD (ed): Handbook of Infant Development. New York, Wiley, 1979
17. Parke RD, Power TG, Fisher T: The adolescent father's impact on the mother and child. J Soc Issues 36:88–106, 1980
18. Osofsky HJ: Expectant and new fatherhood as a developmental crisis. Bull Menninger Clin 406:209–230, 1982
19. Zilboorg G: Depressive reactions related to parenthood. Am J Psychiatry 87:927–963, 1931
20. Jarvis W: Some effects of pregnancy and childbirth on men. J Am Psychoanal Assoc 10:689–700, 1962

21. Freeman T: Pregnancy as a precipitant of mental illness in men. Br J Med Psychol 24:49–54, 1951

22. Ginath Y: Psychoses in males in relation to their wives' pregnancy and childbirth. Isr Ann Psychiatry 12:227–237, 1974

23. Wainwright WH: Fatherhood as a precipitant of mental illness. Am J Psychiatry 123:40–44, 1966

24. Hendricks LE: Unwed adolescent fathers: Problems they face and their sources of social support. Adolescence 15:861–869, 1980

25. Strindberg A: The Father. Boston, International Pocket Library, 1912

26. Moore K, Waite L, Hofferth S, et al: The consequences of age at first childbirth: Marriage, separation, and divorce. Washington, DC, Urban Institute, 1978

27. Osofsky JD, Osofsky HJ: Teenage pregnancy: Psychosocial considerations. Clin Obstet Gynecol 21:1161–1174, 1978

28. Card J, Wise L: Teenage mothers and teenage fathers: The impact of early childbearing on the parents' personal and professional lives. Fam Plann Perspect 10:199–205, 1978

29. Hetzel A, Cuppetta M: Teenagers: Marriages, divorces, parenthood, and mortality. Vital and Health Statistics, Series 21, no. 23, 1973

30. Zelnik M, Kantner J: Sexual activity, contraceptive use and pregnancy among metropolitan-area teenagers: 1971–1979. Fam Plann Perspect 12:230–231, 233–237, 1980

31. Furstenberg F: Unplanned Parenthood. New York, Free Press, 1976

32. Osofsky HJ, Osofsky JD, Kendall N, et al: Adolescents as mothers: An interdisciplinary approach to a complex problem. J Youth Adolesc 2:233–249, 1973

33. Pohlman E: Psychology of Birth Planning. Cambridge, England, Schenkman, 1969

34. Freedman D, Thornton A: The long-term impact of pregnancy at marriage on the family's economic circumstances. Fam Plann Perspect 11:6–21, 1979

35. Stack C: All Our Kin. Chicago, Aldine, 1974

36. McCarthy J, Menken J: Marriage, remarriage, marital disruption and age at first birth. Fam Plann Perspect 11:21–30, 1979

37. Teenage parenting: Social determinants and consequences. J Soc Issues (special issue) 36:1–144, 1980

38. Teenage parenting. Am J Orthopsychiatry 50:403–504, 1980

39. Cherlin A: The effect of children on marital dissolution. Demography 14:264–272, 1977

40. Cutright P: Income and family events: Marital stability. J Marriage Fam 33:291–306, 1971

41. Moles O: Marital dissolution and public assistance payments: Variations among American states. J Soc Issues 34:87–101, 1976

42. Sawhill I, Peabody G, Jones C, et al: Income Transfers and Family Structure. Washington, DC, Urban Institute, 1975

43. Osofsky JD, Osofsky HJ: Final Report on Healthy Start Program. State of Kansas, Department of Social and Rehabilitation Services, 1981

44. Erikson E: Growth and crisis of the "healthy personality," in Kluckholm C, Murray H, Schneider D (eds): Personality in Nature, Society and Culture (rev ed 2). New York, Knopf, 2, 1973

11

Early Mothering by Adolescents

Ruth A. Lawrence

Adolescent pregnancy has been closely scrutinized by medical and social scientists searching for the absolute factors that influence the outcome for both mother and baby.[1-4] The sequelae of adolescent childbearing have been cited as a national crisis that has concerned health care providers and government analysts alike.[5] When early medical care and good nutrition are provided, however, the outcome for mother and baby is comparable to that for older mothers of the same socioeconomic background.[6-8] The biologic vulnerability is minimal except for mothers 14 years old and younger.[9] The seeming disadvantages are attributable to an interaction of many factors: perinatal care, socioeconomic status, race, marital and educational status, parity, geographic location, and maternal prepregnancy height and weight, and not to age alone. The psychosocial risks for the childbearing adolescent herself, however, have been reported as diminished educational attainment, increased marital instability, and long-term welfare dependence.[9-11] The children of adolescents, especially male offspring, have been found by some to be smaller, sicker, slower in school, and more disruptive socially. There is a paucity of information, however, about the mothering skills of the adolescent in the plethora of studies of large groups of adolescents over extended periods of time. The literature is almost silent on the question of when an adolescent is actually ready to mother an offspring. Do the parenting practices of the adolescent differ from those of adult women? Are there long-range effects on the child who is parented by an adolescent? Can an egocentric adolescent assume a responsible parenting role and extend herself emotionally and intellectually to her infant?

MATERNAL ATTACHMENT

Investigation into the maternal behavior of adults led to the study of attachment of mother and infant. *Maternal attachment,* as first suggested by Bowlby[12] and later expanded by Ainsworth,[13] is defined as the affectional tie between mother and infant that develops out of species-specific responses that ensure that the infant will indeed be cared for by the mother. Maternal attachment to her infant is viewed as clinically relevant and identifiable as a critical development phase for a mother.[14]

The attachment of the infant to the parents has been considered essential to the optimal development of the child.[15] It is certainly an accepted principle of child development that warm nurturing and consistent interaction between infant and mother is critical to healthy psychological development. Much attention has been focused on the strength of the bond the parents have to their child. Historically, the initial observations of mother–infant interaction were made in the latter months of the first year of life until the innovative observations of Klaus and Kennel.[15] They began their observations in the first moments after birth and in the immediate neonatal period. From these observations came the suggestion that early contact between mother and baby was critical to good bonding. Bowlby had previously described the affectional ties between human beings and theorized that disturbed relationships follow distorted experiences with parents in childhood and adolescence.[12,16] He identified six infant proximity-seeking behaviors: crying, smiling, following, clinging, sucking, and calling, which are relevant to attachment. Ainsworth further organized such interactive behaviors into three categories:[17] (1) signaling (crying, smiling, vocalizing); (2) orienting (following, approaching); and (3) active physical contact (clambering up, embracing, clinging). Klaus and Kennell described specific activities of the mother toward her baby in the first few days and weeks of life that were associated with evidence of healthy mother–infant attachment at 1 and 2 years of age.[18] These activities included gentle touching, stroking, eye-to-eye contact, high-pitched voice, entrainment, and synchrony.

The term *bonding* has been used most often to refer to the process that takes place immediately after birth on initial contact, is predominantly unidirectional, and is optimized by physical contact. The term *attachment* has been used to describe the quality of the affectional tie between parent and infant that develops gradually over the first year, is reciprocal between parent and infant, and is influenced by timing and quality of the parent–infant encounters.

Both bonding and attachment have been observed in order to evaluate the relationship between the mother and her infant in an effort to predict mothering characteristics at risk as well as demonstrate that early observations have predictive significance. The initiation of these theories of predictability was based on ethnological observations in other species where behavior was highly predictable in response to certain stimuli. The behavior patterns were predicated on the organism being in a state of biologic readiness. [12,15] These subhuman mother–infant pairs were sensitive to certain species-specific cues that were often critical to survival. Observations of disturbed maternal care-taking behavior often followed intervention in certain species, as illustrated by maternal rejection of the offspring when the offspring has been removed from the mother for a period of time following birth. Species-specific maternal and infant behavior patterns in animals are stereotyped, limited in number, and predictable compared to those behaviors manifested by human mothers toward their infants. Furthermore, individual differences in mothers, in their infants, and in cultural practices influence human behaviors. In the numerous observations made by previous observers, the possibility of maternal im-maturity or readiness to mother was not considered a variable. [12,13,15–20]

MATERNAL BEHAVIOR OF ADOLESCENT MOTHERS

A number of investigators addressed the adequacy of adolescents as mothers. [21–23] These studies described adolescent mothers as impatient, in-sensitive, and prone to punish their children; however, they were descriptive and failed to separate the effects of age from those of sociocultural factors such as race and socioeconomic and marital status.

Patterns and determinants of maternal attachment were studied by Robson and Moss in 54 primiparous healthy mothers ranging in age from 18 to 34 years. [24] They observed that mothers who had been happy to be pregnant and were interested in their babies experienced immediate and intense attachments to their infants. Mothers, however, who had not been eager to have a baby developed attachment late or not at all. They did not associate outcome with maternal age in this study.

Observations in Adolescent Support Programs

Although several studies have been conducted to determine the effect of an intensive support system on the outcome of the adolescent mother and her infant, parenting by the young mother has not been studied in depth. The Young Mothers Educational Development Program in Syracuse, New York, described by Osofsky and Osofsky, provided an extensive support program for the low-income adolescent mother and her offspring. [6] Intensive medical, educational, social, and psychological services were provided in an interdisciplinary program that included classrooms, medical facilities, infant care nursery, offices, cooperative kitchen, and cafeteria all under one roof. Data were collected from all disciplines and included infant growth and development mother–child interaction observations. The ratings of the mothers' and infants' behavior before and during the pediatric examination revealed that these mothers showed warmth and physical interaction toward their infants during the observation but little verbal interaction. The infants were described as relatively active but were scored low on affectivity and responsivity. There were no control dyads, however. The authors concluded that young mothers had both strengths and weaknesses, and the interaction of these mothers and infants needs further investigation to determine any implications for child development.

In the controlled 12-year longitudinal study of 86 young mothers and matched-pair adult mothers (over 18 years of age) and their children reported by Oppel and Royston, the mothers under 18 were less likely to remain with their children, were less likely to rear their children in healthy families, and exhibited less nurturing behavior than the adult controls. [25] The adolescent mothers talked less to their children than did the adults. Oppel and Royston concluded that the youth of the mothers was a contributing factor to less adequate nurturing of their children, leading to deficits in the infants' physical, social, and/or psychological development.

Williams studied the child-rearing practices of adolescent mothers by filming them in a group home program.[26] The young mother's interaction with her child was compared to that of the caregiver in the day care center. The younger the mother the less she talked to her child and the less she picked the child up, when compared with the professional. A clear effect of age or singleness, however, was not demonstrated in this setting.

The impact of child health supervision given unmarried, black, primiparous schoolgirls from socioeconomically deprived environments after their babies were born was studied by Gutelius et al. over a 3-year period and compared with the routine child health supervision given matched controls.[27] The study mothers received professional intervention from the seventh month of their pregnancy until 36 months after delivery. Health care, counseling, and individual cognitive stimulation for their babies were all provided in their homes and group sessions. The behavior of the mothers who had received such elaborate care was compared with the behavior of mothers from similar surroundings who had not received such care. Those who had received intervention had improved diet, better eating habits, more success at toilet training their infants, and more abstract qualities, such as self-confidence and vocalization, than those who had not been given child health care. There was no attempt in this study, however, to evaluate the behavior of the adolescent mother as a function of her age. In comparison to younger mothers, older mothers have been described as spending more time with their infants and talking to them more, behavior which has been thought to stimulate infant behavior.

Grow conducted a comprehensive study of early child rearing by young mothers in which the mothers were scored on degree of pleasure in mothering, degree of contentment with their role, use of corporal punishment, and degree of strictness or permissiveness, as well as many other issues.[28] The study followed 448 mother–infant pairs for 3 years. The mothers were white, unwed primiparas under 25 years of age who had chosen to keep their children. The purpose of the study was "to explore deleterious effects of childrearing out of wedlock." Grow examined the relationship of marital status, maternal age, maternal characteristics, experiences, and attitudes. Grow found that more mothers who scored high on the Thomas-Zander Ego Strength Scale[29] found child care easier and were content with their role at 18 months postpartum. Mothers who had been under 17 years of age at the time of the birth found child care more difficult at 18 months than older mothers. The mother's age was not associated with this or any other outcome variable when the child was 3 years old. Contrary to the investigators' expectations, the mother's age at delivery was a relatively insignificant predictor of eventual outcome of the infant. They did observe that the more content the mother, the more problem free the child was at 3 years. An index of parental permissiveness was developed which ranged from no restrictions to controlling behavior at all times. At 3 years, children whose mothers were moderately strict were more likely to be well adjusted as measured by the Louisville Behavior Checklist[30] than were children whose mothers were either very strict or very permissive. Items included aggression, inhibition, cognitive disability, normal irritability, presocial deficit, neurotic behavior, somatic behavior, and severity level. It is significant that Grow's study, unlike many in the literature, was limited to white, young, unwed mothers.

Impact of Psychological Factors on Mothering

The psychological factors of teenage pregnancy and motherhood were studied by Wise and Grossman in a group of 30 adolescent mothers and their infants in whom there were few medical difficulties.[31] They found positive adjustment to motherhood through the first 6 weeks post partum. The ego strength of the adolescent and the infant's behavioral individuality were the factors most closely related to the quality of the early mother–child interaction and attachment. The mothers were healthy, predominantly black, lower socioeconomic class, and unmarried 14- to 19-year-olds who had good health care. The group was heterogeneous as to parity, educational level, and school/work status. There was, however, a high degree of family and peer support for the mothers.

The procedure included contact of the adolescent in two prenatal clinics, where they were approached for the study as "emancipated minors." There was an overall refusal rate of 39 percent (24 of 61). The study took place in the third trimester of pregnancy, immediate postpartum period, and 6 weeks post partum, and included a semistructured interview and direct observations. The Mother–Infant Reciprocity Scale developed by Price was used to rate the mother–infant interaction at a feeding on the second or third day post partum.[32] At the 6-week observation, done either at home or in the clinic, maternal attachment was rated according to the adolescent's reported feelings for the baby. Mother–infant reciprocity was again measured. The mothers who had made plans for the pregnancy and the infant and whose family was supportive did better. At 6 weeks, the adolescents whose babies had greater motor maturity were more attached to their infants, and the mothers of infants who were better adjusted were less depressed. The authors suggested that the important domains of early mother interaction for adolescents are physical and involve motor activity. What adolescents find most important about their newborns perhaps differs from what older mothers emphasize, but this should not make the mother–infant interaction less reciprocal.

The attachment to the infant by adolescent mothers has also been studied by Flick et al.[33] Their sample included 321 low-income mothers with medically normal pregnancy and delivery and their children at 1 year of age. The mothers were 14–43 years of age, 40 percent were married, 70 percent were black, and 50 percent were primiparous. The study included a prenatal interview, a 4-month postpartum interview, and a 12-month postpartum interview plus observations. They found greater differences in attachment at 1 year in younger mothers. The authors concluded that immature mothers have less well developed capacities for coping with life stressors and, therefore, their attachment was more vulnerable to situational influences. They felt that "younger mothers would be at greater risk of transmitting stress to their children through less positive behavior."

Impact of Mothering Skills on Child Development

A wealth of information from recent investigations indicates that the development of cognitive, social, and emotional competence in the child is strongly related to prior mother–child interaction.[34-37] Cohen et al. found that those infants who at 24 months of age had more language competence had caregivers who were more stimulating.[34] Beckwith et al. found that children who achieved higher developmental and intellectual quotients at ages 9 months, 2 years, and 5 years had spent less of their awake time at 1 and 3 months of age receiving physical care and had experienced more mutual caregiver–infant gazing at 1 months of age.[35] These infants had also had more interchanges of smiling during gazing and more continued responses to distress at 3 months of age. Early positive mother–child contact led to greater cognitive and social competence according to work by Clarke-Stewart.[36] The degree of stimulation in the home differentiated those children with and without achievement problems. It appears that social and emotional development is most closely related to the mother's expression of affection. There is also a correlation between maternal stimulation and intellectual development, as overall competence is related to maternal responsiveness to her child and the mother's ability to communicate with her infant.

Differences in maternal behavior on the basis of socioeconomic status of the mothers have been reported. Lewis and Wilson studied the effect of socio-economic status on maternal behavior toward their infants.[37] They reported an increase in frequency of maternal touch as the socioeconomic level decreased. The mothers of lower socioeconomic status touched their infants approximately twice as much as middle-class mothers.

Thompson and colleagues applied the Brazelton Neonatal Assessment Scale to 30 infants of lower socioeconomic, black, adolescent mothers and to 30 infants of black older mothers of similar socioeconomic status. They found that the infants of the adolescent mothers differed markedly from those of the older mothers in their interactive and motor processes.[38] Another study failed to corroborate these findings.[39]

Observations of Early Mother–Infant Contacts

Als, in an ethnological study of the human newborn and the mother, asked the question whether teenagers are less capable as first mothers than women in their 20s.[40] Tabulation of certain typical interaction behaviors— including feeding, burping, making faces, verbalization, holding, and touching—during the first 3 days post partum showed little overall difference between adult and younger mothers. On the first day, the younger mothers fed more and were slightly more active but on the second and third days no differences were found. The study included 30 black Hollingshead V primiparous mothers who delivered normal full-term babies vaginally and were bottle feeding. The mothers were 16–25 years old with a mean age of 20 years. The comparison groups were defined as under 20 years and over 20 years of age at the time of delivery.

In a pilot study of 15 primiparous women 18 years and younger, McAnarney et al. found a relationship between the degree of immaturity of the mother and her ability to interact with her infant.[41] The younger the adolescent mother, the less she utilized typical maternal behaviors of touching, high-pitched voice, synchronous movements, and closeness to the infant—all behaviors previously observed among adult mothers. In a pilot study of 10 Guatemalan mothers 14–17 years of age, Hales and Bergen also reported that the adolescent mothers were less able than adult mothers to establish close contact immediately after delivery.[42] The affectionate and caretaking behaviors were not significantly different. The cross-cultural implications of this study have not been established.

A serendipitous finding of Jones et al. in a study of maternal responsiveness of primiparous mothers during the postpartum period was that the age of the mother was an important factor.[43] They had looked at 40 primiparous mothers with normal full-term infants in the early postpartum period using videotape to record the mother during the discharge physical examination and the first 10 minutes of the subsequent feeding. Maternal responsiveness was rated by assessing five 30-second film clips for the presence or absence of specific maternal behaviors: en face position, lateral trunk contact, maternal fondling, and vocalization.

The original design of the study was randomly to assign mothers into one of four study groups; (1) a control group with traditional contact; (2) a group with only a glimpse of the infant at birth; (3) an additional information group; and (4) an additional physical contact group. Although the mean maternal ages in all groups were similar (18.5, 20.2, 19.3, and 19.4), the range was not given for each group, only for the total, 17–23 years. Because the study was unable to demonstrate any effect of early contact and the age of the mother had a high correlation with maternal responsiveness, the subjects were regrouped by age; 17–18, 19–20, and 21–23 years. Regardless of race, socioeconomic status, or marital status, mothers 17–18 years old showed less maternal responsiveness while feeding their infants and less proximity to their infants during physical examination. The authors concluded that age of the mother was a significant variable in maternal readiness for mothering.

The quality of the interaction between an adolescent mother, here defined as less than 20 years of age, was also examined by Flick using a social-cognitive developmental model.[44] The results suggested that younger mothers in this low-income population exhibit less interaction with their children and seem less accepting and involved than older mothers. The results also suggested that the coping capacities of a given mother are more relevant to interaction than age alone.

Included in the risk factors for outcome of adolescent pregnancy is the potential for producing a premature infant. The degree to which teenage parenting (a caretaking casualty risk factor) and preterm delivery (a reproductive casualty risk factor) contribute to developmental delays in infants of adolescent mothers was studied by Field et al.[45] They provided a home-based, parent-training intervention, and the infant development was then compared with that of nonintervention controls. Both term and preterm infants of adolescent and adult black mothers of low socioeconomic status were included. Being born both preterm and to a teenage mother created greater risk for the infant than being born either preterm or to a teenage mother alone. All preterm infants in this study showed some developmental delays, but the infants of the adolescents were also exposed to less desirable child-rearing attitudes and developmental expectations. Intervention had an effect on study group infants in all categories.

Adolescent mothers were more likely to seek medical advice from their own mothers than from health professionals in a pilot study of attitudes of inner city adolescent mothers reported by Zuckerman et al.[46] They were also more insecure than older mothers in their maternal self-image if caretaking was shared. The authors suggested that further investigation is necessary to establish differences in maternal self-image, child-rearing practices, and available support systems.

Most of these study designs suffered from the use of homogeneous, small populations, so that their results were often not generalizable. There is, therefore, a major need for investigation of adolescent mother–infant interactions using large, heterogeneous populations. In addition, it is important to investigate whether there are specific times in the lives of adolescent mothers when they are less able to handle the rapid development of their children from passive and undemanding infants to active, intrusive toddlers.

It has been shown in studies by Furstenberg[4] and by Mednick[47] that the negative effects of having an adolescent for a mother may be muted by the presence of a father or grandmother in the household. The children whose adolescent mother was not married, not employed outside the home, nor going to school, and thus was the primary caregiver, scored lower on the Preschool Inventory than children whose caregiving was provided by at least one adult. There was an apparent positive influence of more than one caretaker on the child's development. Broman looked at family characteristics 7 years after delivery and found them to be related to maternal age at delivery.[48] The offspring of younger mothers were more often living in foster or adoptive homes. Placement outside the home by age 7 was highly related to maternal age in both ethnic groups and within the same socioeconomic group. The lower the socioeconomic status was, the greater was the probability of placement of the child.

In order to understand better the causes of increased risk for apparent poor outcome in children of adolescents and to examine maternal behavior for long-range predictive qualities, McAnarney et al. initiated studies of the interaction between the adolescent mother and her infant in the neonatal period.[41] Dyads were videotaped in our laboratory in the first few days post partum. A nonfeeding sequence was chosen because the task of feeding masked some of the adolescents' innate behavior. We observed that the younger the mother the less apt she was to hold the baby close or to talk to the baby. These tapes were reviewed by trained observers who counted the interactive behaviors. Adolescents less than 15 years of age mothered their infants differently than did older adolescents and adults. They interacted with less synchrony, verbal communication, and closeness to their infants.

We were subsequently able to show that some mothers in the middle adolescent years demonstrate aggressive behaviors, such as picking, poking, and pinching their infants, that are rarely seen in adult mothers.[49] In addition, some very young mothers were passive and nonverbal toward their infants. Study is currently underway to evaluate the significance of these behaviors and to examine whether they may predict future mother and/or infant morbidity

When we compared frequency of picking, poking, and pinching behaviors among white, Spanish-speaking, and black adolescents, the frequencies were similarly high for white and Spanish-speaking adolescents and low for black adolescents. All the adolescents were of lower socioeconomic level. These data suggest that the highest risk group for parental dysfunction as manifest by aggressive behaviors are 15- to 16-year-old nonblack lower socioeconomic status adolescents.

CONCLUSIONS

Exploration of the mothering behavior of adolescents has opened new avenues of observation and introduced new questions. Long-range studies have shown a difference between infants of some adolescent mothers and those of older mothers. The infants at greatest risk for poor outcome are those born and raised by the very youngest mothers and those with the least adequate family support system.

Further research is necessary to determine if the maternal interactive skill of the biologic mother has major long-range effects on the outcome of the infant. If mothering skills are the critical factor, then it is important to establish that mothering can be learned. If mothering can be learned, it should be taught. Ultimately, intervention programs that will improve infant outcome developmentally and psychologically should be developed.

REFERENCES

1. Baldwin W, Cain VS: The children of teenage parents. Fam Plann Perspect 12:34–43, 1980
2. Hardy JB, Mellits ED: Relationship of low birthweight to maternal characteristics of age, parity, education and body size, in Reed DM, Stanley FJ (eds): The Epidemiology of Prematurity. Baltimore, Urban and Schwarenberg, 1979, pp 1–174
3. Carey WB, McCann-Sanford T, Davidson EC Jr: Adolescent age and obstetric risk. Semin Perinatol 5:9–18, 1981
4. Furstenberg FF Jr: Unplanned Parenthood: The Social Consequences of Teenage Childbearing. New York, Macmillan, 1976
5. Lincoln R: Is pregnancy good for teenagers? Testimony before the Select Committee on Population, 95th Congress, 1979, p 318

12

Adolescent Mothers: How Nurturant Is Their Parenting?

Olle Jane Z. Sahler

C hild rearing is the art of overseeing a child's growth and development. Parenting is a special category of child rearing, since the designation *parent* is uniquely reserved to identify the child's biologic progenitors or adoptive guardians. For biologic progenitors, the fact of parenthood is immutable, even if the individual never assumes actual child-rearing responsibilities. Even though this is a true statement for both mothers and fathers, our society has traditionally held mothers, including unwed mothers, more responsible than fathers for the care and welfare of the child, regardless of the mother's age, physical or mental health, financial assets, or social resources. When our society has allowed, and perhaps at times even encouraged, a mother to relinquish formal guardianship of a child by release for adoption, it has been with the understanding that she will sever all ties and contacts. In fact, until recently, releasing a child for adoption was a frequently advocated solution to the crisis of unwed pregnancy, especially among the middle-class population.

But what of the teenager who elects to keep her child? What conflicts influence her concept of herself as a mother? What skills does she bring to her role as child rearer? What supports can she reasonably expect from the baby's father, from her own extended family, and from society?

TEENAGER'S MATERNAL CAPABILITIES

To mother is defined as "to care for or protect." Mothering is a long-term process that requires the ability to understand the needs of someone else and, on occasion, to put those needs before one's own. In addition to all the other factors that appear to influence success in mothering—the opportunity to have experienced good mothering as a child oneself, adequate knowledge of child behavior and development, confidence in personal ability, financial resources to provide for basic needs—the individual's level of developmental maturity is a significant factor in determining the probability that effective mothering will occur. The often asked question, Can an adolescent be a successful mother? is a reasonable one. The answer is the same as one would give about individuals of any age, Some can and some cannot.

Because there are rapid changes and wide variations in maturational level during adolescence, actual chronological age is not necessarily an accurate indicator of maturity. Indeed, personality traits, cognitive functioning, and emotional responses can be quite unstable over time even in the same individual. Recent research has identified three major stages (early, middle, and late) of adolescence, each of which can be characterized by predominant drives, moods, and abilities. Since maturational differences have been shown to affect parenting behavior,[1] we must discriminate among these stages and estimate a specific maturity level for each young mother if we are to be realistic in predicting her expected child-rearing capabilities.

Impact of Developmental Level on Child Rearing

Hatcher has outlined some characteristic personality traits found at each developmental substage that are relevant to understanding the adolescent's feelings about the event of childbearing. In her work with pregnant adolescents of varying developmental stages, she had each girl "draw a baby." Her results showed that maturationally early adolescents typically drew a stick figure, lifeless looking, unsupported by an arm, cradle, or other structure. Middle adolescents drew an exaggerated, larger than life-size baby with a "bombshell" appearance. Late adolescents drew mother–baby scenes with the baby supported by arms or a crib.[2]

In seeking to understand and categorize the girls who had done these drawings, it was reasonable for Hatcher to suggest that such parameters as cognitive level, behavior, and objects of intrapsychic conflict might be useful in assessing general psychosocial maturity. Indeed, she found the following five aspects of personality development to be particularly good indicators of a teenage girl's overall developmental level:[2]

1. The identity of the parent most related to conflicts
2. The quality and style of her relationships with others
3. Her view of herself
4. Her major defense mechanisms
5. Her goals and interests

Let us extend these concepts and apply them specifically to the task of child rearing, keeping in mind that even though these stages are not necessarily associated with chronological age, we would expect more very young adolescents to be in the early adolescent stage and proportionately more older adolescents to be in the late adolescent stage.

Early Adolescence

1. The early adolescent is beginning to loosen her tie to her mother. She has so much ambivalence about this separation that pregnancy may actually represent the wish to become closer to her mother by becoming a mother herself. At the same time, she has such a strong desire to remain "her own mother's baby" that it may be impossible for her to think of herself as a mother, in the sense of providing ongoing care and concern for another dependent being.

2. Her extrafamilial relationships, usually with other girls, are extremely ardent but, paradoxically, evanescent. She play-acts relationships, trying out what Deutsch termed "as if" personalities.[3] She experiences crushes on unattainable (and therefore safe) men and women.

3. Her view of herself is inconsistent and fluctuating, entirely in keeping with the rapid and dramatic changes in physical appearance and capability that she is experiencing. She has a vague sense of herself as female.

4. The primary defense mechanism of this substage is denial. It is important to consider a comment Hatcher made regarding her own clinical experiences teaching young teenagers about sex: "Although reports in the literature implicate inadequate sex education as an important cause of unwanted pregnancy, our data suggest that sex education is effective only when there is sufficient emotional maturity to absorb the information."[2] Since the early adolescent protects herself through denial (manifested by an unwillingness to hear pertinent information), she is almost invariably unprotected by medical contraception during sexual experimentation. Providentially, the relative biologic immaturity of the young adolescent, expressed as the high incidence of anovulatory cycles during the so-called adolescent sterility period,[4] provides the young girl with some degree of physiologic contraception. Thus, her body, if not her mind, is perspicacious.

5. Her goals and interests are closely allied with her level of cognitive functioning. She tends to be "now" oriented rather than future oriented. There is an immediacy to her needs demanding instant gratification. Because she does not have the ability for abstract thinking, she is tied to the concrete and conventional. Her judgment about the relative morality of actions usually reflects a "law and order" orientation whereby individuals focus on authority and fixed rules in making their decisions about proper action and right behavior: one does one's duty and shows respect for authority. She tends to be very rigid and punitive.[5]

Middle Adolescence

1. The middle adolescent, according to psychoanalytic theory, is struggling with a recrudescence of the oedipal conflict: competition with her mother for the love and attention of her father. The incest taboo, however, is well known to the adolescent and her flirtation with her father is relatively short-lived. Whereas the young adolescent is struggling to break away from her mother, the middle adolescent ultimately struggles to break away from both parents and achieve autonomy.

2. Her relationships with peers are intense since these friendships provide a replacement for (rather than merely an alternative to) her relationship with her parents. Because of this need to free herself from her parents, the middle adolescent has more difficulty with authority figures than any other teenage subgroup. She can neither accept authority as the young adolescent can nor participate in the productive, insight-oriented discussion characteristic of the late adolescent. Whereas at a younger age most, if not all, friendships were same sexed, the middle adolescent now experiments with heterosexual relationships. These relationships, however, are not based on the need to express intimacy, but are part of the search for self-identity: Who am I? How do I relate to others? How do they perceive me?

3. Self-involvement is the most pervasive characteristic of middle adolescence. Extended periods of introspection appear to be a crucial need. The middle adolescent is highly ambivalent and uncertain. Her new ability to commit herself by conscious decision, discovered during this stage, is tempered by the knowledge that real commitments do not yet have to be made and thus she can continue to experiment with giving and demanding. Indeed, she feels panic at the thought of someone else's dependence on her, given the magnitude of her own unresolved dependency needs. Because of the physical changes she has undergone, her femininity is difficult to deny and she is becoming increasingly aware of her own responsibility for certain actions.

4. Magical thinking, and with it an attendant feeling of great power, pervades middle adolescent fantasy. The middle adolescent experiences tremendous mood swings and is constantly "on stage," larger than life. Every-

thing that goes poorly is a tragedy. This hyperbole shields her from accurately representing, considering, and accepting real tragedy.

5. Her goals and interests reflect her increasing ability to problem solve as she seeks autonomy from her parents. She vacillates, however, between being a young adolescent and a late adolescent, making her plans inconsistent over time. Her intense narcissism makes her generally unempathetic and unlikely to tolerate demands from others that detract from her self-focus.

Late Adolescence

1. The late adolescent has achieved some sense of personal identity and with it has won some emotional independence from her parents. Thus, she can participate in increasingly intimate love relationships outside her family.

2. Relationships within her family are less conflict laden than at any other time during adolescence. Love relationships are motivated by a growing need to share feelings and commitment. She demonstrates a rudimentary "motherly ego":[3] nurturant feelings for others emerge as her own needs become less all-consuming.

3. The late adolescent is more realistic about who and what she is. Her behaviors and responses are more predictable because they are more fixed. She is capable of personal reflection and therefore understands her own motivations better. She is, in general, more in touch with her own feelings than either the early or middle adolescent.

4. Her defense mechanisms are more fully developed and tend toward intellectualization and rationalization. In addition, she can reduce stress by developing reality-based strategies to cope with undesirable situations.

5. Her goals and interests are in keeping with the longer-range view that the late adolescent has of herself and her world. She is more likely than the younger adolescent to be concerned about completing her education or developing occupational skills and to recognize her own personal responsibility for herself and anyone who is dependent on her. Thus, it is not until a young mother reaches the late adolescent stage that we would expect her to be able, emotionally and cognitively, to provide even an approximation of warm, consistent parenting to a child.

THE ROLE OF THE FATHER: GENERAL CONSIDERATIONS

We know very little about the male partner's sexual behavior and attitudes, psychosocial characteristics, and feelings about the pregnancy.[6] Our lack of knowledge about these young men stems from society's attribution of a "love 'em and leave 'em" attitude to the unwed father that has essentially robbed him of any official status within the family unit. Indeed, under current welfare laws, a financially destitute mother is penalized for the presence of an employed or employable male within her household, despite the fact that this same welfare system ideologically promotes the concept of the traditional nuclear family as highly desirable for optimal child development. Such a lack of congruence between philosophy and reality permeates many government programs for young parents[7] and contributes to their confusion about proper and expected roles and the long-term responsibilities appropriate for mature parenthood.

Despite governmental, and often family, pressure to the contrary, data from several longitudinal studies of school-aged parents indicate that long-term relationships between mothers and fathers may be quite common, although most remain informal. Lorenzi et al. studied 180 girls in the Young Mother's Program at Yale and found that at 26 months post partum 23 percent of the mothers in their sample had married the child's father, a like number had regular contact with the father, and an additional 18 percent saw the father occasionally. Furthermore, one-half of the fathers were contributing some financial aid as late as 2 years post partum, and a large number of fathers, even though not married to the mothers, visited their children. Lastly, a small number of fathers had ongoing contact with their children despite "never" seeing the mothers.[8] Similarly, in a follow-up study of 404 adolescent mothers, Furstenberg found that more than 60 percent of the fathers continued to have some type of ongoing relationship with their children as long as 5 years after the pregnancy.[9]

Thus, despite social pressure against the continued involvement of the unwed father, he often maintains some personal (emotional and financial) stake in the pregnancy and subsequent child. A substantial number of these relationships, however, might be considered unstable, since the contact or support is often irregular, intermittent, or unreliable.

PARENTHOOD LIFESTYLES

Although we have outlined the developmental sequence of adolescence specifically as it relates to a girl, a boy undergoes a similar maturational process that ultimately allows him to formulate his own identity and to enter into intimate relationships that are responsive to the needs of others. This has important implications for the potential success or failure of the parenthood lifestyle a young mother may choose for rearing her child.

Marriage

Some teenage parents formalize their relationship through marriage. Two factors appear to be particularly important in determining whether or not a young couple will marry: age and subcultural expectation. Vital statistics reveal that the older the pregnant teenager, the more likely she is to marry. Among girls of similar age, there are significant subcultural differences, however, in the rate of marriage to legitimize the birth. Furstenberg and Crawford studied pregnant teenagers in Baltimore, Maryland, and found that whereas 70 percent of the white adolescents in their clinic population married during pregnancy, only 16 percent of their black patients did so.[10,11] Since whites are underrepresented in urban clinic populations, the true incidence of early pregnancy and marital outcome among this population is not well known. This pattern of single parenthood among the nonwhite mothers, however, is consistent with the matriarchal family system long believed to be prevalent in this country among blacks of low socioeconomic status.[12]

The increased incidence of marriage among older teenagers, regardless of ethnic background, may be due to the greater cognitive ability of the more mature couple to make realistic plans and to carry them out. In addition, since the couple has greater emotional stability and usually a higher educational or skill level promising more financial security, family pressure to formalize the relationship may be higher.

Marriage increases the probability of independent living and decreases the chance of obtaining those tangible (room, board, baby care) and intangible (advice, support, affection) supports usually found within families. As Furstenberg and Crawford pointed out, the families of origin may expect that the partners will derive such supports from each other.[11] However, since the overall psychological functioning of the adolescent male is similar to that of the female at the same stage, this may be an unrealistic assumption. Indeed, in the specific family situation of disciplining a young child, the joint effectiveness of immature parents may not be sufficient for success. For example, in some recent research that Oosting and I have done on parenting satisfaction and effectiveness in average middle class, nonadolescent, two-parent families, we found that parents who are able to practice nurturant child rearing (anticipating needs, explaining consequences, providing incentives for desired behavior) often rely on one another to help defuse potentially explosive discipline encounters or to support a point of view. This type of mutual support between spouses diminished the probability that one of the parents would lose self-control and be too physically or verbally harsh when disciplining a child.[13]

In order to be able to provide mutual support, however, caregivers must be able to anticipate each other's needs and be consistent and nonjudgmental when they do intercede. The developmentally appropriate egocentrism and impulsiveness of early and middle adolescence make such cooperative parenting between two young teenagers unlikely. In addition, research on adolescent understanding of child development has shown that teenage boys and girls have serious (but remediable) gaps in knowledge and therefore may be unable to anticipate the child's needs or understand the child's motivations behind certain behaviors.[14-16]

If a young adolescent couple marries and elects to set up an independent household, the stresses of financial insecurity and emotional immaturity, among other factors, may sap much of the energy necessary for a successful marriage, let alone successful parenting. The two- to fourfold higher incidence of divorce among adolescent couples as compared to adult couples[17] clearly reflects the generalized turmoil of these relationships. As was shown by Burchinal, waiting until late adolescence to marry has a significant effect on the endurance of the relationship: in 1960, twice as many males who had married at 15 years of age were separated or divorced than those who had married at 18.[18] Thus, marital stability appears to be directly related to the degree of personality consolidation and identity formation the adolescent has attained. This finding deserves to be brought to the attention of any parents rushing to legitimize the expected child of their young adolescent daughter: a forced marriage may well have very substantial and long-term negative sequelae, including pervasive bitterness over separation and divorce. This outcome needs to be balanced against the immediate crisis of unwed childbearing. All things considered, it is not surprising that Fischman found that many of the young adolescent girls she surveyed considered marriage a much more serious undertaking than motherhood especially if mothering could occur within the support system of extended family.[19]

Remaining with Extended Family

Of all the options, single parenthood within her family home is the one most commonly chosen by the adolescent mother. In their Baltimore study, Furstenberg and Crawford found that more than 98 percent of unmarried teenage mothers lived with their families throughout pregnancy. One year later 88 percent remained in this arrangement, and 5 years later 70 percent of never married mothers still lived with their families of origin. Furthermore, about 50 percent of once married but now separated or divorced mothers and almost 20 percent of currently married mothers lived with their families of origin at the time of the 5-year follow-up.[11]

Such a strong attachment to her family reflects a combination of dependence and adaptability. The level of her dependence and the consequent need for personal and family adaptation vary with the developmental stage of the young mother. If the early and middle adolescent mother is to continue her education, participate in developmentally appropriate behaviors, especially peer-oriented social events, and be free to experience and experiment with the full range of emotions common to her age, she must have personal freedom. She and her family must negotiate how much freedom she can have based on how easily the infant can be accommodated within the household schedule of other family members.

Shared child rearing is not, however, a solution without problems. If we examine the dynamic social equilibrium of the family of an early or middle adolescent, parent–child (especially mother–daughter) conflict is a hallmark of this period. In trying to express her autonomy, the young girl often finds fault with her mother, and no matter how right and reasonable (by adult standards) the mother's limits, threats, entreaties, or rational decisions, the two will be in opposition. If we tried to scale the ideas of the two along some dimension that reflects responsible thinking and good planning, the mother would almost always demonstrate more highly developed cognitive skill and greater experience. If we scaled the two along some dimension that reflected the ability to make a well-thought-out and long-term commitment, the mother, again, would usually score higher. However, such right, reasonable, and logical arguments seldom defuse the developmentally predictable mother–daughter conflict of middle adolescence. Some very deep-rooted, generationally defined, intrapsychic conflicts, as well as cognitive limitations, influence a young teenager's ability to mother within her mother's home. Her inability to accept parental support coupled with her limited ability to provide adequately for herself may put the middle adolescent at a higher psychosocial risk than early or late adolescent mothers.

Some authorities have expressed concern that remaining with her family of origin may negatively affect the teenager's self-image as a mother. Zuckerman and co-workers found that teenagers who shared child-rearing responsibilities with their own mothers were concerned about two issues: that their infants would be confused about roles within the family, and that they, as mothers, would be unable to interpret their infants' communications because of their secondary role in child care.[20] Indeed, resentment at their mothers for being more attuned to the infants' needs and assuming leadership in care has frequently been seen among teenage mothers in our clinical setting as well. Overall, it is interesting that these young mothers were aware of and could articulate the potential difficulties uncovered by Zuckerman et al. The next step for us is to learn from these mothers and their children, in 5- and 10-year follow-up studies, what problems actually do arise from this form of shared parenting.

Independent Living

The adolescent girl who elects to remain single and to live alone may relinquish not only any support she might have derived from marriage, but also those overt and subtle offers of help families extend to girls living at home. The decision to live independently, if made under poor or borderline financial or emotional circumstances, also raises the question of the judgment (and overall mental well-being) of the young mother. If a long-standing parent–child conflict has contributed to the girl's motivation to become pregnant in the first place and then does not permit her and her family to resolve differences enough to provide adequately for the welfare of the infant, the mother–infant relationship may be in special jeopardy.

Social programs play an especially important role in the lives of these particular mothers by acting as family surrogates or complementing assistance extended by the family when some contact is maintained. By design, the most successful of these programs meet practical as well as emotional needs by providing educational opportunities, skill training, day care, health-related services, and social events.

SUMMARY AND CONCLUSIONS

In assessing the capabilities of any individual teenager to contribute to infant care, it is absolutely crucial that our determination be based not on chronological age but on developmental level. It must be remembered that commitment to care is an emotional-cognitive decision that requires the ability to plan, to place oneself in another's position, and to delay gratification. A given 13-year-old may demonstrate a social maturity usually seen among late adolescents. By the same token an 18-year-old may have the social maturity of a young or middle adolescent.

As we have seen, the individual who is developmentally in early or middle adolescence, regardless of chronological age, is not ready to assume the major portion of the responsibility necessary for an ongoing commitment to an infant. A girl who becomes pregnant at one of these stages is typically still trying to resolve some very important parent–child conflicts in which she is the child, *not* the parent. She is in the midst of experimenting with relationships and spends a great deal of time in egocentric, narcissistic reflection because she *must* do so in order to pass on to the next developmental stage. This is not to say that no girl has ever experienced—and survived— an abbreviated childhood; however, if asked to provide a plan that maximizes her growth potential, we must allow the adolescent time to herself. If she is intrigued with and absorbed by her infant one moment and neglectful the next, it is because her attention span is short and needs constant stimulation. If she "promises" to do something and then "forgets" it may be that she is rebelling against that parental authority she loves and hates at the same time. If her mothering skills are very rudimentary, this limitation may merely reflect the brevity of her encounters with child care jobs at home or in the community. If she is not "into" babies—as we might expect, given her very appropriate interests in clothes, hair styles, and teen idols—she has probably observed little of infant behavior and paid little, if any, attention to the rather dry child development courses often taught in school. If this girl happens to become a mother, what can we reasonably expect of her, and what must adult society provide for her and her child?

Theoretically, the most successful child-rearing arrangement for the early or middle adolescent who elects to keep her infant combines continued residence within the parental home and shared child-rearing responsibilities between the biologic mother and one or two others—one of whom is usually the maternal grandmother. Developmentally, it is most appropriate for the growing teenager to remain in her home and for her to profit from the opportunity to experience the role modeling such an arrangement permits. The assumption that this young girl/woman is ready for parenthood merely because she participated in sexual activity (two very different behaviors with widely disparate motivations) has been shown time and time again to be erroneous. The "surprise" many young teenagers register at their pregnancy may reflect lack of information, but it also reflects the fact that, to them, sex and motherhood are not synonymous. The tradition of holding the mother responsible for the infant "regardless" has a punitive tone and contradicts all that we have learned about the emotional and cognitive readiness of the young adolescent to accept such responsibility. She is not necessarily a bad kid; but she is, necessarily, just a kid.

Societies, such as some in the Middle East, that allow early childbearing by encouraging early marriage are usually nonmobile, tradition-bound cultures that rely heavily on extended family support systems. The American home that contains several generations of individuals sharing responsibilities and resources has many of the same communal characteristics seen in these other cultures. Such a living arrangement provides protection to the young and dependent by providing multiple layers of caregivers.

The willingness of many extended families to assume responsibility for the young mother and her offspring deserves careful attention within the medical community. By having granted her all legal custody and rights of guardianship from the moment of the child's birth, we have made the young mother responsible for her child, mandated her autonomy in decision making, and diminished the authority of other family members who still have legitimate moral, if not legal, responsibility for the physical and emotional welfare of the young mother herself. We may or may not have acted in the best interests of those concerned.

We must treat the fostering of individuation and self-identity in the teenage parent as a simultaneous but separate issue from the fostering of an environment conducive to the nurturant parenting of the infant. Thus it is time for the health care system, and society in general, to look more closely at the benefits as well as the risks of (1) allowing more flexibility in the relationship between teenage parents, and (2) encouraging more creativity in designing living arrangements for the young family that promote shared responsibility for child rearing. As a final result we might find that by increasing personal satisfaction and success among these young mothers and fathers, their own offspring may have the self-esteem and social maturity necessary to find fulfillment in ways other than early pregnancy.

REFERENCES

1. Green JW, Sandler HM, Altemeier WA, et al: Child rearing attitudes, observed behavior and perception of infant temperament in adolescent versus older mothers. Pediatr Res 15:442, 1981
2. Hatcher SL: Understanding adolescent pregnancy and abortion. Primary Care, 3:407–425, 1976
3. Deutsch H: Selected problems of adolescence. Psychoanal Study Child Monogr no 3, 1967
4. Montagu A: The Reproductive Development of the Female: A Study in the Comparative Physiology of the Adolescent Organism (ed 3). Littleton, Mass, PSG, 1979
5. Kohlberg L: Stage and sequence: The cognitive-developmental approach to socialization, in Goslin DA (ed): Handbook of Socialization Theory and Research. Chicago, Rand McNally, 1969
6. Elster AB, Panzarine S: The adolescent father. Semin Perinatol 5:39–51, 1981
7. Cannon-Bonventre K, Kahn J: Interviews with adolescent parents: Looking at their needs. Child Today, Sept–Oct 1979, pp 17–20
8. Lorenzi ME, Klerman LV, Jekel JF: School-age parents: How permanent a relationship? Adolescence 12:13–22, 1977
9. Furstenberg FF: The social consequences of teenage parenthood. Fam Plann Perspect 8:148–164, 1976
10. Furstenberg FF: Unplanned Parenthood. New York, Free Press, 1976
11. Furstenberg FF, Crawford A: Family support; Helping teenage mothers to cope. Fam Plann Perspect 10:322–333, 1978
12. Ladner J: Tomorrow's Tomorrow: The Black Woman. Garden City, NY, Doubleday, 1971
13. Oosting RS, Sahler OJZ: Unpublished data, 1980
14. DeLissovoy V: High school marriages: A longitudinal study. J Marriage Fam 35:245–255, 1973
15. Weigle JW: Teaching child development to teenage mothers. Child Today, Sept–Oct 1974, pp 23–25
16. Berger A, Winter ST: Attitudes and knowledge of secondary school girls concerning breast-feeding. Clin Pediatr 19:825–826, 1980
17. Sklar J, Berkov B: Teenage family formation in postwar America. Fam Plann Perspect 6:80–90, 1974
18. Burchinal LG: Trends and prospects for young marriages in the United States. J Marriage Fam 27:243–254, 1965
19. Fischman S: Delivery or abortion in inner-city adolescents. Am J Orthopsychiatry 47:127–133, 1977
20. Zuckerman B, Winsmore C, Alpert J: A study of attitudes and support systems of inner city adolescent mothers. J Pediatr 94:122–125, 1979

13

Adolescent Fathers

Arthur B. Elster and Susan Panzarine

The subject of adolescent fathers has traditionally received little attention in the medical or social science literature. There is a need for increased awareness among professionals of the problems that these men face and the services they need. Public awareness regarding teenage fathers already appears to be increasing; popular movies and television shows have addressed this issue during the past several years. In 1979, the short film "Teenage Fathers" (Children's Home Society of California) won an Academy Award for its depiction of the problems faced by a young man whose girlfriend became pregnant.

During 1978, 554,179 women who were less than 20 years of age had a live birth.[1] Of these births, 113,753 (20 percent) were fathered by adolescents. In total, 134,297 (4.6 percent) live births in 1978 were fathered by men who were less than age 20. The birth rate in 1978 (defined as the number of live births per 1000 people in a specified age group) for males 15–19 years of age was 18.5; this represented a 28 percent decline from the 1970 rate of 25.6. During this interval, the birth rate for adolescent females 15–19 years of age declined by 23 percent, from 68.3 to 52.4. Most likely, the decline in the birth rate for both sexes was due to the increased

This work was supported in part by a grant from the William T. Grant Foundation and by Grant APH 000034-01-0 from the Department of Health and Human Services, Office of Adolescent Pregnancy Programs.

rate of abortions; there are no data, however, to substantiate this notion for adolescent males, as there are for adolescent females.[2]

The exact number of total pregnancies (live births plus abortions) fathered by adolescents is unknown. Coddington[3] and Miller,[4] in studies of selected high school populations, found that 37 of 788 and 10 of 163 boys who were questioned reported that they had fathered an unwed pregnancy. Russ-Eft and associates, in 1975, interviewed 1000 subjects (500 males and 500 females) representative of a nationwide random sample of adolescents who, at the age of 15 during 1960, had participated in Project Talent.[5] These investigators found that 10 percent of these 30-year-old men had had a child before the age of 20. If, after further investigations, the results of these studies prove to be an accurate reflection of the general adolescent population, then approximately 1 teenage boy in 10–20 will father a premarital pregnancy. For comparison, a study by Zelnik and Kantner indicated that approximately 1 teenage girl in 10 has a premarital pregnancy.[6]

Of the approximately 1.2 million first marriages that took place in 1979, 9 percent involved brides and 1.5 percent involved grooms who were 17 years of age or younger; 23 percent of the brides and 12 percent of the grooms were 18–19 years of age.[7] Over 25 percent of the marriages involving girls aged 15–19 in 1976 were associated with either a premarital birth or a birth within 7 months after marriage.[8]

The topic of adolescent fathers is difficult to discuss because of the lack of critical research. We use data from the few studies that have been done on adolescent fathers, results from studies that investigated the sexual behavior of general populations of adolescent males, and other concepts from the literature on adult fathers. We also rely on the results from two studies performed by the authors.

The first study was performed to explore the health-educational and emotional needs of unwed teenage fathers who were partners of girls attending the Rochester Adolescent Maternity Project in Rochester, New York.[9] The 16 prospective fathers in the study were interviewed and administered psychological tests. Extensive demographic, psychological, family, and cognitive information was obtained. The young men ranged from 15 to 19 years of age, with a mean age of 17.4 years. They were predominantly from families of lower socioeconomic status; 10 were black, 5 were white, and 1 was Hispanic. The girlfriends of 2 of these teenagers were in late first trimester at the time of the interview, and the remainder were in their second trimester.

The purpose of the second study, which was conducted in Salt Lake City, Utah, was to investigate the stresses perceived and coping mechanisms utilized by adolescent fathers.[10] The 20 subjects were predominantly white and from middle socioeconomic status families. They were interviewed intermittently throughout the prenatal period and once post partum: 4 boys were interviewed once, 5 had 2 interviews, 9 had 3 interviews, and 2 had

4 interviews. All conceptions had occurred out of wedlock, but 15 teenagers had married by the time of delivery. The average age of the boys was 17.6 years; their partners averaged 16.6 years. The results of this study provided information regarding the trajectory of specific stresses affecting young fathers, and the anticipatory coping mechanism used to prepare for prospective parenthood.

Using information from these various sources, we discuss the following topics: The sexual behavior of adolescent males; contraception among adolescent males; psychosocial characteristics of adolescent fathers; consequences of pregnancy for the adolescent father; and implications for clinical intervention.

SEXUAL BEHAVIOR OF ADOLESCENT MALES

Studies investigating the extent of sexual behavior in adolescents are of questionable value because of sample bias and problems with subject reliability.[11] It is difficult to obtain a random selection of subjects who are willing and able to answer sexually oriented questions. Parental consent is a prerequisite to clinical investigation of adolescent subjects. Thus, in a study by Sorenson that utilized a nationwide random sample of adolescents, 39 percent of prospective subjects were not interviewed because their parents refused to consent; another 14 percent of adolescents declined directly.[12] Studies of older adolescents who are in college can be easier to perform because parental consent is not needed. College students, however, are not necessarily representative of all adolescents; the behavior of adolescents who attend college may differ greatly from that of adolescents who either choose not to or are not able to enter college.

The reliability of adolescents' answers to questions concerning their sexual activity may be poor due to faulty recall, falsified accounts, or misunderstood questions.[11,13] Faulty recall of past events occurs unintentionally. This happens when the adolescent simply does not accurately remember past behavior; there is no purposeful intent to mislead the investigator. Almost all studies investigating coital behavior of adolescents are retrospective in design and, therefore, are subject to producing inaccurate results. Falsified reports of sexual activity occur when the subject states what he thinks is acceptable behavior for members of his peer group and not what actually happened. The social pressures for men to be sexually active may cause a teenager to overestimate his sexual behavior. Finally, the wording of sexual questions can affect the reliability of the answers. The meaning of words such as "intercourse" and "coitus" or a phrase such as "going all the way" may not be understood by all adolescents.

Even though existing studies of male sexual behavior contain methodological problems, when the results of multiple studies are compared some tentative conclusions are suggested. Probably 20–30 percent of teenage males 15 years of age or less, have had sexual intercourse.[4,12,14,15] Some studies have suggested that this figure is closer to 10 percent;[4,15] others have suggested a figure of over 40 percent.[12] Probably 30–50 percent of 16- to 19-year-olds have had sexual intercourse by high school graduation.[4,16–20] Results of recent studies investigating this age group are presented in Table 13-1; there is substantial scatter among study results.

The majority of studies investigating male sexual behavior have involved older adolescents (Table 13-1).[15,21–28] The results of these studies indicate that between 50 and 60 percent of college-aged adolescents have experienced coitus. There is less scatter among results for this age group, and therefore more confidence can be placed in these figures.

Cross-sectional studies in 1958[23] and 1965[24] indicated little secular change in the number of college-aged males who were sexually experienced.

Table 13-1. Frequency of Sexual Behavior among Young Men

Investigator	Year of Study	Percentage Sexually Active
High school age		
Vener et al.[16]	1969	34
Jessor and Jessor[19]	1969–1972	27
Miller[4]	1971	58
Lester and Perez[17]	1971–1974	40
Sorenson[12]	1972	72
Finkel and Finkel[20]	1974	68
Chess et al.[18]	1975	30
College age		
Finger[15]	1943–1944	45
Kinsey et al.[22]	1948	54
Christensen and Gregg[23]	1958	47
Robinson et al.[24]	1965	65
Lewis and Burr[25]	1967–1968	60
Bauman and Wilson[26]	1968	56
Christensen and Gregg[23]	1968	46
Luckey and Ness[27]	1968	58
Finger[15]	1969–1973	75
Robinson et al.[24]	1970	65
Bauman and Wilson[26]	1972	73
Simon et al.[28]	1972	56
Jessor and Jessor[19]	1975	82

Results from other studies, however suggested that coitus is being experienced by males at earlier ages.[15,26] Although the results regarding changes in male sexual behavior are conflicting, there is a clear indication that the sexual activity of adolescent females has risen substantially since 1960.[6,11,14] Males experience sexual activity at earlier ages than do females, but by late adolescence approximately equal numbers of each sex have had coitus.

CONTRACEPTION AMONG ADOLESCENT MALES

Many studies have demonstrated that adolescent males, even if they have had a school course that taught sex education, frequently lack adequate knowledge of reproductive physiology. Finkel and Finkel studied 421 high school males to assess their sexual behavior and their knowledge of, use of, and attitudes toward contraception.[20] The mean age of the subjects was 16.3 years. Six true–false questions were asked regarding reproductive physiology. Only 52 percent of the subjects correctly answered more than one-half of these questions. Of the 285 students who had taken a course on sex education, 60 percent answered four or more questions correctly.

In a study of high school students, Miller found that only 47 percent of the 163 males tested could correctly answer the question, "Do you know when a girl is fertile?"[4] Teenagers of the Youth Values Project in New York City, in a 1976 study of teenage sexuality, distributed questionnaires to 343 young men between 13 and 19 years of age.[29] By their own report, 70 percent of the subjects had "heard a lot about" the pill, 45 percent "knew about condoms," and 30 percent "had heard of a diaphragm"; 51 percent reported that they either did not know enough or else knew nothing about birth control.

In our first study of adolescent fathers, four multiple-choice questions were asked to assess knowledge of reproductive physiology.[9] Only 4 of the 16 subjects correctly answered the question, "When in her cycle is a woman most likely to become pregnant?" Only 1 subject answered all four questions correctly, 3 answered three questions correctly, and 11 answered zero to two questions correctly; 13 of these teenagers had taken a course in school that taught sex education.

Pannor and associates interviewed 91 unwed partners of women enrolled in a maternity program.[30] Subjects in this study were older, in general, than those in the studies previously described; only 57 percent of the mothers and 28 percent of the fathers were less than 20 years of age. Unfortunately, the results were not tabulated by age group. All unwed fathers stated that they "knew about contraception." The quality of this knowledge, however, was not assessed. Only 15.5 percent of the men felt that contraception availability was a major problem that had contributed to the unwed pregnancy.

In order to learn more about the dynamics of unwed fatherhood, Robbins studied four groups of college men: (1) 30 men who were bachelor nonfathers (mean age of 17.6 years); (2) 30 men who were unwed fathers (mean age 20 years); (3) 30 men who were married fathers (mean age 22 years); and (4) 20 men who were divorced fathers (mean age 37 years). No difference among groups was found in the ability to identify sexually related terms such as conception or birth, contraception or birth control, and orgasm or ejaculation.

The results of all these studies strongly suggest that adolescents lack a thorough knowledge of reproductive physiology. Since only a relatively small percentage of sexually active males become involved in a pregnancy, the role that lack of this knowledge may play in contributing to unplanned pregnancy is unclear.

In addition to cognitive factors, an adolescent's sexual behavior and use of contraception are influenced by the attitudes and behavior of significant people in his environment. The attachment that the adolescent has for these people and his perception of their attitudes toward premarital sex affect his own attitudes and sexual behavior.[19,21] Reiss studied the social context of premarital sexual permissiveness among high school and college students.[21] He concluded that an individual's attitude toward premarital sex is determined by the degree of his autonomy from the family, which traditionally has low permissiveness, and the degree of sexual permissiveness of his sociocultural setting, which traditionally has high permissiveness. Thus, the more emotionally independent an adolescent becomes from family influence, whether it results from normal psychosocial development or from estrangement because of conflict, the more he will be influenced by the relatively permissive sexual attitudes of his peer group. Jessor and Jessor conducted a longitudinal study of high school students to determine the relationship between problem behavior and psychosocial development.[19] Among both males and females, the students who had experienced sexual intercourse perceived greater parental and peer group approval for their behavior and also more frequently had sexually active peers as role models than did students who were not sexually active.

Results from the study by Miller involving high school students appear to substantiate the concept that the peer group generally has a permissive attitude toward sexual behavior.[4] Almost 50 percent of the 163 males questioned reported that it was acceptable for a teenager to have sex with someone who was a "good friend"; over 65 percent thought that sex was acceptable "when in love." Only 15 percent felt a male should have sex "only when married," whereas 74 percent approved of a couple living together even though not married. Miller concluded that peer group attitudes among students are relatively supportive of premarital sexual relationships.

In our initial study of unwed adolescent fathers, we found that there were strong role models for premarital childbearing in the family and peer group. Among 16 subjects, 5 were the product of an unwed pregnancy and 8 had a sibling who was born out of wedlock; 8 had a sibling and 11 had a male friend who had borne a child out of wedlock. In all, 14 prospective fathers either had a relative or a friend who had an out of wedlock child.

These unwed fathers were also questioned about attitudinal influences. Ten of 13 subjects reported that their mothers, and 7 of 12 said that their fathers did not object to them having premarital sex. Furthermore, 10 of 15 subjects reported that "most of their friends think it is alright to have sex with someone that they do not know well." Only 5 of 15 teenagers stated that "most of their friends think it is important to wait to be a father until they are married."

The parents' emotional responses upon learning that their son's girl-friend was pregnant are presented in Table 13-2. Eight of 14 mothers and 8 of 12 fathers were perceived by the teenagers to be happy with the announcement of the pregnancy. Three subjects reported that their mothers were disappointed but also happy upon learning about the pregnancy. In general, the parents' response to the pregnancy was quite positive.

The unwed teenage fathers in our study perceived their families and friends to have what could be labeled "permissive attitudes" regarding premarital sexual activity and pregnancy, the parents were generally perceived as responding favorably to the announcement of the pregnancy, and role models for unwed pregnancy were prevalent among family and friends. The results of this study are consistent with those of a study by Robbins and Lynn in which they investigated the family influences and attitudes of unwed fathers.[31,32] The study was performed twice: one group of subjects came from a juvenile detention ward, and the other group came from a college campus. The investigators found that unwed fathers, when compared to nonfathers, more frequently were illegitimate themselves, had a sibling who was ille-

Table 13-2. Parents' Response upon Learning that Their Unwed Teenage Sons Were Involved in a Pregnancy

Reaction	Mothers ($N = 14$)	Fathers ($N = 12$)
Happy	8	8
Ambivalent (both happy and disappointed)	3	0
Disappointed	2	1
Angry	1	1
Other	0	2

gitimate, had a sibling who produced an illegitimate child, and held more sexually permissive attitudes. They concluded that these permissive attitudes, if conveyed to the children, could explain the generational recidivism for premarital pregnancy which is seen among unwed fathers.

Most likely, role models for unwed pregnancy and permissive sexual attitudes among family and peer group serve to reduce the social sanctions against premarital pregnancy. The implicit message conveyed to the teenage male may be that "while premarital pregnancy may not be good, the consequences are not that bad either." The sexually active male may develop an attitude of unconcern regarding the consequences of pregnancy and, therefore, take fewer precautions to prevent a pregnancy from occurring.

Several other factors also appear to influence the initiation of sexual behavior for the adolescent male.[4,14,19,20] The age at which this event occurs is directly related to the age at onset of puberty and the degree of religiosity; the earlier puberty begins and the less strong an individual's religious attitudes and beliefs, the sooner he has his first episode of coitus. In addition, nonwhite males and males from the lower socioeconomic strata appear to initiate sexual behavior at earlier ages than do white adolescents and adolescents from middle-class families.

In association with the recent widespread use of oral contraceptive agents among teenagers, there has been an apparent decline in the use of male-oriented birth control methods. Results of a nationwide survey by Zelnik and Kantner indicated that in 1971 23.8 percent of unmarried, sexually active teenage girls used birth control pills, compared to 43.3 percent in 1976.[6] The percentage of females who stated that their partners had used condoms declined from 32.1 percent in 1971 to 20.9 percent in 1976. Studies of teenage males suggest that 20–40 percent use condoms for contraception.[12,26,33] Condoms are especially well suited for birth control use among adolescents, who tend to have sporadic sexual encounters. In addition, condoms are inexpensive, easily accessible, easy to carry, and provide a status symbol to some adolescent males.[34]

Many factors affect condom usage among adolescent males, who frequently give the following reasons for failure to use condoms: they interfere with pleasure, they seem unnatural, the female partner doesn't like them, they are inconvenient, they make sex seem less spontaneous, and the teenager had not planned on having sex.[25,27] Moreover, the application of condoms necessitates an interval between sexual foreplay and intercourse; this interval occurs only if both partners are able to control impulsive behavior and have planned in advance on condoms as a contraceptive device.

Between 1969 and 1970 Arnold established a free condom distribution program directed at inner city youth.[35] Program evaluation demonstrated that the number of males who reported that they had used condoms with their last episode of intercourse increased from 20 percent to 91 percent.

The investigator concluded that condoms are an acceptable form of contraception for many adolescents. Easy access to free condoms was most likely a major factor in the success of this experimental program.

In a study of predominantly older adolescents and young adult men, Keith and associates found that 84 percent of 438 subjects believed both sex partners had responsibility for contraception.[36] Furthermore, 70 percent answered that they would use a newly developed male contraceptive, if it were other than a condom; 64 percent stated that they would be willing to take a pill, a shot, or both as a contraceptive agent.

Considering the general lack of social acceptance of condoms among adolescents in the United States, a new male-oriented birth control method is needed. Federal support for the development of male contraceptive agents appears, however, to be lacking. In 1975, federally funded population research on males amounted to 25 percent of that spent on females.[37] The percentage of contraceptive research money provided by the government for male fertility studies increased only from 12 percent to 16 percent in 1975. Male contraceptive research has focused on developing agents to change the maturation and fertility capacity of sperm, to suppress sperm production, to block sperm transport, and to change the seminal fluid composition in order to render sperm inactive.[38,39]

PSYCHOSOCIAL CHARACTERISTICS OF ADOLESCENT FATHERS

Results from many sources indicate that only rarely do adolescent pregnancies occur because an adolescent male takes sexual advantage of a seemingly helpless adolescent female. The pregnant teenager and her partner usually are within 3–4 years of age of each other, come from the same socioeconomic background, are equal in educational achievement, and are involved in a meaningful relationship.[40–45] Our clinical experience substantiates these findings.

The data presented in Table 13-3 were obtained during an 8-month period in 1978 from teenagers who were attending the Rochester project. The average age was 16.4 years for the patients and 20 years for their partners; 40 percent of the fathers were less than 20. Almost two-thirds of the couples had been dating for more than 6 months prior to the pregnancy. An indication of the commitment of the relationship is suggested by the finding that 60 percent of the pregnant teenagers stated that their partners had been involved in helping them to make the decision regarding the outcome of the pregnancy, and 84 percent of the couples were still dating when the patients entered the project.

Descriptive data from our Teen Mother and Child Program at the

Table 13-3. Length of Time Couple
Had Been Dating at Time of
Conception ($N = 81$)

Time (months)	Percentage of Couples
Less than 1	5.4
2–6	30.0
7–12	12.5
More than 12	52.0

University of Utah are consistent with these results, even though our patient population (predominantly white and from middle socioeconomic class families) differs substantially from those teenagers served by the Rochester project. Among our first 40 patients, the males averaged only 3.2 years older than their partners, and 33 percent of couples were of school age (both partners 18 years of age or less). Between conception and delivery, 39 percent of the couples had a change in their relationship suggesting increased commitment, 28 percent had a change suggesting less commitment, and 33 percent had no change.

Other studies have also confirmed that a substantial number of fathers continue their involvement with the mother of their child after delivery. In a longitudinal study of 404 adolescent mothers, Furstenberg found that over 60 percent of fathers were maintaining a relationship with their children at the 5-year follow-up: 30 percent of these men were living with their children, 30 percent saw their children on a regular basis, and 30 percent visited their children irregularly.[41] McCarthy and Menken reviewed data from the 1973 National Survey of Family Growth and found that of 2258 adolescents who conceived out of wedlock, 68 percent had married by the time of delivery.[46] Data from the national survey by Zelnik and Kantner indicated that although 78 percent of first births to adolescents in 1976 were conceived out of wedlock, only 46 percent were delivered out of wedlock.[6] Thus 32 percent of adolescents legitimized their pregnancy after conception, and 54 percent of teenagers overall married prior to delivery of their baby. These statistics vary somewhat by locality. For example, 70 percent of the live births to adolescents in Utah during 1973 were conceived out of wedlock, and only 20 percent were born out of wedlock; 50 percent of the teenagers married after conception, and, overall, 80 percent were married by the time of delivery.[47]

Evidence suggests that many adolescent fathers have an established relationship with their girlfriends at the time conception occurs and they maintain some form of relationship following delivery. This is not true for all adolescents, however. Interviews with teenagers have confirmed that some partners used conception to serve their own individual needs, such as proving their masculinity or pressuring their partner into marriage. Surprisingly, interviews also occasionally have revealed that it was the male and not the female who was "taken advantage of." The following vignette is illustrative of this situation.

Dawn, who was 16 years old, and Bob, who was 17, had been dating steadily for 6 months. They had been having sexual relations for the past 2 months. Contraception was a subject that Bob wanted to discuss, but Dawn always told him not to worry because she was protected. Dawn's parents were having severe marital difficulties. They argued constantly and had discussed divorce on several occasions. When the pregnancy occurred, Bob was shocked; Dawn had quit taking her birth control pills without telling him. Her parents took out their anger on Bob, and refused to let him see their daughter. He offered to take a job to help pay for the expenses of the pregnancy. Her parents refused his offer. While he loved Dawn, he felt that he was not ready to marry. Eventually, he was allowed to visit Dawn, but he was continually excluded from helping plan for the baby. Dawn remained passive as disagreements arose between her parents and Bob; she refused to take any side in the arguments.

This case study demonstrates the need to interview both partners before making a decision regarding the reasons the teenage father is apparently not involved in assisting the prospective mother through pregnancy. The pregnancy served a purpose for Dawn in that it tended to focus her parents' attention away from their own problems. This purpose, however, had little to do with Bob; he was caught in the middle of a conflict that he did not understand.

Few studies have investigated the psychological profiles of adolescent males involved in out-of-wedlock pregnancies. Pauker reviewed the results of the Minnesota Multiphasic Personality Inventory (MMPI) administered during 1954 to 5701 ninth-grade males in Minnesota.[48] Pauker matched (by age and socioeconomic status) the 94 teenagers reported to have fathered a child at some time following the testing with control subjects who had not fathered an out-of-wedlock child. The mean age of both groups at the time of testing was 14.6 years. Differences in MMPI scores between the two groups were minimal. The study group did tend toward scores suggesting that these subjects were somewhat more hypomanic than the controls. There was, however, extensive overlap between groups. Pauker concluded that differences in personality characteristics as measured by the MMPI were not major contributors to out-of-wedlock pregnancies.

In Pannor and colleagues' study of unmarried fathers, psychological tests and personal interviews indicated that the men had psychosocial problems surrounding identity formation.[30] The case workers who performed the interviews thought that in 85 percent of the subjects the sex experience represented an effort to prove masculinity. Pannor et al. concluded that there may be an unwed mother–unwed father constellation in which neither partner possesses a strong sexual identity, neither is responsible or mature, and each reinforces the other to satisfy personal needs with little regard for the consequences. In a 1954 study of 32 unmarried couples who were involved in a pregnancy, Vincent reached a similar conclusion regarding the importance of the effect that sexual partners have upon each other.[42] Vincent suggested that sexual relationships may offer mutual benefits: the female may use sex as a means to date, marry, or achieve upward mobility; the male partner may use various means to obtain sex, which serves to reinforce his masculinity and self-identity.

We speculate that a certain interaction of sociocultural and psychological factors between adolescent partners is necessary for unprotected intercourse to occur. Each partner brings into a relationship his or her own set of sexual values and psychological traits. The pattern of these factors may determine an individual's risk for premarital pregnancy. A sexually active adolescent who perceives that social sanctions against premarital pregnancy are low (permissive), lacks adequate knowledge of reproductive physiology and contraception, has not achieved sufficient cognitive ability or is unwilling to consider the long-range consequences of his or her behavior, has a weak sexual and self-identity, and has impulsive behavior would have a high potential for risking unprotected intercourse. The match of risk patterns between partners may determine whether such behavior occurs. If both adolescents have a constellation of factors that places them at high risk for pregnancy, then there is a greater likelihood that this will occur than if only one or neither of the sexual partners has this pattern. Studies investigating antecedents of out-of-wedlock pregnancy, as they relate to one partner or the other, rarely yield consistent, meaningful results—probably because they do not consider the significant interaction of sociocultural and psychological factors that occurs between partners.

CONSEQUENCES OF PREGNANCY FOR ADOLESCENT FATHERS

Adolescent pregnancy may have significant psychosocial consequences for the adolescent father. Adverse affects may be seen in the adolescent's vocational-educational achievement, in divorce rates, and in the amount of stress that he perceives.

Vocational-Educational Achievement

Results of a study by Card and Wise indicated that males who father a child during adolescence achieve less formal education than do classmates who postpone parenthood.[49] A nationwide random sample of ninth-grade students was interviewed in 1960. The same students were interviewed again at 1, 5, and 11 years after their expected date of high school graduation. Teenage fathers were matched for socioeconomic status, academic aptitude, and educational expectations with males who had not fathered a child by age 24. Only 69.5 percent of the teenage fathers had received a high school diploma, as compared to 97 percent of the nonfathers. The teenage fathers entered the labor force earlier than their peers. At both 1 and 5 years after high school graduation, almost all the teenage fathers, compared to 75 percent of nonfathers, were employed. At the 11-year follow-up, however, over 90 percent of both groups were working. Significantly more teenage fathers than nonfathers had jobs in the blue-collar categories; the reverse was true for professional jobs. Although the income at age 29 was similar between groups, the greater opportunity for advancement in professional fields versus nonprofessional jobs makes it likely that adolescent fathers will subsequently be at a financial disadvantage.

Kerckhoff and Panow studied the effect of early marriage on the educational attainment of young men by analyzing data obtained between 1966 and 1970 from the National Longitudinal Surveys of Labor Market Experience.[50] The initial sample included 5225 unmarried men who were 15–18 years of age; 76 percent of these subjects were successfully followed during the 4-year study period. The results showed that, regardless of race, age at marriage had a depressing effect on educational attainment for those teenagers still in high school, but not for those who had graduated. In addition, the younger teenagers who had married were less likely to be enrolled in school and had lower educational goals at the time of the follow-up than older, married teenagers.

Early Marriage and Divorce

The marriage rate for adolescent males increased by over 320 percent between 1910 and 1970.[51] The largest increment in this rate occurred after World War II, between 1940 and 1950. In 1970, the prevalence of males aged 15–19 who had ever been married was 4.1 percent. As stated earlier, premarital pregnancy is a major factor influencing the decision for teenagers to marry; the combination of this and other social factors has an adverse effect on marriage stability.

Card and Wise found a strong, positive correlation between adolescent childbearing and both age at first marriage and family size.[49] Adolescent fathers married earlier than did nonfathers and they tended toward having larger families. At the 11-year follow-up, males who had fathered their first child when 16 years of age or less had an average of 3.3 children, while those men who postponed childbearing until age 20–24 had an average of 2.2 children.

There is clear evidence that teenage marriages are at risk for dissolution and dissatisfaction.[41,52-54] DeLissovoy longitudinally studied 48 married high school couples to determine the effect of early marriage on couple stability and satisfaction.[52] The average age at marriage was 16.5 years for the females and 17.1 years for the males. There had been a premarital pregnancy in 46 of the couples; 41 females and 35 males left high school prior to graduation. By 30 months of marriage, there was evidence of growing personal dissatisfaction when compared to earlier interviews, especially in the areas of family income and child training. Although 37 couples (77 percent) remained married throughout the 3 years of the study, the clinical impression was that they had difficulties in marital competence and satisfaction.

The divorce rate of adolescent couples is two to four times greater than that of adult couples.[53] This number is increased when there is a premarital pregnancy. Furstenberg found that after 48 months twice as many adolescent females who had had a premarital pregnancy were divorced, compared to the control group of married adolescents who had not had a premarital conception.[41] The younger the age of the adolescent groom, the greater the risk of marital dissolution. Burchinal found from national statistics of 1960 that 15-year-old married males had twice the total divorce-separation rate of 18-year-olds.[53]

Less formal education, earlier marriages, and larger families serve to place families headed by adolescent fathers at a financial disadvantage when compared to families in which the parents had postponed childbearing. Furstenberg suggested that the economic disadvantage of adolescent families may be a major factor in the high rate of divorce of these couples.[41] Lack of continued parental support, in addition to premarital conception, also adversely affects the marital outcome of adolescent couples.

Stresses Affecting Adolescent Fathers

Few studies have investigated the stresses perceived by fathers, regardless of their age. McNall, in 1976, reported the results of interviews conducted on the second to third postpartum day with new, adult fathers.[55] The major concerns elicited were feelings of helplessness and apprehension during labor and delivery, changes in the couple's relationship during gestation, and prospective parenthood.

Analyzing the results from our second study on adolescent fathers, we grouped perceived stressors into 12 minor categories and then into 4 major categories.[10] Group 1, vocational-educational concerns, consisted primarily of general worries regarding how the subjects were going to financially support their new families. Specific concerns about maintaining or getting a job and concerns about not finishing school were also included in this group. Group 2 stressors centered around concerns for the health of the mother and the child, and what would happen during labor and delivery.

Concerns about how the subjects would perform as parents comprised group 3 stressors. Group 4 stressors involved problems with relationships, specifically the subjects' problems with their partners, friends, and parents, and their feelings of alienation from their church.

Because we interviewed subjects at various times during gestation and into the postpartum period, we were able to investigate how these stresses changed over time (Fig. 13-1). Vocational-educational stresses were greatest during the first trimester, but remained at a relatively high level through gestation and into the postpartum period. Health concerns peaked during the third trimester and dropped off substantially after delivery. Concerns about parenthood arose during the second trimester, dropped slightly during the third trimester, and increased again post partum. Relationship stresses were greatest during the first trimester and dropped off at each subsequent interval. At both the first- and second-trimester interviews, problems with relationships appeared to cause the most concern; during the third trimester health concerns were most severe; and at the postpartum interview, vocational-educational concerns were the strongest. The trajectory of these concerns is not surprising, for only after resolving the interpersonal conflicts that inevitably surround a premarital pregnancy can a teenager face the realities of labor and delivery and financial responsibility.

During the course of each prenatal interview, the 20 teenage fathers were asked about their current thoughts relating to the baby and fatherhood,

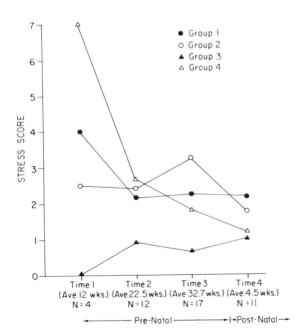

Figure 13-1. Changes in intensity of stress over time. (See text for explanation of groups.)

and any actions that had been taken to prepare for parenthood. This information provided an insight into how the adolescents were coping during pregnancy. The following coping strategies were reported:

- *Assuming role of provider.* During the prenatal course, all teenagers viewed the role of provider as a major component of fatherhood. Each demonstrated some activity directed toward bettering his financial situation—obtaining a first or even a second job, leaving school to get full-time employment, or seeking a higher paying job.
- *Talking with others about fatherhood.* Fourteen teenagers had discussions during the prenatal period with parents, friends, or partners about some aspect of fatherhood. Their discussions often centered around sharing ideas about childrearing and their respective responsibilities regarding child care.
- *Observing and evaluating other parents.* Four teenagers observed how others were performing as parents and identified behavior they wanted either to emulate or avoid.
- *Reading about fatherhood and child care.* This strategy was used by only four prospective fathers.
- *Fantasizing about fatherhood and the baby.* Twelve adolescents reported that they spent time thinking how they would perform as parents in various situations they anticipated would arise. Some worried about the role conflict of being an adolescent and a father.
- *Reviewing and evaluating how they were parented.* Near the end of the pregnancy, 7 of the teenagers began to think more about how they had been raised and to evaluate their parents' performance.
- *Using denial and avoidance.* Three prospective fathers denied ever thinking ahead about fatherhood or the baby. These teenagers maintained that no major changes in their lives would occur as a result of having a baby.
- *Helping with baby preparation.* By the end of the pregnancy, 18 teenagers had helped to buy items necessary for infant care or else had prepared a nursery in the home.
- *Settling down.* Six prospective fathers described how they had participated in fewer peer activities since the pregnancy. They tended to view their new behavior as part of "growing up" and getting ready for parenthood.

Caplan has stated that a crisis occurs, "when a person faces an obstacle to important life goals, that is, for a time, insurmountable to the utilization of customary methods of problem solving."[56] If the teenager is unable to cope successfully with the stresses surrounding pregnancy, he may experience a crisis and subsequent abnormal adaptive behavior. Acute psychosis, severe depression, somatic symptoms, and sexually deviant behavior have been reported to occur in new or prospective adult fathers as a result of the emotional stresses of pregnancy and parenthood.[57-59]

Caughlan, in a report on her clinical experiences with unwed fathers, stated that the emotional response of a man to a premarital pregnancy is not solely the result of the stress of illegitimacy, but also includes stress associated with the integrity of his ego development.[60] Some young fathers, because of immature psychological development, may have great difficulty coping with their situation.

The results of our first study on unwed adolescent fathers demonstrated that some teenagers do have major difficulties adjusting to pregnancy and prospective parenthood.[9] Of the 16 teenagers who were interviewed, 10 were assessed to be coping well with the stresses surrounding pregnancy, 4 were thought to be having moderate difficulty coping, and 2 were coping poorly. Six teenagers were referred for additional counseling because of clinical evidence of depression; 2 of these males had suicidal ideation. Adequacy of coping was not assessed for subjects in our second study.

Parental Behavior

Only recently have studies investigated the role of the father in early infant development.[61,62] Prior to these studies, the socialization of an infant was thought to result predominantly from interaction between the mother and child. Longitudinal studies by Lamb demonstrated that each parent makes a distinct contribution to the socialization process.[63] Fathers interact with their young infants in a quantitively and qualitatively different fashion than do the mothers. Lamb suggested that young infants can distinguish between the two parents on behavioral as well as perceptual criteria.[62] Different behavior patterns are learned from each parent.

Theoretically, fathers who have not reached cognitive and psychosocial developmental maturity may be incapable of providing their children with the quality of parenting necessary for early infant psychological development. This situation may be compounded by the magnitude of stress perceived by teenagers and their separation from a supportive social network. For various reasons, therefore, adolescents may be at risk for parenting failure.[64,65] Parental behavior of adolescent fathers, however, has not been critically studied.

IMPLICATIONS FOR CLINICAL INTERVENTION

Clinical assessment of the adolescent father should be made to determine his health-educational needs and his needs for emotional support and counseling. Our experience supports the opinion of Pannor and associates that the most effective way to interview an unwed father is to enlist the girlfriend's support.[30] With the unmarried mother's active assistance, these investigators had success in contacting 94.3 percent of the unmarried fathers who lived in the local community; the success rate was only 12.1 percent when the woman did not provide assistance. Success at interviewing the unwed father, therefore, depends to a great extent on how willing the pregnant adolescent is to have her partner accompany her to the clinic. An initial interview with both partners is the most effective way of meeting the father of the baby.

Exploration of the social context in which conception occurred usually can elicit the reasons for the pregnancy. In those instances when the pregnancy was anticipated, our clinical experience indicates that the stresses are less severe than when conception was unexpected. In the former situation, the couple frequently had already discussed getting married or how they would earn enough money to afford having a baby. The families of these adolescents also seem to more readily accept the pregnancy. Although the problems that face these couples may be great, they appear to be well tolerated. Counseling should be directed at helping the adolescents to plan effectively for the future and to increase their parenting skills.

An assessment should be made regarding how well the teenager is coping with the stresses surrounding pregnancy and how well he is preparing for fatherhood. A teenager who has dropped out of school or has had a decline in his academic performance, reports that he is feeling depressed, preoccupied, or excessively anxious, or exhibits more acting-out behavior than prior to conception may be having difficulty adjusting to the situation. These adolescents need active counseling directed at helping them cope with their immediate problems.

In the assessment of the adolescent's need for counseling, it is important to determine the availability of supportive individuals. The fathers who need the most assistance are usually those who have few people available for emotional support. They tend to be isolated from their peer group, to have poor relationships with their parents, and to feel alienated from their religion. The health care provider for the adolescent mother may be the only person who is in a position to offer emotional support to the father of the baby.

The teenage couple should be assisted in discussing their future plans for the relationship. It is important that the provider direct this discussion in a neutral, nonjudgmental manner. Both the "costs" and "benefits" of each alternative should be thoroughly examined. Because the communication patterns of adolescent couples are frequently ineffective, they may have never expressed their opinions to each other regarding the future of their relationship. They should be helped to come to a decision regarding what is best for themselves and for their child. Frequently, adolescents need help in realistically appraising their situation: How much money does it take to raise a child and be married? Who will babysit the child while the couple goes to work or school? Where would they live if they got married? This reality-oriented approach can help the adolescent father explore the extent of the involvement he plans to continue with his partner and the baby.

The adolescent father's educational-vocational plans should be explored. If the couple plans to marry, he may need assistance in finding alternative education programs in order to allow him to continue schooling and get a job. He may not know what opportunities are available for vocational training and may need help to understand that this education will lead to better paying jobs in the future.

The adolescent father's knowledge of reproductive physiology and contraception should also be evaluated. It is erroneous to assume that a course in sex education or self-reported familiarity with these topics reflects an adequate understanding of conception or contraception. Myths and false information may need to be dispelled. One of the fathers in our study said during an interview, "I was wondering why a pregnancy had not happened. I went to a doctor in school and he said I had a hernia; I thought that the hernia was stopping me from getting my girl pregnant." In part, this teenager was trying to have a baby to dispel his fear of sterility. He also had a misconception that he was protected from impregnating his partner.

Clinicians can also provide the adolescent male an opportunity to talk about his thoughts of fatherhood and the baby. The role of the health provider in offering supportive counseling to these young men has been long overlooked. If the teenager has not met any other young fathers, these contacts could be made on either a formal or informal basis during clinic visits, thus offering the adolescent an opportunity to expand his support network to include members that share similar experiences.

During the latter part of gestation, if he has not given much thought to what fatherhood will be like for him, the adolescent can be encouraged to review his own childhood as a means of clarifying his own values and goals. He can be encouraged to observe his siblings or relatives in interactions with their own children, and discuss his evaluations with his partner. A prospective teenage father could also be encouraged to fantasize about what his child will be like, and to develop goals and aspirations for his offspring. Teenage fathers should be given the opportunity to learn about childbirth and child care. They should routinely be included in prenatal education classes. In our experience, when given the opportunity, many teenage fathers wanted to become involved in preparing themselves to help their partners through labor and delivery and to learn how to become a better father.[9] These types of anticipatory coping strategies may better prepare the adolescent to undertake his role as a new father by readying him emotionally for his paternal responsibilities.

Many beneficial effects can occur when the father of the baby is included in the clinical services provided to adolescent mothers. Pannor et al. found that when the boyfriends were involved, the unwed mothers reported that they felt less fear of desertion, were more confident in their decision regarding the outcome of the pregnancy, and were better able to discuss their future plans regarding the relationship. The couples were also able to plan for the future more realistically.[30]

Some teenage fathers have their own needs that can be helped by involvement in pregnancy counseling. Adolescent fathers can receive assistance in coping with the stresses surrounding pregnancy and prospective parenthood; they can be helped to prepare themselves both practically and emotionally for their paternal responsibilities; and they can also gain a factual knowledge of how to prevent future, unwanted pregnancies. A pregnancy does not happen to a teenage girl in a void; the causes and effects also involve the teenage father.

REFERENCES

1. National Center for Health Statistics: Final natality statistics, 1978. Monthly Vital Statistics Report [Suppl] 29, 1980
2. Center for Disease Control: Abortion Surveillance—1976. August 1978
3. Coddington RD: The significance of life events as etiologic factors in the diseases of children II. A study of a normal population. J Psychosom Res 16:205–213, 1972
4. Miller WB: Sexuality, contraception, and pregnancy in a high school population. Calif Med 119:14–21, 1973
5. Russ-Eft D, Sprenger M, Beever A: Antecedents of adolescent parenthood and consequences at age 30. Fam Coordinator 28:173–179, 1979
6. Zelnik M, Kantner JF: First pregnancies to women aged 15–19: 1976 and 1971. Fam Plann Perspect 10:11–20, 1978
7. National Center for Health Statistics: Advance report of final marriage statistics, 1979. Monthly Vital Statistic Report [Suppl] 30, July 31, 1980
8. National Center for Health Statistics: Selected demographic characteristics of teenage wives and mothers. Advance Data from Vital and Health Statistics 61, Sept 26, 1980
9. Elster A, Panzarine S: Unwed teenage fathers—Emotional and health educational needs. J Adolesc Health Care 1:116–120, 1981
10. Elster A, Panzarine S: Teenage fathers—A measurement of stress over time. Presented at the meeting of the Society for Adolescent Medicine, October 1981
11. Hopkins JR: Sexual behavior in adolescence. J Soc Issues 33:67–85, 1977
12. Sorenson RC: Adolescent Sexuality in Contemporary America. New York, World, 1972
13. Spanier GB: Use of recall data in survey research on human sexual behavior. Soc Biol 23:244–253, 1977
14. Diepold J, Young RD: Empirical studies of adolescent sexual behavior—A critical review. Adolescence 14:45–64, 1979
15. Finger FW: Changes in sex practices and beliefs of male college students: Over 30 years. J Sex Res 11:304–317, 1975
16. Vener AM, Stewart CS, Hanger DL: The sexual behavior of adolescents in Middle America: Generational and American-British comparison. J Marriage Fam 34:696–705, 1972

17. Lester LF, Perez P: Dimensions of college student behavior. J Am Coll Health Assoc 26:90–93, 1977
18. Chess S, Thomas A, Cameron M: Sexual attitudes and behavior patterns in a middle-class adolescent population. Am J Orthopsychiatry 45:689–701, 1976
19. Jessor R, Jessor SL: Problem Behavior and Psychosocial Development. A Longitudinal Study of Youth. New York, Academic Press, 1977
20. Finkel ML, Finkel DJ: Sexual and contraceptive knowledge, attitudes, and behavior of male adolescents. Fam Plann Perspect 7:256–260, 1975
21. Reiss IL: The Social Context of Premarital Sexual Permissiveness. New York, Holt, Rinehart, Winston, 1967
22. Kinsey AC, Pomeroy WB, Martin CE: Sexual Behavior in the Human Male. Philadelphia, Saunders, 1948
23. Christensen HT, Gregg CG: Changing sex norms in America and Scandinavia. J Marriage Fam 32:616–627, 1970
24. Robinson IE, King K, Balswick JO: The premarital sexual revolution among college females. Fam Coordinator 21:189–194, 1972
25. Lewis RA, Burr WR: Premarital coitus and commitment among college students. Arch Sex Res 4:73–79, 1975
26. Bauman KE, Wilson RR: Sexual behavior of unmarried university students in 1968 and 1972. J Sex Res 10:327–333, 1974
27. Luckey EB, Nass GD: A comparison of sexual attitudes and behavior in an international sample. J Marriage Fam 32:364–379, 1969
28. Simon W, Berger AS, Gagnon JH: Beyond anxiety and fantasy: The coital experience of college youth. J Youth Adolesc 1:203–222, 1972
29. Ross S (director): Report of the Youth Values Project. New York, Population Institute, 1979
30. Pannor R, Massarik F, Evans B: The Unmarried Father. New York, Springer, 1971
31. Robbins MMB: The dynamics of unwed fatherhood. Unpublished doctoral dissertation, University of California, Davis, 1975
32. Robbins MMB, Lynn DB: The unwed father: Generation recidivism and attitudes about intercourse in California Youth Authority Wards. J Sex Res 9:334–341, 1973
33. McNamara V, King LA, Green MF: Adolescent perspectives on sexuality, contraception, and pregnancy. J Med Assoc Ga 68:811–814, 1979
34. Scales P: Males and morals—Teenage contraceptive behavior amid the double standard. Fam Coordinator 26:211–222, 1979
35. Arnold CB: The sexual behavior of inner-city adolescent condom users. J Sex Res 8:298–309, 1972
36. Keith L, Keith D, Bussell R, et al: Attitude of men toward contraception. Arch Gynecol 220:89–97, 1975
37. Diller L, Hembree W: Male contraception and family planning: A social and historical review. Fertil Steril 28:1271–1279, 1977
38. Jackson H, Morris ID: Contraception for the male—Problems with progress. Clin Obstet Gynecol 6:129–155, 1979
39. Barwin BN: Recent advances in the pharmacologic regulation of fertility in men. Can Med Assoc J 119:757–759, 1978
40. Gispert M, Falk R: Sexual experimentation and pregnancy in young black adolescents. Am J Obstet Gynecol 125:459–466, 1976
41. Furstenberg FF: The social consequences of teenage parenthood. Fam Plann Perspect 8:148–164, 1976
42. Vincent CE: Unwed Mothers. New York, Free Press, 1956

43. Kinch RAH, Wearing MP, Love EJ, et al: Some aspects of pediatric illegitimacy. Am J Obstet Gynecol 105:20–31, 1969
44. Pope H: Unwed mothers and their sex partners. J Marriage Fam 29:555–567, 1967
45. Gebbard GO, Wolff JR: The unwed pregnant teenager and her male relationships. J Reprod Med 19:137–140, 1977
46. McCarthy J, Menken J: Marriage, remarriage, marital disruption and age at first birth. Fam Plann Perspect 11:21–30, 1979
47. Van Dyck P, Brockert JE, Heiner CD: Outcomes of teenage pregnancy relating to the interval between marriage and birth. Unpublished report, 1973
48. Pauker JD: Fathers of children conceived out-of-wedlock—Prepregnancy, high school, psychological tests results. Dev Psychol 4:215–218, 1971
49. Card JJ, Wise LL: Teenage mothers and teenage fathers—The impact of early child-bearing on the parent's personal and professional lives. Fam Plann Perspect 10:199–205, 1978
50. Kerckhoff AC, Panow AA: The effect of early marriage on the educational attainment of young men. J Marriage Fam 41:97–107, 1979
51. Sklar J, Berkov B: Teenage family formation in postwar America. Fam Plann Perspect 6:80–90, 1974
52. DeLissovoy V: High school marriages: A longitudinal study. J Marriage Fam 35:245–255, 1973
53. Burchinal LG: Trends and prospects for young marriages in the United States. J Marriage Fam 27:243–254, 1965
54. Lowrie SH: Early marriages—Premarital pregnancy and associated factors. J Marriage Fam 27:48–56, 1965
55. McNall L: Concerns of expectant fathers, in McNall L, Galleener L (eds): Current Practices in Obstetric and Gynecologic Nursing, Vol 1. St. Louis, Mosby, 1976
56. Caplan J: An Approach to Community Mental Health. New York, Grune & Stratton, 1961
57. Trethowan WH, Conlon MF: The Couvade Syndrome. Br J Psychiatry 111:57–66, 1965
58. Savenar JO, Weddington WW: Abdominal pain in expectant fathers. Psychosomatics 19:761–768, 1978
59. Freeman T: Pregnancy as a precipitant of mental illness in men. Br J Med Psychol 24:49–54, 1951
60. Caughlan J: Psychic hazards of unwed paternity. Soc Work 5:29–35, 1960
61. Parke RD, Power TG, Tinsley BR, et al: The father's role in the family system. Semin Perinatol 3:25–34, 1979
62. Lamb ME: The father's role in the facilitation of infant mental health. Infant Ment Health J 1:140–149, 1980
63. Lamb ME: Father-infant and mother-infant interaction in the first year of life. Child Dev 48:167–181, 1977
64. Elster A, Lamb ME: Adolescent fathers—A group potentially at risk for parenting failure. Infant Ment Health J (in press)
65. Parke RD, Power TG, Fisher T: The adolescent father's impact on the mother and child. J Soc Issues 36:88–106, 1980

14

Effects of Early Parenthood on the Cognitive Development of Children

E. Milling Kinard and Lorraine V. Klerman

The problems associated with adolescent pregnancy and childbearing—such as disrupted education, low income, and marital dissolution—have been amply documented. Fortunately, programs have been developed to prevent or reduce the occurrence of these negative consequences.[1] The consequences of adolescent parenting for infants have been studied less often and programs that could have impact in this area are just beginning to be established. Attempts to determine whether physical, emotional, or cognitive deficits in the children of adolescent parents are due to the socioeconomic conditions under which they develop or to the biologic immaturity of their parents are complicated by the fact that adolescent childbearing is more prevalent among low-income populations than among those of higher socioeconomic status. If deficits exist and parental immaturity is the principal cause, remedial programs could be targeted at the children of young parents. If socioeconomic factors are paramount, however, the problem will be more difficult to solve.

This work was supported by Brandeis University Biomedical Research Support Grant 6621.

BACKGROUND

In a recent review of studies of the children of teenage parents, Baldwin and Cain concluded that "children born to teenagers suffer intellectual deficits, largely because of the economic and social impact of early childbearing on the young parents."[2] Among the studies of cognitive development summarized in the review were two based on samples composed largely of black urban adolescent mothers. Marecek analyzed data from the Philadelphia segment of the Collaborative Perinatal Project (CPP),[3] and Furstenberg conducted a longitudinal study of unmarried adolescent mothers in Baltimore.[4] Both found somewhat lower scores on measures of cognitive development among the children of adolescents.

In another study using a sample selected from the complete CPP data set, Broman compared children of two groups of teenage mothers (12–15 years and 16–17 years) with children of older mothers (20–29 years).[5] When they were tested at age 4 years, the children of both white and black teenage mothers had lower mean IQ scores than those of older mothers. At age 7 years, there was a tendency for IQ scores to be associated with maternal age among whites but not among blacks. However, the effects of socioeconomic status on IQ scores were much greater than the effects of maternal age.

Belmont et al, analyzed data from three large studies: the complete CPP data set and Cycles II and III of the Health Examination Survey (HES).[6] In the CPP analysis, their findings were similar to Marecek's and Broman's: when tested at age 7 years, children of teenage mothers had lower mean scores on the Wechsler Intelligence Scale for Children (WISC) than children of older mothers; and children of black mothers in all age groups had lower scores than those of white mothers. The HES analyses showed lower mean WISC scores for children of white adolescent mothers than for children of white older mothers and lower mean WISC scores for children of black mothers in each age group than for children of white mothers. The pattern by age groups among black mothers was inconsistent: children of mothers 14–17 years old had higher mean scores than children of mothers either 18–19 years old or 20 and over.

The researchers were mainly interested in the unique contribution of maternal age to children's WISC scores after the effects of other independent variables were controlled. Using hierarchical multiple regression analysis for each of the three data sets, Belmont et al. found a small but statistically significant contribution of linear maternal age to WISC scores after other relevant social and demographic factors* were entered into the regression

---

*These included the following variables: age, sex, race, birth order, and twin status of the child; family size and income; education and employment of parents or guardians; one or two parents in the family; and area of residence.

equation. Because there were no consistent effects of teenage mother status (young teens versus others; young teens versus older teens versus others), the authors concluded that children of teenage mothers "suffer virtually no depression in intelligence test scores that can be attributed solely and specifically to the teenage status of the mother." Moreover, socioeconomic factors seemed to be more important predictors of intellectual development than maternal age.

To explore further the relationships among these variables, these investigators tested a causal model designed to determine the direct and indirect effects of their two measures of maternal age (teenage motherhood status and linear maternal age) on children's IQ scores.[7] Several family characteristics were selected as intervening variables. Analyses were conducted separately for blacks and whites for each of the three data sets previously used. As expected from the earlier analysis, the effects of linear maternal age on children's IQs were primarily direct, that is, not mediated through intervening sociodemographic factors. On the other hand, teenage motherhood status had no significant direct effect on children's IQs, but did have indirect effects, chiefly through parental education. The authors interpreted these findings as evidence that deficits in the intellectual status of the children of teenage mothers are attributable almost entirely to the lower educational status of the parents.

In another analysis of data from Cycle II of the HES, Edwards and Grossman[8] examined the relationships between children's cognitive development and measures of their health status, including mother's age at the time of the child's birth. Their analysis included only white children living with both natural or adopted parents at the time of the survey and was further restricted to cases with no missing data. Using WISC IQ scores based on the Vocabulary and Block Design subtests as the dependent variable in a multiple regression analysis (controlled for a set of non-health-related demographic variables*), they found that children whose mothers were under 20 years of age at the time of their births had lower WISC scores than children whose mothers were between 20 and 35 years of age at their births. The authors noted that the regression coefficient for maternal age indicated a difference of approximately 2 points between children of teenage mothers and children of older mothers. When the sample was subdivided into low-income (less than $7000) and high-income ($7000 or more) groups, the effect of maternal age on WISC scores in the low-income sample was comparable to the results for the total sample, but maternal age had no significant effect in the high-income group. Despite differences in the HES sample

---

*These included the following variables: sex, birth order, and twin status of the child; family size and income; preschool experience; foreign language spoken in the home; education and employment of parents; and region and size of place of residence.

selection criteria used by Edwards and Grossman and by Belmont et al., their findings appear to be consistent.

In an attempt to clarify further the relationship between the parent's age and the child's intellectual development, we examined the data from HES Cycle II. Although this data set was also used in other studies,[6-8] the analyses reported here differ from previous approaches, particularly with respect to the measures of intellectual status.

STUDY DESCRIPTION

HES Cycle II was conducted by the National Center for Health Statistics from 1963 to 1965. A nationwide probability sample of noninstitutionalized children 6–11 years of age was selected and examined. For a sample of 7119 children (96 percent of the total probability sample of 7417), data were collected through interviews with parents, physical examinations, psychological tests, school reports of behavior and performance, and birth certificates. For children living with one or both natural parents, we used the current age of the parent(s) present in the household at the time of the survey as reported in the parental interview to calculate the age of the parent(s) at the time of the child's birth. For children with one or both natural parents missing from their current households, the age of the parent(s) at the time of the child's birth was obtained from information derived from birth certificates.*

An early report of the survey findings[9] indicated that the children's mean deviation WISC scores increased as the age of their mothers at the time of their births rose, reaching the highest level for those whose mothers had been 25–39 years old when they were born, and then the children's scores decreased as the age of their mothers rose to 40 years and beyond. A similar pattern was found for father's age at the child's birth, with WISC scores reaching the maximum for those whose fathers were 25–44 years of age and then declining for those whose fathers were 45 years and over. In order to preserve a linear relationship between parental age and children's scores, the present analysis of maternal age was restricted to those children whose mothers were under 40 and the analysis of paternal age to those whose fathers were under 45 at the time the children were born.

---

*In the Belmont et al. analysis of the HES data, maternal age at the child's birth was derived entirely from birth certificate information.[7] However, we chose to define parental age according to interview information in order to avoid any systematic bias that might result from the exclusion of the 399 cases with no birth certificate information. Edwards and Grossman used only interview information to determine maternal age at the child's birth.[8]

The calculations of variances reported here are based on an assumption of simple random sampling, although the HES in fact used a complex sampling design. The effect of the complex sample design is to decrease the probability of finding significant sample statistics. Small differences that are statistically significant under the simple random sample assumptions used in the present analysis may not be significant if the complex sample design were taken into consideration. Thus, the findings reported here should be strictly applied only to the population used in the HES.

Three indices of intellectual development previously constructed from the HES data by Dupuy and Gruvaeus to clarify the effects of socioeconomic status on intellectual achievement were used as dependent variables: (1) the index of Intellectual Development (ID); (2) the index of Sociointellectual Status (SIS); and (3) the index of Differential-Intellectual Development (DID).[10] The ID index is comparable to the Full Scale WISC IQ score. The SIS index reflects the contribution of family background factors (parents' education and annual family income per person under 21 in the household) to the ID scores. The DID index represents the child's intellectual achievement independent of the contribution of socioeconomic status as reflected in the SIS index. A more detailed description of the derivation of the three indices is given in Appendix A.

RESULTS

Maternal Age

For the total sample, mean ID and mean SIS scores increased with increasing age of the mother at the child's birth, except for the very small group age 14 and under where mean scores were inflated due to an ID score of 129 for one white child whose mother was 11 years old at the child's birth (Table 14-1). The mean DID scores for children of teenage mothers, with the same exception, were lower than those for children of older mothers, but scores did not consistently increase with increasing maternal age for mothers in the under 20 groups. Moreover, the range of mean DID scores was narrower (again omitting the 14 and under age group) than either mean ID or mean SIS scores. This finding suggests that a substantial contribution to the relationship between maternal age and child cognitive development was due to the association of cognitive development with socioeconomic factors, as reflected by the SIS index, and the tendency for teenage mothers to be overrepresented in lower socioeconomic groups. Also noteworthy is the finding that the correlation coefficients between mother's age in years and the three indices were quite small, and the proportion of variance in the indices accounted for by mother's age was less than 1.5 percent.

Table 14-1. Mean Scores for Three Indices of Intellectual Development by Age of Mother at Birth of Child, with Percentage Variance Accounted for and Pearson Correlations*

| Age of Mother | N | ID | Race Specific | |
			SIS	DID
Total sample				
14 or less	7	98.1	89.3	108.8
15–17	208	92.9	93.5	99.5
18–19	490	95.4	96.7	98.7
20–29	4059	100.6	100.5	100.1
30–39	2087	101.7	102.2	103.4
Total	6851	100.3	99.9	100.4
Percentage variance		1.44	0.92	0.59
Pearson's r		0.1201	0.0960	0.0771
p Value		<0.001	<0.001	<0.001
White and other races				
14 or less	4	108.5	92.8	115.7
15–17	138	96.3	97.1	99.2
18–19	375	98.4	99.8	98.7
20–29	3557	102.5	102.4	100.1
30–39	1844	103.6	102.2	101.4
Total	5918	102.5	102.0	100.4
Percentage variance		0.93	0.44	0.51
Pearson's r		0.0965	0.0665	0.0714
p Value		<0.001	<0.001	<0.001
Black				
14 or less	3	84.3	84.8	99.6
15–17	70	86.3	86.4	99.9
18–19	115	85.5	86.8	98.7
20–29	502	86.5	86.6	99.9
30–39	243	87.5	85.5	101.9
Total	933	86.6	86.3	100.3
Percentage variance		0.48	0.74	1.31
Pearson's r		0.0692	−0.0862	0.1144
p Value		0.017	0.004	<0.001

*The correlation coefficients are based on maternal age in single years rather than the grouped age categories.

When the sample was subdivided by race, the findings for white and other races were similar to those for the sample as a whole: increasing mean ID and SIS scores with increasing maternal age (excluding the under 14 age group); and slight differences in mean DID scores, but no consistent trend for the under 20 age groups. The proportion of variance in the indices explained by maternal age was less than 1 percent. For blacks, all three indices showed very slight differences among age groups with no consistent pattern by mother's age. For each age group, mean ID and SIS scores were consistently lower and the range of these scores was narrower for blacks than for white and other races. On the other hand, mean DID scores did not differ between blacks and white and other races because of the race-specific adjustment in the SIS index. These findings suggest that lower ID and SIS scores for blacks were likely to be due to lower socioeconomic status and not to maternal age.

Paternal Age

For the total sample, mean scores for each of the three indices increased with increasing paternal age at the child's birth, with the exception that mean ID and SIS scores decreased slightly in the 40- to 44-year-old group (Table 14-2). Unlike the inconsistent pattern for mother's age and DID scores, mean DID scores increased, albeit slightly, with increasing paternal age. However, the proportion of variance in the indices explained by age of the father was too small to consider the relationship important.

When the sample was divided according to race, father's age showed no consistent relationship to any of the three indices for white and other races, but children whose fathers were under 20 at the child's birth scored lower on all three indices than children of fathers age 20–39 years. Less than 1 percent of the variance in the three indices was accounted for by paternal age, thus indicating virtually no relationship between the age and indices for this group. For blacks, mean ID and DID scores tended to increase with increasing paternal age, but mean SIS scores tended to decrease. As with maternal age, lower mean ID and SIS scores for blacks than for white and other races seemed to reflect socioeconomic factors. The proportion of variance in the SIS index associated with father's age was higher for blacks than for white and other races. However, lower mean SIS scores were associated with older ages for fathers, suggesting that socioeconomic status was lower for the older fathers. The negative direction of this association suggests a lower socioeconomic status for older childbearing blacks or, more positively, an improvement in socioeconomic status among younger black parents.

Table 14-2. Mean Scores for Three Indices of Intellectual Development by Age of Father at Birth of Child, with Percentage Variance Accounted for and Pearson Correlations*

Age of Father	N	ID	Race Specific	
			SIS	DID
Total sample				
15–17	23	93.4	95.9	97.1
18–19	136	95.1	97.4	97.6
20–29	3294	100.3	100.4	99.9
30–39	2656	101.6	100.7	100.8
40–44	504	100.5	98.4	102.1
Total	6613	100.7	100.3	100.4
Percentage variance		0.30	0.001	0.52
Pearson's r		0.0551	−0.0043	0.0718
p Value		<0.001	0.364	<0.001
White and other races				
15–17	16	97.9	99.7	98.1
18–19	104	97.8	100.3	97.5
20–29	2871	102.3	102.4	99.9
30–39	2362	103.4	102.6	100.8
40–44	441	102.2	100.2	102.0
Total	5794	102.6	102.3	100.4
Percentage variance		0.20	0.05	0.44
Pearson's r		0.0448	−0.0229	0.0667
p Value		<0.001	0.04	<0.001
Black				
15–17	7	83.1	87.3	95.9
18–19	32	85.9	87.9	98.0
20–29	423	86.9	87.4	99.5
30–39	294	86.8	85.6	101.1
40–44	63	88.0	85.5	102.5
Total	819	86.8	86.6	100.2
Percentage variance		0.05	3.34	1.16
Pearson's r		0.0228	−0.1828	0.1078
p Value		0.257	<0.001	0.001

*The correlation coefficients are based on paternal age in single years rather than the grouped age categories.

Other Sociodemographic Factors

In order to explore further the influence of parental age on cognitive development, a set of independent variables in addition to parental age was selected from those previously reported as affecting intellectual development.[9] These independent variables—birth order of the child, length of the child's stay in the hospital at birth, age at which the child first walked alone, age at which the child first spoke a word, preschool experience (nursery school and/or kindergarten), and parent structure of the household (mother and/or father)—along with mother's age (for mothers under 40) and father's age (for fathers under 45) at the child's birth were then used as predictor variables in multiple regression analyses for the ID, SIS, and DID indices. Information on the total number of dependent and independent variables was available for 5534 cases; thus, the sample for this portion of the analysis is smaller than that previously presented.

The predictive model explained 11.6 percent of the variance in the ID index (Table 14-3). The two most powerful predictors were mother's age at the child's birth and birth order of the child. ID scores increased with increasing maternal age and decreased with later birth order. Higher ID scores were also associated with having had preschool experience, having both natural parents in the household, having spoken the first word and taken the first step at younger ages, and having a shorter length of stay in the hospital at birth. The coefficient for father's age was not significant. However, the large number of statistically significant coefficients must be interpreted with caution because of the large sample size.

Table 14-3. Standardized Regression Coefficients and R^2 Coefficients

Independent Variables	Dependent Variables		
	ID	SIS	DID
Preschool experience	−0.144*	−0.204*	−0.032‡
Household composition	0.117*	0.202*	—
Birth order of child	−0.198*	−0.346*	—
Mother's age at child's birth	0.224*	0.305*	0.059†
Child's age at first word	−0.086*	−0.041*	−0.075*
Child's stay in hospital at birth	−0.053*	—	−0.064*
Child's age at first step	−0.028‡	0.019	−0.047*
Father's age at child's birth	−0.031	−0.098*	0.031
R^2	0.116*	0.243*	0.022*

*p ≤ 0.001.
†p ≤ 0.01.
‡p ≤ 0.05.

The explanatory power of the predictor variable set was greatest for the SIS index, accounting for 24.3 percent of the variance. The two most powerful predictors were again the age of the mother at the child's birth and birth order of the child. For this index, the coefficient for father's age was significant, although small, but mother's age had three times the predictive power of father's age. Moreover, higher SIS scores were associated with younger ages for fathers, as noted in the findings of the previous analysis. The independent variable set explained only 2.2 percent of the variance of the DID index, thus indicating that these variables have little predictive power once the effects of parental education and income as reflected in the SIS index are removed.

SUMMARY AND CONCLUSIONS

The assumption that children of teenage mothers are at significantly increased risk for substantial deficits in intellectual development is not supported by the data presented here. Although this analysis of the relationship between parental age at child's birth and three indices of cognitive development showed a relatively consistent pattern of lower scores in the children of mothers or fathers who were under 20 years of age as compared to those whose mothers or fathers were no longer teenagers, the absolute magnitude of the differences in scores among age groups was less than 1 standard deviation. In the ID scores, where socioeconomic factors are not eliminated, the difference between the highest and lowest mean scores for maternal and paternal age groups was about 9 points for the total group (excluding the under 14 age group), less than 8 for white and other races (excluding the under 14 age group), and less than 5 for blacks. Moreover, when the influence of education and income were removed in the DID scores, the differences became less marked, except for blacks: 5 points or less for the total group, less than 5 for white and other races, and less than 7 for blacks.

Furthermore, in several of the analyses the trends were not consistent, that is, children of younger teenagers did not always score lower than children of older mothers. This finding suggests that factors other than parental age may be of greater importance. One possible explanation for this inconsistency is that children of mothers under 18 years old may be more likely to live in extended family settings with grandparents or other relatives and therefore may receive more cognitive stimulation than children of 18- and 19-year-olds who may live with their mothers only.

Empirical support for such an explanation was provided by Card in an analysis of cognitive development in 15- and 17-year-olds from Project Talent data.[11] Children of adolescent parents had lower scores on cognitive measures than children of older parents, even after sociodemographic and family structure variables were controlled. These findings showed a direct effect of adolescent parenthood on cognitive ability. Further analyses restricted the two groups to first-born children matched on sex, race, socioeconomic status, and size of community of residence. These matched groups were significantly different in family structure: children of adolescent parents were less likely than children of older parents to live in families with both mother and father present. Furthermore, cognitive differences between the groups disappeared when family structure was controlled. In analyses controlled for adolescent parenthood, family structure had a significant effect on cognitive measures, with children from homes with both mother and father having the highest scores and children moving between separate homes headed by mother and by father having the lowest. Card interpreted the findings as indicating that the effect of adolescent parenthood on the cognitive development of children is primarily indirect, operating through family structure.

The analyses reported here, as well as the other studies reviewed, make it abundantly clear that sociodemographic variables contribute more to a child's cognitive development than either maternal or paternal age at the child's birth. Thus, the effects of parental age are apparently not biologic, but instead are due chiefly to the impact of sociodemographic factors and the tendency for young mothers, especially blacks, to be overrepresented in lower socioeconomic groups and in female-headed households. The association between teenage pregnancy and socioeconomic status has been well documented, particularly by Zelnik et al. in their research on teenage sexual activity. Teenage females whose parents were in lower socioeconomic groups were more likely to be sexually active and were less likely to use contraceptives (and thus were at greater risk of pregnancy) than those whose parents were in higher socioeconomic groups.[12] Edwards and Grossman pointed out that in the HES data, the proportion of births to young mothers was more than twice as high in the low income group as in the high income group (9.7 compared to 4.1 percent).[8]

The association between teenage parenting and low socioeconomic status may operate in two ways: low socioeconomic status may lead to an increased risk of teenage parenthood; or becoming a teenage parent may increase the likelihood of low socioeconomic status. In an analysis of factors explaining geographic differences in birth rates among teenagers, Perlman et al. found that median income was the most important factor, with lower incomes associated with high birth rates for teenagers.[13] Regardless of socioeconomic status, teenagers who become parents may be underachievers in school or may have low educational aspirations. Once they become parents, teenagers tend to drop out of school, thereby lowering their educational attainment and increasing the likelihood of obtaining low-income jobs. The lack of education among teenage parents is also likely to contribute to a lack of understanding of child development and thus less ability to maximize their children's cognitive functioning. Furthermore, the early childbearing and limited education may reduce chances for an enduring marriage, thus increasing the possibility that children may be raised in single-parent households—another potential negative influence on cognitive development.

Although the observed cognitive loss in children of teenage parents is small, it has important implications for program development with respect to both parent and child. The children of teenage parents remain at high risk for cognitive deficits, not because of their parents' biologic immaturity, but because of their parents' low income and incomplete education. Programs directed toward this target group should be concerned with helping and encouraging young parents to complete their education and to delay additional pregnancies until they have sufficient economic resources.

The children themselves would benefit from interventions, such as infant stimulation programs, cognitive development programs incorporated in day care, and preschool programs. A review of longitudinal follow-up studies of early intervention programs offers compelling evidence for the positive effects of these programs, particularly with respect to the reduction in the proportion of children retained in grade or placed in special education classes.[14] Early intervention programs for infants of adolescent parents are likely to be more cost effective, both financially and socially, than special education programs directed toward these children in their later years.

REFERENCES

1. Klerman LV: Evaluating service programs for school-age parents: Design problems. Evaluation Health Professions 2:55–70, 1979
2. Baldwin W, Cain VS: The children of teenage parents. Fam Plann Perspect 12:34–43, 1980
3. Marecek J:Economic, Social and Psychological Consequences of Adolescent Childbearing: An Analysis of Data from the Philadelphia Collaborative Perinatal Project. Final report to National Institute of Child Health and Human Development. Bethesda, Md, 1979
4. Furstenberg FF: Unplanned Parenthood: The Social Consequences of Teenage Childbearing. New York, Macmillan, 1976
5. Broman SH: Longterm development of children born to teenagers, in Scott KG, Field T, Robertson EG (eds): Teenage Parents and Their Offspring. New York, Grune & Stratton, 1981, pp 195–224
6. Belmont L, Cohen P, Dryfoos J, Stein Z, Zayac S: Maternal age and children's intelligence, in Scott KG, Field T, Robertson EG (eds): Teenage Parents and Their Offspring. New York, Grune & Stratton, 1981, pp 177–194
7. Cohen P, Belmont L, Dryfoos J, Stein Z, Zayac S: The effects of teenaged motherhood and maternal age on offspring intelligence. Soc Biol 27:138–154, 1980
8. Edwards LN, Grossman M: The relationship between children's health and intellectual development, in Mushkin SJ, Dunlop DW (eds): Health: What Is It Worth? New York, Pergamon Press, 1979, pp 273–314

9. Roberts J, Engel A: Family Background, Early Development, and Intelligence of Children 6–11 Years Old. Rockville Md, National Center for Health Statistics, 1974
10. Dupuy HJ, Gruvaeus G: The Construction and Utility of Three Indexes of Intellectual Achievement. Hyattsville, Md, National Center for Health Statistics, 1977
11. Card JJ: Long-term consequences for children of teenage parents. Demography 18:137–156, 1981
12. Zelnik M, Kantner JF, Ford K: Sex and Pregnancy in Adolescence. Beverly Hills, Calif, Sage, 1981
13. Perlman SB, Klerman LV, Kinard EM: Using socioeconomic data to explain variations in teenage birth rates: An exploratory study in Massachusetts. Public Health Rep 96:335–341, 1981
14. Palmer FH, Andersen LW: Long-term gains from early intervention: Findings from longitudinal studies, in Zigler E, Valentine J (eds): Project Head Start: A Legacy of the War on Poverty. New York, Free Press, 1979

APPENDIX A:
DERIVATION OF THREE INDICES OF
INTELLECTUAL DEVELOPMENT

ID Index

The ID index was obtained by transforming raw scores on the Vocabulary and Block Design subtests of the WISC to age- and sex-independent normalized scores (T scores) and summing the adjusted scores. The ID index was set to a mean of 100.0 and a standard deviation of 15.0, both of which are similar to the mean and standard deviation of the WISC Full Scale IQ Score.

SIS Index

From a set of family background variables that could be considered independent of the child's own contribution and that were not considered of substantive interest for future analyses, variables were selected that best fit the criteria of representing factors that could to some extent be controlled or influenced by the parent and that accounted for the largest proportion of variance in the ID index. Four variables were chosen: education of each parent, annual family income, and number of persons in the household under 21 years of age. From these four variables, two new variables were constructed: (1) sum of both parents' education, and (2) annual family income per person under 21 years of age in the household. Values for these constructed variables were then developed by using the technique of criterion scaling. SIS scores were calculated from a multiple regression equation of the two constructed variables with the ID index. Two race-specific equations were developed: one for white and other races and one for blacks. For all races combined, the mean for the SIS index was set to 100.0; the standard deviation obtained from the observed sample was 9.04.

DID Index

The DID index consists of ID scores independent of the SIS contribution, that is, the ID score minus the SIS score (DID = ID − SIS). Since race-specific formulas were used for the SIS, the DID indices were also race specific. For all races, the mean for the DID index was set to 100.0; a standard deviation of 11.98 was obtained from the observed sample distribution.

Psychosocial Risk

15

Psychosocial Risk to Mother and Child as a Consequence of Adolescent Pregnancy

Stanford B. Friedman and Sheridan Phillips

Systematic research on the consequences of adolescent parenthood is virtually nonexistent.[1]

U nfortunately, the above statement, made by Furstenburg in 1976, is still a fairly accurate summary of the "data base" regarding the outcome of teenage pregnancy and parenthood. Although there is practically universal agreement in the United States, among professionals and the general public alike that adolescent girls should not become pregnant or achieve motherhood, it is difficult to divorce moral and ethical beliefs from the evaluation of scientific findings. Indeed, those involved in improving programs for pregnant teenagers are commonly plagued with the admonition: "Do not reward sin."

Those attempting to be objective find the professional literature confusing and inconclusive. Nevertheless, data are accumulating which indicate that teenage motherhood has adverse and long-term implications for the young mother, and probably for her child. Possible effects on teenage fathers are unknown. Lack of complete and definitive information regarding the consequences of adolescent pregnancy and parenthood, however, does not mean that the potential problems are unimportant. The number of teenage parents—and their children—in itself demands attention to adolescent sexual activity and resultant pregnancy.

269

DEVELOPMENTAL CONSIDERATIONS

The major developmental task of adolescence, according to Erikson, is establishing an "identity."[2] This is the process by which the adolescent establishes a relatively stable self-concept and defines his or her uniqueness from others in the environment. Individual, social, and vocational goals are broadly defined.[3] Peer acceptance is crucial for adolescents attempting to establish independence from adults, particularly their parents. Although increasing detachment from adults and adult values is typical during adolescence, teenagers also seek "models" in their environment for patterning their own behavior.

Erikson also maintained that a given task must be mastered, at least to a significant degree, before the individual can succeed with the next task.[4] As noted in Table 15-1, the task of "intimacy" is that of the young adult. This entails the ability to have intimate sexual and social relationships with others, including the sharing of thoughts and feelings.

Psychological difficulties related to teenage pregnancy and motherhood may reflect the developmental stage of the early or midadolescent girl. Identity formation, characteristically emerging toward the end of adolescence, is vital for a close, meaningful relationship with one's sexual partner if it must precede the task of "intimacy." Furthermore, developing a close relationship with one's child may be difficult for a very young parent, as it is difficult to have long-range expectations and hopes for the child when such futuristic thinking is undeveloped in one's self. The authors contend that these are the factors alluded to when teenagers are described as "not emotionally mature enough" to enter parenthood.

Table 15-1. Developmental Tasks

Stage	Developmental Task
Infancy	Trust versus mistrust
Early childhood	Autonomy versus shame, doubt
Play age	Initiative versus guilt
School age	Industry versus inferiority
Adolescence	Identity versus identity diffusion
Young adult	Intimacy versus isolation
Adulthood	Generativity versus self-absorption
Mature age	Integrity versus disgust, despair

Modified from Erikson.[4]

SEXUAL ACTIVITY AND PREGNANCY

Adolescent sexual behavior is complex and determined by numerous interacting factors—personal, social, and cultural. To consider sexual intercourse as only satisfying physical desires obviously is far too simplistic. It is generally acknowledged that even young teenagers usually engage in intercourse with partners who represent relatively stable relationships, and that continuing promiscuous sexual activity reflects psychological problems. Thus, sexual activity of adolescents is typically associated with some degree of interpersonal investment in the partner.

In addition, teenagers often engage in sexual intercourse for reasons that have been described as "the use of sexual behavior for non-sexual reasons."[5] The adolescent may perceive sexual intercourse as enhancing his or her acceptance by peers, thus allowing for greater independence from adults and their values. Such "independence" may be far broader than issues related to sexuality and may be associated more with feelings of parental rejection, poor self-concept, past experiences with social or academic failures, and isolation from peers. The adolescent equates sexual activity with more general acceptance and often "love," which, unfortunately, is frequently an unwarranted assumption. Thus, in the quest for acceptance the teenager may enter into what is ultimately self-destructive, promiscuous sexual behavior, or she may "buy" affection with sex.

Adolescents also may be motivated by conscious needs to express hostile feelings. Sexual activity, among a wide range of teenage behaviors, including delinquency and drug abuse, frequently distresses parents and brings discredit to the family. Illustrative of this was one suburban teenager who, in describing her sexual practices and resulting pregnancy, said to one of the authors: "The look of horror on my mother's face makes it all worthwhile."

As with sexual intercourse, pregnancy may also be a manifestation of the psychological needs of the adolescent. Even though adults view pregnancy as socially deviant behavior, the adolescent may see pregnancy and motherhood as having "self-enhancing potential."[6] Pregnancy and parenthood, therefore, cannot be understood without considering how the adolescent is attempting to cope and adapt.

It seems clear that pregnancy and motherhood are not random phenomena, and that teenage mothers differ from their never pregnant peers. Since they are more likely to have experienced social and/or academic failure, teenagers who become mothers tend to view family, school, and peers as persistent sources of self-devaluing experiences.[6] These adolescents may thus find it difficult to establish an identity by defining their role and goals in socially acceptable ways. They may cope with this developmental task by becoming a mother, which provides an identity and a purpose. Teenage parenthood can be viewed as a coping strategy, possibly the only one that the adolescent anticipates will enhance her self-esteem. This acknowledges the potentially advantageous aspects of parenthood for an adolescent, as well as possible deleterious effects.

ABORTION

Pregnancy may not lead to the delivery of a child. Little is known about the psychological effects of abortion on the teenage girl—not to mention her partner. There is increasing interest, however, in the psychological impact of abortions and stillbirths on women,[7,8] and awareness that potential parents may experience a profound grief reaction under such circumstances. Elective abortion may be associated with feelings of guilt, and with anger that the abortion was "necessary." Varying degrees of depression are common, and may be almost universal in girls having undergone an elective abortion. Ethical and moral blame may be placed upon the girl by her partner and family—and by herself. Spontaneous abortion may be viewed by the girl, and others, as "just punishment" for her sexual behavior.

The teenager's reactions seem to be less severe when her parents or partner have not forced her to have an abortion[9,10] or when they offer her emotional support.[11] Psychological reactions, however, are generally only measured in the hospital or clinic immediately after the abortion. There is probably no psychological issue related to teenage pregnancy that has been more ignored by researchers than the long-term psychosocial aftermath of abortion.

IMPACT ON THE MOTHER

Numerous studies have documented some major negative consequences of teenage motherhood.[1,12-14] Cross-sectional and longitudinal research indicates that teenaged mothers, in comparison to older mother or nonmother "controls," generally reach a lower educational level and are less successful vocationally. Marriage, if it occurs, is associated with a high rate of separation and divorce. There is a strong tendency, over time, for teenage mothers—especially those with two children—to become the only adult in the household. This evolution toward "mother aloneness" is much more pronounced for women who became pregnant while adolescents. Furthermore, mothers who live alone, regardless of their age, are less likely than others to receive help with child rearing or to belong to social, religious, or political organizations. Thus, while early motherhood may be an easy route to an identity, the subsequent socioeconomic consequences may foreclose access to other roles.

The incidence of emotional or psychiatric problems of adolescent mothers is virtually unknown. One study reported that teenage mothers experience an unusually high incidence of life crises during their pregnancies,[15] although interpretation of this finding is not possible at this time, nor is it known whether an increased incidence of life crises continues into motherhood. A second study, a large epidemiologic project, has collected prospective data on the psychological status of mothers who became pregnant while adolescents, in contrast to those who became pregnant at age 20 or above.[12] Self-ratings of feelings of sadness and tension indicated that early childbearing substantially increases feelings of distress, and that this effect is likely to continue through later stages of life. While the evidence is sparse, these data suggest that the "stress" of early motherhood contributes to an increased frequency of emotional problems, or precipitates symptoms that reflect underlying psychological maladjustment. On the other hand, as proposed earlier, motherhood may actually help teenaged girls cope with an unsupportive or even hostile environment.

Some teenage mothers adapt substantially better than others. In general, the older the adolescent is at the time of conception, the more apt she is to complete high school or be gainfully employed. Marriage per se does not appear to predict a successful outcome, although the outlook is far more optimistic if the husband has a high school education or is employed.[1] There is some evidence that married adolescent mothers have a more positive self-concept than their single counterparts.[16] A key factor is the availability of family members for financial, psychological, and child care assistance—the existence of such a support system can greatly aid teenaged mothers to cope with parenthood.[17] For example, family members can assist at times of crisis when one-parent families have great difficulty—this would include such crises as a child's illness or the death of a family member.

Economic and social support not only reduces the demands of adolescent parenthood, but also increases the potential for psychological development. Eliminating some of the environmental sources of stress can enhance the teenager's emotional satisfaction and her self-concept as "mother." If she is not satisfied with this as her "identity," family support can also provide access to continued development, enabling her to attend school or work. In either case, such support can promote satisfactory completion of this developmental task and thus pave the way for the next task—intimacy.

IMPACT ON THE CHILD

To the clinician, a basic and crucial issue is: Are teenage mothers capable of successfully raising children? If, in general, the answer is affirmative, it is difficult to invoke the child-rearing perspective as support for opposing adolescent parenthood. Several areas of research have recently generated data that appear promising for addressing this aspect of teenage pregnancy and motherhood.

One important area of research considers prenatal maternal psychological distress and its effect on delivery and the infant's health and behavior. Animal research has repeatedly demonstrated that prenatal psychosocial factors influence subsequent psychological status and behavior of the offspring,[18] and recent data strongly suggest that similar effects also occur in humans.[19] For instance, it has been noted that "the Apgar scores of babies born to highly-anxious mothers were significantly less than those born to mothers of normal anxiety scores."[20] Another study, however, found that "anxiety measures" were *not* related to labor complications, including Apgar scores.[21] While it would clearly be premature to generate conclusions from this area of research, the *assumption* that many young mothers experience more environmental stresses than older mothers make such studies highly relevant to the issue of teenage motherhood.

Mother—infant attachment, or bonding, has recently received considerable scientific attention.[22-24] It has been suggested that the first few days of life (especially the first 12 hours) are critical for optimal bonding to occur and, hence, this is a developmentally "critical period." Young adolescent mothers, perhaps due to developmental issues discussed earlier, may have difficulty in establishing close mother—infant attachment. Support for this speculation comes from a study by Jones et al., who reported that "mothers 19 years of age and older demonstrated significantly more maternal responsiveness toward their infants than did mothers 18 years and younger."[25] In another study, the Ainsworth-Bell Strange Situation observational model was used to investigate the attachment behavior of low-income, teenage mothers and their infants. Comparing their behavior with data previously obtained from middle-class mothers, Howell et al. noted behaviors that "suggest that the ineffectual mothering skills of these teenage girls increase their infants' chances for becoming vulnerable for disturbed socio-emotional development."[26]

The adequacy of teenage mothering has also been investigated by comparing the infants or children of adolescent mothers with the offspring of older mothers. These two groups of mothers are often "matched" for key variables such as marital and socioeconomic status, although the degree of equivalence varies from study to study. In their comprehensive review of this research, Baldwin and Cain noted consistent findings that "show deficits in the cognitive development of children (especially male children) born to teenagers" but further commented that "while statistically significant, the effect on measures of aptitude is small and may be trivial in terms of later achievement."[27] They also reported that "less consistent effects are found for the children's social and emotional development and school adjustment." In general, the better the socioeconomic "match" was between teenage mothers and the control mothers, the fewer differences were noted between the offspring of the two groups. In summarizing findings related to the socioemotional development of children of teenage mothers, Baldwin and Cain stated: "Again, evidence suggests that the effect does not result from the mother's age at birth directly, but rather is transmitted through other factors associated with early child-bearing, such as educational and economic disadvantage and greater likelihood of marital breakup."[27]

These studies, then, suggest that children of teenage mothers are not *markedly* different from children of older mothers who are similar with regard to marital and socioeconomic status. Such results, however, only indicate that age per se is not a vital factor. They do not address the quality of mothering. It may well be that the "matched control" children are receiving inadequate mothering themselves: The older, matched control mothers might also reveal multiple problems—similar to or different from those of teenage mothers—if they were scrutinized with the same intensity. While they are an appropriate comparison group to determine age effects, it also appears advisable to compare teenage mothering and its effects with that of "random controls" (older mothers who are unmatched) to assess adequacy of mothering.

It is sometimes assumed that teenagers *cannot* be adequate mothers. As discussed previously, this attitude may reflect general disdain for adolescents who engage in coitus. While it is true that adolescents are more likely to experience parenting problems, there are individual differences in the quality of care they provide. What emerges as important is how much support the teenage mother receives from her family—especially from her husband or her mother. Kellam et al., in their longitudinal study of children's social adaptation and psychological well-being, found that the negative effect of a teenage mother was ameliorated by the presence of a father or grandmother in the household: mother-alone families entailed the highest risk—"alone" being more important than father absence—while mother–grandmother families were nearly as effective as mother–father families.

CONCLUSIONS

To professionals working with pregnant teenagers it seems obvious that these girls have numerous and complex psychological, social, and school problems. Nevertheless, there is little evidence that *youth itself* contributes *substantially* to psychological problems for either the mother or her child. We have suggested that adolescent mothers and their children are at greater risk for psychosocial problems due to a combination of factors: (1) the increased difficulty of successfully completing a major developmental task (identity formation), and (2) the more stressful demands of parenting without adequate economic and social support. Providing such support improves the prognosis for both the adolescent mother and her child. Currently, the most pressing need appears to be the development and expansion of service programs that can provide longitudinal intervention, promoting the necessary economic and social support system for teenage parents and their children.

REFERENCES

1. Furstenburg FF Jr: The social consequences of teenage parenthood. Fam Plann Perspect 8:148–164, 1976
2. Erikson E: Identity: Youth and Crisis. New York, Norton, 1968
3. Leichtman SR: Psychosocial Development of Adolescents, in Friedman SB, Hoekelman RA (eds): Behavioral Pediatrics: Psychosocial Aspects of Child Health Care, New York, McGraw-Hill, 1980, pp 350–356
4. Erikson E: Psychological Issues, vol 1: Identity and the Life Cycle. New York, International Universities Press, 1959
5. Cohen MW, Friedman SB: Nonsexual motivation of adolescent sexual behavior. Hum Sex, Sept 1975, pp 9–31
6. Kaplan HB, Smith PB, Pokorny AD: Psychosocial antecedents of unwed motherhood among indigent adolescents. J Youth Adolesc 8:181–207, 1979
7. Davidson GW: Death of the wished-for child: A case study. Death Educ 1:265–275, 1977
8. Peppers LG, Knapp RJ: Maternal reactions to involuntary fetal/infant death. Psychiatry 43:155–159, 1980
9. Barglow P, Weinstein S: Therapeutic abortion during adolescence: Psychiatric observations. J Youth Adolesc 2:331–342, 1973
10. Evans J, Selstad G, Welcher W: Teenagers: Fertility control behavior and attitudes before and after abortion, childbearing or negative pregnancy test. Fam Plann Perspect 8:192–200, 1976
11. Bracken MB, Hackamovitz M, Grossman G: The decision to abort and psychological sequelae. J Nerv Ment Dis 158:154–162, 1974
12. Brown H, Adams RG, Kellam SG: A longitudinal study of teenage motherhood and symptoms of distress: The Woodlawn Community Epidemiological Project, in Simmons R (ed): Research in Community and Mental Health, vol 2. Greenwich, Conn, JAI Press, 1981, pp 183–213
13. Moore KA, Hofferth SL, Wertheimer R II, et al: Teenage childbearing: Consequences for women, families, and government welfare expenditures. Presented at the 87th annual

convention of the American Psychological Association, New York, September 1–5, 1979

14. National Institute of Child Health and Human Development: Excerpt from the Annual Report, 1979, in Adolescent Pregnancy and Childbearing: Rates, Trends and Research Findings from the Center for Population Research. Social and Behavioral Sciences Branch, NICHD, Bethesda, Md

15. Sugar M: At-risk factors for the adolescent mother and her infant. J Youth Adolesc 5:251–269, 1976

16. Zongker CE: Self-concept differences between single and married school-age mothers. J Youth Adolesc 9:175–184, 1980

17. Furstenburg FF Jr, Crawford AG: Family support: Helping teenage mothers to cope. Fam Plann Perspect 10:322–333, 1978

18. Archer JE, Blackman DE: Prenatal psychological stress and offspring behavior in rats and mice. Dev Psychobiol 4:193–248, 1971

19. Ferreira AJ: Prenatal Environment. Springfield, Ill, Charles C Thomas, 1969

20. Crandon AJ: Maternal anxiety and neonatal wellbeing. J Psychosom Res 23:113–115, 1979

21. Jones AC: Life change and psychological distress as predictors of pregnancy outcome. Psychosom Med 40:402–412, 1978

22. Klaus MH, Kennell JH, Plumb N, et al: Human maternal behavior at first contact with her young. Pediatrics 46:187–192, 1970

23. Klaus MH, Jerauld R, Kreger NC, et al: Maternal attachment: Importance of the first post-partum days. N Engl J Med 286:460–463, 1972

24. Brazelton TB, Als H: Four early stages in the development of mother–infant interaction. The Psychoanalytic Study of the Child, vol 34, New Haven, Conn, Yale University Press, 1979, pp 349–369

25. Jones FA, Green V, Krauss DR: Maternal responsiveness of primiparous mothers during postpartum period: Age differences. Pediatrics 65:579–584, 1980

26. Howell V, Teberg AJ, Wingert W: Variations in attachment behaviors among low-income teenage mothers and their infants (abstract). Presented at the national meeting of the American Federation for Clinical Research, Washington, DC, May 10–12, 1980

27. Baldwin W, Cain VS: The children of teenage parents. Fam Plann Perspect 12:34–43, 1980

28. Kellam SG, Ensminger ME, Turner RJ: Family structure and the mental health of children. Arch Gen Psychiatry 34:1012–1022, 1977

16

Education and Childbearing among Teenagers

James McCarthy and Ellen S. Radish

I t is now well documented that women who begin their childbearing while still teenagers experience a host of social and economic disadvantages throughout the rest of their lives. These women tend to have more children more quickly than do their counterparts who delay the start of childbearing. They experience more marital disruptions, achieve lower levels of schooling, earn lower wages, and have lower levels of participation in the labor force.[1] Furthermore, evidence suggests that the level of schooling a teenage mother achieves has a substantial indirect impact on her labor force experience.[2] Other studies have shown that controlling for academic aptitude, expectations, and achievement reduces the differences between adolescent parents and later childbearers in terms of both their future fertility and martial careers.[3] These studies point to education as a crucial factor in mediating the negative influence of early childbearing on a woman's future well-being. Many young mothers do suffer disadvantages because of the timing of their first births, but for those who manage to avoid these disadvantages, education may be one of the factors responsible for their success. Successful efforts to encourage teenage mothers to stay in school or return to school might well have important positive consequences for the lives of young mothers.

In this chapter we present a comprehensive review of issues surrounding

This work was supported by a grant from the Mellon Foundation to the Department of Population Dynamics at The Johns Hopkins University School of Hygiene and Public Health.

the relationship between early childbearing and educational achievement. Earlier research on the link between age at first birth and level of completed schooling is examined first. Recent changes in government policies that had as their goal the improvement of educational opportunities for young mothers, and a sample of the educational programs established to provide services to young mothers are discussed. Finally, the most recent national data on early childbearing and educational attainment are used to determine the extent to which these recently established programs have influenced the amount of education received by young mothers.

REVIEW OF EARLIER STUDIES

The association between early childbearing and low levels of schooling among women has never been seriously questioned. It had been long assumed that pregnancy, childbearing, and child rearing were incompatible with continued schooling. This assumption was reflected in policies that barred pregnant girls or young mothers from regular school classes, or in some cases from access to any schooling at all.

Although the existence of an association between early childbearing and low levels of education has been widely recognized and accepted, the causal relations responsible for this association have been a matter of considerable debate. The debate centers on the question of whether the event of a birth to an adolescent girl actually *causes* the low levels of education typical among young mothers. One argument states that teenage mothers differ in many ways from those who delay the start of childbearing, and that it is these differences which are responsible for the low levels of education achieved by teenage mothers. The social, economic, and cultural factors that are responsible for early childbearing are also responsible for low levels of education, and all the negative social and economic correlates of early childbearing as well. According to this argument, the correlation between early childbearing and low levels of education exists not because childbearing causes low education, but because both conditions are caused by the same socioeconomic forces. An opposing argument recognizes that teenage mothers are in fact different from older mothers, but states that early motherhood itself is sufficient to ensure that adolescent childbearers will never be like women who become mothers at later ages. They will be different not only because they were different to start with, but because that early first birth has consequences that influence the rest of their lives.

Although these hypotheses have been stated often, it has been quite difficult to test them. Most of the literature on the social consequences of adolescent childbearing, including the literature on educational consequences, has not been able to show conclusively whether early childbearing is itself causally related to these consequences. Most studies have recognized the limitations of the available data, and often include a caveat to the effect that "for the sake of precision, we consider the correlates, rather than the consequences, of early childbearing."[4]

Fortunately, there is one data set that does allow researchers to disentangle the causal structure of the relationship between early childbearing and educational achievement. Card and Wise analyzed data from Project Talent, a study that started administering a number of tests and questionnaires to a national sample of high school students in 1960.[3] These students were reinterviewed 1, 5, and 11 years after their expected date of high school graduation. Because these students were first interviewed before any of them had had a child, Card and Wise were able to compare those who had children as teenagers with classmates who delayed childbearing, and were able to match parents with a sample of nonparents who had similar levels of academic aptitude and achievement, socioeconomic status, educational expectations at age 15 years, and were of the same race. Card and Wise found not only that young mothers had substantially less education than their classmates, but also that the negative impact of early childbearing remained when the characteristics at age 15 were included as controls. They concluded that "early childbearing appears to be a direct cause of truncated schooling, independent of other influences."[3]

RECENT CHANGES IN ADOLESCENT LIFE

Although Card and Wise provided a conclusive analysis of the impact early childbearing had on the lives of women who were teenagers around 1960, we cannot be certain that the same relationships hold true for teenagers today. Many aspects of adolescent life, particularly adolescent sexual and reproductive life, have changed drastically in the past 10 years. The change has been so drastic that adolescent childbearing in 1980 may well represent a very different social situation than that represented by adolescent childbearing in 1950 or 1960.

Fertility rates among adolescents have declined substantially in recent years. In 1960, the birth rate per 1000 women aged 15–19 was 89.1; in 1977, the same rate was 53.7. The decline among the 18- to 19-year-olds has been particularly sharp. In 1960, contraceptive knowledge and availability among teenagers were certainly less than they were in 1980. Zelnik and Kantner reported that between 1971 and 1976 sexual activity among teenagers increased in frequency and was initiated at younger ages.[5,6] Along with these changes in sexual activity there were changes in contraceptive use. Overall use and use of the most effective methods of contraception increased substantially in the 5 years between the surveys. Although the proportion of sexually active teenagers who became pregnant remained constant, subsequent pregnancies did decline over the 5-year period. In addition, those teenagers who consistently used the most effective methods were only one-tenth as likely to get pregnant as nonusers. Finally, in 1980 a teenager who does become pregnant can choose to have a legal abortion. This option was not available before 1973.

All this evidence supports the claim that a teenage mother in 1980 is not at all like the teenage mother of 1960. The more recent mother did not use the effective methods of contraception that were used by many of her peers; and unlike many other young, pregnant girls, the young mother in 1980 did not obtain an abortion. These two differences make any attempt at predicting the consequences of recent adolescent childbearing difficult. The young mothers are a select group because they were not effective users of contraception. If this pattern of nonuse or ineffective use persists, they may continue to suffer the negative consequences, including reduced education, associated with early childbearing in the past. However, these young mothers also did not get abortions. They may be a select group who had a child because they wanted one, or they may be select because they did not have ready access to abortion services. To the extent that the former is the case, these mothers may be more highly motivated toward their role, and less likely to suffer negative consequences.

In addition, the educational system that a young mother faces in 1980 is quite different from the one a young mother faced in 1960. In 1960, it was common for pregnant adolescents to be forced to leave school. Some school systems provided alternative classes, but others did not. By contrast, it is now illegal in the United States to exclude married or pregnant girls, or girls with children, from public schools. This is a fairly recent development, and was implemented in 1976 as one of the provisions under Title IX of the Educational Amendments passed by Congress in 1972. Therefore, teenage girls who had children in the past 5 years should have had more access to opportunities to remain in school and complete their high school education. Have they taken advantage of these increased opportunities, and are more adolescent mothers remaining in school while pregnant and after the birth of their children? By reviewing recent changes in educational policies and programs, and by examining recent national data on the relationship between age at first birth and educational attainment, we hope to provide an answer to this question.

SERVICES FOR ADOLESCENT MOTHERS

Comprehensive services, "based on a nucleus of educational, health and social service components" have become the model for programs provided for pregnant teenagers.[7] A series of amendments, Titles VI, VII, and VIII, commonly referred to as the Adolescent Pregnancy Act, was passed by Congress in 1978. The passage of these amendments established "a competitive grant program focused on providing 'linkages' and filling service gaps" in the programs that have been created.[8] However, the decision to assign administrative responsibility for this act to a new unit within the Federal Health Administration, the limits imposed by the 3-year authorization period, and the mandatory phasing out of grant funds allocated to projects after 5 years, have all been criticized. In addition, the ongoing needs of pregnant adolescents, and the need to integrate comprehensive services into the total services offered by a community, have made the competitive funding approach a questionable practice.

Two surveys have provided a broad overview of the services being offered to pregnant teenagers since 1970. Questionnaires were mailed to the health officers and superintendents of schools in approximately 150 cities with a population of 100,000 or more according to the 1970 census.[9,10] The 1970 survey showed major unmet needs, with education being cited as the most frequently unmet need for pregnant teenagers in these cities. By 1976, however, educational services had become the sixth most frequently unmet need.

In 1970, the most frequent sponsors of programs, as well as the major funding sources for programs, were local, state, or federal departments of education. Special education was then the third most frequent service provided, while for all services, caseloads were small and waiting lists were often reported. In 1970, 86.2 percent of the cities provided special education, usually in a special school or through home instruction. A waiting list was reported by one-fourth of these cities, and this waiting list was found most often in the large cities. The size of the city was related to the degree of service comprehensiveness, with larger cities being more likely to provide comprehensive programs.

In 1976, the most frequent sponsors and the most frequent funding sources were again the local, state, and federal departments of education. The second most frequent service offered was now special education. The percentage of cities providing special education, however, had only grown to 88 percent. Waiting times for services were somewhat shorter in 1970 than in 1976, although waiting lists still occurred most often in the largest cities. In 1970, waiting lists were reported to vary from 2 to 426 girls, and waiting time varied from 1 day to 1 school semester. In 1976, waiting lists varied from 30 to 169 girls, and the waiting period varied from 2 weeks to 2 school semesters.

Jekel examined comprehensive service programs for pregnant teenagers and noted:[8]

By the mid-1970's the community programs available were said to number about 1200, although most did not offer all 3 of the basic service components [medical, educational, and social] . . . . A 1976 study of 1128 programs showed that only 5% provided all 3 components, 36% provided 2 of 3 components and 59% provided only 1 of 3 components.*

Failure to reach or to know the size of the target group to be served has been an important problem for these programs. Many programs have more work than can be handled efficiently and thus cannot be too concerned with the pregnant teenagers whose needs are not being met. In fact, it has been estimated that fewer than one-half of pregnant adolescents are now being served by any type of program.

The comprehensive service programs found in an examination of the published studies from about 1970 to 1980 are summarized in Table 16-1. The programs were conducted in hospitals, schools, or social service institutions and contained some type of educational component. Most of the comprehensive programs for pregnant adolescents have targeted their services to inner city, low-income teenagers. While this type of target population does have special needs and should not be ignored, many pregnant adolescents will not be able to benefit from these programs unless services are extended to other populations. For example, rural and suburban teenagers have not been cited as a target population in any of these programs; comprehensive programs may have to undergo major modifications if they are to benefit these teenagers. Comprehensive programs targeted to rural or suburban teenagers might also add new insights into the best ways to provide services to low-income, inner city adolescents.

Most of the programs described in Table 16-1 used special classrooms or special schools in order to provide educational services to pregnant adolescents. When classes were offered in a regular classroom setting, however, such as in St. Paul, Minnesota, or Baltimore, Maryland, program results tended to be beneficial in terms of educational achievement. It would have been helpful if more information about other services, educational aspirations and goals, and other program outcomes had been provided in order to facilitate comparisons between regular classroom and special classroom programs. In addition, a longer follow-up period, comparisons between different age groups in terms of program outcomes, and more information on the effects of marriage or family life would have been helpful in assessing these programs.

A consensus seems to have developed since 1970 that the best way to provide the services needed by pregnant teenagers is through comprehensive service programs. The findings from studies of comprehensive services, how-

---

*From Jekel JF: Evaluation of programs for adolescents, in McAnarney ER, Stickle G (eds): Pregnancy and Childbearing During Adolescence: Research Priorities for the 1980s. New York, Alan R. Liss, 1981, pp 107–122. With permission.

ever, have pointed to some key variables that still need to be researched. In the past it was usually assumed that the use of special schools was the best way to provide services for pregnant teenagers; however, this assumption has been questioned by program coordinators and evaluators. Special schools may only increase the pregnant teenager's feeling of isolation from her peers, and the intensive counseling and attention offered may make it harder for her to return to her regular school. In addition, funds must often be used to duplicate services and personnel that can be found in a regular school. In fact, Berg et al. believed that their findings in St. Paul, Minnesota, showed positive outcomes for students who were given prenatal care and stayed in their regular classroom.[14] Jekel suggested, however, that for "some younger or less mature young mothers a special school in a separate setting may offer distinct advantages."[8]

The coordination of activities between the medical, educational, and social service components, and especially the provision of day care services, have been found to be crucial variables in allowing pregnant teenagers and young mothers to continue their education. The programs in San Francisco, California, St. Paul, Minnesota, and Kalamazoo, Michigan, provided day care services, whereas others, such as the program in Baltimore, Maryland, noted a lack of people available to provide care for the infant was a major barrier to the teenagers' staying in school.

The effect of being a single mother or a married mother on these girls' educational achievements needs to be further researched. In the programs at Baylor College of Medicine and Johns Hopkins Hospitals, single girls found it easier to stay in school, whereas in the San Francisco program married girls were more likely to stay in school. It may be that single mothers receive more family support and have more people around to provide child care during school hours, but this may vary for different communities and different time periods. More programs have begun to include the pregnant teenager's sex partner and family, but it is not known whether this has had an impact upon the educational achievements of these girls. The type of activities in which family members and fathers participate, as well as the girl's feelings about their inclusion, may be an important factor in this area.

Because there has often been a lack of long-term follow-up study data, it has been difficult to assess the effectiveness of programs cited in the literature. Success has most often been measured by whether or not a girl stays in school for a few months after delivery. Real success, however, has not been achieved unless the services provided have had an effect upon long-term educational attainment. More follow-up data, at least until the age of high school graduation, are needed in order to determine the effectiveness of a program. Follow-up data are also needed to compare the effectiveness of components, such as home visits and day care centers, within and among different programs.

Table 16-1. Programs Providing Educational Services to Adolescent Mothers

Location and Reference	Target Population	Services Provided Educational	Services Provided Other	Evaluation Activities*	Program Outcomes Educational Aspirations/Goals*	Program Outcomes Educational Achievement	Program Outcomes Other
Kalamazoo, Mich.[11]	Emphasis on dropouts who wish to continue their schooling	Classes provided in a special school	Free day care program; outreach to help girls who dropped out or never participated in the program; help for girls' families	1963–1979	Availability of child care seemed to be very important in decision to stay in school		
Yale–New Haven Hospital, Conn.[12]	Residents of New Haven, 18 years old or younger	Encouraged to attend classes directed by City Board of Education at McCabe Community Center		Sept. 1967–June 1969: retrospective, followed to 2 months post partum. A. Examined 151 girls who delivered in clinic and attended McCabe classes. B. Looked at 150 girls attending McCabe or regular classes. C. Looked at 23 girls who did not attend school	A. Those who stated educational goal was college were the most likely to enroll in McCabe classes, whether or not they were in school when they registered for clinic services	A. 77% were in school or had graduated. B. 86% still in school or had graduated. C. 13% still in school or had graduated	A. 1. 92% of girls in school and 23% of girls not in school when registered for services, also enrolled in McCabe classes. 2. Girls 15 years old, with low educational goals, and below their appropriate grade level, were most likely to attend class infrequently
Baylor College of Medicine, Texas[13]	Indigent girls 18 years old or younger	Special school on hospital grounds for about 100 girls, built after program established		1968–1973. A. Questionnaires mailed at 8 months post partum to all participants; 50% response rate		A. 76% of single, 23% of married girls were still in school	
St. Paul, Minn.[14,15]	Girls in the schools in which clinics were located	Stayed in regular classrooms	Prenatal, post partum, and day care provided in school; delivery provided at St. Paul–Ramsey Medical Center	1968–1979. A. Retrospective: all participants. B. Sample of participants (N = 36) matched to control group (N = 36)			A. 1. 85 girls delivered during 1978–1979. 2. 40% decline in deliveries from 1976–1977 to 1978–1979 school year. 3. No repeat pregnancies for 90.4% of girls who remained in school. B. Controls began care later, had fewer prenatal visits

Program (location)	Target population	Program description	Evaluation activities	Outcomes
San Francisco, Calif.: six hospital centers[10,17]	City and/or county residents, over 700 school-aged girls	Vocational counseling, work-study program / In-hospital classrooms, staff provided by city school district; students can return to hospital school for 1 month after delivery with day care provided	1969–1973 A. Examined program begun in 1969 at San Francisco General Hospital; success seen as girl staying in school after leaving the program or graduating from the program	A. 1. 3.2% of those referred, 47% of those who actually entered, achieved success 2. Married girls and those closest to graduation were more likely to achieve success
New Brunswick, N.J.[18]	Inner-city school-aged girls	Special classes in Family Learning Center	1969–1975 A. Participants (N = 86) compared with matched controls (N = 30)	A. Participants completed significantly more schooling
Cincinnati General Hospital, Ohio[19]	Teenage welfare population who delivered at the hospital	High school credit for those attending weekly classes on care and stimulation of the infant / A control group received monthly visits; not weekly classes; no high school credit given to this group	1973–1975 A. Compared 15- to 16-year-old with 18- to 19-year-old mothers: all received services during Jan.–Feb. 1973. B. Examined black experimental (N = 18) with control (N = 16) mothers who participated in extended project begun Sept. 1974	A. At recruitment, younger mothers felt they could more easily manage a class one night a week than did older mothers. B. 1. Participants in classes had higher aspirations and more upward mobility than did controls 2. Significant difference between the two groups in the realization of school and/or employment goals
Crittenton Hastings House, Boston, Mass.[20,21]	Inner-city teenagers, about 450 served in 1973–1979	Classes under direction of Board of Education / After 1976, extended program offered counseling (through home visits) to all participants whether or not they asked for help	1973–1978 A. Examined girls who participated before 1976, until 2 years after services were received. B. Examined participants (N = 67) who received services Mar. 1976–Sept. 1977, $\frac{1}{2}$–3 years after delivery.	A. Academic goals generally higher after participation. B. 1. 80% returned to school after delivery 2. 50% had dropped out after 2 years; 64% dropped out by 2 years after delivery. 50% of this occurred immediately after delivery
Johns Hopkins Hospital, Baltimore, Md.[22]	Adolescents, 18 years old or younger, residing in Baltimore	Classes offered in special classrooms or regular classrooms / Included family and partner in some education and family planning activities; follow-up care (if needed) for 3 years	1974–1979 A. Examined participants at 1 year post partum. B. Participants matched to control group by age, race, and delivery date; no comparison results given	A. 1. 8% of participants graduated or remained in school 2. The few mothers who married tended to drop out. B. All but 6 of the 43 who dropped out had entered a job training program or an alternative academic program, or had obtained full-time employment
Fort Worth, Texas[23]	Students, 12–20 years old; about 425 served yearly	Continuing education unit offering credits toward a high school diploma	Jan. 1977–Dec. 1978 A. Examined sample (N = 17) of those pregnant for first time and enrolled in school	A. Strong progress was made in attaining educational goals / A. Lack of people to care for child was a major barrier to staying in school / A. Findings (not given) showed program encouraged high school completion, job market entry, and avoidance of repeated pregnancies.

•In each program summary, lettered evaluation activities correspond to goals and outcomes bearing the same letter.

POPULATION STUDIES

Although this review has covered very few programs, and these programs were often not evaluated fully, it is clear that the programs discussed did succeed in keeping pregnant adolescents or those with children in school for some time. The questions of interest, however, cannot be answered completely by reviewing individual programs. We need to know the extent to which educational programs have influenced the educational careers of young mothers throughout the entire population. We also need to know the long-term consequences of these programs—not just how successful they were in the few months following the birth of a teenager's baby.

A recent study by Mott and Maxwell can provide some answers to the first question.[24] Mott and Maxwell, using national surveys of labor force experience, compared young mothers in 1968 and 1979, focusing on the percentage enrolled in school in the interval from 5 months before birth to 9 months after the birth. Their results showed conclusively that "pregnant high school girls who went on to have a first child were much more likely to remain in school during their pregnancies in 1979 than in 1968. . . . In addition, in 1979, a larger proportion of young women returned to school after the birth of their children."[24] These results suggest that changes in attitudes toward young mothers, reflected in recent legislation and new service programs, have had at least a short-term impact on the education of those girls.

Table 16-2. Mean Number of Completed Years of School by Current Age and Age at First Birth

Current Age	Age at First Birth				No Births
	17 or Less	18–19	20–24	25 or More	
18–19	10.3	10.9	—	—	11.8
20–24	10.6	11.5	12.0	—	13.2
25–29	10.8	11.5	12.5	13.9	13.9
30–34	10.6	11.6	12.5	14.0	13.9
35–39	10.6	11.5	12.5	13.6	13.3
40–44	10.2	11.4	12.3	12.7	12.5
45–49	9.9	11.3	12.0	12.2	11.9
50–54	9.3	10.6	11.7	12.0	11.6
55–59	8.5	10.2	11.4	11.9	11.6
60 or more	8.0	9.2	10.3	11.2	10.9

Data from U.S. Bureau of the Census, Current Population Survey, June 1980.

To assess the long-term effect of those changes, we can use the June 1980 Current Population Survey, one in a series of monthly surveys conducted by the U.S. Bureau of the Census, which asked questions about a woman's childbearing history and her level of education. The mean number of years of school completed among women classified both by their current age and the age at which they had their first child is shown in Table 16-2. It is important to note that the education older women report is likely to represent their completed lifetime education, whereas younger women, particularly those 24 years old and younger, may still be in school or may return to school.

The first two columns of Table 16-2 indicate that the level of education received by young mothers has increased. Those currently 25–29 years old who had a first birth before they were 19 had more than 2 years more education than did women currently 60 or older who gave birth at a young age. Among the youngest group of mothers, the increase was from 8.0 years to 10.8 years, and among those 18–19 at their first birth, the increase was from 9.2 years to 11.5 years. Although young mothers, on the average, do not complete 12 years of education (the time usually required for high school graduation), they are receiving more education now than they did in the past.

Lest we become too optimistic based on this improvement, we should examine changes in the level of education received by women who were older at the time of their first birth (Table 16-2). Older mothers and childless women also gained at least 2 years of education. The largest gain was experienced among women with no children: those currently 25–29 had 3 more years of education than those currently 60 or older. Young mothers, therefore, do not appear to have gained any educational ground relative to either older mothers or childless women. Although young mothers have shared in the trend toward increasing education among all women, their share has been no greater than that of other women. The result is that their absolute level of education has improved but their disadvantage relative to other women has not changed.

The youngest women, however, are the most likely to have been influenced by recent programs and are young enough to be still in school or may return to school. New programs may well have an influence on their educational attainment in the near future, but the results in Table 16-2 suggest that these programs face a difficult task. In order to reduce the relative educational disadvantage suffered by young mothers, programs must produce a gain that exceeds the gain being experienced by others in the population. The educational gap between the youngest and the oldest mothers is slightly more than 3 years—this gap presents a considerable challenge to educational programs for young mothers.

CONCLUSIONS

Our review of selected programs for young mothers, and our examination of the most recent data on the association between age at first birth and educational attainment lead to both optimism and discouragement about the consequences of adolescent childbearing. We can be optimistic because the programs reviewed and the research by Mott and Maxwell show that young mothers are now more likely than in the past to stay in school while pregnant and to return to school immediately after giving birth.[24] It may be discouraging that while young mothers were improving their educational achievement, other women were improving theirs at an equal or greater rate, leaving the relative disadvantage of young mothers unaffected. However, programs to aid young mothers have been in place for a very short period of time, and it is possible that they will soon begin to have an effect on the education of young mothers in the total population. These programs face the challenge of improving not only the absolute number of years spent in school by young mothers, but also their educational achievement relative to that of other women in the population.

The long-term influence of recent programs to improve the education of young mothers cannot be ascertained with certainty for some time, not until these women are past the age when most will have completed whatever formal education they are likely to receive. As we await such definitive analyses, are there other issues that warrant consideration?

There are several lines of inquiry that emerge from the issues raised here. First, we need to know much more about the workings of the programs that have been set up to help young mothers. A probing and extensive analysis of the effect of individual programs might lead to insights not revealed by a broad review.

We can also learn more about the demographic and social correlates of teenage parenthood. Young girls who have recently become mothers may be quite different from those who became mothers some time ago. Changes in the prevalence of sexual activity and the use of both contraception and abortion are but some of the factors that suggest the existence of differences. Recent data could be examined to see if the socioeconomic, regional, or ethnic characteristics of teenaged mothers have changed over time.

Finally, we might gain a considerable amount of insight by comparing recent young mothers who did manage to achieve a certain level of education, such as graduation from high school, with those who did not. It may be fruitful to identify any characteristics that are associated with high levels of education among young mothers. There might be regional variations, variations by size of city or place of residence, variations among racial or ethnic groups, or variations associated with characteristics of the households in which young mothers live. In our review of programs, one factor that was identified as being important was the availability of day care facilities. Perhaps young mothers who live in extended families have day care services available within the household and are therefore able to return to school or to stay in school. Data that may answer at least some of these questions are available in surveys such as the June 1980 Current Population Survey.

Although the birth rate among teenagers has declined in recent years, and more services are available to teenage mothers, our analysis suggests that the negative social and economic consequences of adolescent childbearing are likely to persist. Previous research has shown that education may be a key factor in determining the extent to which an individual young mother suffers any of these social and economic consequences. Our analysis of both recent programs and recent data for the whole population suggests that low educational achievement is still associated with early childbearing and that the strength of the association has not changed over time. These conclusions require additional analysis before they can be accepted without qualification, but indications are that the problems faced by young mothers still exist and will continue to exist.

REFERENCES

1. McCarthy J: Social consequences of childbearing during adolescence, in McAnarney ER, Stickle G (eds): Pregnancy and Childbearing During Adolescence: Research Priorities for the 1980s. New York, Liss, 1981, pp 107–122

2. Trussell J, Abowd J: Teenage mothers, labor force participation and wage rates, in Menken J, McCarthy J, Trussell J (eds): Sequelae to Teenage Childbearing. Final Report. National Institute of Child Health and Human Development, Bethesda, Md, 1979

3. Card JJ, Wise LL: Teenage mothers and teenage fathers: The impact of early childbearing on the parents' personal and professional lives. Fam Plann Perspect 10:199–205, 1978

4. McCarthy J, Menken J: Marriage, remarriage, marital disruption and age at first birth. Fam Plann Perspect 11:21–30, 1979

5. Zelnik M, Kantner JF: Contraceptive patterns and premarital pregnancy among women aged 15–19 in 1976. Fam Plann Perspect 10:135–142, 1978

6. Zelnik M, Kantner JF: First pregnancies to women aged 15–19: 1976 and 1971. Fam Plann Perspect 10:11–20, 1978

7. Washington VE: Models of comprehensive service—Special-school-based. J Sch Health 45:274–277, 1975

8. Jekel JF: Evaluation of programs for adolescents, in McAnarney ER, Stickle G (eds): Pregnancy and Childbearing During Adolescence: Research Priorities for the 1980s. New York, Liss, 1981, pp 139–153

9. Wallace HM, Gold EM, Goldstein H, et al: A study of services and needs of teenage pregnant girls in the large cities of the United States. Am J Public Health 63:5–13, 1973

10. Goldstein PJ, Zalar MK, Grady EW, et al: Vocational education: An unusual approach to adolescent pregnancy. J Reprod Med 10:77–79, 1973

11. Sung K, Rothcock D: An alternative school for pregnant teen-agers and teen-age mothers. Child Welfare 59:427–430, 1980

12. Foltz A, Klerman LV, Jekel JF: Pregnancy and special education: Who stays in school? Am J Public Health 62:1612–1619, 1972

13. Smith PB, Mumford DM, Goldfarb JL, Kaufman RH: Selected aspects of adolescent postpartum behavior. J Reprod Med 14:159–165, 1975

14. Berg M, Taylor B, Edwards LE, et al: Prenatal care for pregnant adolescents in a public high school. J Sch Health 48:32–35, 1979

15. Edwards LE, Steinman ME, Arnold KA, et al: Adolescent pregnancy prevention services in high school clinics, in Furstenberg FF Jr, Lincoln R, Menken J (eds): Teenage Sexuality, Pregnancy and Childbearing. Philadelphia, University of Pennsylvania Press, 1981, pp 372–381

17. Grady EW: Models of comprehensive service—Hospital-based. J Sch Health 45:268–270, 1975

18. Bennet VC, Bardon JL: The effects of a school program on teenage mothers and their children. Am J Orthopsychiatry 47:671–678, 1977

19. Badger E: Effects of parent education program on teenage mothers, in Scott KG, Field T, Robertson E (eds): Teen Parents and Their Offspring. New York, Grune & Stratton, 1981, pp 283–310

20. Cartoof VG: Postpartum services for adolescent mothers. Child Welfare 57:661–666, 1978

21. Cartoof VG: Postpartum services for adolescent mothers: Part 2. Child Welfare 58:673–680, 1979

22. Hardy JB, King TM, Shipp DA, et al: A comprehensive approach to adolescent pregnancy, in Scott KG, Field T, Robertson E (eds): Teen Parents and Their Offspring. New York, Grune & Stratton, 1981, pp 265–283

23. Enos R, Hisanaga M: Goal setting with pregnant teenagers. Child Welfare 58:541–551, 1979

24. Mott FL, Maxwell NL: School-age mothers: 1968 and 1979. Fam Plann Perspect 13:287–292, 1981

Part V

INTERVENTION APPROACHES

17

Comprehensive Service Programs for Pregnant and Parenting Adolescents

James F. Jekel and Lorraine V. Klerman

S ufficient evidence has accumulated to indicate that child rearing should be delayed until both parents are sufficiently mature to enable the experience to be safe and beneficial to them, the child, and society. No specific age can be stated before which this is impossible or after which child rearing is always positive or desirable. Many young men and women in their late teens have graduated high school, have a steady income, and are able to satisfy both the physical and emotional needs of a child. This may occasionally be true for younger adolescents, but the evidence accumulated since 1965 strongly suggests that few adolescents under age 18 are fully prepared for child rearing. Those who become parents during these years usually need considerable assistance to maximize their social and economic ability in order to provide an adequate environment for a new child. This is not to imply that childbearing is desirable for all women age 18 or over. In fact, young women in their late teens having their second or higher birth order children are often in particular need of assistance. Women in this age group who are single, separated, or divorced, and who are trying to create a family without other adults in the household, are especially vulnerable to nutritional, medical, and social problems.[1]

It has been argued that the main focus of public programs should be to assist young women to avoid unwanted pregnancies.[2] Unfortunately, progress in this direction, although substantial, is still inadequate considering the magnitude of the problem. Major changes in societal attitudes concerning sex education and contraceptive provision, and the development of new contraceptive technology are needed to encourage adolescent family planning efforts. The mere availability of contraceptive services does not eliminate the problem. In many communities, such as the Hill area of New Haven, Connecticut, there are many easily accessible sources of contraception and contraceptive advice and yet these communities continue to have high rates of adolescent pregnancy.

In addition, many adolescents, as well as adults, see childbearing as a creative and exciting prospect, and often the full impact of this responsibility on their future life and resources is not appreciated. Adolescent pregnancy will continue to be a frequent occurrence unless society does something to make the adolescent period one in which teenagers feel they are useful and productive members of their communities. Continued efforts and research directed toward prevention should be emphasized, but special efforts to help those already pregnant or parents will continue to be needed. The history and present status of efforts to provide comprehensive services to adolescents who are or are soon to become parents are reviewed in this chapter.

HISTORICAL OVERVIEW

Prior to the 1960s, adolescent pregnancy was perceived as a problem more because of legitimacy status than because of the mother's age. Therefore, the major service programs were maternity residences for unmarried mothers operated, in most cases, by the Salvation Army (Booth Homes) or by the Florence Crittenton organizations. During the 1960s, the focus changed and the mother's age became the primary concern. More people began to see adolescent pregnancy as a community-wide problem requiring community-wide solutions, rather than as something to be hidden. In the early 1960s the efforts of such pioneers as Lyons, Wright, and Washington, and in the mid-1960s those of Sarrel and Sherlock, Osofsky and Braen, Nix, and others, resulted in a model of community programs for pregnant adolescents based on the now classical triad of services: medical, social, and educational. By the mid-1970s the known community programs for pregnant adolescents numbered more than 1100, although most of these did not offer all three services.[3,4]

In 1978, Congress passed Public Law 95-626, which included three titles dealing with the issue of adolescent pregnancy. This became known as the Adolescent Health Services and Pregnancy Prevention Act. Title VI provided funding, through a competitive grant mechanism, to public or private nonprofit organizations to improve coordination and linkages between community agencies serving pregnant or parenting adolescents. Ten core services were required of all grantees:

- Pregnancy testing, maternity counseling, and referral services
- Family planning services
- Primary and preventive health services, including prenatal and postnatal care
- Nutritional information and counseling
- Referral for screening and treatment of venereal disease
- Referral to appropriate pediatric care
- Educational services in sexuality and family life (including sex education), and family planning information
- Referral to appropriate educational and vocational services
- Adoption counseling and referral services
- Referral to other appropriate health services

Other services were encouraged but not required:

- Child care
- Consumer education and homemaking
- Counseling for family members
- Transportation

These services were considered most important by the experts who worked on the legislation and testified before Congress and, therefore, may be seen as defining a service program as of the late 1970s. Abortion was not included because of its controversial nature. It was tacitly understood, however, that a grantee could counsel and refer a pregnant adolescent to an agency that did provide abortions, if that was the adolescent's choice.

The small amount of funds actually appropriated, and the small number of programs funded, suggest that the Adolescent Pregnancy Act was more a statement of national policy than a major federal grant program.[5] Evidence for this is seen in the statistics on funding levels and grants approved presented in Table 17-1. Clearly, the commitment of the federal government to the funding of comprehensive programs for pregnant and parenting adolescents has been limited. The influence of the Act, and the Office of Adolescent Pregnancy Programs (OAPP), which administered it, however, probably extended beyond the few programs that received financial assistance. The presence of the grant program caused many communities to think about their pregnant and parenting adolescents and the services that were, or were not, available to meet their needs. In many communities, agencies met and planned coordinated programs that would satisfy the grant requirements and attract federal funds. Boston's Alliance for Young Families is an example of an organization that has developed in response to the Act.

The Adolescent Pregnancy Act would have been considered for renewal in 1982, but prior to that it was incorporated into the Maternal and Child Health Services Block Grant authorized by the Omnibus Budget Reconcil-

Table 17-1. Funding of Title VI, The Federal Adolescent Pregnancy Program: 1979–1981

Fiscal Year	Funding (millions of dollars)		New Programs	
	Authorization	Appropriation	Applications Reviewed	Funded
1979	50	1.0	210	4
1980	50	7.5	390	23*
1981	50	8.0	†	12*

Adapted from Cornely[5] and from personal communication with L. Eddinger (Public Information Officer, Office of Adolescent Pregnancy Programs, Washington, DC).
*With continued funding for most of the previous awardees.
†No new applications were sought. Previous unfunded applications were reviewed again to determine the FY 81 awards.

iation Act of 1981. All future grants to programs for pregnant and parenting adolescents, presumably, would have to be awarded by states from their block grants—except that Title XX of the same Omnibus Act authorized "adolescent family life demonstration projects." This title was promoted by Senator Jeremiah Denton and was dubbed "the chastity bill" because of some of its original language. One of its provisions is very similar to the earlier act: "to establish innovative, comprehensive, and integrated approaches to the delivery of care services for pregnant adolescents . . . and for adolescent parents, which shall be based upon an assessment of existing programs and, where appropriate, upon efforts to establish better coordination, integration, and linkages among such existing programs."[6] The Act authorized a grant program and provided a list of "necessary services" that may be provided by the grantees. Although this list was similar to the list in the previous act (see above), several new items indicate both awareness of additional problems and the interests of the Act's sponsors:

• Referral to licensed residential care or maternity home services
• Mental health services and referral to mental health services
• Outreach services to families of adolescents to discourage sexual relations among unemancipated minors

This act places considerably more emphasis on families and the adoption alternative than did the previous one. It also has provisions for research and evaluation. The authorization is for $30 million each year for 3 years, of which at least two-thirds is to be for demonstration projects. However, as of August 1982, no money had been appropriated to carry out the provisions of this act. (The supplemental appropriations bill vetoed by President Reagan in August 1982 contained $10.3 million for this purpose.)

PRESENT STATUS OF COMPREHENSIVE PROGRAMS

The current status of comprehensive service programs for pregnant and parenting adolescents is unclear. It is difficult both to define "comprehensive" services, and to obtain adequate, up-to-date data. The earliest definitions of "comprehensive" programs required a triad of medical, educational, and social services. However, from one program or study to another, the criteria varied for the type and number of services required in each area. For example, if a special school was provided for only the "regular" academic subjects, and there was no special effort to teach nutrition, childbearing, child rearing, or family life courses, was that a comprehensive program? A study by the National Alliance Concerned with School-Age Parents (NACSAP) in 1976 added a time dimension to the criteria: to be considered fully comprehensive, a program not only had to offer the triad of services, but also had to offer them for a defined period post partum.[3,4] (They did not, however, as implied in the JRB Associates report,[7] have to have residential facilities.) Later, after the passage of the Adolescent Pregnancy Act, a "comprehensive" program became one that offered the 10 core services previously listed. Presumably, a comprehensive program in 1982 would offer the 16 services listed in the new Act.

NACSAP Directory

The first effort to develop a program-by-program inventory of the continental United States was made by the Cyesis Programs Consortium in the early 1970s. This effort consisted largely of a short description of each new program that came to the Consortium's attention. These descriptions were usually published in the organization's newsletters. In 1976 NACSAP produced a national inventory of 1132 programs providing some services to pregnant adolescents.[3] Of the programs listed in this directory, only 54 (4.8 percent) had the full triad of services and a clear commitment to pregnant teenagers for a defined period of time following delivery. (The duration of the commitment was not an issue here, just the existence of a clear commitment.) These were called type A programs.[4] Another 405 programs (type B programs, 35.8 percent) had two of the three services (or the full triad without any postdelivery commitment), and 311 (type C, 27.5 percent) offered only one of the three services. Thus 770 known programs were providing one or more of the triad of services, but most of these programs were not truly comprehensive. Another 176 programs (15.6 percent) were abortion clinics serving adolescents, 169 (14.9 percent) were family planning clinics serving teenagers, and 17 (1.5 percent) were both family planning and abortion clinics. Not all of the agencies were new: in 1976, one agency had been serving unmarried mothers (many of whom were teenagers) for 147 years!

Many of the type A programs were maternity homes. The type B programs usually had counseling and/or social services (98 percent), and most of them (79 percent) had an alternative school. In addition, 53 percent of the type B programs had transportation, 31 percent had infant day care, 36 percent had follow-through counseling, and a nurse was on location at least part of the time in 24 percent. About one-quarter (23 percent) provided medical services and counseling, but no educational program. In most cases, the "other" services, either medical or educational, were available in the community but were not incorporated into one "program."

The type C programs had a strong unitary focus—usually social services. For example, 79 percent provided counseling and social services as the primary service. Other services by type C programs were infant day care (18 percent), follow-through counseling (17 percent), instruction in childbearing and child rearing (13 percent), and transportation (10 percent).

Under contract from the Joseph P. Kennedy, Jr., Foundation, NACSAP studied 42 of the programs more intensely.[4] The programs were selected by random sampling (50 were chosen, and 42 of these agreed to participate). Each program was sent a detailed questionnaire, which was followed up by a site visit. This study confirmed the general impressions obtained from analyzing the program directory, namely, that most programs were not truly comprehensive. This lack was due to the history and focus of the agencies (schools, social service agencies, or hospitals, for example) and to problems in financing and coordinating services in the community. It was also clear that the existing services varied greatly from community to community, in part, due to the lack of federal and/or state policy as to what the programs should be doing. The lack of policy was both caused by, and contributed to, piecemeal and inconsistent funding support.

Funding sources were quite varied, and included federal, state, and local governments and private sources. Of the local voluntary sources, the United Way was clearly the most important in most of the programs. No clear funding pattern emerged, except that of a mosaic of sources. This should not be surprising, given the history of the development of most of these programs.

Due to the lack of both adequate data and necessary data skills at the local level, it was very difficult to determine the penetration rates for the programs, that is, the proportion of the target population that was reached by the programs. Local programs often had not clearly defined the target population, and were just taking all eligible applicants they could. This usually kept them so busy that they did not worry about a theoretical target population and did not know its size.

A disturbing lack of service follow-through was seen; that is, services were usually available for only a few weeks following delivery. The agencies, however, were aware of this need and were committed to providing such services if resources increased. Family planning services after delivery were usually not provided by the agency that assisted the pregnant adolescent and were encouraged only through referral elsewhere, often without a monitoring system to ensure that appointments were kept. Putative fathers were not usually included in the programs in any official way. The study revealed significant service gaps, which needed better linkages, more resources, or both. The Adolescent Pregnancy Act was an attempt to provide both.

JRB Associates Directory

Title VIII of the 1978 Adolescent Pregnancy Act required the Secretary of Health, Education and Welfare to contract with an independent agency to perform a study of the problem of adolescent pregnancies. JRB Associates was awarded the contract and, as a part of its obligations, analyzed the results of a nationwide survey.[7] The six-page survey instrument was developed by the OAPP in 1979–1980 and mailed in the spring of 1980 to approximately 2000 agencies and projects. These were identified as comprehensive service providers, or intending to become so, on a list of over 3000 organizations that had requested information from OAPP. The mailing also included those agencies listed in the earlier NACSAP directory. A second mailing 1 year later included projects in the directories of the Young Women's Christian Association, Kennedy Foundation, and National Conference of Catholic Charities.

From 1117 completed survey forms, 274 were selected for inclusion in the Directory on the basis of meeting the following criteria for comprehensiveness:

- Offered all "core" services
- Delivered services to teenagers 17 years old and younger
- Followed clients for at least 1 year after delivery

For each of these projects, the Directory provides program name, director, address and telephone number, whether services are provided directly or through linkages, the age and range of adolescents served, and the number of pregnant adolescents served during the 1978–1979 school year.

Based on a separate analysis of all responses, the JRB Associates study concluded that 941 programs more or less corresponded to the 770 programs in the earlier NACSAP Directory. The lack of exactly comparable methods, however, prohibits the conclusion that the number of teenage pregnancy programs increased from 770 to 941 (i.e., by 22 percent) from 1976 to

1981. The JRB Associates report also noted that 207 programs (22 percent of the study sample) were more or less comparable to the NACSAP type A programs.

A comparison of the data from the two studies suggests that there was an improvement in the comprehensiveness of programs in the 5 years between the studies. One hypothesis, discussed previously, is that in the process of applying for the OAPP grants, many communities perceived gaps and linked program components that previously had been separate.

JRB Associates was able to obtain a better estimate of the national penetration rates than was NACSAP. They found that the 541 programs were serving an estimated 194,000 pregnant teenagers, or about 35 percent of the total teenage deliveries in 1979. The number of deliveries, however, may not be the correct denominator, since many of the persons served could have been adolescents who came for pregnancy testing (some of whom probably were not pregnant), and some may have obtained abortions. Therefore, the 35 percent overall figure is probably high. However, if only adolescents under age 18 (who are much more likely to be served by these programs) are included, the conclusions change. The denominator becomes 210,836 deliveries and the 194,000 teenagers served represents 92 percent of that figure. Due to uncertainties about the accuracy of the number served and about the appropriate denominator, it can only be tentatively concluded that the proportion of younger pregnant teenagers receiving services is probably moderately high, but the proportion of older teenagers receiving such help is probably low.

The JRB Associates study also analyzed the proportion of programs providing various services, either directly or through referral. For example, 89 percent provided primary pre- and postdelivery medical care: 48 percent directly and 41 percent through other agencies. The proportion of programs providing particular services in any way is shown in Table 17-2. These figures also suggest that the program linkages had improved since 1976, perhaps because of the adolescent pregnancy legislation and the efforts of the OAPP.

Little information has been available on the extent to which rural pregnant adolescents have access to comprehensive programs. The JRB Associates study showed that many programs serve combinations of urban, rural, and suburban teenagers. The percentage of the study programs claiming to serve at least some rural residents was 53 percent, and 45 percent claimed to serve some suburban clients; 70 percent served urban young women. The more important question of the proportion of rural adolescents for whom services are not available remains unanswered.

The JRB Associates study also provided data on the extent to which the programs were based in different kinds of agencies: 13 percent in hospitals, 17 percent in schools, 31 percent in social agencies, 10 percent in

Table 17-2. Percentage of Comprehensive Programs Providing Various Services

Service	Percentage
Sex education and family planning education	97
Pregnancy testing	96
Birth control	96
Nutritional education	95
Prenatal care	94
Venereal disease testing and treatment	94
Health education	93
Educational counseling	92
Child development/parenting and family life education	92
Adoption arrangements	91
Women, Infants, and Children Nutritional Program services	90
Vocational guidance	88
Financial aid	88
Counseling for fathers	86
Homemaking services	82
Pediatric care	82
Vocational education	81
Job placement	80
Residential care	77
Regular school curriculum	76
Abortions	76
Transportation	75
Dental care	73
Day care	55–59*

Data from JRB Associates: Final Report on National Study of Teenage Pregnancy. McLean, Va, 1981.
*Depending on the age of the child.

health departments, 2 percent in community health centers, and 27 percent in other kinds of agencies/settings. Even though most of the programs provide medical care and education, the programs as such are not technically "based" in these types of institutions. There seems to be a trend for programs to use "regular" or existing community services of a wide variety, with a separate coordinating person or agency that refers and links these various services together into a "program." This appears to be an adaptive approach to survival during a time of restrictions on public and private funds, but it also represents a departure from the earlier development of complete, detached, and self-contained programs.

EDUCATIONAL PROGRAMS

Educational issues have always been a major concern of comprehensive programs. Two recent studies provide some new information in this area.

Rand Study

A Rand Corporation study of school programs in 1981 classified them into three types:[8,9] The *inclusive curriculum programs* offered students general education (English, mathematics, and social sciences) and other special courses, such as parenting or nutrition classes, plus various types of support services such as counseling, health monitoring, and breakfast snacks. These programs usually provided their education and services in a separate environment (i.e., outside of school), but few provided continuing services after delivery. By contrast, *integrated programs* were much more likely to provide services after delivery, and, in fact, to emphasize the postdelivery period more than the predelivery period. Two types of integrated programs were the *supplementary curriculum* programs, which provided parenting-related courses for credit in lieu of other electives plus supportive services within regular school settings; and the *noncurricular* programs, which provided services only, also in regular school settings.

The report suggested that detached programs are one way that school administrators and teachers can make the problem of adolescent pregnancy "disappear." By transferring students to special schools, they no longer need to deal with their educational and other needs. Unfortunately, this attitude may continue through the postdelivery period and result in inadequate arrangements for the transition to regular school or for the adaptation of school programs to the needs of parenting students. Another important insight from this study is that the more resources are used to maintain a special, detached program, the less resources are available for follow-up. If this proves to be true in a larger sample, it would provide a strong argument for the "regular-plus" approach in community-based, comprehensive programs.

NASBE Study

The National Association of State Boards of Education (NASBE) also completed a study of school programs in 1981.[10] It compared "exemplary" school programs with a control group of less exemplary programs. The exemplary programs tended to have a better balance between teachers and other professionals compared to the nonexemplary programs, which employed teachers almost to the exclusion of other types of professionals. The exemplary programs also tended to spend about twice as much time in outreach activities as did the others.

CURRENT ISSUES

As the number of and interest in comprehensive service programs increases, several basic questions are being asked more often:

- Which is the best setting for comprehensive services: medical, educational, or social service setting?
- Should education for pregnant adolescents and young mothers be continued within a regular school with special services, or should there be a separate school in a separate setting?
- How important are additional support services such as transportation, day care, and residences?
- Are medical services best provided in a private medical setting or a clinic? If a clinic, should it be a special clinic for teenagers or is a general obstetric clinic sufficient?
- Is the ideal program a highly organized one with a wide variety of services easily available under one roof, or does this produce a "hothouse" client incapable of functioning independently in a community setting and unable to find and demand needed services?
- How long should the services be continued after delivery—months, years, or to a defined period such as until the end of the school year?
- Should putative fathers be included in the programs?
- What is the cost of these services; in particular, what is the ratio of benefits to costs?

These issues have not yet been fully resolved; however, general wisdom and some of the studies just reviewed suggest tentative answers to most of these questions.

Setting

The setting in which a program is operated is probably less important than the quality and coordination of the services. School systems, however, provide a continuity of contact and support (except during the summers) that is lacking in medical settings. This consideration does not necessarily imply that the program should be coordinated from the school, but it suggests that it may be important to make as many services as possible available at or through the school. On the other hand, during the summers (and at all times for those not attending public schools) the needed services should be available elsewhere, and coordination of services should continue.

Type of School

Most pregnant adolescents are capable of continuing in their usual schools. Exceptions are those with medical or social problems that might make it unwise or unsafe for them to be exposed to the turmoil of senior high schools. Moreover, fellow students, as well as teachers, may be uncomfortable with very young pregnant adolescents. In this case, they should be considered for education outside the regular school. Others who may benefit from a separate school, even though it is not essential for their well-being, are those who are behind grade or having other educational problems. Their performance often improves in a setting with a low student-to-teacher ratio and a concerned faculty.

No separate school, however, can provide the wide diversity of courses and facilities available in the regular school. Therefore, students who need or are capable of benefiting from these resources should not be denied them because of their pregnancy. Such exclusion is expressly forbidden by Title IX of the 1972 Education Amendments.

Both regular and special schools should be encouraged to supplement their educational programs with special services for pregnant and parenting adolescents, including classes in health, nutrition, and childbearing, counseling and referral services, and possibly child care. All educational programs should make arrangements for a smooth transition from the prenatal period to the postpartum period—one in which the young woman loses no academic input and adaptations are made to her special needs as a mother.

Support Services

Support services are essential. For many, education and medical care may be impossible without transportation and/or child care. Transportation may be especially crucial in rural areas, and for the older pregnant adolescent who needs prenatal care and already has one or more children at home. Indeed, lack of transportation and child care may be one cause for inadequate prenatal care for this population, which in turn may play a role in the higher perinatal mortality of the higher birth order children born to teenagers.[1]

Child care, particularly for infants, is a service required by many young mothers in order to continue their education or to work. While some can find grandmothers or others to babysit, a significant number must drop out of school because this service is unavailable at rates they can afford.

Some have advocated special residential facilities for unmarried teenagers after they have chosen to leave their own homes or have been forced out. Although such facilities have been tried in a number of cities, they are very expensive, and documentation is lacking to show that expected benefits, such as completion of high school and the prevention of subsequent pregnancies, have occurred.

Medical Care

The source of medical care does not seem to be the crucial variable; those who prefer private care and are able to obtain it should be encouraged to seek it. When a clinic is used by a large number of adolescents, however, a separate adolescent clinic should be developed in order to provide peer support and staff members who are particularly sensitive to the needs of pregnant adolescents. For example, nurse-midwives performed exceedingly well in the New Haven study.[11] For obstetrically uncomplicated pregnancies, the outcomes were identical for nurse-midwives and for obstetricians. Moreover, the young mothers cared for by nurse-midwives showed better compliance, especially in returning for postpartum checkups. Patient satisfaction with care was clearly higher with the nurse-midwives than the obstetricians, although it was generally good for both groups.

Dependence

No studies have dealt with the question of the dependence of pregnant adolescents and young mothers under different service patterns. While normal casework practice seeks to promote client independence, this is especially difficult during the adolescent period when dependence–independence issues are being worked out. Young mothers should be taught to use the available community services when they need them, but the first priority of service providers should be to make sure that their clients receive essential services, even if dependency is fostered temporarily.

Duration

Several studies have suggested that short-term (crisis intervention) services have an immediate effect that declines rather rapidly after the services are ended. Moreover, some studies have shown that maintaining contact and services for years after the first pregnancy helps to promote schooling and reduce subsequent pregnancies during adolescence.[7,12] For these reasons, many experts now urge programs to continue services for 2–3 years after delivery.

Father's Role

Many agencies seek to include the putative fathers as fully as possible into their programs, believing that these young men are an important part of the dyad that produced the child, and that they usually continue to be an important source of financial and emotional support. Data from the New Haven study, however, suggested that the adolescent mother usually does not marry the putative father, nor even necessarily continue a close relationship with him for very long. It would seem unwise to encourage a relationship unless both the young woman and her male partner feel it is in their best interests and that of their child. Sensitive casework is needed (1) to determine when the father wants to, and is able to, play a positive role, (2) to encourage his participation if he is willing and able, and (3) not to force the continuation of a relationship in those cases where it may have negative results, including rapid subsequent pregnancies.

Benefit-to-Cost Ratios

As funds become less available at all levels of government and in the private sector, some form of cost–benefit analysis, whether formal or informal, is being applied to budget decisions. Political and social costs are considered, but increasingly the concern is simply that because the financial costs of these programs are outstripping resources, programs must be cut back or eliminated. Sometimes it is not sufficient to demonstrate that benefits exceed costs; it must be shown that the benefits accrue to the *same* treasury that must pay the costs, and often in the *same* budget period (i.e., that a program saves a city or state budget as much as it costs in the same budget period.) That may be difficult in the case of adolescent pregnancy, because many of the costs occur later in the form of unwanted pregnancies, incomplete education, problem children, welfare dependency, etc.

Budget constraints may reduce the scope of comprehensive programs, affecting particularly detached schools—but even special teachers and classes within regular educational programs may suffer. Budget cuts may also reduce public health nursing services from health departments, social workers in hospitals and clinics, and Medicaid for prenatal care during a first pregnancy. Child care programs are very vulnerable.

Advocates for maintaining and expanding comprehensive service programs should utilize information from the few cost–benefit analyses that have been done. The Johns Hopkins Adolescent Pregnancy Program reported that averted costs were $1440 per mother–child pair, as compared to $775 in program costs for each pair for the first 100 clients in its 2 year follow-up program.[7] The JRB Associates study showed benefit-to-cost ratios of 2:1 or 3:1 in favor of the comprehensive service programs, but the benefits often came later than the special program costs. Because it can be expected that within a very few years, after some equilibrium has been reached, the public treasuries will be receiving the benefits of past programs, the dismantling of programs that currently appear effective should be resisted.

CONCLUSIONS

The helping professions must continue to expect several hundred thousand adolescent pregnancies per year in the United States and be prepared to provide the wide variety of services needed to enable young parents to overcome the extra burdens a premature pregnancy brings. This must be accomplished despite the evidence that the coming decade will continue and increase the chaotic nature of the funding of comprehensive service programs for adolescents. Although to date research on comprehensive service programs has been sparse, some consistent patterns have emerged. One is that programs are moving toward the model of integrating and supplementing "regular" community educational, medical, and social services as opposed to creating detached special programs that provide all needed services under one roof. This trend may be adaptive in times of financial limitations. Moreover, there is some evidence that this type of program may do a better job of long-term follow-through. Hopefully, other adaptations to shortages of funds and inadequate public policies will also be positive in nature. Community comprehensive programs for pregnant and parenting adolescents have survived and, in fact, grown in number and strength since the early 1960s, despite a general lack of public enthusiasm and support. The unusual dedication of most of the workers, despite decades of hardship, suggests optimism for the future despite obvious problems.

REFERENCES

1. Jekel JF, Harrison JT, Bancroft DRE, et al: A comparison of the health of index and subsequent babies born to school-age mothers. Am J Public Health 65:370–374, 1975 1975
2. Vinovskis MA: An "epidemic" of adolescent pregnancy? Some historical considerations. J Fam History, Summer, 205–230, 1981
3. National Alliance Concerned with School Age Parents: National Directory of Services for School-Age Parents. Washington, DC, National Alliance Concerned with School Age Parents, 1976
4. Forbush JB, Jekel JF: A survey of programs for pregnant adolescents in the United States. Presented at the annual meeting of the American Public Health Association, Washington, DC, Nov 2, 1978

5. Cornely DA: Title VI funding for adolescent pregnancy: What have we learned? in McAnarney ER, Stickle G (eds): Pregnancy and Childbearing During Adolescence. New York, Liss, 1981
6. Adolescent Family Life Act of 1982, Title XX, Section 2001(b)3.
7. JRB Associates: Final Report on National Study of Teenage Pregnancy. McLean, Va, JRB Associates (mimeographed), 1981
8. Zellman GL: The Response of the Schools to Teenage Pregnancy and Parenthood. Santa Monica, Calif, Rand Corporation, 1981
9. Zellman GL: A Title IX Perspective on the School's Response to Teenage Pregnancy and Parenthood. Santa Monica, Calif, Rand Corporation, 1981
10. Alexander SJ: Suggested Services and Policies Related to Adolescent Parenthood. Washington, DC, National Association of State Boards of Education, 1981
11. Klerman LV, Jekel JF: School-Age Mothers: Problems, Programs, and Policy. Hamden, Conn, Linnet Books, 1973
12. Cartoff VG: Postpartum services for adolescent mothers, Part 2. Child Welfare 58:673–680, 1979

18

Approach to Adolescents by the Perinatal Staff

Lisa B. Handwerker and Christopher H. Hodgman

I ncreasing numbers of 15- and 16-year-old mothers and fathers are coming in contact with a perinatal staff heretofore inexperienced and unprepared to deal with adolescents. Because teenagers are now frequent visitors to obstetric wards and neonatal centers, their health providers are rapidly learning how to approach these unique patients.

In order to care effectively for the adolescent patient, caretakers require (1) an understanding of adolescent physical, psychological, and social development, (2) knowledge of their own values, stereotypes, and attitudes that may affect their responses to the adolescent, and (3) skills in communicating with and interviewing adolescents. As a framework for addressing these requirements, we discuss adolescent development in relation to hospitalization, caretakers' views and behaviors toward adolescents, and problems commonly encountered by perinatal staff working with adolescent patients. Throughout, adolescents and caretakers are discussed in terms of generally expected behavior. It is, however, important to stress that each person is an individual, with his or her own life experiences; statements concerning adolescents in general may not apply to any particular patient, nor will any single treatment modality lead to success in every case. Each

The authors wish to thank Mary Ann Colamarino for her assistance in preparation of this manuscript.

individual must be assessed in the context of his or her family background, cultural experiences, and personality; these are the influences upon which future interactions are based.

OVERVIEW OF ADOLESCENT DEVELOPMENT

Adolescents of the same age exhibit numerous variations in size, emotional maturity, and sexual development. For this reason, the adolescent patient is frequently classified by developmental rather than chronological age.

The stages of adolescent development are classically defined as early, middle, and late. The adolescent progresses from one stage to another by the accomplishment of certain developmental tasks. The major task of *early adolescence* (13–15 years of age) is the awareness and achievement of comfort with *body image*. As adolescents mature biologically, their physical appearance changes; they begin to resemble (physically mature) adults. An adolescent's body image, "the image of our bodies we form in our mind—the way in which our body appears to ourself,"[1] must change as well. Frequently, the internalization of these outward changes lags far behind the changes themselves. This process is dependent on a number of factors: the adolescents' ideal body image, input they receive from bodily sensations, awareness of how parents and peers see them, and their own interpretation of these evaluations. Young teenagers constantly compare themselves to peers and to an ideal; they may be frustrated if they imagine that their rate of maturation is particularly slow. Any alteration in physical appearance that requires a continually changing body image, such as in pregnancy, is even more difficult for adolescents to understand.

Middle adolescence (15–17 years of age) is characterized by the task of establishing *independence*. Adolescents must move from being dependent and obedient children to becoming autonomous adults who make their own decisions. However, middle adolescents have not yet reached full adulthood; they are constantly vacillating between the two worlds. Adulthood may be frightening and confusing; adolescents may perceive it as a time of being alone, unsupported, and unloved. At the same time, they no longer want to be treated as children. The struggle for independence frequently arises out of their desire for the "privileges" of adulthood without an awareness of the added responsibilities.

The establishment of identity, a process begun in early adolescence, continues in middle adolescence and culminates in *late adolescence. Identity* refers to adolescents' own understanding of who they are as well as an awareness of how others see them.[2] There are many dimensions to an individual's identity, including intellectual, sexual, and interpersonal. As part of establishing an identity, adolescents may experiment with various roles, using peers or, for example, movie stars as role models. Fantasy is an important mechanism for adolescents to "try out" a particular identity. Sexual roles may be practiced with the parent of the opposite sex, or, if this is too threatening, with a teacher. Middle adolescents gain partial identity from peers; they are anxious to be "the same," to identify with a group. For example, a girl who is not having sexual intercourse may say that she is sexually active in order to feel that she is "one of the crowd."

Late adolescents (17–19 years of age) must become fully independent, productive citizens, with the ability to sustain intimate relationships with peers. The task of establishing relationships also begins in early adolescence, as young teenagers begin to place less emphasis on their families, and more on their peer group. Adolescents must define their social group, and then initiate contact; when this behavior is reciprocated, it reflects back onto teenagers and helps them to establish an identity.[3] In developing this capacity for intimate, long-term relationships, adolescents have to accomplish several tasks. They develop a realistic self-image that is well accepted, the ability to give as well as to receive love, and the capacity to compromise and to be committed to a single lasting relationship. The completion of these tasks makes it possible for adolescents to become socially functioning adults.

ADOLESCENTS IN THE HOSPITAL

Ordinarily, the maturation process proceeds in a steady, although seemingly all too slow, manner. However, the process may be interrupted and, therefore, disrupted, by an untimely event such as pregnancy, which may require some time spent away from the home environment in the hospital. The effect this experience has on the adolescent girl depends on past experiences, anxieties, support from family and peers, and support from the hospital staff. The goal of the staff is to make hospitalization as positive an experience as is possible.

It is useful to look at the adolescent girl's reactions to hospitalization from a developmental perspective: How is it different for an early, middle, or late adolescent? Although an adolescent girl in the hospital experiences stress from a variety of sources, her anxieties can be divided into two types: external and internal. External anxiety is that which stems from the removal of the familiar environment, the separation from family or friends, the strangeness of the new environment, and the anticipation of possibly painful procedures. Internal anxieties are derived from developmental concerns. The adolescent's feelings about her body image or identity contribute to the amount of anxiety she experiences.[4] The manner by which she handles the experience may depend on her physical condition, as well as her perceptions of how much control she has over circumstances. Those situations for which the adolescent needs to feel "in control" will depend on where she is developmentally.

Early Adolescents

The key issue for early adolescent girls in the hospital is that of body image. At this stage of her psychosocial development, the adolescent has no clear idea of what she is supposed to look like; her image of herself is constantly changing. The pregnant early adolescent is even more confused. She may look at herself in the mirror several times a day to assure herself that her abdomen has not tripled in size. She is concerned over what she will look like after she has a baby. The postpartum adolescent may be annoyed and feel some loss of control when she has not reverted to her prepregnancy weight immediately after delivery.

This concern for body image makes it particularly important for the early adolescent to be assured of some degree of privacy in the hospital. She needs to have time for herself to adjust to new bodily sensations and physical changes. She needs others to respect her privacy; typical bedside rounds may be inappropriate for an early adolescent, especially if an examination is an expected procedure. The idea of exposing her yet unformed body to a large group of observers may be extremely anxiety provoking.

The early adolescent in the hospital is concerned about procedures and their effects on her body: Will a venipuncture leave a large bruise? How long is it before I can wash my hair? Cognitively, early adolescents struggle with the here and now: pain must be relieved immediately; feeling better tomorrow has no relation to feeling bad today.

Middle Adolescents

Middle adolescence is probably the most difficult time both for the adolescent and the adults with whom she interacts. At this stage the adolescent is most awkward, both in social skills with peers and in relationships with those who are older. Independence conflicts and identity formation are at their peak. In the hospital the adolescent's battles with parents may be transferred to interactions with hospital staff. Such battles may even be intensified, as hospitalization may be perceived as an infringement of the right to independence. The adolescent who has been experimenting with being "on her own" will feel threatened by hospitalization. She is "placed in a position of forced dependency."[5] Her life is no longer completely under her control. Many adolescents are extremely conflicted; to allow oneself to remain dependent is contradictory to one's emerging adult self-concept.

Unable to clearly express or understand this confusion, the adolescent patient may respond with regression and avoid the conflict by returning to the dependent status of a child. Others may continue to strive for control; a few will simply give up.[3]

Many middle adolescents equate dependency with exploitation. The mere idea of being confined in a hospital triggers a need to revolt.[3] This may be particularly true when the peer group visits: in an effort to remain important to her peers, to maintain her "sameness," the middle adolescent may ignore the restraints the hospitalization has placed on her. She may appear stoic when her friends are visiting, only to cry for pain medication as soon as they leave. The adolescent patient may be boisterous and rambunctious in lounge areas, at times to the point of destructiveness, but be meticulous about the appearance of her own room. "Showing off" may also be apparent in the use of profanity and obscene gestures.

Late Adolescents

By late adolescence the teenager usually is comfortable with her body image and has some idea of who she is and what she wants to be. Hospitalization and illness in late adolescence is often viewed as interfering with future plans. The pregnant late adolescent is concerned with her career opportunities or how well she will maintain her own home. She may be worried about her relationship with her baby's father. Her cognitive development is complete; conversations take on adult themes, and planning ahead is foremost in her mind.

CULTURAL SHAPING

The presentation thus far has stressed the differences among adolescents from a developmental perspective. Youth do not, however, develop in a vacuum; they are a product of their culture. Society has a profound impact on adolescent development: it is her cultural background which shapes the adolescent girl in terms of values, regulations, rules, and familial priorities. These learned experiences and values may be very different from those of the health caretaker, and an awareness of these influences is just as important to the communication process as an understanding of psychosocial development.

The health care provider cannot work effectively with the adolescent from a different ethnic group without the ability to foster that adolescent's self-esteem. Adolescents from minority groups in the United States have more difficulty maintaining a high self-esteem than those in majority groups. Blacks, Latinos, Orientals, and lower socioeconomic adolescents see fewer role models in the popular media. They have less of an idea than majority group adolescents of who they are in relation to others in society. Health workers need to understand that the adolescent's priorities, values, and rules may be different from theirs. Miller studied 21 groups in a lower class section of a large city.[6] In his examination of blacks and whites, males and females, and early, middle, and late adolescents, he identified six focal concerns of lower class cultures: trouble, toughness, smartness, excitement, fate, and autonomy. The dominant concern was trouble, i.e., getting into trouble. Youths "in trouble" received attention and prestige. Toughness was essential to the male identity, as was smartness, or the ability to outwit another. Together, these six concerns offered the deprived adolescent something positive, something of which to be proud. This is not to say that all lower class adolescents wish to be in jail; but it does point out that some youth may have different priorities in life and base their behavior on these priorities.

The adolescent girl from a minority ethnic group in the United States is brought up in conflict: Should her behavior reflect the values of her cultural background or those of the general society to which she belongs? In any general discussion of these areas of conflict and confusion there is some tendency to overgeneralize and to stereotype. The reader is reminded that within any group there are both similarities and variations. It is hoped that this presentation of the more common, well-documented beliefs about various groups will enable the caretaker to examine adolescent patients as individuals.

In working with minority families, the health provider must take into consideration a number of factors that influence the degree of acculturation: socioeconomic level, geographic location, and length of time in the United States. In general, higher socioeconomic levels and longer time in the United States are associated with greater acculturation.[7-9]

The stigma of out-of-wedlock pregnancy remains for any cultural/ethnic group; however, the impact that it has on family relationships and interactions, and hence on the adolescent herself, differs in the Latino, black, and Oriental communities. Most Latinos are reared as Roman Catholics; many of the attitudes and values of this group stem from this religious perspective. Sex roles are taught in the home; the expected behaviors of both males and females are learned early in life. Both boys and girls are taught that, above all, one must respect one's parents; bringing shame to the family is taboo. For Latino women, loss of virginity prior to marriage is a most shameful behavior. Because of these intense teachings, a Latino teenage girl may not talk to adults about sexual matters. She is taught to be extremely modest about her body; examinations by male doctors or nurses may be terrifying, as she has been taught that no one is to touch her genitals until she is married.[7] She may be particularly distressed when the examination relates to her sexual activity—she will have to admit her shameful behavior to an adult! To avoid this shame, the Latino adolescent may deny pregnancy until it becomes obvious to all.

Although Latino parents feel shock, shame, and anger when faced with an adolescent pregnancy, the illegitimate child is usually accepted as family and the shameful daughter eventually returns to her previous position in the family.

Adolescent pregnancy among black families is also viewed with disapproval. In a study of 306 black mothers of pregnant teenagers, Furstenberg found that only 4 percent actually approved of the daughter's pregnancy; 69 percent were decidedly negative, and 65 percent of the teenagers themselves also felt unhappy. Those teenagers who were happy about their pregnancies were very likely to have friends with children. Pregnant black teenagers are more likely to have feelings of despair, worthlessness, and social isolation than their nonpregnant peers.[10,11]

Although having an illegitimate child is somewhat shameful, marrying after giving birth has less stigma in the black community. This may be the result of the response to the adolescent—she is not disinherited nor "thrown out of the house," as might be expected in a different culture. Black families have strong feelings of self-preservation and strive to preserve family unity as well.[9]

Although Orientals in the United States are not a homogeneous group, most adolescents are taught that family and cultural development are most important; development of the individual may be less emphasized. For this reason, many Oriental youths complain that there is little or no communication between them and their parents. When major problems are faced, the family tends to solve them on its own, without outside help. Such is the case with an adolescent pregnancy—the family, usually the father, decides the outcome, frequently without consulting the baby's father in the decision to marry early or to adopt.[8] The traditional values of obedience, devotion to parents, and respect for authority hold for all Oriental cultures.

In summary, minority groups in the United States hold different values than those in the majority. These can be extremely conflicting for the minority adolescent as she develops in a majority culture quite different from that which she expects. Her subsequent behavior and adjustment to life depend on her ability to resolve that conflict successfully.

STEREOTYPING BY CARETAKERS

Previous sections in this chapter have addressed the development and behaviors of adolescents themselves; however, the adolescent's experience in the hospital also depends on how hospital personnel react to her. Mercer suggested that those who work with adolescents ask themselves several questions: Do I look at adolescents as a group or as individuals? Am I comfortable working with this age group? Can I be flexible enough to be tolerant of indecisiveness, and not inflict my own values or beliefs on the young person?[12] The answers to these questions may be revealing to the caretaker who heretofore viewed him- or herself as responsive to adolescents.

Treating all adolescents as if they were one person is a common pitfall of adults working with this age group. Rarely are adolescents viewed through a bias-free perspective. Stereotypes include the adolescent as victim and victimizer; dangerous yet nearly endangered, requiring intense overprotection; sexually precocious and sexually inadequate, needing information and encouragement; and emotionally disturbed.[13,5] Adults often do not view teenagers as individuals, just as many adolescents see all adults as hypocritical and unable to understand the problems of teenagers. Stereotypes are perpetuated by both sides of the generation gap.

Unfortunately, the stereotypes of adolescence are not true of even a minority of youths. The so-called "headline intelligence" of society has led the majority of adults to view all adolescents as delinquent, irresponsible, hypersexual, or hedonistic.[13]

In a recent study at a university-based medical center, Finkelstein et al. polled employees as to their opinions of adolescents.[14] More than 90 percent of respondents (of whom 89 percent were white, 4 percent black, 5 percent Mexican-American, and 2 percent Oriental) characterized *all* adolescents as imaginative, critical of adults, and easily influenced by peers; 60 percent of respondents described qualities of all adolescents as well as qualities of adolescents of different ethnic groups. At least 75 percent stated that all adolescents were likely to engage in petting and necking and to drink beer.

White adolescents were described as using contraceptives or tranquilizers, smoking pipes or cigars, self-confident, self-centered, open to new ideas, critical of adults, smoking marijuana, imaginative, using stimulants, smoking cigarettes, and drinking beer. More than 50 percent of respondents described black adolescents as hostile, getting into trouble, rebellious, uninterested, unable to delay gratification, exhibitionistic, boisterous, having sexual intercourse, aggressive, using hard drugs, and lackadaisical. Orientals were stated to be shy, easily influenced by adults, and cooperative. Mexican-Americans were not characterized by more than 25 percent of the respondents.

In general, in this study population, whites and Orientals were viewed as having positive behaviors, and blacks as having negative behaviors. Although white teenagers were characterized as having more sexual activity, black youths were viewed as more likely to have intercourse. White adolescents were described as being more likely to use an illicit substance, but black teenagers were thought to be more likely to use hard drugs.

In comparing these results to self-reports by teenagers of the different ethnic groups, Finkelstein et al. found serious discrepancies, thereby substantiating their hypothesis that adults stereotype adolescents as a group, particularly adolescents of various ethnic groups.

What are the implications for caretakers in the hospital? First, they must be aware that these stereotyped ideas do exist. Second, adolescents are also aware of their existence, and respond by setting up barriers to communication; they want to act, look, and talk differently from adults, and thus exclude adults from their culture. Caretakers must realize that in being different the adolescent is simply trying to delineate his or her identity and is trying just as hard to be different from the child as from the adult.[13]

RESPONSES TO ADOLESCENTS IN THE HOSPITAL

For any caretaker, the critical issue in dealing with patients is establishing rapport. This establishment of trust, comfort, and communication[2] may be viewed as nearly impossible with some adolescent patients. If, however, interactions are based on an understanding of normal adolescent growth and development, and sufficient time and empathic listening techniques are utilized, this extremely frustrating experience may become one of fulfillment for staff and patient alike.

It is difficult for some adults to relate well to adolescents because of their own past experiences and attitudes. Many find it confusing to talk to adolescents; teenagers do not respond as we expect them to based on our experiences with children or adults. Frequently, the most frustrating part of working with adolescent patients is the beginning, "getting acquainted" period.

Most adolescents also experience a certain degree of discomfort in relationships with adults. Personal insecurities, anxieties about an unfamiliar situation, or uncertainties about appropriate behavior frequently lead adolescents to be uncommunicative. Sider and Kreider suggested some guidelines to help establish good rapport with adolescent patients.[2] At the outset, the caretaker must avoid being judgmental. If the health provider cannot refrain from imposing on the adolescent his or her own views about a particular situation, he or she should not work with the patient. Health professionals need to recognize those areas in which they hold strong feelings and attitudes and not allow these feelings to interfere with the care they provide their patients.

Being judgmental also refers to stereotyping individuals by their dress or mannerisms. Adults sometimes make errors in judging a person because of dress, hair length, or superficial appearance. The well-dressed, polite 14-year-old seen for amennorrhea will be reassured, and her pregnancy will be missed, while a sloppy, arrogant 17-year-old will get a pregnancy test as soon as she walks in the door. Adolescents are as individual as adults; appearances do not always reflect actions.

When caring for the adolescent girl in general, there are some approaches that may help to establish good rapport:[2,15,16]

- Treat the adolescent as a person—she is one! It may take longer for the adolescent to explain what is on her mind, but it is important that what she is saying be taken seriously. This will help to establish an honest, trusting relationship.
- Respond emphatically at appropriate times. The adolescent needs more encouragement than a simple nod of the head.
- Don't patronize or infantalize the teenage patient. Teasing or using childish names will only serve to disavow whatever trust you have secured.

Difficulties with adolescent patients are not limited to initial encounters. Some caretakers, although they have the best intentions, cannot work with this age group. It may be that their own experiences interfere with their ability to care effectively for the adolescent patient. Others have a tendency to "go overboard"—they may attempt to relate to adolescents by using their language or imitating their mode of dress. Adolescents are extremely sensitive to inconsistencies and may react in a negative or mocking manner to such behavior. It is difficult for staff members to present themselves as professionals and, at the same time, be perceived by the teenager as responsive to her lifestyle.

Younger staff generally work better than older staff with the adolescent patient. Older staff seem to be less able to cope with the boisterous activities, obscene gestures, or profane remarks that are likely to occur.[3] Younger staff may also experience problems in response to adolescent patients. The proximity of age of a younger staff member to the adolescent patient can often lend itself to overidentification. While this unusual level of empathy is a positive experience for the adolescent, it may make it difficult for the staff member to perform painful procedures or to be completely honest with the patient. Frequently, working with adolescents reminds caretakers of their own adolescence—that it, too, was a painful experience—and leaves them with a hesitant, defensive approach to the patient.[5,15]

When adolescent behaviors do not meet adult expectations, staff members may become angry and frustrated. Independence struggles, stemming from the adolescent's desire to remain in control, may be perceived by staff members as a threat to their professional autonomy. From the developmental perspective, hostility toward adults increases in middle adolescence; this battle for independence may be transferred to the nurse or doctor, even though they may view themselves as the "good parent." The staff person may then become extremely frustrated because the patient's response is disappointing. This may lead to feelings of helplessness, inadequacy, and anger at the patient.

Such feelings and responses to her behavior need to be discussed with the adolescent in a communicative manner. Approaching her in an authoritative, inflexible manner frequently "turns her off," and is counterproductive. That is not to say that the adolescent should be given free reign in the hospital; this would be intolerable for staff, other patients, and the adolescent herself. However, the adolescent should be allowed to continue her psychosocial development, even though she has assumed a somewhat dependent posture in the hospital.

Whether the pregnant adolescent is hospitalized in the obstetric unit or a separate adolescent ward, the staff needs to be prepared to respond appropriately to her sometimes erratic, inconsistent behavior. Hoffman et al. suggested the following guidelines in caring for adolescent patients:[5]

- Medical care should be a collaborative effort. The adolescent needs to feel as if she has some power over what is happening to her. It may be something as simple as having an intravenous solution flow into her right rather than her left hand, but to the teenager who is struggling with conflicting ideas of independence and body image, this may make the difference between a "good" and a "bad" day.
- Respect the youth as an individual. The caretaker must avoid stereotyping and must take time to communicate with the patient.
- An understanding of adolescent development is essential.
- Confrontations and power struggles should be avoided. This is best accomplished if limits are set in advance, e.g., lights out at 11 P.M. for all patients on the unit. This needs to be done with some flexibility and should be constantly reevaluated as to its effectiveness.
- All medical and nursing care should take into account the adolescent's intense need for privacy.

The ideal staff–adolescent relationship includes a sincere, direct, warm, and interested approach to the patient in a nonjudgmental manner.[16] The staff member who is knowledgeable about adolescent development and who enjoys encouraging teenagers in their growth process will also recognize the need to encourage responsible behavior.

PROBLEMS SPECIFIC TO THE PERINATAL UNIT

In this section problems specifically encountered by perinatal staff are presented with an emphasis on the adolescent's developmental stage.

Adolescents during Labor, Delivery, and the Postpartum Period

Teenagers have long been considered high-risk obstetric patients. Factors implicated in their poor outcome include lack of prenatal care and high anxiety levels.[17-19] In any case, the goal of the obstetric team is to enable the adolescent to have a successful delivery; this becomes difficult when the team is faced with an adolescent patient who is both physically and psychologically unprepared for the experience.

Psychological stressors play an important part in the individual's response to labor. Most women have some fears and anxieties about the delivery of their babies. This is true for adolescents, as well, but often the adolescent is less able to express these fears. The degree of this anxiety depends on how adequate the mother's coping mechanisms are; adolescents, with fewer emotional supports, less life experience, and less ability to communicate, have less sophisticated coping mechanisms.[18]

What effect does this heightened anxiety have on obstetric outcome? As anxiety increases, epinephrine is released into the blood stream. The ensuing physiologic responses may decrease blood flow to the fetus and may depress or increase uterine tone.[20] Crandon studied 146 women in labor and found that higher anxiety levels (as measured by the IPAT Anxiety Scale Questionnaire) were significantly correlated with the incidence of preeclampsia, forceps deliveries, prolonged labor, precipitous delivery, fetal distress, and postpartum hemorrhage.[17] Mean Apgar scores were significantly lower in infants born to mothers who were highly anxious. It follows, therefore, that by lowering a woman's anxiety level, one may alter her obstetric outcome.

The major objective, then, in working with the adolescent during labor and delivery is to enable her to lower her level of anxiety. The staff must recognize that the teenager who has a poor sense of identity and who is feeling totally helpless will be the most anxious, and therefore have the most difficulty in labor.[18]

The early adolescent in labor is likely to be the most dependent. She may be extremely demanding, requiring frequent, concrete explanations of what is happening. Her fantasies about labor and delivery may be unrealistic; hence she may be more anxious than older teenagers. A supportive, clear approach by the health professional with frequent attempts at allowing the patient to remain in control is most helpful. It may be most difficult to establish rapport with the middle adolescent. In her independence struggle, she wants to do things on her own; attempts by health care staff to help ease the pain or to teach relaxation techniques may be rejected. The staff should realize that her behavior may only be a front and should not relinquish efforts to decrease the middle adolescent's anxiety. She, too, needs concrete explanations of procedures and her progress in labor.

The late adolescent, although perhaps more physically prepared for labor and delivery, may be as psychologically immature as her younger counterparts. She may lack information on the process of labor and delivery, especially if her cultural background is one in which such discussions are forbidden. The health care provider needs to look at patients as individuals and respond to them in terms of their own needs. Patients in labor, at any age, are most responsive to the staff they perceive as most supportive. Mothers perceive labor as a much more positive experience when they feel they have a caretaker who is able to recognize and respond to their need for a supportive presence.[21] With a knowledge of adolescent development, the caretaker in labor and delivery is more capable of assessing this need in teenage patients.

The labor and delivery experience can be traumatic for the adolescent or it may be a positive part of her psychosocial development. The latter result can be facilitated if we respect her abilities and personal attributes but recognize that she is an adolescent. According to Mercer, "the teenager's rights to grant informed consent and to refuse treatments must be continually acknowledged, along with her right to be informed of her progress and of both her own and her infant's health status. According the youthful parents their rights fosters their self-esteem and personal development."[18]

The postpartum period is that time immediately following delivery through the next 6 weeks. This may be an anxious time for the teenager. She is adjusting to her new role as mother, and adjusting to her new body image. As with any adolescent, she may be unrealistic in her expectations of her body size and weight; she may brag that she will be down to her prepregnancy weight within 1 week. The middle adolescent may be concerned about her stitches or scars—will they spoil the way she looks or her ability to have sexual intercourse? The late adolescent may behave more like her adult counterparts.

The adolescent's response to her infant in the immediate postpartum period depends, of course, on her expectations and her feelings toward the infant. It is important to note, however, that infants of adolescent mothers may be different in their interactive and motor processes. In one study, in the first 5 days of life infants of teenage mothers were observed to be less capable of responding to social stimuli, less alert, and less able to control motor behavior than infants of older mothers.[22] In combination with a mother who feels inexperienced and doubts her mothering abilities, such an infant's behavior may become a negative reinforcement to its mother's efforts to care for her baby. Perinatal staff must be aware of these interactive difficulties and make an extra effort to point out positive experiences with the infant.

As the adolescent feels more comfortable with herself and her baby, she will once again become a "normal" adolescent, with the added responsibility of having a baby to care for. Mother–infant interactions are covered elsewhere in this volume (see Chapter 11); suffice it to say that the adolescent's behavior post partum will be stage appropriate. The staff may expect her to act as an early, middle, or late adolescent in the hospital; the tasks of establishing body image, identity, and independence will be resumed.

High-Risk Infants

The birth of a high-risk infant is a traumatic experience for any parent. The adolescent's response to this experience parallels that of an adult but is molded by her developmental stage. Kaplan and Mason presented four psychological tasks posed by the birth of an infant born at risk.[23] In order to cope successfully with the experience of a problem infant, and to have a sound basis for a future healthy mother–child relationship, the mother must complete these four tasks.

The first task, anticipatory grief, should take place at the time of delivery. It involves a withdrawal from the previously established relationship with the coming child; the mother still hopes the infant will live, but at the same time becomes prepared for its death. This task may be difficult for the early adolescent. Her cognitive state may allow her only to think of the baby as being ill, or having difficulty breathing. That illness today may mean death tomorrow can be incomprehensible. Especially with the early adolescent, caretakers may need to stress the negative aspects of the infant's present health, such as low blood pressure or respiratory distress. Future implications may go unheard.

As the mother realizes her infant is at risk, she must also come to realize her failure to deliver a normal, full-term baby. For an adolescent who is struggling with the concepts of identity and body image, this failure may be viewed as all-encompassing. She may see herself as totally unable to be an adult, as she has been unable to function as one. This is particularly true for that adolescent who has seen the pregnancy as a means to establish herself as a woman. Health professionals in the neonatal and obstetric units must be aware of these feelings and allow adolescents to ventilate their concerns.

As the infant's condition improves, the mother must resume the process of relating to her baby. The early adolescent who has viewed the baby as nearly dead may be reluctant to initiate contact. She may have already excluded the infant from her lifestyle and may need tremendous encouragement from the neonatal staff to resume the relationship. The middle adolescent, although fearful and wary of the neonatal unit, may exhibit a false bravado and behave as if she "knows it all." This should not prevent perinatal staff from offering thorough explanations of equipment and the infant's condition. Such an adolescent, in trying to be an independent adult, may often want to touch and feed the baby immediately, but may experience intense disappointment and feelings of failure when the infant does not respond as she had anticipated. Caring, concrete information from the staff about normal infant behaviors helps to alleviate this anxiety. Late adolescents may be concerned and frightened and may feel inadequate. Their reactions may be similar to those encountered in adult parents, and the staff may treat them similarly.

Kaplan and Mason's fourth psychological task is that of recognizing that the infant has special needs as a high-risk infant and that this is a temporary state which should end well. The adolescent must be made aware that the infant differs in its growth patterns and behavioral responses from normal newborns. This is the time for learning how to care for a high-risk infant. The early adolescent may be unable to understand the importance of preventive care, such as physiotherapy. The middle adolescent may want to "do it all." Both will look to perinatal staff members for role models and will imitate their behavior with the infant. Frequently, mothers of high-risk infants are observed to feed their babies with the infants in their laps, rather than cuddled close; this is a behavior they copy from neonatal nurses, who may have fed the infant in this position early in its life.[24]

The ultimate goal in working with high-risk infants and their adolescent parents is to ensure the development of an attachment to the baby. With an understanding of the adolescent's fears and needs, this is a goal perinatal staff can usually accomplish effectively.

Adolescent Fathers

The paucity of literature on adolescent fathers in no way reflects their role in adolescent pregnancy. Fathers are becoming more involved in prenatal care and delivery.[25] Perinatal staff need to recognize their importance both as support for the mother and as fathers to the infants.

If an adolescent father is present in the perinatal period, it is highly likely that he will maintain contact with the mother for at least the first 3 months post partum.[26] Just as adult fathers are proud of their children, the adolescent father may boast of his child and show the child off to kin and peers.[25] He needs to be treated as an integral part of the family unit. (See Chapter 13 for further discussion of adolescent fathers.)

Perinatal staff members need to recall that just as adolescent mothers present at various stages of development, so, too, do adolescent fathers. Although most adolescent fathers are chronologically older than their partners,[26] this is no assurance that they are more mature in the psychosocial realm. The approach to the adolescent father needs to be individualized and based on open and honest communication.

CONCLUSIONS

Perinatal staff members need to learn approaches to a specific and unique group of patients: pregnant adolescents. Adolescents, when viewed in general, can be frightening, unapproachable, arrogant, and totally frustrating; however, when approached as individuals, they may favorably modify notions previously held by staff members. The individual approach to adolescents requires a knowledge of adolescent development. Regardless of chronological age, developmentally early, middle, and late adolescents differ in cognitive and psychosocial abilities. For a caretaker to communicate effectively with any teenager, these differences must be recognized.

Health providers must be aware of their own attitudes; their stereotypes of various cultural/ethnic groups, attitudes toward premarital pregnancy, and feelings about abortion might influence their behavior with adolescent parents. Caretakers need to learn how not to impose such views on adolescent patients.

Caring for pregnant adolescents in the hospital setting can be a difficult, frustrating, and rewarding experience. It is most often rewarding when staff members approach these patients with a knowledge of adolescent development, an understanding of their own biases and attitudes in relating to this age group, and a willingness to communicate openly.

REFERENCES

1. Kolb LC: Disturbances of the body image, in Arieti S (ed): American Handbook of Psychiatry, vol 4. New York, Basic Books, 1975, pp 539–547
2. Sider RC, Kreider SD: Coping with adolescent patients. Med Clin North Am 61:839–854, 1977
3. Schowalter JE, Anyan WR: Experience on an adolescent in-patient division. Am J Dis Child 125:212–215, 1973
4. Conway B: The effect of hospitalization on adolescents. Adolescence 6:77, 292, 1971
5. Hofmann AD, Becker RD, Gabriel HP: The Hospitalized Adolescent. New York, Free Press, 1976
6. Miller WB: Lower class cultures as a generating milieu of gang delinquency, in Winder AE, Angus DL (eds): Adolescence: Contemporary Studies. New York, Van Nostrand Reinhold, 1968, pp 189–204
7. Bello TA: The Latino adolescent, in Mercer RT (ed): Perspectives in Adolescent Health Care. New York, Lippincott, 1979, pp 57–64

8. Fong CM: The Chinese adolescent, in Mercer RT (ed): Perspectives in Adolescent Health Care. New York, Lippincott, 1979, pp 64–72

9. Hayes CA: The black adolescent: Attitudes and reflections, in Mercer RT (ed): Perspectives in Adolescent Health Care. New York, Lippincott, 1979, pp 49–57

10. Furstenburg FF: The social consequences of teenage parenthood. Fam Plann Perspect 8:148–164, 1976

11. Gispert M, Falk R: Sexual experimentation and pregnancy in young black adolescents. Am J Obstet Gynecol 126:459–466, 1976

12. Mercer RT: The adolescent and health professional, in Mercer RT (ed): Perspectives on Adolescent Health Care. New York, Lippincott, 1979, pp 387–401

13. Anthony J: The reactions of adults to adolescents and their behavior, in Caplan G, Lebovici S (eds): Adolescence: Psychological Perspectives. New York, Basic Books, 1969, pp 54–78

14. Finkelstein JW, Medina M, Vegehla M: Hospital-based employees' opinions about adolescents of four racial-ethnic groups. J Adolesc Health Care 2:1–7, 1981

15. Rosenthal MB: Sexual counseling and interviewing of adolescents. Primary Care 4:291–300, 1977

16. Smith MS: An approach to the adolescent for the primary care clinician. J Fam Pract 8:63–66, 1979

17. Crandon A: Maternal anxiety and neonatal wellbeing. J Psychosom Res 23:113–115, 1979

18. Mercer RT: The adolescent experience in labor, delivery and early post-partum, in Mercer RT (ed): Perspectives on Adolescent Health Care. New York, Lippincott, 1979, pp 302–347

19. Ryan GM, Schneider JM: Teenage obstetric complications. Clin Obstet Gynecol 21:1191–1197, 1978

20. Zuspan FP, Cibils L, Pose SV: Myometrial and cardiovascular responses to alterations in plasma epinephrine and norepinephrine. Am J Obstet Gynecol 84:841–851, 1962

21. Shields D: Nursing care in labor and patient satisfaction. J Adv Nurs 3:535–550, 1978

22. Thompson J, Cappleman MW, Zetschel KA: Neonatal behavior of infants of adolescent mothers. Dev Med Child Neurol 21:474–482, 1979

23. Kaplan DM, Mason EA: Maternal reactions to premature birth viewed as an acute emotional disorder. Am J Orthopsychiatry 30:539–547, 1960

24. Devitto B, Goldberg S: The effects of newborn medical status on early parent–infant interaction, in Field TM, Sostek AM, Goldberg S, et al (eds): Infants Born at Risk. New York, Spectrum, 1979, pp 311–332

25. Earls F, Siegel B: Precocious fathers. Am J Orthopsychiatry 50:469–480, 1980

26. Lorenzi ME, Klerman LV, Jekel JF: School age parents: How permanent a relationship? Adolescence 12:13–22, 1977

19

Birth Alternatives for Adolescents

Nancy Jo Reedy

Traditional hospital care for childbirth is changing. New alternatives are developing to meet demands of childbearing families. Since the late 1950s consumers of maternity care have challenged the traditional health care system. Women have demanded care that recognizes their emotional and psychological needs as well as their physical needs during childbirth. Family-centered care, rooming-in, support for breastfeeding, psychoprophylaxis, and active participation in birth by a chosen support person have been accomplished within hospitals under consumer pressure. These changes did not adequately meet the needs, however. In the mid-1970s many women who had become totally disenchanted with the traditional health care system chose to deliver at home with untrained attendants. The health care system struggled to modify rigid traditional hospitals and at the same time maintain safety for mother and baby. The late 1970s saw a dramatic change in philosophy and facilities available to childbearing families; consumers and health care providers joined resources to develop alternatives to traditional care. The alternatives share a philosophy that recognizes childbirth as an inherently normal, healthy, physiologic process. Alternative facilities were designed to reflect the philosophy of health in medically safe environments.

Homelike birthing rooms, alternative birth centers, and hospital birth centers evolved in previously traditional facilities. New out-of-hospital birth centers developed to provide comprehensive family-centered care for prenatal through postpartum visits. The key to alternatives is the provision of flexible options for the pregnant woman and those important to her: her partner, extended family, mother, friends, or siblings. The family is actively involved in decision making concerning the place, emotional environment, and management of the childbirth. Alternatives are predicated upon a well-informed mother, partner, and/or other support person.

Too often adolescents are automatically barred from participating in alternatives—they are considered "too young," "too high-risk," "too inappropriate," etc. They often lack the support to seek out childbirth alternatives. Adolescents, however, benefit from a policy of appropriate access to alternatives. Choosing, preparing for, and using an alternative method of childbirth requires responsible thought, decision making, active preparation, and follow-through by the adolescent. The new skills and behaviors required to utilize the alternatives are the very activities that can assist positive development and growth in the adolescent. Young people are not all alike. Their capabilities and needs are dependent upon their maturity. Each adolescent must be considered individually. Encouraging adolescents to consider and utilize appropriate alternatives can enhance their development. Forcing adolescents into environments they are not prepared to manage can lead to increased dependence, and, perhaps, have an adverse effect on their self-image and development.

Alternatives and adolescents must be carefully and thoughtfully matched. In order to do this the health care professional must have a thorough knowledge of the essential preparation and skills necessary for a safe, effective childbirth in an alternative facility, and an understanding of adolescent development; this combination is the key to effectively utilizing alternatives in order to enhance positive adolescent development.

ADOLESCENT DEVELOPMENTAL TASKS

Mastering the adolescent developmental tasks signals the end of adolescence and beginning of adulthood. The tasks serve to chart the progress of the adolescent moving from childhood to adulthood. Just as the goal of adolescence is to attain adulthood, the goal of supportive adults is to assist the young person in this development. The pregnant adolescent experiences change and stress from two perspectives: as an adolescent she is moving from childhood to adulthood, and as a pregnant woman she is moving from individual to parent. The pressure of these two major developmental changes can be overwhelming to the young person, however, many adolescents respond to pregnancy by rapidly accomplishing the developmental tasks of adolescence. It is necessary for the young person to master the tasks of adolescence in order to move into a stable role as an effective adult and parent.

Experts have not established one single set of adolescent developmental tasks. Helms published a set of tasks consistent with other experts and particularly suited to assessment of the individual adolescent.[1] The tasks are described below, with implications for the adolescent who is pregnant.

To Develop Cognitive Abilities Further

The ability to think abstractly and solve complex problems develops slowly during middle and late adolescence. Piaget stated that the final stage of cognitive development is reached in adolescence.[2] Abstract thinking is essential for the adolescent to be able to identify her personal values and comprehend the impact of those beliefs on her daily life and pregnancy. Cognitive abilities are necessary to consider, evaluate, and follow through with alternative birth plans. Cognitive abilities should be fostered in all discussions of pregnancy. Health care providers must give support and guidance to each adolescent as she considers her options. The process of making the decision is at least as important as the decision itself.

Traditional childbirth leaves decision making with the physician and/ or institution from pregnancy through delivery; alternatives require decision making by the adolescent. The goal is to guide the adolescent toward a mature decision-making process. The adolescent who learns a positive way to investigate options and make decisions will have grown and will carry her skill into adulthood.

Early adolescents tend to choose a birth alternative based on how they are feeling "now" rather than what they think they would like "later"—at the time of birth. Early adolescents are just beginning to be able to look at themselves and often have an unrealistic view of their capabilities. The early adolescent needs extensive guidance in making appropriate plans for childbirth. Middle adolescents need less assistance in assessing their own capabilities and their commitment to preparation for the alternative. They are developing the ability to think "what if I choose this or that facility." They need guidance, however, because of gaps in their thinking process. For example, a middle adolescent might choose to deliver in a hospital birthing room because it looks less "hospitally" but forget that she must attend childbirth classes to prepare for her birth. Late adolescents often have developed skills in decision making and may need only minimal guidance. They are capable of seeking out alternatives because they have the ability to plan abstractly for the future. Late adolescents function independently in choosing alternative birth centers, early discharge home, and other options that require complex thinking, planning, and preparation. For all adolescents, looking ahead to the time of the birth encourages "future orientation."

To Establish Their Own Identity

"Who am I?" is a recurring question of adolescents—especially during pregnancy. In fact, pregnancy may be a result of the young person's attempt to answer this question. Identity plays a minor role in choosing alternatives for early and middle adolescents but may play a major role in the decision of a late adolescent. The late adolescent who has rejected traditional institutions for a "back to nature" lifestyle may be attracted to an out-of-hospital birth center. Another late adolescent who has chosen an Eastern religion may seek out a birth environment that allows the participation of members of her religious group. Adolescents often exhibit inconsistencies within their newly adapted value system. For example, a middle or late adolescent may adopt a "natural" approach to food and drink by shunning "artificial chemicals and drugs" and yet continue to smoke cigarettes. Resolution of the inconsistencies is part of the process of developing a personal identity. The health care system is challenged to provide alternatives that allow the adolescent freedom to choose options appropriate to her emerging identity but remain within parameters of medical safety.

To Achieve Independence from Parents

Adolescents often state "independence from parents" as a goal of their teenage years. The struggle for independence is an emotional turmoil for both the young person and the parents. Vacillation between periods of dependence and independence is the norm.

To Develop Relationships with Peers of Both Sexes

Early adolescents move from family ties to close friendships with peers of the same sex. An early adolescent girl seeks the advice and support of her "best girlfriend" before turning to her family. The opposite sex becomes important as the young person moves into middle adolescence. Middle adolescents run in "herds" of boys and girls, relying on the peer group for security; conformity is the rule. Middle to late adolescence brings dating, and the peer group becomes less important as individual relationships become more important. Late adolescents are able to establish lasting relationships with one person of the opposite sex.

Peer relationships play a major role in the provision of birth alternatives. Peer counselors are received well by early and middle adolescents, who are in the stage of development that relies on peers for information. In time of crisis, early and middle adolescents turn first to peers. For this reason, peer support in labor and/or in outpatient areas can be accepted by the young people and are effective in promoting optimal health.

The late adolescent may have a stable partner. Late adolescent couples function like their older married counterparts—indeed marriage could be in their plans. The young man is an active participant in planning, preparing, and participating in birth and child rearing. The prescence of a stable partner can provide support to an adolescent experiencing stress within her family and enable her to maintain her emotional independence. The participation of a stable supportive person is especially important if the pregnant adolescent chooses nontraditional childbirth. She needs the partner to help shoulder the responsibility of classes, preparation, birth, and early discharge.

To Prepare for Self-Sufficiency

The major choice the adolescent must make is that of her or his life work. Educational preparation and/or work are the first steps toward self-sufficiency. Late adolescents may remain financially dependent upon parents during their education; this dependency may last into early adulthood. The most important preparation for self-sufficiency is learning to make decisions. Birth alternatives are an excellent ground for adolescents to exercise their decision-making skills. Responsibility for decisions and choices are inherent in the utilization of alternatives. Decision making involves the following steps:

1. Recognize need for decision
2. State the options
3. Gather data on all options
4. Analyze risks and benefits of each option
5. Consider personal values
6. Discard unacceptable options
7. Make reasoned decision from acceptable options

Adolescents should be guided patiently through each step by the health care professional. Decision making and responsibility are keys to successful parenting. Fostering good decision-making processes and a sense of personal accountability for the outcome should be a priority for health care providers. Self-sufficiency is the necessary base upon which to build parenting skills.

Adolescents normally grow into self-sufficiency through the process of maturation as described. Some adolescents may be forced into premature self-sufficiency by childbearing. Families may reject them emotionally or literally. Early and middle adolescents may be forced to establish their own apartment, support themselves and their child financially, and abandon any educational or career plans. The forced self-sufficiency may appear to be a giant leap into maturity, however, the young person has not completed the required tasks. At some time in her or his life, the adolescent developmental tasks will have to be completed.

ROLE OF THE PROFESSIONAL IN PROVIDING BIRTH ALTERNATIVES

Health care providers should be adolescent advocates; this advocacy extends beyond traditional health care to the fostering of growth and development. Assisting the childbearing adolescent to grow into a mature adult, effective parent, and productive citizen must be the goal. Birth alternatives provide a unique opportunity to enhance her emotional and psychological maturation as well as provide quality health care. Cost is a major concern of many adolescents and their families, and alternatives are often less costly than traditional care. A birth alternative a young person can afford contributes to the development of her independence and responsibility.

The health care professional should offer appropriate alternatives to adolescents rather than wait for young people to inquire. Adolescents may be unaware of their options and their right to participate in those options. The health care provider functions as a guide and support through the decision-making process. It is essential that proper guidance be given so that the adolescent makes choices that she is capable of achieving. Negative messages bombard the adolescent who is pregnant or parenting a young child. The adolescent needs positive accomplishments to enhance her self-image. For example, an early adolescent should not be encouraged to choose an early postpartum discharge, but a late adolescent may do well with this alternative. The key to success is preparation for the chosen option. Professionals must be certain that the young person is participating in and understanding whatever class, reading, or other preparation is necessary.

Adolescents vacillate in their development and move back and forth between childhood and adulthood. Middle adolescents are particularly unpredictable. Flexibility and continual reassessment of the adolescent's developmental status are essential. Birth plans are modified periodically as appropriate. An early adolescent may elect a hospital birthing room with an older peer as support; the plans are reassessed near term, however, if the health care professional discovers the girl has become totally dependent on her mother for support and decisions. The return to a dependency role is normal, but it may conflict with plans for peer support in labor. The girl would need to be guided through rethinking her birth plan and making any appropriate changes. Should her mother become her coach and attend preparation classes with her? If she wishes to retain her peer coach, what role will her mother assume during labor and delivery? The important aspect of this situation is that it provides an opportunity to teach decision making to the early adolescent. The outcome—who actually coaches at delivery—is secondary to the process of arriving at a conscious, considered decision.

Alternatives in childbirth might be described as anything nontraditional or "a choice apart from the usual." Alternatives are neither good nor bad in and of themselves. A nontraditional method is not necessarily better or worse than the traditional method. Each option must be considered on its own merit and matched with the needs and capabilities of the individual. For example, a hospital birthing room is not medically better than family-centered labor and delivery rooms. Emotionally and developmentally, however, the birthing room may be better for a late adolescent. It is imperative to match the alternative and the adolescent appropriately to achieve a positive growth experience.

MONITRICE SYSTEM—PEER SUPPORT

It is well established that emotional support in labor is essential to a positive birth experience. With such support women are able to manage their labors better and use their chosen preparation method more effectively. Lamaze, Bradley, and other psychoprophylactic preparation methods emphasize the role of the father as the provider of psychological support, comforter, and nurturer during labor and birth. Adolescents usually lack the stable partner upon which Lamaze and other childbirth preparation methods are based. No woman should ever be alone in labor; adolescents certainly are no exception. Since adolescents usually do not have stable partners, other methods of providing supportive companionship are necessary. Sosa et al. reported that a supportive companion in labor led to shorter labors and the enhancement of some early mother–infant interaction behaviors.[3]

Nurses provided emotional support as well as physical care before fathers were permitted in labor and delivery. Now fathers often fill the supportive role with nurses as guides. Staffing problems, unexpected emergencies, unpredicatable patient loads, nonnursing duties and other factors prevent nurses from providing the constant one-to-one nurse-to-patient care that is optimal. Traditional health care institutions, such as hospitals, rarely provide opportunities for nurses to care for patients on both an outpatient and inpatient basis. The division between inpatient and outpatient eliminates the possibility of the nurse establishing a positive, supportive "companion" relationship prior to the woman's admission to the labor and delivery unit.

Monitrice Services

Manchester Memorial Hospital, Manchester, Connecticut, has implemented a "monitrice" system to ensure that every laboring woman or couple will have a supportive companion in labor. At Manchester, the monitrice is an addition to the hospital maternity service staff—not a replacement. The monitrice is an experienced obstetric nurse with additional training in the psychoprophylactic method of childbirth. Continuity between inpatient and outpatient care is achieved because the monitrice also teaches Lamaze classes. The monitrice role is to provide emotional/psychological support, companionship, and basic comfort measures (back rub, cool cloth, etc.) to the laboring woman. The monitrice supplements the support given by the father and staff. Hospital nursing and medical staff provide nursing and medical care such as taking vital signs and giving medications. The monitrice comes to the hospital as a "private duty" nurse when the patient is admitted and remains with her continuously until 4–6 hours after birth.

It is not essential that monitrices be nurses. Childbirth educators, nursing students, physical therapists, and other committed individuals can be prepared to fill the role of labor companion. The requirements are a thorough knowledge of and experience in prepared childbirth and a commitment to providing one-to-one psychological support in labor. The precedent for this was set by women with husbands who travel or are away in the military and single women who have turned to women relatives and friends to serve as labor coaches. Coaches attend psychoprophylactic classes and provide supportive care in labor. Both coach and patient report great satisfaction.

The monitrice system is especially suited for the care of adolescents. Health care facilities cannot be certain that one individual can be devoted exclusively to the care of a young girl. It is uncommon for a single person to stay from admission through recovery—nurses change as the shift changes. The disruption in personnel is very disturbing and certainly contrary to the goal of a companion in labor; it is unusual for nurses to know their patients prior to labor. Late adolescents may have a partner interested in assisting them in labor, but early and middle adolescents rarely have these individuals. Family members and friends, however, may well be available and interested in assisting the girl and participating at birth.

Monitrices participate in preparation for labor and delivery, alleviate fear by reinforcing education and psychoprophylactic preparation, provide companionship and supportive care in labor, encourage participation by the father if present, and serve as an advocate with the staff when necessary. Moreover, the monitrice can continue her educational and supportive role by calling and visiting the new mother during the postpartum period. A study by Trause et al. suggested that the benefits of a labor companion extend beyond birth itself into the postpartum period.[5] If the monitrice is a family member, certainly all involved—new mother, infant, monitrice, family—can benefit from the positive, supportive interaction.

Monitrices may be paid on a fee-for-service basis by the patient or may be made available as a service through the hospital or birth center. In view of the limited financial resources of adolescents and the special need they have for this service, it seems reasonable to include the monitrice fee in the institutional cost.

Monitrices need to be recruited and trained. Two approaches are available to professionals. The first approach is to seek monitrices from obstetric nurses in the community. Inactive or retired nurses may welcome the opportunity to become active on a part-time basis. It is important that these nurses be well versed in psychoprophylaxis and adolescent development. Interest and commitment to the care of the adolescent is understood.

Peer Monitrices

A second approach to providing monitrices is to recruit from the adolescent peer group. Peer counseling has been shown to be effective in several settings.[6] Both the pregnant adolescent and peer monitrice can grow from the experience: the pregnant adolescent gains the benefits derived from any monitrice; the peer monitrice grows in responsibility and has an opportunity to share and teach that which she has learned from her birth and parenting experience.

Peer monitrices should be recruited from late adolescents who demonstrate the maturity and interest in serving their younger "sisters" as monitrices. Dependability and ability to follow through with the personal commitment to be available for their clients is essential. Peer monitrices attend a series of classes to prepare them to apply the psychoprophylactic techniques in a coaching role rather than as a laboring woman. In the author's experience, carefully chosen peer monitrices have been most effective in calming fear, promoting compliance with preparation classes, and postpartum teaching. Middle and late adolescents are particularly receptive to a peer monitrice. The peer group is the security and source of information for the middle adolescent; she finds peers more credible and trustworthy than most adults. A peer monitrice supplementing the regular hospital or birth center staff provides the adolescent with an advocate with whom she can communicate easily.

Late adolescents may have a partner who serves as the "coach" or monitrice. If the baby's father is no longer in her life, the late adolescent often asks a close relative or friend to "be with me when I have my baby." This selected person should attend psychoprophylactic classes as would a partner. If the late adolescent has no person available, a monitrice should be offered.

Early adolescents may not gain as much from the monitrice system as their older adolescent counterparts. Early adolescents usually prefer a close female relative to assist them in labor. Peers have not achieved high importance in their lives yet. Because of their immaturity, early adolescents are not ready to function as peer monitrices.

The institution of a peer monitrice system is not a massive program undertaking; the system can start with one or two individuals. An adolescent who is skilled in psychoprophylactic techniques and mature in her approach to preparation and participation in childbirth can be taught to support a woman in labor. Since the peer monitrice will have to work closely with the professional staff, potential monitrices must be comfortable with adults as well as other adolescents. Attending psychoprophylactic classes as the "coach" rather than the "patient" serves as a good basis for support in labor. Additional reading from a basic obstetric nursing text and childbirth education literature provides an additional foundation. Careful guidance with her first patients affords her another important opportunity to learn. The peer monitrice supports and coaches her patient, but must never assume (or be forced to assume) any responsibility for nursing or medical observation and care of the laboring adolescent. In the author's experience, as Hommel found in her monitrice program,[7] two monitrices later entered nursing education programs.

Peer monitrices are expected to attend psychoprophylactic classes with their clients. Getting to classes, practicing techniques, and preparing for labor promotes individual responsibility and a mutual dependence between patient and monitrice. Early and middle adolescents have a difficult time in maintaining a commitment to childbirth education or prenatal classes if participation in those classes requires extra planning and effort. Classes held in the evening, at a location and time apart from the school or clinic, or instead of social activities with peers are especially difficult for early and some middle adolescents. Late adolescents are better able to prioritize and may consciously decide to forego a social activity in favor of childbirth classes. Childbirth classes designed specifically for adolescents with active participation by adolescents are more acceptable to the young person. Pregnant adolescents (with the possible exception of late adolescents who are married) express great discomfort in participating in childbirth classes attended primarily by older married couples. Classes limited to and/or designed with adolescents in mind are received best. Childbirth classes—in the form of Lamaze, Bradley, International Childbirth Educators Association classes, and/or a modification of these—are essential to enable the pregnant adolescent and her monitrice to understand and to participate in birth. With the support of a well-prepared peer monitrice who has "been there," the pregnant adolescent is motivated to attend class and actively participate and cooperate in her labor.

HOSPITAL BIRTHING ROOM

General Description

A *hospital birthing room* is defined as a combined labor and delivery room for the patient and her husband or supporting other during a normal labor and delivery.[8] Most hospitals permit mother and infant to recover together in the birthing room in the presence of their support person or persons. The purpose of the birthing room is to provide a "homelike" atmosphere for a "natural" birth within an environment prepared for careful observation and rapid intervention at the first sign of a problem for mother or infant. The birthing room is designed to meet the emotional needs of the family within a medically safe environment. The most important component of the birthing room is the philosophy. All too often, furniture or setting is seen as the key to a successful birthing room, but philosophy as implemented by the staff is primary. Sumner and Phillips gave an excellent summary of birthing room philosophy:

> [Birthing rooms] were developed on the premise that childbirth is basically a normal physiologic event and a powerful emotional experience. However, since childbirth is occasionally abnormal, these birthing rooms provide an appropriate milieu in which many different support systems are synthesized to reduce risks, minimize intervention, and maximize the joy of childbirth— all within the hospital setting.*

It is the role of both medical and nursing staff to be certain that all care is provided consistent with the birthing room philosophy.

Of secondary importance are facilities or setting for the birthing room; the room itself is a reflection of the philosophy. Birthing rooms often are converted labor or delivery rooms. The room is decorated to resemble a home and camouflage the typical hospital atmosphere. The decor is designed to create a comfortable and relaxing atmosphere for birth. Birthing room facilities vary from rudimentary or primitive to elaborate and plush. Curtains, rugs, rocking chair, double bed, bright wall paper and bed linen, home

---

*From Sumner PE, Phillips CR: Birthing Rooms: Concept and Reality. St. Louis, The C. V. Mosby Co., 1981, p 12. With permission.

furnishings rather than hospital furniture, and pictures on the wall set the mood. Technology is minimized in a birthing room. Medical equipment such as fetal monitors, intravenous poles, oxygen, suction, delivery equipment, and resuscitation equipment are hidden but easily accessible if needed. Birthing rooms are located within easy transfer distance to the delivery room, operating room, and newborn nursery should an emergency arise.

Medical and nursing literature is replete with documentation of the safety and, indeed, potential medical benefit of a hospital birthing room. Sumner and Phillips reported a fetal complication rate of 2.3 percent and a maternal complication rate of 2.47 percent in their birthing rooms,[4] and Schmidt reported a cesarean section rate of 3.3 percent in Stanford University's Family Birth Room.[9] Faxel compared statistics from the birthing room in Phoenix Memorial Hospital, Phoenix, Arizona, with the traditional services.[10] In the birthing room the maternal problem rate was 21 percent and the infant problem rate was 17 percent, whereas in the traditional facility the rates were 48 percent and 30 percent, respectively. Certainly, birthing center statistics should reflect a healthier outcome because the initial population is screened to rule out patients at risk; however, the difference is dramatic and cannot be ignored. Safety is not a reason to counsel healthy patients—including adolescents—away from birthing rooms.

Eligibility requirements for the birthing room are (1) that the mother is healthy, (2) that she is expecting a term, healthy newborn, and (3) that the mother and coach are appropriately prepared. The mother must have no history of medical or obstetric factors that place her or her infant at risk. An adolescent should not be excluded on the basis of age alone; she should be evaluated on medical/obstetric criteria, not age. Preparation for the birth must include satisfactory completion of a psychoprophylactics in childbirth course for the mother and her identified coach. The coach is expected to be present for the entire labor and birth. The mother must agree to the philosophy and educational preparation requirements of the birthing room and must agree to be moved to a traditional labor or delivery room if problems are suspected or identified.

Medical intervention and traditional medical procedures are minimized in the birthing room. Laboring women rely on their prepared childbirth training as the primary technique for management of their labor. Analgesics are available and used if needed. Parenteral narcotics, paracervical and pudendal blocks, and local anesthetics are commonly used. Sumner and Phillips reported that 28 percent of primigravidas and 62 percent of multiparous women required no analgesia in labor.[4] Hewitt and Hangsleben reported that at the Henepin County Medical Center in Minneapolis, Minnesota, 72 percent of women did not need analgesics in labor.[11] Local anesthetics for episiotomy are more common. Intravenous fluids, perineal shave, fetal monitor, delivery in stirrups, and other nonessential interventions are avoided in the birthing room. The woman in labor is encouraged to be ambulatory, take oral fluids, wear her own clothing, and choose a birth position comfortable for her. Whenever possible, noninvasive interventions are used in labor: for example, verbal support is used to preclude the need for large doses of analgesics. Changing maternal position is used to encourage natural rotation of an occiput posterior presentation and avoid the need for forceps.

Patients developing complications requiring the use of continuous fetal monitor, regional anesthesia, or oxytocin augmentation are moved to traditional labor and delivery rooms for continued care. Birthing rooms are equipped to handle emergencies in mother or newborn but are not intended to be used for intensive care. For this reason, mothers or newborns developing problems in labor or at the time of delivery are moved out of the birthing room to a traditional facility. Sumner and Phillips transfer equipment into the birthing room rather than move the mother with problems out,[4] but cesarean section always requires transfer to the operating room.

The laboring mother and her chosen support person are encouraged to participate actively throughout the labor and birth. Psychoprophylactic techniques in labor, ambulation in labor, choosing positions for birth, touching the baby during birth—including helping to lift the baby out of the birth canal—immediate skin-to-skin contact with the newborn, early breastfeeding, and extended parent–newborn contact post partum are encouraged in the birthing room. The facility itself is designed to promote these activities. Families using the birthing room report positive experiences that reflect the families' participation.

Benefits of the birthing room, as perceived by the participants, include the following: elimination of transfer from labor to delivery; no separation of mother and baby; option to breastfeed early; personal involvement in the birth and the philosophy of nonintervention in the normal birth process.[12,13] Mothers and partners report a feeling of control in the birthing room that is not perceived in traditional units. Multiparous women who had had both traditional and birthing room deliveries in Maloni's study mentioned freedom to interact and react as they felt appropriate as a positive aspect of the birthing room.[12] Enhancement of the attachment process is often reported as a benefit although no one has directly linked the birthing room with enhanced mother–father–infant interaction. Enhanced attachment has been associated with early, extended mother–infant contact,[3,5,14] which is certainly a central feature of the birthing room.

Appropriateness for Adolescents

Hospital birthing rooms provide many opportunities for growth in the adolescent and should be offered to appropriate young women. Aspects of birthing room care appeal to all adolescents. The environment, by design, is less threatening than that of traditional units. Rules are more lax and there are fewer traditional hospital routines. Birthing room patients often may have two or three chosen support people for birth, while the traditional units permit only one. All these factors are attractive to adolescents who are struggling for control, independence, and freedom from traditional authority. Selling the pregnant adolescent on the idea of an alternative facility is rarely a problem, but preparing her appropriately requires some degree of maturity on her part and a commitment to the potential benefits on the part of the professional staff.

The adolescent who wishes to use a hospital birthing room must be able to meet the eligibility criteria of normal, healthy, term pregnancy as well as other criteria. She must have successfully completed a series of prepared childbirth classes in psychoprophylactic techniques for labor and birth with her chosen support person. The adolescent must have attended the orientation session offered by the birthing room staff and demonstrate understanding of the rules governing transfer out of the facility. Finally, the physician or nurse-midwife caring for the adolescent must agree that she and her fetus demonstrate no risk characteristics. Age alone is not a reason to rule out the use of a birthing room.

Early adolescents need careful guidance before choosing a hospital birthing room. The very young girl (10–12 years of age) is at a high risk for complications during her pregnancy. Developmentally, early adolescents are poor planners with little ability to visualize the future—they live for today only. Planning is extremely difficult for the early adolescent because she is unable to grasp the future for which she is preparing. Childbirth classes and serious preparation for birth are hard for the early adolescent even in late pregnancy when labor is imminent. The early adolescent may fear the delivery process and seek alternatives to traditional delivery in an attempt to allay her fears. Psychoprophylaxis classes offered at school, classes with peers, or a monitrice to go with her to class help provide encouragement to stay involved with the preparation. Sometimes her mother, older sisters, or other relatives the girl wishes to participate in her birth go to class with her. This also serves to prepare the relatives. Whether or not the early adolescent ultimately uses an alternative facility, she will benefit from the education.

Early adolescents are romantics with a fascination for media figures. Recently, a news magazine published an article on movie stars who were having babies. One popular figure reported her delivery in a hospital birthing room, and many young adolescent pregnant girls began looking for the same type of experience to imitate their idol. The early adolescent has to separate her true feelings from her desire to imitate a favorite movie star.

Middle adolescents are the most emotionally labile and unpredictable of the teenagers. They have ultrahigh and superlow moods with little stability between. Wide, rapid, mood swings make middle adolescents the most difficult to guide. They may be totally committed to a birthing room one day and be totally opposed to the concept the next day. It is important to work toward consistency with a middle adolescent. Putting her preferences in writing, repeatedly reviewing her decision-making steps, and focusing her thoughts on one decision at a time can help her achieve consistency.

When stressed, middle adolescents first react emotionally and later react with reason or thought. The health care professional should allow time for the emotional outburst, and then refocus the middle adolescent on her impending decision. For example, a middle adolescent planned to attend a birthing room orientation session on a Wednesday morning and discovered the session was full—with the next available opening 2 weeks away. She became so angry at the delay and the need to change her plans that she told the clinic nurse "I'm not going to use that stupid birthing room—they don't want me in there and I don't want to be there." Talking with the teenager later, the nurse helped her to separate her anger at the inconvenience from her basic plan to prepare for the birthing room. The adolescent focused her attention on preparation, registered for the next open session, and continued her plans to use the birthing room.

Peers are extremely important to the middle adolescent, and peer relationships can be harnessed as a positive force during pregnancy. Prenatal and nutrition classes, preparation for labor and other activities—if they are group events—attract and hold the middle adolescent as a participant. The middle adolescent is tempted to "go along with the crowd" instead of making her own decisions; if her friends plan to use the birthing room, she will too. Peer disapproval of the birthing room, however, makes it very difficult for the middle adolescent to break away, deviate from her peers, and prepare for the alternative facility.

Middle adolescents appreciate the privacy and intimacy provided by the birthing room. This is often a major factor in their choice of a birthing room. They are attracted to the opportunity of including peers as coaches or an older peer as monitrice.

Middle adolescents who choose the birthing room need a clear delineation of their responsibilities for preparation and participation. They need to know the rules for what they may and may not do during labor and delivery. For example, middle adolescents readily plan for a celebration during the recovery stage after the baby is born. They need to be reminded that the "celebration" is predicated upon a healthy pregnancy and birth. They must, therefore, eat well during pregnancy, learn psychoprophylactic techniques, and enter labor rested and in good health.

Late adolescents do well in birthing rooms. They are mature enough to plan and prepare for the birthing experience. For the young couple, preparing for the birth together is practice in the decision-making techniques that they will need later as parents. Assuming responsibility for her birth experience reinforces the independence of the late adolescent. She gains confidence in her own ability to plan, follow through, and accept responsibility for her actions. A late adolescent couple benefits in the same way. Late adolescents have identified a lifestyle, philosophy, and personal identity. The birthing room is a safe environment to "try out" their chosen lifestyle.

All adolescents are attracted to the more relaxed environment of the birthing room. Freedom from hospital rituals such as hospital clothing, routine intravenous fluids, and restriction to bed are appealing too. Adolescents benefit from the decision-making process and exercise of responsibility. Peer supports/monitrices are a valuable assistance. Young people grow in confidence and independence as they master skills and support each other in labor.

Mother–infant contact is early, intimate, and extended in the birthing room. Such contact soon after birth repeatedly is associated with enhanced mother–infant interaction into infancy.[3,14]

EARLY POSTPARTUM DISCHARGE

Traditional hospitalization following normal delivery ranges from 2 to 4 days. Many hospitals are permitting discharge within 24 hours. Hospital birthing rooms and free-standing birth centers typically encourage discharge within 24 hours—some as early as 4–6 hours post partum.[15] The reasons women and families opt for early discharge are varied. One reason is the desire for total family involvement with minimal family separation. Adolescents express the desire to be in the familiar, supportive environment of home. Second, the need to relieve overcrowded postpartum facilities has led hospitals to initiate an early discharge program.[16] A third reason for early discharge is economic: mothers avoid costly hospital days by going home in 1 day instead of 3. Economics are a major concern to the adolescent only if she is personally responsible for her own care.

Early discharge has been shown to be safe when appropriate criteria are followed.[15,16] The family is prepared for early discharge with extensive parent education during the prenatal period. The emphasis is on preparation for the first few days at home. Instruction is focused on the identification of common problems and their solutions. Danger signs in mother or infant that should be reported to professionals are reviewed. The woman planning early discharge is required to have help at home after discharge. Her partner, family, or friends can fill this need. Both mother and infant must be healthy immediately post partum to qualify for early discharge. A visiting nurse follows all mothers and babies who go home early.

Potential benefits to adolescents are the same as the benefits observed in older families. Separation of mother–infant–family is eliminated, thereby enhancing attachment. Advance preparation provides an opportunity to learn observation and care skills for newborns that will be important for child health care. Adolescents may derive more benefit from the "on the job" reinforcement provided by postpartum hospitalization in a rooming-in setting than from early discharge. The potential benefit of inpatient care should be assessed for each adolescent. All adolescents benefit from the in-home visits of the nurse.

Early adolescents think concretely. For this reason, this age group especially learns best by "doing." Supportive health care professionals in a rooming-in setting is the ideal learning environment for the early adolescent. Early discharge deprives the young teenager of this opportunity. It is recommended that early adolescents remain in a positive hospital setting and not be encouraged to choose an early discharge.

Middle adolescents are the unpredictable teenagers. They tend to have unrealistic estimates of their own capabilities. Open communication between health care provider and middle adolescents must be ensured before the middle adolescent is permitted an early discharge. Should problems arise with the newborn, the adolescent has to be comfortable calling the appropriate health care professional and not just her best friend. The family serves as a valuable support for the middle adolescent if she chooses early discharge but a danger of being "taken over" exists. Her home situation deserves close scrutiny before early discharge.

Late adolescents have developed the skills necessary to prepare for early discharge. The late adolescent who is adequately prepared and manages well with her planned resources gains self-confidence and self-esteem. The late adolescent is apt to be concerned about finances and seek ways to cut costs. The primary danger in early discharge is that the late adolescent may become overwhelmed with the 24-hour work load. If the late adolescent then is forced to turn to family in ways she had not planned, she may sacrifice some of her newly developed independence. An example of this risk is a situation in which the newborn becomes fussy at 2 A.M. and is inconsolable for 2–3 hours. The adolescent, in desperation, calls her mother down the street for help. Mother rushes in to "take over" because her daughter "just doesn't know how to take care of babies." The adolescent is forced into a dependency role during the vulnerable postpartum period.

FREE-STANDING BIRTH CENTERS

Out-of-hospital or free-standing birth centers are the complete alternative to traditional hospital care. The Maternity Center Association in New York developed the prototype Childbearing Center in 1975. The Childbearing Center was described as "an out-of-hospital unit that offers comprehensive care in a homelike atmosphere to healthy families anticipating a normal birth experience. Uniquely, the unit is a maxi-home and not a mini-hospital."[17] The impetus to develop free-standing birth centers came from families who demanded a level of control, involvement, psychological support, and freedom during childbearing that was not available in hospitals. Famiies insisted upon active participation in the birth and were willing to accept responsibility for unattended home birth if no alternative were available.

Free-standing birth centers are independent of hospitals although they have transfer agreements to accommodate patients who develop problems. They are physically and philosophically removed from traditional care. Physically, the free-standing birth center is located in a converted house or specially designed facility near but completely separate from the hospital maternity service. Typically, the free-standing birth center provides prenatal care, prenatal education, psychoprophylaxis classes, labor and birth, early discharge home, and visiting nurse services. Education is a strong component of care. Interconceptional care is offered by some but not all free-standing birth centers.

Philosophically, the free-standing birth center differs dramatically from traditional hospital care. Traditional care emphasizes the role and responsibility of the health care providers—the patient is simply expected to comply. Traditional hospital care approaches childbirth as a medical event. The free-standing birth center views childbirth as an essentially normal, healthy process that needs a safe environment with minimal or no intervention. Parents are expected to assume a major share of responsibility for health maintenance. Parents who fail to prepare actively for birth and early parenthood may be declared ineligible for further care at the birth center and be referred to a more traditional facility.

The safety of free-standing birth centers has been well documented. In 1979, Lubic and Ernst reported 244 births at the Childbearing Center with no major emergencies.[17] The transfer to hospital rate prior to delivery was 24.8 percent. Three neonatal deaths occurred—none occurred in the birth center. Barton et al. reported statistics from an alternative birthing center within a hospital medical center: the transfer rate was 23.8 percent and there were no major emergencies.[18]

The free-standing birth center includes all the alternatives discussed to this point; the considerations in adolescent participation include those discussed in the context of each previous alternative and an additional measure of maturity. Free-standing birth centers require extensive participation and responsibility from clients. Adolescents choosing the birth center must be able to meet these requirements. Early adolescents are not good candidates—they lack the maturity necessary to manage the responsibility. Other alternatives are better for younger teenagers. Lubic and Ernst reported a 16-year-old enrolled at the Childbearing Center;[17] this is the youngest mother reported in free-standing birth center statistics. Barton et al. reported that 7.3 percent of their population was under age 20; exact ages were not stated, but given other parameters of this population they were probably late adolescents.[18]

Middle adolescents must receive careful direction if they consider a free-standing birth center. The risk-taking behavior of middle adolescents influences their reason. This age group is emotionally unpredictable with wide mood swings, and these traits are not desirable in clients planning to use an out-of-hospital facility. Early discharge can be difficult for middle adolescents, as discussed earlier. The total responsibility of a new baby is more than the middle adolescent is able to handle without elaborate support systems. Some middle adolescents have included their family in their free-standing birth center experience. Older sisters, grandmothers, and friends have prepared and participated in the birth. On discharge home, the involved extended family shares responsibility for care of the new mother and baby. This extended family is an option for the adolescent who desires a free-standing birth center but is unable to accept total responsibility for care. The health professional guiding the middle adolescent in her decision making needs to ascertain that the extended family would be supportive of the young mother and not simply take over the new baby.

Late adolescents possess the skills necessary to choose and participate in free-standing birth centers. They are able to consider the differences between traditional hospital care and the birth center, and are able to evaluate critically the implications of their choice for themselves and their newborn. They can manage the responsibility of the newborn but lack the experience to handle the baby comfortably 24 hours a day. Late adolescents who have chosen a philosophy that emphasizes individual responsibility for health and rejects traditional medicine seek dramatic alternatives. Too often, they see unattended home birth as their only option. The free-standing birth center is an acceptable alternative to all but the most radical counterculture groups. The birth center supports the individuality of the late adolescent, reinforces the role of responsibility, and provides preparatory education to ensure a safe birth and postpartum/neonatal period.

OTHER ALTERNATIVES AND CONSIDERATIONS

Adolescents have many choices for their childbirth—some as simple as which hand an intravenous line is placed in and some as complex as whether or not to give birth in a hospital. The majority of choices to be made are small ones. Small choices are as important to adolescent growth and devel-

Table 19-1. Options in Childbirth

Delay of newborn eye prophylaxis
Choice of labor coach/monitrice
Location of intravenous line if indicated
Timing of shave, enema if indicated
Position for labor
Position for birth
Breast or bottle feed
Circumcision or not
Rooming-in or central nursery
Timing of cord clamping
Birthing room or traditional labor and delivery
Early discharge or longer stay
Free-standing birth center
Leboyer bath

opment as are larger choices—adolescents learn from the process of decision making. Indeed, small choices are more appropriate and more "real" to younger adolescents than the location of birth.

Each potential choice is an opportunity for the adolescent to grow intellectually and increase her sense of responsibility. The options listed in Table 19-1 are examples of choices to be discussed with the pregnant adolescent. The health professional should match the options with the individual adolescent and encourage her to use good decision-making skills to arrive at her choice.

Adolescents at Risk

All too frequently, the adolescent develops problems during pregnancy or labor that place her or her infant at risk. Plans for a hospital birthing room or free-standing birth center are discarded for the technology and intensive care capability of traditional labor and delivery. Both adolescent and health care provider are disappointed with the change in plans, but the safety and health of mother and baby are primary. Early and middle adolescents are apt to see the move to traditional care as punitive for an imagined failure on their part—their failure in not remaining normal. The younger adolescents need help in understanding that the development of complications is not their fault nor are they being punished with the addition of necessary technology. A young girl who received magnesium sulfate injections for preeclampsia late in labor told her nurse one day, "They moved me to the delivery room and gave me horrible shots because I yelled in labor." In reality, the patient had been in very active labor at 9 cm and was moaning with contractions when it was determined she also needed magnesium sulfate. The transfer to delivery and injections occurred simultaneously with the moaning. The young girl saw events in a cause-and-effect relationship.

Elimination of one alternative should not necessarily negate all other birth choices. Adolescents may "risk out" of an alternative facility but continue other alternatives such as breastfeeding, early contact with the newborn, and ongoing participation by their chosen support person/monitrice. As with older high-risk families, the separation of patient and her chosen support person during a crisis increases rather than decreases anxiety. Whenever possible, the support person should be permitted to continue assisting the adolescent mother during intensive care or in the operating room during cesarean section.

Alternatives are a series of choices. The changing condition of the mother requires reassessment but no discontinuation of the process of alternatives. The adolescent mother at risk has many alternatives open to her; the teenager with complications has a right to expect the opportunity to exercise her decision-making skills.

Adolescent Fathers

The place of the adolescent father in the birth and early parenting of his children has been unclear. In the past, the adolescent father was seldom seen in the health care facilities. Today a few young men are actively participating in childbearing and child rearing with the adolescent mother.[19] The young father is demanding his rightful place not only as partner/support of his mate in labor and birth but also as father to his children.

Alternatives provide an opportunity for the young father to participate in decisions that affect his mate and child. Just like the young mother, the adolescent father benefits from the process of making the decision. Developmentally, the adolescent father needs the same assessment and guidance as his female counterpart.

CONCLUSIONS

Childbirth is moving rapidly from a single traditional health care model to a system of birth alternatives. The goal of alternatives is not only to provide safe options in childbirth but also to meet the psychological and emotional needs of the family. Alternatives should be made available to adolescents. Making decisions, assessing values, evaluating options, planning for parenthood, and taking responsibility for self-care are inherent in alternatives. When used appropriately, birth alternatives can be a valuable tool to assist adolescent development.

Adolescents view life with optimism and an unfailing sense of wonder and discovery. Every minute is new—the future is forever. The health care professional should approach the pregnant adolescent with a commitment to her potential for positive growth and development. With the help of concerned adults, young people can mature through their childbearing experience. The "disaster" of adolescent pregnancy can be minimized for the ultimate benefit of the young mother, father, and newborn.

REFERENCES

1. Helms C: What is a normal adolescent? Matern Child Nurs 6:405–406, 1981
2. Ginsberg H, Opper S: Piaget's Theory of Intellectual Development (ed 2). Englewood Cliffs, NJ, Prentice-Hall, 1979
3. Sosa R, Kennell J, Klaus M, et al: The effect of a supportive companion on perinatal problems, length of labor, and mother–infant interaction. N Engl J Med 303:597–600, 1980
4. Sumner P, Phillips C: Birthing Rooms: Concept and Reality. St. Louis, Mosby, 1981
5. Trause MA, Kennell JH, Klaus MH: A fresh look at early mother–infant contact (abstract). Pediatr Res 12:376, 1978
6. Zapka JM, Mazur RM: Peer sex education training and evaluation. Am J Public Health 67:450–454, 1977
7. Hommel F: Nurses in private practice as monitrices. Am J Nurs 69:1447–1450, 1969
8. Interprofessional Task Force of Health Care of Women and Children: Joint position statement on the development of family-centered maternity/newborn care in hospitals. Chicago, 1978
9. Schmidt J: The first year at Stanford University's family birth room. Birth Fam Journal 7:169–174, 1980
10. Faxel AM: The birthing room concept at Phoenix Memorial Hospital, Part I: Development and eighteen month's statistics. J Obstet Gynecol Neonat Nurs 9:151–155, 1980
11. Hewitt MA, Hangsleben KL: Nurse-midwives in a hospital birth center. J Nurse Midwifery 26:21–29, 1981
12. Maloni J: The birthing room: Some insights into parents' experiences. Matern Child Nurs 5:314–319, 1980
13. Kieffler M: The birthing room concept at Phoenix Memorial Hospital, Part II: Consumer satisfaction during one year. J Obstet Gynecol Neonat Nurs 9:155–159, 1980
14. Kennell J, Klaus M: Maternal–Infant Bonding. St. Louis, Mosby, 1976
15. Carr KC, Walton VE: Early postpartum discharge. J Obstet Gynecol Neonat Nurs 11:29–30, 1982
16. Scupholme A: Postpartum early discharge; An inner city experience. J Nurse Midwifery 26:19–22, 1981
17. Lubic RW, Ernst EM: The Childbearing Center: An alternative to conventional care. Nurs Outlook 26:754–760, 1978
18. Barton JJ, Rovner S, Puls K, et al: Alternative birthing center: Experience in a teaching obstetric service. Am J Obstet Gynecol 137:377–384, 1980
19. Hendrick LE: Unmarried adolescent fathers: Problems they face and ways they cope with them: Final Report, Mental Health Research and Development Center. Institute for Urban Affairs and Research, Howard University, Washington, DC, September 1979

20

Abortion in Adolescence

Donald E. Greydanus

Abortion in adolescence is a complicated, controversial, and highly emotional issue, bringing into perspective various issues of adolescent sexuality. It is a problem all concerned individuals wish did not occur, but one that must be addressed. Unfortunately, abortion is currently a well-documented occurrence for many adolescents.[1-3] Recent statistics indicate there are over 400,000 adolescent abortions each year in the United States, and abortions are more common than deliveries for individuals under age 15.[4-6] Of the 1.3 million abortions occurring each year in the United States, approximately one-third are in those under 20 years of age. Such enormous figures have spurred public opinion and stimulated considerable debate. Many agree it is far better for teenagers to avoid pregnancy than face the possibility of abortion. Some individuals now seek to stop abortion altogether.

It must be acknowledged that anyone writing about teenage abortion has some bias, one way or another. For example, is sexual activity by youth "wrong"? Is abortion immoral for youth? Does it produce psychological effects in teenagers? Should the law regulate abortion or even totally ban it? Should pregnant youth who wish an abortion tell their parents or obtain their permission? Unfortunately, these issues are complicated by religious, legal, financial, and personal considerations. The reader is urged to evaluate the literature discussed here and form his or her own opinions. It is the author's own view that all efforts must be made to avoid pregnancy in youth and reduce the number of teenagers having to make this difficult decision.

It is important to note that the mortality rate for pregnancy is indeed far greater than for legal abortions, especially those performed early in gestation.[7-9] For example, Tietze noted a mortality rate of 11.1/100,000 individuals 15–19 years old who undergo pregnancy and childbirth;[10] this is in marked contrast to a rate of 1.2/100,000 legal abortions. How such data are interpreted depends on the particular bias of the observer. It is clear, however, that although pregnancy and abortion are relatively safe events, there is a marked difference between the two in terms of mortality rates. The lowest complication rates for pregnancy are noted if the teenager is diagnosed and placed under adequate prenatal care early in the gestation.[11] Likewise, legal abortion becomes increasingly dangerous the later in gestation it is performed.[5] Thus, the earlier the pregnancy is diagnosed, and the earlier the abortion is done, the lower is the eventual medical complication rate.

It is also clear that illegal abortions are very dangerous and are to be avoided in all women. Tietze noted a 100-fold greater mortality from illegal abortions than from legal abortions.[12] Cates and Rochat described a decrease in abortion-induced deaths among women after legal abortions were permitted, starting in 1973.[13] Although there is intense disagreement as to whether legal abortion is acceptable for youth, there is considerable agreement among health care professionals that illegal ones are to be totally banned. The performance of such a procedure by untrained individuals results in tremendous rates of infection, hemorrhage, laceration, and maternal death. Of course, many argue that legal abortions should be allowed or else the number of illegal abortions will dramatically rise, as will the resultant rates of maternal morbidity and mortality. Opponents argue that abortions of all kinds are wrong and should be banned. Unfortunately, the teenager sits in the middle of this heated debate and is often confused about the entire issue.

Abortion is a complex issue for most teenagers confronted with the choices of delivery, adoption, or abortion. Although generalities are often made in the literature about various groups, the decision remains an individual one, dependent on the specific circumstances of the adolescent's life at a particular time.[14] The individual may or may not be aware of the abortion option, or where to go in the health care system to obtain it. Some receive adequate backup and support from family, while others do not. Many youth involve their parents in the decision-making process,[15] if it is at all possible. Some adolescents (especially the young ones) may deny the reality of the gestation until an abortion is difficult or impossible to obtain; others wish to be pregnant and reject the possibility of an abortion from the start. Counseling sexually active youth involves exploring the underlying reasons for the coital activity and, in some cases, identifying reasons for wishing to become pregnant.[16] It is startling to note that some youth wish to become pregnant and that the gestation often appears to meet their developmental or psychological needs.[17,18] These developmental needs have an impact on the ability of the teenager to consider and implement an abortion.

Religious background clearly has an influence in this regard.[19] It is very difficult for those brought up in some religious environments actively to consider or seek an abortion. Youth who are persistently taught that any abortion is immoral and that it is an act of murder have a very difficult time accepting such an option. The current intense debate in our society over this very issue only reinforces the negative feelings the teenager has. In order to choose abortion, she must be willing to understand her own background, and then essentially reject it to some degree. This necessitates a great deal of insight if she retains other values of her family. The youth who rejects her family values completely may be more likely to accept the abortion. However, as previously noted, each adolescent's decision is based on many variables that are specific for her. General trends do not necessarily apply to her.

As previously noted, the number of abortions is increasing.[20] If contraceptives services are not readily available, the abortion rate may increase in some areas.[21] Abortion remains a common procedure among pregnant teenagers. Current data show that more than 50 percent of pregnant 10- to 14-year-olds have an abortion.[22] Legal abortion services are not available to all teenagers, sometimes due to monetary, travel, or family considerations.[5,23] Fortunately, this has not increased the number of illegal abortions as yet, and thus the number of deaths from illegal abortions has not recently increased.[20,24]

A very disturbing fact is that teenagers account for many of the second-trimester abortions performed in the United States.[25] There are many reasons for this, including a delay in the diagnosis or ambivalence about the pregnancy and possible abortion.[26] There may be a delay in the diagnosis because neither teenager nor physician may consider pregnancy as a possibility when symptoms first develop. Some youth present with a "smoke screen" appearance—they come with vague complaints, hoping the physician will inquire about the possibility of pregnancy. Some young teenagers are unable to discuss openly aspects of sexuality. Some physicians fail to inquire about their patient's sexuality, assuming their medical role should not include such questions, or the youth may deny being sexually active; thus "suspicious" symptomatology is not screened with a serum pregnancy test. There may be a history of irregular menstrual periods and both patient and physician may assume pregnancy is not possible. The health care professional should always remain suspicious if there is a history of sexual activity, irregular menses (especially if delayed), and/or specific pregnancy symptomatology (such as nausea, breast tenderness, breast swelling, urinary frequency, etc.). Early diagnosis is important whether delivery or abortion is the outcome.

The increase in adolescent second-trimester abortions results in a marked increase in abortion complications. It is clear that second-trimester abortion is more dangerous than first-trimester abortion.[5,27] The later the abortion is performed, even in expert hands, the higher the morbidity and mortality rate. This should reinforce the goal of early diagnosis and early medical care.

An option that has been underutilized is that of adoption.[14] This alternative should be presented to any youth who is pregnant and must decide what to do. The choice of keeping the baby or abortion is often discussed, but the possibility of adoption is frequently neglected. There are agencies that can assist the youth and family in offering the baby for legal adoption. It is not a popular choice, but it should not be ignored.

Another phenomenon to be noted is that of the repeat aborter.[28,29] This is an individual who essentially uses abortion as a contraceptive method and refuses attempts at pregnancy prevention. Fortunately, only a small number teenagers do this. The abortion experience is a difficult one for most individuals and produces enough negative feelings that they eventually develop some motivation for contraception. Thus it is worthwhile to include contraceptive information and services as part of the postabortion counseling process. Most individuals profit from the experience of abortion and learn to delay subsequent pregnancies until a more appropriate time arises. A limited number of women, however, refuse to use contraceptive methods and rely on abortion. This is a diverse group of individuals who have complex reasons for their repeat abortions. Some remain markedly ambivalent about their sexuality, using it in various power struggles with their environment. Some remain angry about life and consciously or unconsciously use the pregnancy as the means of expressing this anger. Others have a psychiatric disorder (such as a personality trait disorder, schizophrenia, severe depression, etc.). Careful behavioral and psychiatric evaluation is recommended for such women. Unfortunately, attempts to intervene are often not effective, and such situations are very frustrating to health care professionals and to society in general. The existence of repeat abortions is also used as an argument to ban all abortions—since some do abuse their availability. When such an individual is encountered, it is best to adopt the attitude that she should receive all possible help, but she is not representative of the vast majority of youth in this regard.

MINORS' LEGAL RIGHTS

Induced abortion has been performed for centuries, and was well described by Hippocrates.[30] The era of Christianity has introduced the concept that abortion is immoral and should be legally banned. Although abortion has been discussed for centuries, the concept of minors' legal rights is only a recent phenomenon.[31] Only recently has the law openly acknowledged that individuals under the age of 21 have any legal rights comparable to those of adults. This concept can be traced to a Supreme Court decision in 1967 (*In re Gault*)[32] 387 which stated that a 15-year-old youth who was accused of a crime had the right to receive a fair trial before any possible sentencing could occur.[33] This was the first of many important legal cases further defining the legal rights of youth (Table 20-1).

On July 1, 1970, New York State liberalized its abortion laws, making it much easier for women to obtain an abortion if a physician consented.[41] This was followed in January 1973 by a landmark Supreme Court decision (*Roe* vs. *Wade* and *Doe* vs. *Bolton*)[34,35] in which the right of women to obtain a first-trimester abortion was protected.[42] This decision also noted that a licensed physician must perform the procedure for a consenting patient, and added the possibility of restrictions in the second trimester. especially as the age of fetal viability was approached and surpassed. The current legal climate favoring abortion probably peaked in 1976 with another landmark Supreme Court decision (*Danforth* vs. *Planned Parenthood of Central Missouri*).[36,40,43] In this decision the court ruled that third-party individuals (including parents)

Table 20-1. Important Legal Cases and Laws Involving Legal Rights of Minors

Case	Year	Significance
In re Gault[32]	1967	Minors have right to fair trial before sentencing
Tinker vs. *The Des Moines Independent School District*[34]	1969	Minors cannot be removed from school unless their rights are protected.
Roe vs. *Wade, Doe* vs. *Bolton*[35]	1973	Women have the right to obtain a first-trimester abortion
Planned Parenthood of Central Missouri vs. *Danforth*[36]	1976	Mature minors have the right to obtain an abortion regardless of third-party (e.g., parental) disapproval
Bellotti vs. *Baird*[37]	1979	Judge can grant a minor an abortion with parental notification but without parental consent
Hyde Amendment[38]	1979	Restricted use of federal funds to pay for legal abortions
H. L. vs. *Matheson*[39]	1981	It is legal to require immature and dependent minors to inform parents before abortion is obtained

could not stop an abortion of a consenting mature minor and her physician. The language of the court was startling:

> The state may not impose a blanket provision requiring the consent of a parent or person in loco parentis as a condition for abortion of an unmarried minor during the first twelve weeks of her pregnancy. . . . [T]he state does not have the constitutional authority to give a third party an absolute, and possibly arbitrary, veto over the decision of the physician and his patient to terminate the patient's pregnancy. Minors, as well as adults, are protected by the constitution and possess constitutional rights. . . . Any independent interest the parent may have in the termination of the minor daughter's pregnancy is no more weighty than the right of the competent minor mature enough to become pregnant.[36]

This was also the time that the concept of the mature minor became formulated.[44] Individuals who are married, a parent, serving in the armed forces, or living away from home with parental permission and earning their own way are considered "emancipated" minors—mature enough to consent to their own health care. If they are runaways or still at home but acting essentially independent of parents, they may also be considered as "emancipated" to some extent. Whether these individuals have a right to seek health care on their own has been a matter of debate. A mature minor doctrine has been suggested by some as a way of dealing with such a problem. If an individual requests medical help and is mature enough to understand the suggested therapy, medical care has been rendered in some cases. The youth must refuse to allow parents to be involved and the clinician can document the reason(s) that the youth does not want parents informed. It is a complex doctrine and each medical center or medical office sets up its own guidelines. It is not necessary to notify parents for permission to treat a youth with suspected pregnancy or sexually transmitted disease. Individuals over age 16 years who are classified as emancipated minors are often treated without parents' consent for other medical problems if the youth wishes and the clinician agrees. The individual under age 16 remains in a gray zone, since legal guidelines are often unclear. In general, it is always best to involve parents in medical care decisions if at all possible.

What about the issue of abortion and the teenager? The Supreme Court decision of 1976,[36] indicated that a pregnant minor could have an abortion in the first trimester if a physician agreed, even if parents disagree. This seemed to be the culmination of changes in the law allowing abortions with minimal restrictions for youth.[45] The Hyde Amendment has been added to the Annual Health and Welfare Appropriations Bill of Congress since 1976;[38] consequently, since August 1977, the federal government has restricted the use of federal (i.e., Medicaid) funds for legal abortions and only allows such monies for those who are pregnant due to rape or incest or in whom the pregnancy constitutes a danger to life. Thus, although an adolescent can still legally obtain an abortion, she often cannot use federal money to pay for it. Thus, most youth are now dependent on parents, boyfriends, or others to support the cost of the procedure. This has severely reduced the access of the poor to a legal abortion.[45]

Legal battles continue between various groups about the legal rights of women (including teenagers) to an abortion. In 1979, the Supreme Court declared as unconstitutional a Massachusetts statute that required parental consent for the abortion of an unmarried minor.[37] In this statute the minor could still obtain the abortion if a judge granted it, but the parents would always be notified of the abortion. In 1981, the Supreme Court upheld a Utah statute which required that "immature and dependent" minors must tell parents before an abortion is obtained.[39] New decisions can be expected as this dynamic situation remains in constant flux. There is currently a strong climate that seeks to ban abortions for all women, including teenagers. This intense legal climate may clearly remind teenagers that there are many individuals who feel abortion is wrong and should not be allowed at all. Perhaps this will compel some to evaluate carefully the consequences of their own sexuality and avoid the necessity for an abortion. Most health care professionals do agree that prevention of the pregnancy is a far better plan than abortion. It reminds one that early and complete education about sexuality is an important part of the education of any youth. The health care profession should assist parents and the educational system in this regard. Whether the decade of the 1980s will witness a total ban or severe restriction on abortion remains to be seen.

ABORTION METHODS

Many methods of abortion are available to the pregnant individual, depending on the gestational age (Table 20-2).[46-53] Methods of choice during the first trimester (gestation under 12 weeks) include menstrual extraction, suction curettage, or dilatation and curettage. Controversy exists regarding the best abortion method during the second trimester.[54] Methods used include dilatation and evacuation, intraamniotic saline injection, intraamniotic prostaglandin injection, prostaglandin vaginal suppository, hysterotomy, and others. Dilatation and evacuation is a very popular method up to approximately 18 weeks of gestation, and intraamniotic saline instillation procedures are also common between 16 and 20 weeks. Considerable disagreement exists regarding which method(s) to use during the late second trimester (20–24 + weeks).

First-trimester abortion is generally recognized as a safe procedure if it is done by a well-trained clinician.[55] The major complication rate for first-trimester abortion is about 1 percent.[51] Abortion complications include in-

Table 20-2. Methods of Abortion

General methods
  Menstrual extraction
  Vacuum aspiration
  Dilatation and curettage or evacuation
  Intraamniotic instillation procedure
    (hypertonic saline, prostaglandin, or urea)
  Intravaginal instillation of prostaglandin
  Hysterotomy
  Hysterectomy

Usual first-trimester methods
  Menstrual extraction
  Vacuum aspiration
  Others

Usual second-trimester methods
  Dilatation and curettage
  Dilatation and evacuation
  Intraamniotic fluid instillation
  Hysterotomy
  Others

fection (e.g., endometritis), bleeding, Rh sensitization, genital trauma (to the vagina, cervix, or uterus), retained products of conception, continued pregnancy, and death. The complication rate can be minimized by careful evaluation of each patient and performance of the abortion as early as possible. The mortality rate is 0.3/100,000 abortions if the gestation is 8 weeks or less; 2–3/100,000 for 9–12 weeks; 11–12/100,000 for 13–15 weeks; and over 16/100,000 for 16 weeks or longer.[51,56] Since there are over 100,000 second-trimester abortions done in the United States each year, and since many of these patients are teenagers, the morbidity as well as the mortality rate for adolescent abortion remains considerable. Psychological trauma to the individual undergoing abortion is considered later, but it is generally agreed that emotional sequelae to the abortion, if present, usually are worse with procedures done in later gestation. Thus clinicians are challenged to attempt early diagnosis of the pregnancy and early referral of the patient for prenatal care or abortion.

Menstrual Extraction

Menstrual extraction is done within a few weeks of a missed menstrual period.[57,58] It is also called menstrual regulation, menstrual aspiration, miniabortion, endometrial aspiration, and other names. Some clinicians perform this method after confirming the pregnancy with a positive serum pregnancy test, whereas others perform it without laboratory confirmation of the gestation. Because it is done early in the pregnancy, complications are few and the procedure itself is relatively easy. Paracervical anesthesia is used to prepare the individual, and thus general anesthetic complications are prevented. A flexible cannula is placed within the uterus and suction aspiration of the uterine lining then done. This procedure only takes a few minutes and can be done as an outpatient procedure. Follow-up is necessary to reduce the complication rate, especially to ensure that the pregnancy does not continue.[58]

It has been suggested in the literature that trained paraprofessionals can easily learn this technique. However, the health care professional should be careful not to allow abuse of this technique. If the procedure is done on demand to any teenager by a paraprofessional—especially if it is used repeatedly by a youth—then in the author's opinion the technique is being abused. If it done because of a missed period and the pregnancy is not confirmed with laboratory testing, there may also be some abuse of this procedure—but this may be a bit more controversial. The act of abortion should precipitate a series evaluation by the teenager of her sexual practices and of her need for contraception. The fact that an abortion is occurring should not be hidden by failing to confirm the gestation or calling it a "miniabortion." It should not become the contraceptive choice of the repeat aborter, and become misused the way the postcoital contraceptives (e.g., diethylstilbestrol) were by some in the early 1970s.[59] On the other hand, an abortion procedure should not be established to be merely punitive either. This is an excellent method and the method of choice for abortion during early gestation.

Vacuum Aspiration (Suction Curettage)

Vacuum aspiration is a late first-trimester (8–12 weeks) abortion method that many clinicians use as the method of choice for this gestational period. Paracervical block is the type of anesthesia used for most patients, in which 1 percent xylocaine (lidocaine) is injected into several cervical sites. General anesthesia is needed in a few patients, such as the mentally retarded or those who are unable to tolerate the procedure while awake. The cervix may have to be dilated to allow safe introduction of the cannula or currette. This may be done with traditional dilators (as the Pratt or Hegar types) or with laminaria tents.[60] The latter are rigid, thin twigs of dried seaweed that are placed into the cervix; as they gather moisture they swell, slowly dilating the cervix. Laminaria are placed several hours (usually within 24 hours) prior to the anticipated procedure. Once adequate cervical dilatation has occurred, a cannula is introduced into the uterus, negative pressure is developed, and the uterine contents are gently but thoroughly suctioned out. A curette can then be introduced after the suction to finish the procedure. The removed uterine contents should be carefully examined to see if all the conceptus has been obtained.

Such a procedure involves more complications than menstrual extraction, but it is considered a very safe procedure in well-trained hands. More hemorrhaging is to be expected than with the miniabortion, and infection as well as genital trauma are also possible. An incomplete abortion occasionally occurs, but uterine perforation should be rare. RhoGam may be needed if Rh sensitivity is a factor. The patient may be sent home that day if the complications have been kept to a minimum. Careful observation is necessary over the next few days, with the patient checking for fever, leukorrhea, and other symptomatology. She is usually instructed to avoid tampons, douching, and coitus for several days to 2 or more weeks. Some patients are routinely started on antibiotics, although their role in the absence of overt infection is unproven. A postabortion examination is done 2–4 weeks after this procedure. The exact postprocedure rules are dependent on the particular patient, her physician, the duration of the gestation, and how the procedure went. Postabortion counseling is always recommended, as well as attention to contraceptive needs.

Dilatation and Curettage or Evacuation

Dilatation and curettage or evacuation are done in the late first trimester and more commonly during the second trimester of gestation. The procedure may involve the use of general anesthesia, and thus the overall complication rate is increased. Careful evaluation and preparation of the patient is necessary. Extensive cervical dilatation is a necessity, and thus trauma to the young cervix is a real possibility. The term *dilatation and curettage* implies that curetting is the main method of conceptus removal. The term *dilatation and evacuation* connotes a variety of means used to remove the uterine contents: vacuum aspiration, curettage, and/or ring forceps. Although there is no agreement on the best (or safest) method of abortion at 13–16 weeks of gestation, the current method of choice is some form of a dilatation and evacuation technique.[54] It is preferred over intraamniotic saline instillation, which was more popular a decade ago (discussed below).

Because the gestation is longer and the necessary technical skills are greater in these procedures than in those previously discussed, major and minor complications are not rare. These are, however, considered safe procedures and have far lower mortality rates than pregnancy and childbirth. Uterine hemorrhaging can be extensive, especially if parts of the conceptus are left behind. A thorough curettage and/or evacuation is necessary, with extreme caution aimed at preventing uterine perforation and infection. Oxytocin and methergine are used frequently to reduce uterine bleeding. General anesthesia, hospitalization, and prophylactic antibiotics are common for these procedures when used in later gestation. The patient is to avoid douching, tampon use, and sexual activity for at least 3 weeks. Strenuous activity is also to be avoided and a careful postabortion evaluation is recommended at 2–3 weeks postabortion.

The entire procedure is emotionally traumatic for most patients and thus adequate pre- as well as postabortion counseling is important. The clinician should carefully observe the patient who quickly decides in the second trimester to have an abortion but does not wish any kind of counseling. The individual should carefully work through her feelings with a counselor she chooses before and after the abortion procedure. A delayed, previously unsuspected grief reaction may occur and she should not be left on her own. The counselor need not be and probably should not be the individual performing the abortion. A team approach is recommended in which the health care professional who performs the abortion has others helping with the counseling role. This counseling is just as important as the actual abortion.

It is also very important that contraception be discussed directly and that some form of effective contraception be offered. One should not listen to the notion that "it will not happen again." The individual wishing a second-trimester abortion may be especially vulnerable in this regard, since there may be considerable personal ambivalence about her sexuality and coital activity. If accepted, contraception (e.g., oral contraception or intrauterine device) is started with 7–10 days after the abortion.[52] It must be acknowledged that some individuals simply will not accept contraception, although they remain at high risk for pregnancy. This attitude reflects the many reasons behind adolescent pregnancy—some of which are not affected by the abortion or counseling services. As previously noted, repeat aborters are a very frustrating subgroup of individuals. However, they should not prevent the health care professional from providing contraception to those individuals who wish to remain sexually active but are (or can be), motivated to use effective contraception. Most teenage pregnancies are unwanted and the abortion experience (especially in the second trimester) can be used as a helpful experience in this regard.

Intraamniotic Instillation Procedure

Direct instillation of chemicals into the amniotic sac is another common second-trimester procedure.[46,51,55] Injection of hypertonic saline is popular, although prostaglandins are also frequently used; urea has been advocated by some. This procedure is usually not possible before 16 weeks of gestation due to the lack of sufficient amniotic fluid.[60] There are many variations of this technique but the basic principles remain the same. A needle is introduced through the abdomen into the amniotic cavity. Sometimes a needle is placed into the cervix or transabdominally into the extraovular space. With the needle into the amniotic sac, 150–200 cc fluid (clear, not bloody) is removed and a similar volume of 20 percent saline is injected into the sac. This causes uterine contractions and the release of uterine prostaglandins. It may also cause the release of oxytocin from the pituitary gland, causing more uterine motility. The placental synthesis of progesterone is reduced, again resulting in more uterine contractions.[56] The hypertonic solution directly kills the fetus and the dead conceptus is usually delivered 1–2 (occasionally 3) days later. The time from saline instillation to actual abortion can be shortened by the use of laminaria tents to dilate the cervix and oxytocin to increase uterine contractions.

The complications are many, due to the prolonged gestational stage and the technique itself. Problems to observe for include hemorrhaging, genital laceration (especially the cervix), hypernatremia, coagulation disorders, intravascular coagulopathy, retained placenta, maternal intravascular saline injection, maternal intraperitoneal extravasation of saline, endometritis, and others.[47] Delivery of a viable fetus is not a rare event, especially when the technique is used in the late second trimester. Individuals with severe anemia, cardiac disease, or renal disease should not be given this method. The emotional trauma to the patient is also increased, as it is clearly a direct fetus-killing method occurring at a time when the chances for viability outside the womb are increasing. The issue of abortion becomes very difficult at this point to all but those using extreme denial for the entire process.[61]

Intraamniotic instillation of prostaglandins has been advocated by some over the use of hypertonic saline.[56,62] Prostaglandins are an important class of fatty acids that are involved with uterine contractions. The intraamniotic instillation of prostaglandin $F_{2\alpha}$ may result in abortion of a dead fetus in a shorter time than with saline. Various side effects are described including uterine perforation, gastrointestinal dysfunction (such as nausea, emesis, or diarrhea), hemorrhage, and others. There may be delivery of more live fetuses than with saline.

Other Abortion Techniques

Intravaginal instillation of prostaglandin has been used to induce labor after spontaneous fetal death or a missed abortion. This vaginal suppository has also been used as treatment for hydatidiform mole and as an induced abortion method in the second trimester.[63] A 20-mg suppository is placed high into the vagina every 3 hours and the abortion may occur within 4 hours (or up to 2.5 days) later. It may induce abortion in 90 percent of individuals, while a complete abortion is noted in 75 percent.[63] Live births may occur, as well as maternal complications such as gastrointestinal dysfunction, chills, fever, rare seizures, and others that are prostaglandin induced. The use of this method for first-trimester abortion is uncertain at this time.

Occasionally hysterotomy or hysterectomy is used as an abortion technique in teenagers. Hysterotomy involves general anesthesia followed by surgically opening the uterus and physically removing the conceptus. Once the immature uterus has been cut, cesarian section will be necessary for subsequent pregnancies.[43] Hysterotomy is considered in unusual cases when other methods are contraindicated or have failed. The complication rate of such a method is considerable. Hysterectomy is a method of sterilization that has rare application to youths. In unusual cases it has been used as an abortion method.[52]

PSYCHOLOGICAL EFFECT OF ABORTION

One of the concerns shared by all those involved with the health care of teenagers is that abortion in this age group might prove to be psychologically detrimental to those undergoing the procedure. Isolated or anecdotal reports of behavioral or psychiatric difficulties arising postabortion can indeed be found; however, a careful review of the existing literature indicates that such adverse reactions usually do not occur.[6,30,64,65] Most teenagers do well psychologically after the abortion.[64,65] Postabortion psychoses are unusual in contrast to the well-known syndrome of postpartum psychosis.[66,67] Good results are usually noted in those who have had some preparation for the procedure and have chosen it after considering all other alternatives. For many the outcome after the abortion can be a feeling of relief and of happiness.[68,69]

A major point that much of the abortion literature makes is that the abortion can be a positive step in the lives of many women who are adequately prepared to take this step.[70–74] This is a concept that individuals adamantly opposed to abortion would find very difficult or even impossible to accept— that such a "negative" (in their view) process could have anything but devastating effects. Those in favor of abortion readily accept this concept, on the basis that carrying the pregnancy to term, delivering, and raising the child would have devastating effects on many women.

The teenager is usually not at a time in her life when motherhood is advisable, although she may remain ambivalent about her sexuality and its consequences. The shock of the abortion may force her to view her life realistically and stimulate her to take better charge of herself. This would be seen more with the older, more insightful adolescent than with the younger, cognitively immature individual. The abortion may force her to carefully review her life and evaluate what direction it is taking. Although the procedure can be painful physically and psychologically, the eventual outcome may be positive—if future pregnancies are then postponed until a more appropriate time. Psychosocial adjustment several months after the abortion may be better than that before the procedure,[74] and the carefully performed abortion does not adversely affect subsequent fertility.[75-77]

Proponents for abortion sometimes note a beneficial effect of this procedure on infant care in general—since open, legal abortion may lead to fewer abandoned infants[78] and lower infant mortality rates.[79] This may be stretching the positive aspects of abortion too much. One can argue with the various published papers or completely reject such a concept. The literature does note, however, that women (including teenagers) who are prepared for the procedure may experience a growth process that can positively affect their lives. This does not occur if adequate counseling is not provided— the adolescent must not be left alone to make her own progress in this regard.

Counseling, whether individual or group, allows the teenager to reflect on her pregnancy and the options available to her.[64,80] It is important to explore fully her various reactions to the pregnancy and the possible abortion or the option of keeping the baby. It is usually difficult, if not impossible, for the teenager to be aware of the realities confronting each decision. It is necessary to explore the positive and negative aspects of all options. Negative feelings and reactions are normal and need to be brought out in the open. Adoption, although unpopular, may be an option for a few.[14,81] The counselor can also explore past coping mechanisms and help the individual learn better coping skills. There may be some resistance to the counseling, but it should be offered nonetheless. A rapid decision serves no one and can have devastating effects.

Those who counsel youth—physicians, psychologists, social workers, nurses or other health care professionals—should not be judgmental toward teenagers.[84] As noted by the Committee on Adolescence of the American Academy of Pediatrics, the counselor should keep his or her morality out of the discussion.[51] The counselor may have a strong moral attitute or opinion, but should be attempting to help the adolescent decide what is best and acceptable to her at a particular time in her life. Of course one's attitude become obvious to some degree,[83] but its expression should be kept to a minimum. The counselor should be a neutral observer—neither strongly advising for nor strongly advising against the abortion on emotional grounds. There are enough individuals in the teenager's life who will urge her one way or another. The counselor should not be the parent figure—whether discussing sexuality, contraception, or abortion. Certainly, the teenager will encounter intense disagreement about this particular topic, since it involves an area where so many aspects of her life meet—religion, minors' rights versus parents' rights, sexuality, socioeconomic status, cognitive development, psychological development, and many others.

The health care professional who cannot provide neutral factual information about the options available to the pregnant individual should refer her to someone else who is capable of doing this important task. The counselor should be very knowledgeable about contraceptive information and contraceptive services; this information should be included in the pre- and postabortion counseling sessions. These sessions should aim at helping the youth cope with the current pregnancy and with the prevention of other pregnancies at inappropriate times in the future. It does no good to abort a pregnancy now only to be presented with another gestation in the near future. All health care professionals agree that prevention of the pregnancy is a far better approach than having society argue whether or not the young mother-to-be should or should not abort the fetus and how it should or should not be done.

Abortion is not an easy issue for most women. It is a difficult issue that presents some psychological pain to most who are forced to consider it. Some authors have noted that abortion is more psychologically difficult for teenagers than for adult women.[84,85] According to one study, this may be especially true for young teenagers who lack sufficient maturity to cope effectively with this situation.[84] Transient psychological difficulties are noted in many individuals,[51,65,86-88] and thus counseling before as well as after the procedure is important. Increased anxiety or some depression is not unusual during the period between deciding to have the abortion and having it done.[89] A particularly difficult time for some women after the abortion is the time the aborted fetus would have turned 1 year of age if he or she had lived.[47,86] Tighler reported two cases of adolescent suicide attempts reflective of this phenomenon.[90]

Thus a careful preabortion assessment is necessary for anyone requesting an abortion. Certain factors leading to a more negative emotional reaction have been identified in various studies. An increased psychological reaction has been noted with later gestation abortion,[30,87] preexisting mental illness,[30,86] strong religious beliefs,[91,92] limited coping skills,[91] limited family support,[91] and other conditions. There may be increased guilt or depression in those having an abortion for genetic reasons,[93] or those seeking an illegal abortion.[94] A negative reaction may be induced by direct fear of the surgical procedure itself.[91] There is also concern on the part of some clinicians that abortion may cause cervical trauma to the young teenager with resultant obstetric-gynecologic sequelae later in her life.[95] Although most clinicians feel that abortion in well-trained hands is safe, fear of the known medical complications certainly can worsen anxiety and depression.

How one interprets such data depends on the particular view one has regarding abortion in general. The author's view is that there are transient negative behavioral reactions noted in individuals contemplating and undergoing abortion, and thus careful screening as well as emotional support is necessary for these individuals. Those at high risk for anxiety, guilt, or other psychological problems are those who are very young, are in strong conflict with their religious views, have limited support from their family or sexual partner, have a history of using negative coping skills to deal with stress, and are not fully prepared for the abortion or the consequences of this procedure. Psychological problems tend to be transient for most women, but each individual should be carefully assessed in this regard. The relevance of various studies of many women to the individual teenager's reactions remains to be determined.

CONCLUSIONS

Abortion techniques currently available include menstrual extraction, vacuum curettage, dilatation and curettage, dilatation and evacuation, intraamniotic fluid administration (hypertonic saline, prostaglandins, or urea), hysterotomy, and hysterectomy. A vaginal suppository for abortion has also been used by some individuals. The complications of abortion (infection, hemorrhage, uterine perforation, or incomplete removal of the conceptus) can be greatly minimized by having a well-trained individual performing the procedure during early pregnancy in a well-screened teenager.

Safe surgical techniques are available, but the subject of abortion remains embedded in many ethical, moral, and legal difficulties. Despite these problems, many abortions do take place annually among teenagers and adult women. Recent court decisions have generally upheld the right of a mature minor and the adult female to decide with her physician whether abortion or delivery follows a pregnancy. Youths who decide on abortion have neither been shown to be very different than their peers, nor to have resultant long-term psychological or fertility difficulties.

What then is the clinician to do with a youth presenting for an abortion? Certainly it is important to confirm the pregnancy and estimate the gestational age by means of a pelvic examination and a pregnancy test (urine or serum). Then the individual *must* receive professional counseling to enable her to make her own decision about the outcome of her pregnancy (keeping her baby, adoption, or abortion.) Such help may come from the physician or other health care professionals. It is important for the clinician to keep his or her own morality out of the patient's decision-making process. This is not to deny that physicians or other professionals have specific moral views; but the youth must be helped to make her own decision—hopefully but not inevitably with the help of her boyfriend or family.

A full review of the patient's situation can be very helpful to her. Often the choice of an abortion or delivery depends on the teenager's particular circumstances and not on specific characteristics of the patient herself. This is also a time to advise the patient about adequate methods of contraception and help her to gain valuable insight into reasons for previous contraceptive failure. Those who utilize repeat abortions as their main contraceptive method require more study. Mature youths have the right to select abortion as an option but it should not be seen as a method of contraception per se. One should also not forget that adoption is also a good alternative for some individuals. Finally, it is also the opinion of many that first-trimester abortions should be provided for teenagers who select this option after careful consideration of all current and future options. Whether the decade of the 1980s will witness a change in current abortion laws remains to be seen.

REFERENCES

1. Sullivan E, Tietze C, Dryfoos JG: Legal abortion in the United States, 1975–1976. Fam Plann Perspect 9:116–129, 1977
2. Teenage Childbearing and Abortion Patterns—U.S., 1977. Morbid Mortal Week Rep 29(14):157–160, 1980
3. Cates W Jr: Adolescent abortions in the United States. J Adolesc Health Care 1:18–21, 1980
4. Forrest JD, Sullivan E, Tietze C: Abortion in the United States, 1977–1978. Fam Plann Perspect 11:329–341, 1979
5. Alan Guttmacher Institute: Teenage Pregnancy: The Problem That Hasn't Gone Away. Section 8: Abortion Services. New York, AGI, 1981, pp 50–57
6. Eisenberg L: Social context of child development. Pediatrics 68:705–712, 1981
7. Tietze C, Bongaarts J, Schearer B: Mortality associated with the control of fertility. Fam Plann Perspect 8:14–15, 1976
8. Rosenfield A: Oral and intrauterine contraception: A 1978 risk assessment. Am J Obstet Gynecol 132:92–106, 1978
9. Cates W Jr, Tietze C: Standardized mortality rates associated with legal abortion: U.S. 1972–1975. Fam Plann Perspect 10:109–112, 1978
10. Tietze C: New estimates of mortality associated with fertility control. Fam Plann Perspect 9:74–76, 1977
11. McAnarney ER, Greydanus DE (eds): Adolescent pregnancy: A risk condition? Semin Perinatol 5:1–103, 1981
12. Tietze C: The effect of legalization of abortion on population growth and public health. Fam Plann Perspect 7:123–126, 1975
13. Cates W Jr, Rochat RW: Illegal abortions in the U.S.: 1972–1974. Fam Plann Perspect 8:86–90, 1976
14. Bracken MB, Klerman LV, Bracken M: Abortion, adoption or motherhood: An empirical study of decision-making during pregnancy. Am J Obstet Gynecol 130:251–262, 1978
15. Rosen RH: Adolescent pregnancy decision-making: Are parents important? Adolescence 15(5):43–54, 1980
16. Greydanus DE: Alternatives to adolescent pregnancy: A discussion of contraceptive literature from 1960–1980. Semin Perinatol 5:53–54, 1981

17. Greydanus DE: The health system's responsibility toward the sexually active adolescent, in Wells CF, Stuart IR (eds): Pregnancy in Adolescence: Needs, Problems and Management. New York, Van Nostrand Reinhold, 1982, pp 48–65

18. McAnarney ER, Greydanus DE: Adolescent pregnancy—A multifacited problem. Pediatr Rev 1(4):123–126, 1979

19. Kramer M: Legal abortions among New York City residents: An analysis according to socioeconomic and demographic characteristics. Fam Plann Perspect 7:128–137, 1975

20. Abortion Surveillance, 1979—Provisional statistics. Morbid Mortal Week Rep 31(4):47–50, 1982

21. Jaffe FS: The pill: A perspective for assessing risks and benefits. N Engl J Med 297:612–614, 1977

22. Kreipe RE, Roghmann KJ, McAnarney ER: Early adolescent childbearing: A changing morbidity? J Adolesc Health Care 2:127–131, 1981

23. Scales P: Teenage pregnancy—What next? J Curr Adolesc Med 2:44–46, 1980

24. Cates W Jr: The Hyde Amendment in action: How did the restriction of federal funds for abortion affect low-income women? JAMA 246:1109–1112, 1981

25. Tyrer LB, Josimovich J: Contraception in teenagers. Clin Obstet Gynecol 20:660–662, 1977

26. Burr WA, Schulz KF: Delayed abortion in an area of easy accessibility. JAMA 244:44–48, 1980

27. Cates W Jr, Grimes DA, Smith JC, et al: Legal abortion mortality in the U.S.: Epidemiologic surveillance, 1972–1974. JAMA 237:452–455, 1977

28. Schneider SM, Thompson DS: Repeat aborters. Am J Obstet Gynecol 126:316–320, 1976

29. Steinhoff PG, Smith RG, Palmore JA, et al: Women who obtain repeat abortions: A study based on record linkage. Fam Plann Perspect 11:30–38, 1979

30. Green KW, Resnick R: The abortion issue: Past, present and future. Curr Probl Pediatr 7(10):1–44, 1977

31. Hofmann AD, Pilpel HF: The legal rights of minors. Pediatr Clin North Am 20:989–1004, 1973

32. In re Gault, 387 US 1, 1967

33. Hofmann AD, Becker RD, Gabriel HP: Consent and confidentiality, in Hofmann AD, Becker RD, Gabriel HR (eds): The Hospitalized Adolescent. A Guide to Managing the Ill and Injured Youth, New York: Free Press, 1976, pp 211–232

34. Tinker vs The Des Moines Independent School District, 393 US 503, 1969

35. Roe vs Wade, Doe vs Bolton, 410 US 113, 179, 1973

36. Danforth vs Planned Parenthood of Central Missouri, 428 US 52, 1976

37. Belotti vs Baird. 443 US 662, 1979

38. Hyde Amendment: Appropriations year 1980—Continuence Public Law 96-123, 109, 93 Stat 926, 1979

39. HL vs Matheson, 101 S Ct 1164, 1981

40. Danforth vs. Planned Parenthood of Central Missouri. Fam Plann/Popul Rep 5:53–58, 1976

41. McLean RA, Cochrane NE, Mattison ET: Abortion and mortality study, twenty-year study in New York State exclusive of New York City. NY State J Med 79:49–52, 1975

42. Paul EW, Schaap P: Legal rights and responsibilities of pregnant teenagers and their children, in Wells CF, Stuart IR (eds): Pregnancy in Adolescence: Needs, Problems, and Management. New York: Van Nostrand Reinhold, 1982, pp 3–24

43. Kreutner AK, Langhorst DM: Abortion and abortion counseling, in Kreutner AKK, Hollingsworth DR (eds): Adolescent Obstetrics and Gynecology. Chicago, Year Book, 1978, pp 79–119.

44. Hofmann AD: A rational policy toward consent and confidentiality in adolescent health care. J Adolesc Health Care 1:9–17, 1980

45. Cook RJ, Dickens BM: A decade of international change in abortive law: 1967–1977. Am J Public Health 68:637–642, 1978

46. Hausknecht RU: The termination of pregnancy in adolescent women. Pediatr Clin North Am 19:803–810, 1972

47. Rauh JL, Johnson LS, Burket RL: The reproductive adolescent. Pediatr Clin North Am 20:1017–1018, 1973

48. Wentz AC, Burnett LS, King TM: Techniques of pregnancy termination. Part I. Obstet Gynecol Surv 28:2–19, 1973

49. Burnett LS, Wentz AC, King TM: Techniques of pregnancy termination. Part II. Obstet Gynecol Surv 29:6–42, 1974

50. Burnett LS: An evaluation of abortion: Techniques and protocols. Hosp Pract 10:97–105, 1975

51. Baldwin WH: Adolescent pregnancy and child bearing—Growing concerns for Americans. Popul Bull 31:14–15, 1978

52. Niswander KR: Obstetric and Gynecologic Disorders. Flushing, NY: Medical Examination, 1975, pp 153–155

53. Committee on Adolescence, American Academy of Pediatrics: Pregnancy and Abortion Counseling. Pediatrics 63:920–921, 1979

54. Berger GS, Brenner WE, Keigh LG (eds): Second-Trimester Abortion: Perspectives After a Decade of Experience. Littleton, Mass: Wright, PSG, 1981

55. Hodgson JE: Major complications of 20,248 consecutive first trimester abortions: Problems of fragmentary care. Adv Plann Parent 9:52–56, 1975

56. Chaudry SL, Hunt WB, Wortman J: Pregnancy termination in mid-trimester. Review of the major methods. Popul Rep F(5):65–83, 1976

57. Van der Vlugt T, Piotrow PT: Menstrual regulation: What is it? Popul Rep F(2):9–21, 1973

58. Key TC, Kreutner AKK: Menstrual extraction in the adolescent. J Adolesc Health Care 1:127–131, 1980

59. Greydanus DE, McAnarney ER: Contraception in adolescence: Current concepts for the pediatrician. Pediatrics 65:1–12, 1980

60. Hanson MS: Abortion in teenagers. Clin Obstet Gynecol 21:1175–1190, 1978

61. Youngs DD, Niebyl JR: Adolescent pregnancy and abortion. Med Clin North Am 59:1419–1427, 1975

62. Bygdemon M, Bertstrom S: Clinical use of prostaglandins for pregnancy termination. Popul Rep G(7):65–76, 1976

63. A vaginal suppository for abortion. Med Lett Drugs Ther 19(22):89–90, 1977

64. Nadelson C: Abortion counseling: Focus on adolescent pregnancy. Pediatrics 54:765–769, 1974

65. Olson L: Social and psychological correlates of pregnancy resolution among adolescent women. A review. Am J Orthopsychiatry 50:432–445, 1980

66. David H: Abortion in psychological perspectives. Am J Orthopsychiatry 42(5):61–68, 1972

67. Brewer C: Incidence of post-abortion psychosis. A prospective study. Br Med J 1:476–477, 1977

68. Bracken MB, Grossman G, Hachamovitch M: Contraceptive practice among New York abortion patients. Am J Obstet Gynecol 114:967–977, 1972
69. Osofsky H, Osofsky J: Psychological effects of legal abortion. Clin Obstet Gynecol 14:215–234, 1971
70. Barnes AB, Cohen E, Stoeckle JD, et al: Therapeutic abortion: Medical and social sequels. Ann Intern Med 75:881–886, 1971
71. Ford C, Castelnuovo-Tedesco P, Long K: Abortion: Is it a therapeutic procedure in psychiatry? JAMA 218:1173–1178, 1971
72. Perez-Reyes M, Falk R: Follow-up after therapeutic abortion in early adolescence. Arch Gen Psychiatry 28:120–126, 1973
73. Addelson F: Induced abortion: Source of guilt or growth? Am J Orthopsychiatry 43:815–823, 1973
74. Greer HS, Lao S, Lewis SC, et al: Psychosocial consequences of therapeutic abortion: King's Termination Study. III. Br J Psychiatry 128:74–79, 1976
75. Daling JR, Emanuel I: Induced abortion and subsequent outcome of pregnancy in a series of American women. N Engl J Med 297:1241–1245, 1977
76. Daling JR, Spadoni LR, Emanuel I: Role of induced abortion and secondary infertility. Obstet Gynecol 57:59–61, 1981
77. Harlap S, Shiono PH, Ramcharan T, et al: A prospective study of spontaneous fetal loses after induced abortion. N Engl J Med 301:677–681, 1979
78. Lanman JT, Kohl SH, Bedell JH: Changes in pregnancy outcome after liberalization of the New York State abortion law. Am J Obstet Gynecol 118:485–492, 1974
79. Pakter J, Nelson F: Factors in the unprecedented decline in infant mortality in New York City. Bull NY Acad Med 50:839–868, 1974
80. Urman J, Meginnis SK: The process of problem pregnancy counseling. J Am Coll Health Assoc 28:308–315, 1980
81. Hollingsworth DR, Kreutner AKK: Teenager pregnancy—Solutions are evolving. N Engl J Med 303:516–518, 1980
82. Silber TJ: Physician–adolescent patient relationship. Clin Pediatr 19:50–55, 1980
83. Nathanson CA, Becker MH: The influence of physicians' attitudes on abortion performance, patient management and professional fees. Fam Plann Perspect 9:158–163, 1977
84. Hatcher S: The adolescent experience of pregnancy and abortion: A developmental analysis. J Youth Adolesc 1:52–102, 1973
85. Margolis A: Therapeutic abortion: Follow-up study. Am J Obstet Gynecol 110:243–249, 1971
86. Walter GS: Psychological and emotional consequences of elective abortion. Obstet Gynecol 36:482–491, 1970
87. Ford CV: Emotional response to abortion. Contemp Obstet Gynecol 1:15–20, 1973
88. Lipper I, Cvejic H, Benjamin P, et al: Abortion in the pregnant teenager. Can Med Assoc J 109:852–856, 1973
89. Freeman EW: Abortion: Subjective attitudes and feelings. Fam Plann Perspect 10:150–155, 1978
90. Tighler CL: Adolescent suicide attempts following elective abortion: A special case of anniversary reaction. Pediatrics 68:670–671, 1981
91. Braken MB: Psychosomatic aspects of abortion: Implications for counseling. J Reprod Med 19:265–272, 1977
92. Osofsky JD, Osofsky HJ: The pscyhological reaction of patients to legalized abortion. Am J Orthopsychiatry 42:48–60, 1972

93. Blumberg RD, Golbus MS, Hanson KH: The psychological sequelae of abortion performed for a genetic indication. Am J Obstet Gynecol 122:799–808, 1975
94. Bridwell M, Tinnin L: Abortion referral in a large college health service. J Am Med Wom Assoc 27:420–421, 1972
95. Russell JK: Sexual activity and its consequences in the teenager. Clin Obstet Gynecol 1:683–698, 1974

Part VI

SUMMARY: A DECADE OF PROGRESS

21

Adolescent Pregnancy and Childbearing: What We Learned during the 1970s and What Remains to Be Learned

Elizabeth R. McAnarney and Henry A. Thiede

National concern recently has been directed toward the morbidity associated with adolescent pregnancy and childbearing. As a result, in 1979, Public Law 95-625 directed that the Secretary of Health, Education and Welfare issue rules for grants for the establishment of projects to provide needed comprehensive community services to assist in preventing unwanted initial and repeat pregnancies among adolescents and to assist pregnant adolescents and adolescent parents to obtain health, social, educational, and other services. This legislation was implemented under Title VI grant funds.[1]

This legislation was very important as it focused national attention and priorities on the problems associated with adolescent pregnancy and childbearing. It acknowledged that comprehensive health, psychosocial, and educational services provide improved outcome for mothers and infants.

This work was supported in part by the New York State Department of Social Services and National Institute of Mental Health Grant 1 TO1 MH 15275-01. The views expressed by the authors do not necessarily reflect policies or positions of the New York State Department of Social Services.

RISKS OF PREGNANCY AND
CHILDBEARING DURING ADOLESCENCE

Factors Affecting Medical Outcome

The improvements in overall maternal and infant outcomes in the United States over the past 40 years have been dramatic. In 1940, the maternal mortality rate was 376/100,000 live births compared to 12.3/ 100,000 live births in 1976. The neonatal death rate was 28.8/1000 in 1940 compared to 10.9/1000 in 1976. Despite the overall improvement in maternal and infant outcomes, nonwhites still suffer greater maternal and neonatal morbidity than whites.[2] This is now thought to be due to the greater percentage of black persons in the lower socioeconomic group rather than genetic predisposition to poor outcome.

There are multiple factors that determine maternal and infant outcome. Dott and Fort identified three major categories: intrinsic patient factors, such as child spacing, legitimacy status, socioeconomic status, race, educational attainment, and maternal age; health care delivery factors, such as the availability and utilization of prenatal clinics, hospitals, and medical personnel; and the quality of medical care.[3] Recent data also have underscored the influence of health habits, such as smoking,[4] drinking behavior,[5] and personal hygiene, and medical conditions, such as untreated urinary tract infections,[6,7] on obstetric and neonatal outcome.

We briefly examine what is known about each of the intrinsic patient factors and then focus on maternal age as a specific and critical factor related to maternal and infant biologic and psychosocial outcome.

Child Spacing

The National Natality Study of 1964–1965 showed that infant mortality rates rose with the parity of the mother. Greater than average mortality rates were noted for the second child of mothers less than 20 years of age and the fifth child of mothers 20–24 years old.[8] Jekel and colleagues reported that for children of primigravida adolescents, the risk of perinatal death was 6/1000; for second births to adolescents it was 71/1000, and for third births to adolescents it was 143/1000.[9] Thus, increasing parity carries greater risk of perinatal death for infants of adolescent mothers.

Legitimacy Status

In 1961, Pakter and colleagues reported that the death rate for infants born out of wedlock was 48.2/1000, compared to a death rate of 23.9/1000 for babies born within wedlock.[10] When the data were analyzed according to ethnic group, the following information emerged: for white infants born to unmarried mothers, the death rate was 35.0/1000, and for white infants born to married mothers it was 20.1/1000; the rate was 51.9/1000 for nonwhite infants born to unmarried mothers and 38.3/1000 for nonwhite infants born to married mothers. They concluded that ethnic origin, when related to poor social and economic conditions, had a greater influence on increasing infant mortality than the lack of marital status.

In their analysis of the relationship of legitimacy status to infant outcome, Dott and Fort concluded that the infant mortality rate for illegitimate offspring was greater than that of legitimate offspring, although whites fared better than blacks despite their marital status.[3] When maternal age was considered, the infant mortality rate was greatest for married mothers under 16 years of age, regardless of race. The highest infant mortality rate in this series was 64.5/1000, for the infants of white, married mothers less than 15 years of age.

An interesting finding was that the infant mortality rate for births to unmarried mothers 10–14 years of age, regardless of race, was *less* than of births to unmarried women 15–19 years of age. The authors suggested that the families of very young, unmarried mothers take care of the infant more often than the families of mothers who are married and may live away from their extended families.[3]

As we examine outcome data, we must be sensitive to changing societal attitudes. O'Connell and Moore reported in 1980 that since the mid-1950s the fraction of first births premaritally conceived had more than doubled among white adolescents and had increased by about one-half among blacks, even though there is some slight decrease now.[11] Between 1975 and 1978, more than 60 percent of first births to white adolescents and 90 percent of first births to black adolescents were conceived premaritally. There has been a sharp increase in the rate of premaritally conceived first births to white adolescents that are legitimized by marriage, as well as a decrease in births that are postmaritally conceived. About 50 percent of marital first births to adolescents in the 1975–1978 period were premaritally conceived.[11] Thus, new studies of infant outcome are needed that consider the changing legitimacy status of children.

Socioeconomic Status

The relationship of poverty to poor neonatal outcome is well recognized. Pakter et al. reported that the prematurity rate was 9.2 percent for infants born to women who received care in a shelter prior to delivery, compared to 17.1 percent for nonshelter women. The authors concluded that environmental factors influence the incidence of prematurity more than racial or ethnic origin.[10]

Individuals who are of lower socioeconomic status are more likely than those of higher socioeconomic status to be chronically undernourished, practice poor nutritional habits during pregnancy, have poor personal hygiene and sanitation, and receive inadequate prenatal care. Some think that poverty rather than racial differences accounts for the relatively poor outcome seen among the infants of poor, black mothers. Since the very young adolescent who becomes pregnant and bears her child is likely to be poor, black, unmarried, and not receive adequate prepartum care, poor outcome for both mother and child is highly possible.

Race

In general, infants born to nonwhites have greater mortality rates than infants born to whites. Dott and Fort concluded that even though race is a risk factor, its relationship to poverty is probably the main contributor to risk. Racial differences became less obvious when women of similar socioeconomic groups are compared.[3]

Educational Achievement

Educational achievement is closely related to socioeconomic status. There is a steady decline in neonatal and postneonatal infant mortality rates with increasing maternal education, regardless of race. Mortality was 27.0/1000 for infants of women with only an elementary school education, compared to 12.9/1000 for infants of women with some college education.[3] Women who are pursuing formal education beyond high school are more likely to delay childbearing until their adult years than women who do not continue their education. They may delay sexual activity until they finish their education; or if they are sexually active, they are likely to use contraception or choose an abortion if they become pregnant.

Medical Risk Secondary to Adolescent Age

We have learned a great deal since 1970 about the relationship of adolescent age to maternal and infant outcomes. In order to discuss the inherent risk of being an adolescent and bearing a child, we have had to look carefully at all the other intrinsic factors—child spacing, legitimacy status, socioeconomic status, race, and educational achievement—and consider only those studies that attempted to control for those factors and isolated age as a variable. A number of frequently quoted studies from the 1960s did not isolate the effects of age from race, socioeconomic status, legitimacy status, etc., and concluded that by virtue of being an adolescent, the mother was at high risk of poor outcome, as was her baby.

Adolescent mothers, even those less than 15 years of age, who receive adequate prenatal care are not at substantially greater obstetric risk than older adolescent or adult women of similar race, socioeconomic, and legitimacy status. New data suggest that the ideal time to bear a child, from the biologic standpoint, is between 16 and 19 years of age, provided the mother receives adequate care.[12]

The infants of girls less than 15 years of age are more likely to weigh less than 2500 g than infants of older adolescents and adult mothers of similar backgrounds.[13] Baldwin and Cain, however, proposed that the newer findings suggest that the increased risks of low birth weight babies and perinatal infant mortality among young adolescents reported earlier were almost entirely a function of the quality of prenatal care the mother received.[14]

We now review only those studies of obstetric, neonatal, and psychosocial outcome of adolescents and their infants in which the controls were sufficiently rigorous to allow a scientific comparison of data. The studies are presented sequentially, as data developed a decade or two ago may now be outdated because of the changing milieu in which today's youth live. We first address medical risk secondary to adolescent age (Table 21-1).

In an early, well-controlled study in Baltimore, Maryland, Battaglia and associates compared three groups of mothers: black adolescents less than 15 years of age; black adolescents 15–19 years old; and all clinic patients.[15]

Table 21-1. Summary of Data of Well-Controlled Studies Comparing Adolescent and Adult Outcomes of Pregnancy

Study	Age (years)	Toxic Conditions (%)	Birth Weight under 2500 g (%)	Perinatal Mortality of Entire Group (per 1000)
Battaglia et al., 1963[15]	Under 15 (black)	27.8*	23.4	82
	15–19 (black)	21.1*	18.3	50
	Total clinic	11.2*	16.3	—
Duenhoelter et al., 1975[16]	Under 15	34.2†	19.2	30
	19–25	25.3†	15.9	38
Spellacy et al., 1978[17]	Under 15 (black)	20.0*	23.5	52
	20–24 (black)	18.5*	9.6	19
	20–24 (white)	10.8*	8.1	22
Hutchins et al., 1979[18]	Under 17	9.3‡	15.8	40
	17–19	6.7‡	15.4	40
	20–24	3.9‡	14.4	33

*Preeclampsia, eclampsia, or chronic hypertension.
†Pregnancy-induced hypertension.
‡Preeclampsia.

The incidence of toxemia was 27.8 percent for girls less than 15 years old, 21.1 percent for those 15–19 years old, and 11.2 percent for the total clinic population. Prematurity rates were 23.4 percent for those under 15, 18.3 percent for those 15–19, and 16.3 percent for women of all ages. The perinatal mortality rate was 82/1000 for adolescents less than 15 years of age and 50/1000 for blacks 15–19 years old. These differences were all statistically significant. Battaglia and associates concluded that the poor outcome was related to the young age of the mother, rather than her primiparity and nonwhite membership.

Duenhoelter and colleagues reported on the obstetric and neonatal outcome of adolescents less than 15 years of age and young adults 19–25.[16] Adolescents less than 15 had a 34.2 percent incidence of pregnancy-induced hypertension compared to 25.3 percent for older women (a statistically significant difference); the prematurity rate was 19.2 percent girls under 15 compared to 15.9 percent for older women (not statistically different). No significant differences were found between groups for the infant and perinatal mortality and average birth weights.

Spellacy and associates reported that the incidence of all toxic conditions (preeclampsia, eclampsia, chronic hypertension) of pregnancy was 20.0 percent for black adolescents less than 15 years old, 18.5 percent for black adults 20–24, and 10.8 percent for white adults 20–24.[17] These differences were statistically significant. The authors concluded that the difference was secondary to racial and not age differences. Prematurity rates were 23.5 percent for black adolescents less than 15, 9.6 percent for black adults 20–24, and 8.1 percent for white adults 20–24; thus, girls less than 15 bore proportionately more prematures than adult women of either race. There were no significant differences in fetal, neonatal, and perinatal mortality among groups. Significantly more adolescents had poor prenatal care: of those less than 15 years old, 6.3 percent had no prenatal visits compared to 3.8 percent of the adults ($p < 0.05$).

Hutchins and colleagues reported that 9.3 percent of teenagers less than 17 years of age had preeclampsia, compared to 3.9 percent of women 20–34.[18] Of the babies born to mothers less than 17 years of age, 15.8 percent weighed less than 2500 g; 15.4 percent of babies born to mothers 17–19 and 14.4 percent of babies born to mothers 20–34 weighed less than 2500 g. Thirty percent of those less than 17, 22 percent of those 17–19, and 18 percent of those 20–34 failed to register for prenatal care prior to the third trimester of pregnancy. The authors concluded that adolescent pregnancy among the urban, nonwhite poor is characterized by poor outcome, primarily as a reflection of the high-risk obstetric population from which it derives, and only secondarily as a result of maternal age.

Merrittt et al. reported that mothers 14 years old or under were six times more likely to bear an infant weighing less than 2500 g than mothers 15 and older.[12] When compared by race, the increase in low-weight preterm infants was found primarily among infants of black adolescents. Perinatal mortality was 51.7/1000 live births for infants of girls 10–15, 37.6/1000 for infants of adolescents 16–19, and 48.2/1000 for women 20–34.

In order to clarify why mothers less than 15 years of age bear more low birth weight infants, several areas warrant investigation. First, the question should be addressed whether the infants are small for gestational age or premature. In our series in Rochester, New York, we examined statistics from 180 births of babies to adolescents mothers cared for in a special maternity project and found that 15 percent of the babies weighed less than 2500 g; of those, 85 percent were premature and 15 percent were small for gestational age. We also examined the data for 490 infants born to adolescent mothers who were delivered in the same hospital: 16 percent weighed less than 2500 g, and 77 percent of those were prematures.[19]

The factors associated with low birth weight are multiple: lack of prenatal care, low socioeconomic status, previous premature births, previous fetal deaths, child spacing, toxemia, poor nutrition, asymptomatic bacteriuria, chronic illness, smoking, alcohol abuse, infections during pregnancy such as rubella, toxoplasmosis, cytomegalic inclusion disease, mother's height and weight, placental abnormalities such as infarcts, thrombosis of the vessels, and premature separation of the placenta.

We, as providers of adolescent health services, are most interested in differentiating whether the mother less than 15 years old has a biologic predisposition for bearing small infants (fixed factor) or whether patient factors (changeable factors) are responsible. A review of each of the possible causes of prematurity of the infants of adolescent mothers is beyond the scope of this chapter, however, several recent findings are of particular interest.

Biologic (Fixed) Factors

Adolescents who bear children when they are very young have experienced early menarches. Some of these adolescents have experienced an earlier menarche than some of their nonpregnant peers. Roche and Davila reported that a girl who experienced her menarche at 11.6 years grew more and for a longer period after menarche than a girl who experienced her menarche at 15.2 years. The total stature increments after menarche were associated with the age at which menarche occurred ($p < 0.0005$).[20] There may be some other subtle portions of the girl's maturation, such as endometrial and hypothalmic-pituitary maturity, that are not entirely complete at the time the very young adolescent carries and bears her child.

The concept of gynecologic age suggests that the very young adolescent may not be entirely mature at the time she bears her child. Gynecologic age is defined as the difference between the mother's age at either conception or delivery and her age at menarche. The Zlatnik and Burmeister[21] and Erkan and colleagues[22] both reported that the percentage of low birth weight babies was significantly greater for teenagers who bore children at a low gynecologic age. Zlatnik and Burmeister reported that 13 percent of mothers with gynecologic ages of 2 years or less had low birth weight babies, compared to 6 percent of those who had gynecologic ages of 3–9 years.[21] Erkan and associates reported that 31.4 percent of mothers who were 2 years postmenarchal or less bore babies who weighed less than 2500 g compared to 16 percent of mothers who were more than 2 years postmenarchal.[22]

New data suggest that the very young adolescent is not too immature to sustain a pregnancy to full term. Forbes reported that adolescents have experienced the majority of their physical growth—as measured by lean body mass, thickness of the cortex of the bone of the wrists, and by bi-iliac diameter—by a short time after menarche.[23]

Hollingsworth and Kotchen reported no relationship between gynecologic age and birth weight in their study in Kentucky.[24] We recently found no relationship between the gynecologic age of 415 young mothers and their infants' birth weights at Strong Memorial Hospital in Rochester, New York.[25]

We believe that even the very young adolescent who bears a child is biologically mature and should be able to sustain a full-term pregnancy if she receives prenatal care.

Patient (Changeable) Factors

Several conditions may adversely affect obstetric and neonatal outcome and may be reducible through excellent prenatal care. Some may be implicated in causing the higher incidence of low birth weight babies among very young adolescents.

Nongonococcal infections. Some studies have shown between the presence of mycoplasma infections in the mother and low birth weight of the infant.[26,27] The birth weight of children of mothers who experienced mycoplasma infections was significantly lower than that of noninfected children. The relationship between mycoplasma infections and low birth weight may not be causative, however. We know little about the incidence of nongonococcal infections in adolescent populations, particularly among pregnant adolescents.

Maternal urinary tract infections. Naeye reported that 26 percent of the mothers who had both pyuria and bacteruria delivered before the 37th week of gestation compared to 21 percent of those who had no pyuria ($p < 0.02$).[6]

Naeye suggested that poor maternal nutrition (known to exist among some adolescents) might interact with urinary tract infections to adversely affect outcome.

Coital behavior during the last trimester of pregnancy. Naeye analyzed data from 26,886 pregnancies to determine whether coitus the week before delivery was related to amniotic fluid infections.[28] The frequency of infections was 156/1000 births when mothers reported having had coitus once or more the week before delivery. In contrast, 117/1000 of those who had not had coitus had infections ($p < 0.001$). The frequency of low Apgar scores, neonatal respiratory distress, and hyperbilirubinemia was doubled among mothers who reported having had coitus.

Maternal cigarette smoking. Cigarette smoking has been implicated as a factor that places the fetus at increased risk for a significant reduction in birth weight, among other poor outcomes.[29,30] The exact cause of the relationship between maternal cigarette smoking and low birth weight is unclear, but it may be related to reduced maternal caloric intake. Miller and Merritt also reported that nicotine and carbon monoxide are being studied as possible etiologic agents.[31] There has been an increase in cigarette smoking among adolescent females in recent years.

Maternal alcohol usage. Mothers who drink to excess during pregnancy are more liley to bear low birth weight babies than mothers who abstain or drink small amounts. Ouellette and colleagues reported that 17 percent of heavy drinkers, 3 percent of moderate drinkers, and 5 percent of light drinkers or abstainers had premature babies ($p < 0.05$).[5]

Correction of changeable factors. These five potential causes of prematurity may be changeable if the pregnant woman receives adequate prenatal care, intervention, and education. Pakter and associates reported that for every ethnic group in their series the incidence of prematurity was greatest for those women who received no prenatal care.[10] Dott and Fort reported that the infant mortality rate was eight times greater for infants of mothers who received no prenatal care than for those who had nine or more visits.[32] Prenatal care is not the only factor in determining outcome—socioeconomic status and the psychosocial milieu are probably of greater importance.

Psychosocial Risk

Most authors agree that the gravest morbidity for adolescent mothers and fathers and their children is in the psychosocial area. The morbidity for mothers, fathers, and children increases with the decreasing age of the adolescent parents, and the problems are greatest for individuals of the lowest socioeconomic status.

Education

Moore and Waite reported that adolescent mothers had a lower level of educational achievement than adolescents matched for race and socioeconomic status who delayed childbearing.[33] Card and Wise found there was a definite correlation between a student's age at the birth of the first child and the amount of education the student completed: 50 percent of adolescent mothers and 70 percent of adolescent fathers received high school diplomas, compared to 97 percent of adolescent women and 96 percent of adolescent men who delayed parenthood. Both adolescent mothers and fathers, as adults, had lower incomes and held less prestigious jobs than control adults who did not bear children as adolescents.[34]

Adolescents as Parents

Recent data indicate that there may be differences in the way adolescents and adults parent their children.

Early interaction. McAnarney and colleagues reported that the younger the age of the adolescent mother, the less likely she was to display the typical adult maternal behaviors of touching, synchrony with the baby, vocalization, and closeness of the infant to the mother.[35]

Jones and associates reported that there were definite differences in maternal responsiveness for mothers aged 17–18 years, 19–20 years, and 21–23 years.[36] Older mothers demonstrated significantly more maternal responsiveness than young mothers in the following four variables: distress of the infant during the examination; proximity of the infant and the mother during the infant examination; amount of lateral trunk contact of mother with the infant during nursing; total of all maternal behaviors scored during the infant examination. These differences were not secondary to race or socioeconomic status.

Thompson and colleagues reported that infants of adolescents differed markedly from infants of older mothers in interactive and motor processes on the Brazelton Neonatal Assessment Scale.[37] Infants of adolescent mothers were less cuddly, exhibited a poorer capacity for responsiveness to repeated disturbing visual stimuli, and had more startles than infants of older mothers.

Infants and children. Oppel and Royston reported that children born to mothers less than 18 years of age were more likely than controls to be distractible, to have infantile behavioral problems, to be underweight and short, and to be deficient in reading grade level and intelligence quotient.[38] Baldwin and Cain reported that the effect of the mother's age on her child's social and emotional development is not as clear as that on the child's cogniive development.[14] They emphasized that the effect on outcome does not result directly from the mother's age at delivery, but rather is transmitted through other factors associated with early childbearing, such as educational and economic disadvantage and marital dissolution. (See Baldwin and Cain for greater detail about the children of teenage parents.[14])

Child abuse and neglect. The data are sparse to support the contention that adolescent mothers abuse their children more than adult mothers of similar backgrounds. Gil reported on 421 incidents of suspected child abuse obtained from a California central registry of child abuse from September 1965 through mid-February 1966: 8 percent of the female heads of households and 1 percent of the male heads of households were less than 20 years of age.[39] As noted by Sahler in her review of the literature concerning whether adolescents are abusive parents, "by far the greatest incidence of child abuse occurs in the families whose parents are in their mid-to-late 20's."[40] This is consistent with the fact that most childbearing occurs during those years, and also suggests that parents who began childbearing as adolescents may become abusive parents as adults when they then have several children for whom to care. Solomon noted that the majority of abusive parents were married, living together, and socially isolated—factors which, in general, do not describe adolescent parents.[41] Thus, the data do not support the popular notion that adolescents are abusive parents.

Neglectful parenthood is a far more subtle measure of inadequate parenting than obvious physical abuse of a child. Perhaps we should be searching for evidence of neglect of children by adolescent parnts more rigorously than we are, as the developmental stage of the adolescent parent may suggest her inability to be an active parent. Adolescents who have not reached the stage of formal operations in their cognitive development may not be able to think ahead about the consequences of the child's behavior or a child's deteriorating physical condition. For example, the preformal operational adolescent may not fully appreciate why it is important to protect the child from dangerous settings—e.g., the adolescent parent may fail to intervene when the toddler puts his or her hand in a dog's mouth. Likewise, the adolescent may not be able to recognize that the child's medical condition, such as bronchiolitis, is worsening and that medical intervention is imperative. There are little data to support these concepts, but our clinical experience indicates that most adolescents do not try to hurt their children actively, but may hurt them passively through developmental immaturity and inexperience in child rearing.

Repeat Pregnancies during Adolescence

Once pregnant adolescents are at high risk for repeat pregnancy during the adolescent years. In 1966, Sarrel and Davis reported that 100 clinic patients who were pregnant at age 15 years and followed for 5 years had an average of 3.4 deliveries, or 340 children.[42] The younger the adolescent at the time of her initial pregnancy, the more likely she will become pregnant again as an adolescent. A 2-year follow-up study of 27 patients cared for in the Rochester Adolescent Maternity Project (RAMP) revealed that adolescents who were the youngest of the group at delivery, in comparison to those who became pregnant late in adolescence, were more likely to become pregnant again during adolescence and to have made suicidal gestures in the interval between first delivery and follow-up; they were less likely to have returned to school, to be financially independent, to be in contact with the father of the child, and to use contraception.[43]

Repeat pregnancies during adolescence are particularly problematic as there is greater morbidity and mortality for the subsequent children born to adolescents and there are spiraling psychosocial problems. Jekel and colleagues found that subsequent infants born to adolescent mothers were at a higher risk of perinatal death and prematurity than first-born children of adolescents.[9] For children of primigravid adolescents, the risk of perinatal death was 0.6 percent and the risk of low birth weight was 10.7 percent; the risks for second-born children were 7.1 percent and 21.1 percent, respectively; and the risks for third-born children were 14.3 percent and 42.8, respectively.

Dickens and associates reported that return to school was positively correlated with a decrease in repeat pregnancies.[44] Our experience at RAMP corroborated this finding.[43]

Psychosocial problems escalate as the adolescent mother's childbearing responsibilities increase. Some adolescents may be able to handle childbearing responsibilities for one child, but few are able to cope effectively with responsibilities for more than one child. Adolescents who have more than one child may find it more difficult to return to school, develop a vocation, and hold a job than when they had one child. Those who marry run the distinct risk of having the burden of children contribute to the failure of the marriage.

Attempts have been made—through the development of comprehensive maternity projects—to decrease the likelihood of subsequent pregnancies to once pregnant adolescents, and increase the likelihood of a healthy mother and child and the return of the young mother to her tasks of adolescence.

COMPREHENSIVE PROGRAMS FOR THE CARE OF PREGNANT ADOLESCENTS AND THEIR FAMILIES

During the 1960s, adolescents, particularly the very young, and their children had been considered at higher medical and psychosocial risk than women in their 20s. As a result of this belief, special programs delivering comprehensive obstetric and psychosocial care to pregnant adolescents were developed. Examples of such programs were the Young Mothers' Program in New Haven, Connecticut,[45,46] The Young Mother's Educational Program in Syracuse, New York,[47] the Atlanta Maternity Project in Atlanta, Georgia,[48] and RAMP in Rochester, New York.[49]

Since we have been closely involved with RAMP, we shall discuss its design and results. RAMP evolved from the interests of staff in the Adolescent Program (Department of Pediatrics) and the Department of Obstetrics/Gynecology at the University of Rochester Medical Center—Strong Memorial Hospital. Initially, the project was developed as part of the Adolescent Program as it was felt that the obstetric and neonatal concerns of pregnant adolescents should be considered within the context of adolescence as a developmental phase. Initial funding was secured from the Rochester—Monroe County Youth Bureau, which previously had only funded recreation programs in the Monroe County, New York, area.

As the project developed with outside funds, we developed several priorities: continuity of care, groups, staff education, family-centered approach to care, the use of certified nurse-midwives and a family counselor, and the evaluation of outcome.

Continuity of care for the pregnant adolescent was critical in order to maintain patient compliance. Since the medical staff (obstetricians, pediatricians) was drawn from individuals who were spending the majority of their time in their parent departments, the RAMP nurses became the continuity persons for the patients. On each visit to RAMP the patient would see the same nurse who was to be present at her labor and delivery. The nurse functioned as a medically supportive person, health educator, and coordinator of the patient's total obstetric and psychosocial care. The social worker saw any patients whom the obstetrician and/or nurse thought required intervention. Examples of adolescents who were seen by the social worker were those young people who wanted to place their babies after birth, those pregnant adolescents who were in foster care, or those young people with whom there were major family and/or personal problems.

Gradually, as the number of patients in RAMP increased, groups were developed to provide teaching and peer-related activities. Initially, the groups were led by the social worker exclusively; gradually, the groups were co-led by a social worker and a nurse. (A detailed description of the groups is available elsewhere.[50])

As the program developed, we became aware of the fact that staff members who were dedicated to the complex care of pregnant adolescents need ongoing support and teaching. Burn-out seemed to be a potential problem among the staff of maternity projects, and thus active inservice educational programs were developed for the RAMP staff.[51]

As the project grew and our research continued, we became convinced that each patient did not require the same level of services and that a greater emphasis on the care of families was critical. We decided to change the emphasis of the program to that of a family-centered approach to care. We began to utilize the services of certified nurse-midwives to deliver the majority of the obstetric care to adolescents whose pregnancies were proceeding normally and a family counselor to develop outreach into the community.

We thought that the certified nurse-midwives were well trained to address the complex medical and psychosocial needs of the pregnant adolescents. They managed normal pregnancies, labors, and deliveries, and were adept at addressing the complex psychosocial aspects of adolescent pregnancy. They provided preventive health teaching and anticipatory guidance to the adolescents. Adolescents who were having particular obstetric problems or were deemed at high medical risk by the staff were seen by the obstetrician.

The family counselor was specifically trained to develop outreach services for the highest risk pregnant adolescents in our population (those 10–14 years of age) through the auspices of a special new project, Project START. The family counselor was a high school educated person who was chosen for the position because of her warmth, maternal skill, and interest in providing services to pregnant adolescents. She functioned in Project START as a community outreach person and was directly supervised in her activities by the social worker in RAMP.

As an extension of the family-centered approach to health care, a major effort was made to reach the fathers of the babies and the families of the babies' parents. Our efforts directed toward the adolescent fathers are described in Chapter 13. During the initial telephone contact with prospective patients, the staff communicated that the family members and/or boyfriend would be welcome to join the pregnant adolescent at her initial intake appointment and to participate in the adolescent's prenatal care. The initial intake interview, which was jointly performed by the social worker and the nurse, allowed the staff to make a psychosocial assessment of the pregnant adolescent and those closest to her, and to facilitate communication about the pregnancy among all those present. The fathers of the babies were encouraged, if they were interested, to participate in the activities of RAMP. Thus, the focus of RAMP has changed from the obstetric and psychosocial needs of the pregnant adolescent to include her family and her partner.[52]

Adolescents who receive adequate prenatal health care should not have any substantially higher risk for obstetric problems than women of similar racial and socioeconomic backgrounds. Utilization of certified nurse-midwives is appropriate as long as there is excellent obstetric consultation available in the clinic for adolescents who have obstetric problems. Since a mjaor issue in assuming excellent outcome for adolescents and their children is their compliance with regular, prepartum care, the community outreach activities of the family counselor encourage adolescents to seek and receive care early in their pregnancies.

The formal evaluation of the outcome of adolescent maternity projects has evolved over the last decade. Klerman and Jekel developed an excellent outline for determining outcome of adolescent pregnancy projects.[45] Obstetric outcome parameters include the number of prenatal visits kept, the percentage of patients who experienced pregnancy-induced hypertension, the percentage of patients who necessitated special prepartum procedures, the average amount and duration of analgesia and/or anesthesia before delivery, and the length of labor. Neonatal data include the birth weight, Apgar score at 5 minutes after birth, average week of gestation at delivery, and percentage of babies born alive. Psychosocial outcome parameters include the percentage of adolescents who have returned to school and/or graduated, the percentage of adolescents who receive public assistance, and the percentage of adolescents who are using contraception at follow-up.

The obstetric and neonatal outcome was similar for patients attending RAMP, those attending a community health center, and those attending a traditional obstetric clinic. Twenty-four percent of the RAMP patients had repeated pregnancy at 2-year follow-up, compared to 45 percent at the community health center and 43 percent at the hospital obstetric clinic; this difference was statistically significant.[53] Other evaluations of RAMP have included a consumer evaluation of the program[54] and a telephone follow-up to determine how the adolescents are managing post partum and whether they have experienced any problem.

Our overall impression from having developed and managed a maternity project for over a decade is that the major issues in the health care of pregnant adolescents are the following: to encourage them to receive early prenatal care; to provide comprehensive obstetric, psychosocial, and outreach services in one setting; and to utilize creative forms of health care delivery to maximize the services to all pregnant adolescents and their families.

THE FUTURE

No matter what the trends are in funding for adolescent pregnancy and adolescent childbearing over the next several years, pregnancy and childbearing during the adolescent years will continue to present problems to concerned health professionals. Efforts must continue in several areas.

Services

Preventive Services

Prevention of adolescent childbearing is the ideal. Since the earlier age of biologic maturity and sexual activity among adolescents will not change in the foreseeable future, prevention through contraception is a critical issue.

Several problems still interfere with ideal contraception on the part of sexually active adolescents.

There is no ideal contraceptive method for developing adolescents. The success of the birth control pill, which is the most frequently used method among adolescents, depends on the individual's compliance with its use. Adolescents, who may have difficulty remembering routine responsibilities such as feeding the dog at home, may have difficulty remembering to take their birth control pills. Diaphragms depend on the person's thinking ahead to plan on their use, and thus the preformal operational adolescent may not have acquired the cognitive ability to use this method. Intrauterine devices have received some negative press because of their association with a higher incidence of infections, but the Cu-7 and others have recently been reported to be of use among nulliparous adolescents.[55] Thus, they may be useful in postpartum adolescents free of gynecologic infections.

Accessibility to and availability of contraceptive services have been problematic for adolescents. Greater appropriation during the 1970s of monies to family planning programs and the development of truly accessible programs in the high schools have resulted in an increasing number of adolescents utilizing contraception. In a high school–based health clinic in St. Paul, Minnesota, pregnancies declined by 40 percent in 3 years, indicating the importance of the accessibility of contraceptive services for adolescents.[56]

Thus, the ideal from the medical and public health perspectives is to prevent adolescent pregnancies through improved utilization of contraceptive services.

Comprehensive Adolescent Pregnancy Services

Adolescents, as well as adults, who receive prepartum care experience better obstetric, neonatal, and psychosocial outcomes than those who do not receive adequate prepartum care. We think that certified nurse-midwives can deliver the majority of the prepartum, delivery, and postpartum care to adolescents who have no preexisting medical conditions nor any pregnancy-related medical problems. An attending obstetrician should be available on site to provide immediate consultation for any adolescent for whom there is question of a medical or obstetric problem.

Certified nurse-midwives are trained to provide health education and psychosocial services to pregnant women. The majority of certified nurse-midwives are women and they provide excellent female role models for pregnant adolescents who are in the midst of their own identity formation and who may not have a strong female role model with whom to identify.

Community health nurses and family counselors can provide the majority of the community outreach. They can identify pregnant adolescents, encourage their participation in early prenatal care, provide outreach from the clinical setting into their homes, and establish supportive and trusting relationships with their young patients. Social workers provide direct services for adolescents in need of special services as well as superivison and guidance of the family counselors.

Groups are a cost-efficient way of providing health education and affective sessions for pregnant adolescents and their families. Postpartum groups can focus on resolution of the labor and delivery experience and parenting education.

A streamlined adolescent maternity project of the future may place emphasis on the utilization of certified nurse-midwives for obstetric care supported by immediate obstetric consultation, community health nurses and family counselors for outreach into the community, social work services for the complex social problems of adolescents and their families, and group work for adolescents. Families would be encouraged to participate extensively in the programing.

Flexible programs should be developed for individual adolescents, so that those who have the greatest personal or financial resources might have a different service delivery package than those who have fewer personal or family resources.

Community-wide efforts, such as those being developed under the incentive of possible Title VI Adolescent Pregnancy Services funding, are mandatory, so that duplication of services within a community and barriers to health care for adolescents are minimized. Evaluation from the outset of the program should be included in the development of services.

Training

Training of those who will service pregnant adolescents—family physicians, internists, obstetricians/gynecologists, pediatricians, certified nurse-midwives, registered nurses, social workers, psychiatrists, and psychologists—should focus on the development of skills to care for their special needs.

The general curriculum for all groups should include information on normal adolescent growth and development and the common medical and psychological problems of adolescence. They all need to know how to interview and evaluate adolescents psychologically. They should know how to perform breast and pelvic examinations.

Primary care providers should know how to diagnose pregnancy and how to discuss the options of keeping the child, adoption, or abortion with the adolescent. Expedient referral to an adolescent maternity project, an obstetrician, or a certified nurse-midwife for the patient's obstetric care is imperative. Some primary care providers will want to provide psychosocial support to the adolescent at the same time as an obstetric colleague provides the prenatal care. Most adolescent maternity projects provide comprehensive services in one setting, which means that the primary care person would probably relinquish the care of the adolescent to that group.

Obstetrician/gynecologists and certified nurse-midwives have excellent knowledge of the obstetric and gynecologic needs of adolescents, but they need greater emphasis in their training on the special developmental needs of adolescents. The training of nurses, social workers, and mental health workers should focus primarily on the complex psychosocial problems of pregnant adolescents and their families. Interdisciplinary efforts among professionals from varied backgrounds provide broad services to pregnant adolescents and their families and have the advantage of preventing the burnout that may occur among providers who deliver comprehensive services.

Research

Research should focus on several questions about the risks of adolescent childbearing secondary to young age:

- Why do subsequent babies born to adolescents have a greater incidence of prematurity and perinatal mortality than first-borns?
- Do adolescent parents neglect their infants more frequently than adult parents of similar backgrounds?
- Do adolescents, particularly the very young, mother their children differently than adult mothers of similar backgrounds?
- Is there a "critical" period of ideal mothering which is age-related?
- Can poor mothering among adolescents be predicted on the basis of observations of early mother–infant interaction?
- What is to be learned about the fathers of babies born to adolescent mothers?

Research about comprehensive services for pregnant adolescents and their families should focus upon the relationship of optimum obstetric, neonatal, and psychosocial outcome to cost-efficient and effective services.

Studies of adolescent pregnancy provide the ideal research model to explore biologic and psychological concerns of individual patients as well as to utilize the community laboratory to develop better services for pregnant adolescents and their families.

Since 1970 we have become more knowledgeable than previously about the risks of adolescent childbearing secondary to the young age of the mother. We now know that compliance with comprehensive prenatal care is critical for optimum outcome for adolescents and their infants. Comprehensive prenatal programs have been effective on a short-term basis in improving obstetric and neonatal outcome, decreasing immediate repeat pregnancies, and providing incentive for adolescents to return to school and develop financial

Subject Index

Author Index

a
2 b
3 c
4 d
5 e
6 f
7 g
8 h
9 i
8 0 j